D1429275

KA 0158472 3

Introductions, Notes, and Commentaries to texts in
'The Dramatic Works of Thomas Dekker'

Introductions, Notes, and Commentaries to texts in
'The Dramatic Works of Thomas Dekker'
edited by Fredson Bowers

VOLUME I

VOLUME II

VOLUME III

VOLUME IV

CYRUS HOY

Introductions, Notes, and Commentaries to texts in 'The Dramatic Works of Thomas Dekker'

EDITED BY
FREDSON BOWERS

VOLUME I

SIR THOMAS MORE: DEKKER'S ADDITION

THE SHOEMAKERS' HOLIDAY

OLD FORTUNATUS

PATIENT GRISSIL

SATIROMASTIX

SIR THOMAS WYATT

CAMBRIDGE UNIVERSITY PRESS
CAMBRIDGE
LONDON   NEW YORK   NEW ROCHELLE
MELBOURNE   SYDNEY

Published by the Press Syndicate of the University of Cambridge
The Pitt Building, Trumpington Street, Cambridge CB2 1RP
32 East 57th Street, New York, NY 10022, USA
296 Beaconsfield Parade, Middle Park, Melbourne 3206, Australia

First published 1980

Printed in Great Britain at the
University Press, Cambridge

Library of Congress cataloguing in publication data
Hoy, Cyrus Henry.
Introductions, notes, and commentaries to texts in
The dramatic works of Thomas Dekker.
Includes bibliographical references.
1. Dekker, Thomas, *c.* 1572–1632 – Criticism, Textual.
I. Bowers, Fredson Thayer. II. Dekker, Thomas, *c.* 1572–1632
Works. III. Title.
PR2495.H68   822'.3   77–80838
ISBN 0 521 21786 5 vol. 1
ISBN 0 521 23647 9 set of two volumes

CONTENTS

PREFACE

These four volumes of Introductions, Notes and Commentaries provide critical and explanatory material to accompany, respectively, the four volumes of texts in *The Dramatic Works of Thomas Dekker*, edited by Fredson Bowers (Cambridge, 1953–1961).[1] Professor Bowers' introductions to the plays in his edition of the *Dramatic Works* are exclusively concerned with textual matters. The introductory essays in the four present volumes place the plays in their critical contexts, and treat of the issues concerning dates, sources and attributions as these arise in connection with them. Taken together, the twenty-five pieces that comprise the canon of Dekker's *Dramatic Works* pose a formidable range of problems that must be faced by anyone who attempts to place these plays in the history of the late sixteenth- and early seventeenth-century English theatre. There are complex problems concerning the relation of individual plays: e.g. of *The Wonder of a Kingdom* and *The Noble Spanish Soldier* to John Day's *The Parliament of Bees*, or of *Lust's Dominion* to the lost *Spanish Moor's Tragedy*, or of *Satiromastix* to the stage quarrel between Marston and Jonson and the plays associated with that celebrated affair. The dates of a number of plays (e.g. *The Roaring Girl, Match Me in London, The Wonder of a Kingdom, The Noble Spanish Soldier, Lust's Dominion*) have been much debated and are difficult to assign with certainty. There is the recurrent problem of attempting to estimate Dekker's share in his collaborations with other dramatists: with Chettle and Haughton in *Patient Grissil*, with Webster in *Sir Thomas Wyatt, Westward Ho* and *Northward No;* with Middleton in *The Honest Whore*, Part One, and *The Roaring Girl*; with Massinger in *The Virgin Martyr*; with William Rowley and Ford in *The Witch of Edmonton*; with Ford in *The Sun's Darling* and

---

[1] Act-, scene- and line-numbers for Dekker's plays cited throughout these volumes are based on the 1970 reprint of vol. I of Bowers' edition, the 1964 reprint of vol. II, the 1966 reprint of vol. III, and the 1968 reprint of vol. IV.

The Welsh Embassador. This is to say nothing of the more tangled authorial claims that must be considered in connection with any effort to determine Dekker's share in *The Wonder of a Kingdom, The Noble Spanish Soldier,* and *Lust's Dominion.* None of these matters have gone unregarded by previous scholars, but the factual record of Dekker's plays is beset with the speculation of such nineteenth- and early twentieth-century scholars as Collier and Fleay and Dugdale Sykes. In my efforts to establish grounds for reasonable conjecture concerning these several issues, I have attempted to incorporate what seems valuable in the conclusions of past investigators, while rejecting what subsequent scholarship has deemed untenable. In addition to attempting to establish the factual record concerning dates, sources and attributions as firmly as the evidence for the various plays will permit, the Introductions in the present volumes provide a record of critical response to the plays, and an account of the stage history of those relatively few plays of the Dekker canon that have had one.

In defining and illustrating the language of any one of Dekker's plays in the Commentary, the practice has here been to provide a widening range of reference that begins with the evidence that is available in parallels from Dekker's other plays, moves on to evidence afforded by his non-dramatic works, and comes to rest in the evidence furnished by works (principally dramatic) of contemporary Elizabethan and Jacobean authors. The numerous cross-references in the Commentary to Dekker's other works, both dramatic and non-dramatic, are intended to aid the cause of relating his separate plays, poems and prose pamphlets into a corpus, and thus to suggest something of the inner connections that characterize his total literary output.[1] The references to the work of his contemporaries will suggest some of the relations of his plays to the language of the

---

[1] Concerning the corpus of Dekker's dramatic works, it may properly be said to consist of the twenty-five pieces collected in Bowers' edition, to which I would add only the comedy of *Blurt, Master-Constable, or The Spaniard's Night Walk,* published anonymously in 1602. Though traditionally included in editions of Middleton, the play is certainly Dekker's in part, and probably is entirely his. The parallels cited from it in these volumes should make clear its relation to the Dekker canon. Edward Pudsey's quotation of two passages from it among quotations from *Satiromastix* in his Commonplace Book provides external evidence for Dekker's authorship. See the Appendix to *Satiromastix.*

contemporary stage, and to the poetic and dramatic conventions of his age.

Since in preparing a Commentary on such a scale as this identical items of information must often be cited, cross-references must also be used to avoid excessive repetition. Whenever possible, passages requiring the same information by way of explanation are referred to a note on a single passage; this will contain as well a listing of all the other passages that have been referred to this single one. The Index to the Commentary at the end of vol. IV is on similar lines, with each entry containing in most cases but a single Commentary reference, where all additional references will be found. Reference is made by abbreviated play title (for which, see Abbreviations: Dekker's dramatic works) followed by act-, scene- and line-numbers. When these in turn are followed by 'n.', it is to be understood that the reference contains a Commentary note that has some substantive bearing on the passage in question. Act-, scene- and line-references without the accompanying 'n.' refer to passages exhibiting identical or comparable verbal features; these, too, are regularly grouped together at a single point in the Commentary, to which all other occurrences are referred. References without an 'n.' do not usually refer to notes containing substantive information; rather, they contain information concerning the prevalence of a given word or image in the corpus of Dekker's work, both dramatic and non-dramatic. Apart from the interest such a record may have for the student of Dekker's vocabulary and his descriptive style, it has seemed appropriate – in a canon that contains as much collaborative work as Dekker's does – to provide information of this kind for whatever value it may possess as authorial evidence.

I wish to express my appreciation to the John Simon Guggenheim Foundation for the award of a fellowship in 1962, and to Vanderbilt University for granting me leave throughout the academic year 1962/3, when work on these volumes was in its initial stage. I am grateful to the Folger Shakespeare Library for two fellowships, one in the summer of 1962 that helped me to launch this project, another that permitted a longer stay in that grand place during the first six months of 1970 and which enabled me to get this work into

PREFACE

a shape that permitted of the hope that someday it might be finished. Finally, I want to acknowledge my gratitude to the University of Rochester for a generous summer grant (in 1967) and for two years of academic leave (1969/70, 1976/7) that were of crucial importance in carrying the work forward and eventually completing it.

For help with foreign languages in Dekker's plays, I want to thank Peter Dunn of Wesleyan University, Connecticut (for translating the Spanish), T. Arwyn Watkins of the University College of Wales and Hadley Tremaine of Hood College, Maryland (for translations of the Welsh), and Frederick Locke of the University of Rochester (for help in identifying Latin quotations).

I am much indebted to Jane Hodgart of the Cambridge University Press for the care and the patience she has expended on a difficult manuscript.

C.H.

Rochester, New York
February 1980

ABBREVIATIONS

DEKKER'S DRAMATIC WORKS

B.H.	*Britannia's Honor*
1 H.W.	*The Honest Whore, Part I*
2 H.W.	*The Honest Whore, Part II*
I.T.B.N.	*If This Be Not a Good Play, the Devil Is In It*
L.D.	*Lust's Dominion*
L.T.	*London's Tempe*
M.E.	*The Magnificent Entertainment*
M.M.L.	*Match Me in London*
N.H.	*Northward Ho*
N.S.S.	*The Noble Spanish Soldier*
O.F.	*Old Fortunatus*
P.G.	*Patient Grissil*
R.G.	*The Roaring Girl*
Sat.	*Satiromastix*
S.D.	*The Sun's Darling*
S.H.	*The Shoemakers' Holiday*
S.T.M.	*Sir Thomas More*
S.T.W.	*Sir Thomas Wyatt*
T.T.	*Troia-Nova Triumphans*
V.M.	*The Virgin Martyr*
W.B.	*The Whore of Babylon*
W.E.	*The Welsh Embassador*
W. of E.	*The Witch of Edmonton*
W.H.	*Westward Ho*
W.K.	*The Wonder of a Kingdom*

DEKKER'S NON-DRAMATIC WORKS

A.G.	*The Artillery Garden* (1616)
B.L.	*The Belman of London* (1608 ('The third impression, with new additions'))

B.R.W.R.	*The Blacke Rod and the White Rod* (1630)
D.D.	*Dekker his Dreame* (1620)
D.P.	*The Double PP* (1606)
D.T.	*The Dead Tearme* (1608)
E.V.	*English Villanies* (1632)
F.B.N.A.	*Foure Birds of Noahs Arke* (1609)
G.H.	*The Guls Horne-booke* (1609)
J.M.M.	*Jests to make you Merie* (1607)
K.C.	*A Knight's Conjuring* (1607)
L.C.	*Lanthorne and Candle-light* (1609 ('The second edition, newly corrected and amended')
L.L.B.	*London Looke Backe* (1630)
M.G.	*The Meeting of Gallants* (1604)
N.F.H.	*Newes from Hell* (1606)
N.G.	*Newes from Graves-end* (1604)
O.P.	*O per se O* (1612)
P.W.	*Penny-Wise, Pound-Foolish* (1631)
R.A.	*The Ravens Almanacke* (1609)
R.R.	*A Rod for Run-awayes* (1625)
S.D.S.	*The Seven deadly Sinnes* (1606)
S.H.R.	*A Strange Horse-Race* (1613)
V.D.	*Villanies Discovered by Lanthorne and Candle-light* (1616)
W.A.	*Worke for Armorours* (1609)
W.W.W.	*Warres, Warres, Warres* (1628)
W.Y.	*The Wonderfull yeare* (1603)

Quotations from Dekker's non-dramatic works are drawn from the editions indicated above with the following exceptions: quotations from *The Wonderfull yeare*, *Newes from Graves-end*, *The Meeting of Gallants*, *A Rod for Run-awayes*, *London Looke Backe*, *The Blacke Rod and the White Rod* are based on the texts in F. P. Wilson's edition of *The Plague Pamphlets of Thomas Dekker* (Oxford, 1925); page references cited with quotations from these pamphlets in the Commentary are to this edition. Quotatons from *Foure Birds of Noahs Arke* are from the edition of F. P. Wilson (Oxford, 1924), to which page references are made in the Commentary. Quotations from *The Artillery Garden* are based on the facsimile edition prepared by F. P. Wilson (Oxford, 1952) from the only extant copy (now preserved at the University of Göttingen), to which reference is made in the Commentary by quarto signature.

SECONDARY SOURCES
AND MOST FREQUENTLY CITED EDITIONS

The following list identifies abbreviations, surnames of authors and editors, and short titles frequently used in these volumes.

Annals	*Annals of English Drama, 975–1700*, by Alfred Harbage, revised by S. Schoenbaum (London, 1964).
Arber	*A Transcript of the Registers of the Company of Stationers of London, 1554–1640*, ed. Edward Arber (5 vols., London, 1875–1894).
Beaumont and Fletcher	*The Dramatic Works in the Beaumont and Fletcher Canon*, General Editor, Fredson Bowers (3 vols., Cambridge, 1966–1976). (Quotations from *Wit Without Money, Monsieur Thomas* and *The Loyal Subject* are based on texts in *The Works of Francis Beaumont and John Fletcher*, Variorum Edition, General Editor, A. H. Bullen (4 vols., London, 1904–1912.) Quotations from *Rollo Duke of Normandy or The Bloody Brother* are from the edition of J. D. Jump (Liverpool, 1948). Quotations from other plays in the Beaumont and Fletcher canon are based on seventeenth-century texts, as indicated in their individual citations in the Commentary.)
Bentley	Gerald Eades Bentley, *The Jacobean and Caroline Stage* (7 vols., Oxford, 1941–1968).
Bond	*Early Plays from the Italian*, ed. R. W. Bond (Oxford, 1911).
Brome	*The Dramatic Works of Richard Brome*, ed. R. H. Shepherd (3 vols., London, 1873). (Quotations from *The Antipodes* and from *A Jovial Crew* are

	based on the editions of A. Haaker (Lincoln, Nebraska, 1966 and 1968).)
Brooke	*The Shakespeare Apocrypha*, ed. C. F. Tucker Brooke (Oxford, 1918).
Bullen	*A Collection of Old English Plays*, ed. A. H. Bullen (4 vols., London, 1882–1885).
Chambers	E. K. Chambers, *The Elizabethan Stage* (4 vols., Oxford, 1923).
Chapman	*The Tragedies and Comedies of George Chapman*, ed. Thomas Marc Parrott (2 vols., London, 1910–1914).
Chappell	W. Chappell, *Popular Music of the Olden Time* (2 vols., London, 1855–1859).
Cotgrave	Randle Cotgrave, *A Dictionary of the French and English Tongues* (London, 1611).
Crawford	*Englands Parnassus*, ed. Charles Crawford (Oxford, 1913).
Day	*The Works of John Day, Reprinted from the collected Edition of A. H. Bullen (1881) with an Introduction by* Robin Jeffs (London, 1963).
Deloney	*The Works of Thomas Deloney*, ed. F. O. Mann (Oxford, 1912).
D.N.B.	*Dictionary of National Biography.*
Drayton	*The Works of Michael Drayton*, ed. J. W. Hebel, K. Tillotson and B. H. Newdigate (5 vols., Oxford, 1961).
Dryden	*The Dramatic Works of John Dryden*, ed. Montague Summers (6 vols., London, 1931–1932).
Field	*The Plays of Nathan Field*, ed. William Peery (Austin, Texas, 1950).
Fleay	F. G. Fleay, *A Biographical Chronicle of the English Drama, 1559–1642* (2 vols., London, 1891).
Florio	John Florio, *A World of Words, or Most copious, and exact Dictionary in Italian and English* (London, 1598).

Ford   *The Works of John Ford, with Notes Critical and Explanatory by* William Gifford, *revised with additions to the text and to the notes by* Alexander Dyce (3 vols., London, 1895). (Quotations from *Perkin Warbeck* and from *The Broken Heart* are based on the editions of D. K. Anderson, Jr (Lincoln, Nebraska, 1965 and 1968); quotations from *'Tis Pity She's a Whore* are based on the edition of N. W. Bawcutt (Lincoln, 1966).)

Greene   *The Plays & Poems of Robert Greene*, ed. J.
(Dramatic   Churton Collins (2 vols., Oxford, 1905).
Works)

Greene   *The Life and Complete Works in Prose and Verse*
(Non-   *of Robert Greene*, ed. A. B. Grosart (15 vols.,
Dramatic   London, 1881–1886). (Referred to in the Com-
Works)   mentary by volume- and page-numbers following the title of individual works.)

Hall   *Collected Poems of Joseph Hall*, ed. Arnold Davenport (Liverpool, 1949).

Halliwell   James Orchard Halliwell [-Phillipps], *A Dictionary of Archaic and Provincial Words* (London, 1924).

Harrison   William Harrison, *Description of England*, ed F. J. Furnivall (London, 1877).

Haughton   William Haughton, *Englishmen for my Money*, ed. W. W. Greg (Oxford (Malone Society), 1912).

Hazlitt,   *A Select Collection of Old English Plays, originally*
Old Plays   *published by Robert Dodsley in the year 1744*, 4th ed., revised and enlarged by W. Carew Hazlitt (15 vols., London, 1874–1876).

Hazlitt, *Popular*   *Popular Antiquities of Great Britain, edited from*
Antiquities   *the Materials Collected by John Brand, with very large corrections and additions by* W. Carew Hazlitt (3 vols., London, 1870).

Henslowe's   *Henslowe's Diary*, ed. R. A. Foakes and R. T.
Diary   Rickert (Cambridge, 1961).

Herbert   *The Dramatic Records of Sir Henry Herbert*,

Master of the Revels, 1623–1673, ed. J. Q. Adams (New Haven, 1917).

Heywood *The Dramatic Works of Thomas Heywood,* ed. R. H. Shepherd (6 vols., London, 1874). (Quotations from *A Woman Killed With Kindness* are based on the edition of R. Van Fossen (London, 1961); quotations from *The Fair Maid of the West* are based on the edition of R. K. Turner (Lincoln, Nebraska, 1967).)

Hunt Mary Leland Hunt, *Thomas Dekker, a Study* (New York, 1911).

Jones-Davies M. T. Jones-Davies, *Un peintre de la vie londonienne: Thomas Dekker (circa 1572–1632)* (2 vols., Paris, 1958).

Jonson *Ben Jonson,* ed. C. H. Herford and Percy Simpson (11 vols., Oxford, 1925–1952).

Kyd *The Works of Thomas Kyd,* ed. F. S. Boas (Oxford, 1901).

Lamb Charles Lamb, *Specimens of English Dramatic Poets,* ed. Israel Gollancz (2 vols., London, 1893).

Linthicum M. Channing Linthicum, *Costume in the Drama of Shakespeare and his Contemporaries* (Oxford, 1936).

Lyly *The Complete Works of John Lyly,* ed. R. W. Bond (3 vols., Oxford, 1902).

Marlowe *The Complete Works of Christopher Marlowe,* ed. Fredson Bowers (2 vols., Cambridge, 1973). (Quotations from *Doctor Faustus* are based on the parallel-text edition of W. W. Greg (Oxford, 1950).)

Marston (Dramatic Works) *The Works of John Marston,* ed. A. H. Bullen (3 vols., London, 1887). (Quotations from *Antonio and Mellida* and *Antonio's Revenge* are based on the editions of G. K. Hunter (Lincoln, Nebraska, 1965); quotations from *The Malcontent* and from *The Dutch Courtesan* are based on the editions of M. Wine (Lincoln, 1965); quotations from *The Fawn* are based on the edition of G. Smith (Lincoln, 1964); quotations from *Histriomastix, Jack Drum's Entertainment,* and *The Insatiate Countess* are based on the texts in vol. III of H. Harvey Wood's edition of *The Plays of John Marston* (Edinburgh, 1939).)

Marston (Non-Dramatic Works)
The Poems of John Marston, ed. Arnold Davenport (Liverpool, 1961).

Massinger
The Plays and Poems of Philip Massinger, ed. Philip Edwards and Colin Gibson (5 vols., Oxford, 1976).

Middleton
The Works of Thomas Middleton, ed. A. H. Bullen (8 vols., London, 1885). (Quotations from *Michaelmas Term* are based on the edition of R. Levin (Lincoln, Nebraska, 1966); quotations from *A Mad World, My Masters* are based on the edition of S. Henning (Lincoln, 1965); quotations from *A Trick to Catch the Old One* are based on the edition of H. Spencer in his *Elizabethan Plays* (Boston, 1933); quotations from *A Chaste Maid in Cheapside* are based on the edition of R. B. Parker (London, 1969); quotations from *No Wit, No Help Like a Woman's* are based on the edition of L. E. Johnson (Lincoln, 1976); quotations from *Women Beware Women* are based on the edition of R. Gill (London, 1968); quotations from *The Changeling* are based on the edition of G. W. Williams (Lincoln, 1966); quotations from *Anything for a Quiet Life* are based on F. L. Lucas' text in vol. IV of his edition of Webster's *Works* (see below); quotations from *The Witch* are based on the Malone Society Reprint prepared by W. W. Greg and F. P. Wilson (Oxford, 1950 (for 1948)); quota-

tions from *A Game at Chess* are based on the edition of R. C. Bald (Cambridge, 1929); quotations from *The Ghost of Lucrece* are from the edition of J. Q. Adams (New York and London, 1937); quotations from *The Second Maiden's Tragedy* are from the Malone Society Reprint prepared by W. W. Greg (Oxford, 1909); quotations from *The Puritan* are based on the edition of C. F. Tucker Brooke in his *Shakespeare Apocrypha* (see above).)

M.S.R.   Malone Society Reprint.

Nares   Robert Nares, *A Glossary; or, Collection of Words, Phrases, Names, and Allusions to Customs, Proverbs, etc. which have been thought to Require Illustration, in the Works of English Authors, particularly Shakespeare, and his Contemporaries* (London, 1822).

Nashe   *The Works of Thomas Nashe*, ed. Ronald B. McKerrow, reprinted with corrections and supplementary notes by F. P. Wilson (5 vols., Oxford, 1958). (Referred to in the Commentary by volume- and page-numbers following the title of individual works.)

Nichols, *Progresses of Queen Elizabeth*   John Nichols, *The Progresses and Public Processions of Queen Elizabeth* (3 vols., London, 1823).

Nichols, *Progresses of King James*   John Nichols, *The Progresses, Processions, and Magnificent Festivities of King James the First* (4 vols., London, 1828).

O.E.D.   *Oxford English Dictionary.*

Peele   *The Dramatic Works of George Peele*, General Editor, C. T. Prouty (2 vols., New Haven, 1961–1970).

Porter   Henry Porter, *The Two Angry Women of Abingdon*, ed. W. W. Greg (Oxford (Malone Society), 1912).

Price | George R. Price, *Thomas Dekker* (New York, 1969).

Rollins | *An Analytical Index to the Ballad-Entries (1557–1709) in the Registers of the Company of Stationers of London*, compiled by Hyder E. Rollins (Chapel Hill, North Carolina, 1924).

Rowley | William Rowley, *All's Lost by Lust*, and *A Shoemaker, a Gentleman*, ed. C. W. Stork (Philadelphia, 1910).

Roxburghe Ballads | *The Roxburghe Ballads*, ed. W. Chappell and J. W. Ebsworth (9 vols., London and Hertford, 1871–1897).

Shakespeare | *The Riverside Shakespeare*, Textual Editor, G. Blakemore Evans (Boston, 1974).

Shakespeare's England | *Shakespeare's England: An Account of the Life & Manners of his Age* (2 vols., Oxford, 1916).

Simpson | Claude M. Simpson, *The British Broadside Ballad and Its Music* (New Brunswick, New Jersey, 1966).

Skeat and Mayhew | *A Glossary of Tudor and Stuart Words*, collected by Walter W. Skeat, ed. with additions by A. L. Mayhew (Oxford, 1914).

Spenser | *The Works of Edmund Spenser*, A Variorum Edition, ed. E. Greenlaw, C. G. Osgood, F. M. Padelford *et al.* (8 vols., Baltimore, 1932–1947).

S.T.C. | Short-Title Catalogue.

Stow, *Survey* | John Stow, *A Survey of London*, ed. Charles Lethbridge Kingsford (2 vols., Oxford, 1908).

Strutt | Joseph Strutt, *The Sports and Pastimes of the People of England*, A New Edition, Much Enlarged and Corrected by J. Charles Cox (London, 1903).

Stubbes | Philip Stubbes, *The Anatomy of Abuses*, ed. F. J. Furnivall (2 parts, London, 1877–1882).

Sugden | Edward H. Sugden, *A Topographical Dictionary to the Works of Shakespeare and his Fellow Dramatists* (Manchester, 1925).

Swinburne   Algernon Charles Swinburne, *The Age of Shakespeare* (London, 1908).

The Three Parnassus Plays   *The Three Parnassus Plays*, ed. J. B. Leishman (London, 1949).

Tilley   Morris Palmer Tilley, *A Dictionary of the Proverbs in England in the Sixteenth and Seventeenth Centuries* (Ann Arbor, 1966).

Tourneur   *The Works of Cyril Tourneur*, ed. Allardyce Nicoll (London, [1929]). (Quotations from *The Revenger's Tragedy* are based on the edition of L. J. Ross (Lincoln, Nebraska, 1966).)

Webster   *The Complete Works of John Webster*, ed. F. L. Lucas (4 vols., London, 1927).

Wheatley and Cunningham   *London Past and Present, Its History, Associations, and Traditions*, by Henry B. Wheatley, based upon *The Handbook of London* by Peter Cunningham (3 vols., London, 1891).

Wright   Joseph Wright, *The English Dialect Dictionary* (6 vols., London, 1898–1905).

SIR THOMAS MORE

INTRODUCTION

Sir Thomas More is preserved as Harleian MS 7368 in the British Library, and in its present state it represents a heavily revised version of a play that seems to have run into objections from two quarters: from the members of the theatrical company for which it was written, and who apparently found it lacking in dramatic effectiveness; and from Sir Edmund Tilney, the Master of the Revels, who objected to it for political reasons. The manuscript contains six passages of additions intended to supplement or replace scenes in the original text, supplied presumably in an effort to make the deficient drama stageworthy. No effort at all seems to have been made to answer the objections of the censor; to have complied with his demands, as W. W. Greg has noted, would have been to eviscerate 'the play in a manner fatal to its success on the stage. The manuscript was consequently laid aside and the play never came on the boards.'[1]

In addition to the written comments in Tilney's hand, the manuscript contains six other different hands: Hand *S* in which the original version of the play is written, and the five hands (designated *A*, *B*, *C*, *D*, *E*, according to the order in which they occur in the manuscript[2]) which are found in the six additions to the original play. Hand *S* has been identified as that of Anthony Munday,[3] Hand *A* as that of Henry Chettle,[4] Hand *B* may be that of Heywood

---

[1] From the introduction to Greg's Malone Society edition (1911) of *Sir Thomas More*, p. xv. Line numbers in the discussion of the text that follows refer to this edition.

[2] The designation of the Hands by letters of the alphabet was devised by Greg; see the introduction to his edition, pp. vii–viii.

[3] W. W. Greg, 'Autograph Plays by Munday', *Modern Language Review*, 8 (1913), 89–90.

[4] S. A. Tannenbaum, '*The Booke of Sir Thomas Moore*', *A Bibliotic Study* (New York, 1927), pp. 53ff.

I

but this identification is by no means regarded as certain,[1] Hand C is that of a theatrical scribe,[2] Hand D has been attributed to Shakespeare,[3] Hand E has been identified as Dekker's.[4] Opinions differ as to whether Munday wrote the original play by himself, or in collaboration with one or more other dramatists. Greg felt that the writer of Hand B was 'undoubtedly an original author'.[5] E. H. C. Oliphant viewed the original play as the work of Munday together with Dekker and Hands A and B.[6] J. M. Nosworthy attributed it to Munday, Chettle (Hand A) and Dekker.[7] But most recent studies regard the original play as the work of Munday alone.[8]

[1] The suggestion that Hand B might be Heywood's was first made by Greg in *Shakespeare's Hand in the Play of 'Sir Thomas More'*, ed. A. W. Pollard (Cambridge, 1923), p. 44, n. For a summary of subsequent views, see Harold Jenkins, 'A Supplement to Sir Walter Greg's Edition of *Sir Thomas More*', Malone Society *Collections*, 6 (1961), 181–182.

[2] First suggested by Greg in the introduction to his edition, pp. xvii–xviii, and subsequently confirmed by him when he found the same hand in two theatrical 'plots' (the plot of *The Seven Deadly Sins* at Dulwich College, and a fragmentary plot which may represent the lost play *Fortune's Tennis* in the British Library). See *Shakespeare's Hand in 'Sir Thomas More'*, p. 55.

[3] A share in the additions had first been claimed for Shakespeare on internal evidence by Richard Simpson in 1871 (*Notes and Queries*, 4th series, 8 (1871), 1–3). Sir Edward Maunde Thompson pronounced Hand D to be Shakespeare's on paleographical evidence in *Shakespeare's Handwriting* (Oxford, 1916). For the subsequent controversy that has swirled around the identification, see Jenkins, 'Supplement', pp. 182–184.

[4] Greg first suggested the identification in the introduction to his edition, pp. ix–x, where he found 'a strong resemblance' between Hand E and Dekker's acknowledged hand (p. ix). Later, he dropped all reservation; see *Shakespeare's Hand in 'Sir Thomas More'*, p. 53. The identification has never been challenged.

[5] Introduction, p. xvii.

[6] '*Sir Thomas More*', *Journal of English and Germanic Philology*, 18 (1919), 230.

[7] 'Shakespeare and *Sir Thomas More*', *Review of English Studies*, new series 6 (1955), 13. Nosworthy considered it 'unthinkable that these two practising dramatists [Chettle and Dekker] were dragged in as an afterthought to contribute seventy lines and thirty lines respectively, especially as there is ample testimony that they often worked in harness with Munday'. But he gives no evidence of their work elsewhere in the play beyond the Additions previously ascribed to them. And he seems not to realize that Dekker was called in for more than thirty lines. He revised the whole of scene viii, to which the last thirty-one lines in his hand are a continuation.

[8] E.g. I. A. Shapiro, 'Shakespeare and Munday', *Shakespeare Survey*, 14 (1961), p. 32; MacD. P. Jackson, 'Anthony Munday and *Sir Thomas More*', *Notes and Queries*, 10 (1963), 96. See also Karl P. Wentersdorff, 'The Date of the Additions in the *Booke of Sir Thomas More*', *Shakespeare-Jahrbuch* (Heidelberg), 101 (1965), 305–325; Scott McMillin, 'The Book of Sir Thomas More: A Theatrical Review', *Modern Philology*, 68 (1970), 10–24.

Dekker certainly had nothing to do with it, his contribution to *Sir Thomas More* being confined to Addition IV.

The play has been variously dated from 1590 to 1605. The available evidence suggests a date of *c.* 1590–1593 for the composition of the original play, and *c.* 1594–1595 for the revision.[1]

Addition IV of the *More* manuscript contains 242 lines and replaces scene viii of the original text. The first 211 lines are written by Hand *C*, that of the theatrical scribe. Lines 212–242 are in Hand *E*, which has been identified as Dekker's. The first 211 lines are Dekker's revision of the original scene viii, presumably the work of Munday; his work of revision has been transcribed by *C*. But following line 211, Dekker added 31 lines in his own hand which correspond to nothing in the original text and amount, not to revision, but to original composition.

In the original text, scene viii begins with More arranging for Randall, his servant, to impersonate him when Erasmus comes for a visit in the company of the Earl of Surrey. The entire scene is not preserved in the original version; it begins at lines 735 and breaks off at line 796; when the original text resumes, the joke on Erasmus has been played out, and we are in the midst of the Faulkner scene. The sheriff has brought Faulkner before More, who comments on his 'Ruffinlike disguise' (line 797); Faulkner tells of his vow not to have his hair cut for three years; More commits him to Newgate until the expiration of the period of his vow; Faulkner is taken away and More has a brief exchange with Surrey (who is still on stage). Now Morris, the master of Faulkner, appears, and announces that Faulkner has seen fit to cut his hair; he is brought in; More compliments him on his appearance and leaves the scene; Faulkner confesses to his master that he has 'bin much misgouernde,/and led by ydle spleenes' (lines 866–867) but has learned the error of his ways, and the scene ends at line 876.

In Addition IV, the revised scene opens as in the original, with More and his man making ready for the jest on Erasmus; but before Erasmus and Surrey appear, the sheriff brings in Faulkner, and More dispatches him to Newgate. Then Surrey, Erasmus and attendants arrive, and their scene is played with the disguised

[1] Jenkins, 'Supplement', p. 189.

servant, whose disguise is soon penetrated, and More appears to welcome his guests. As he is about to depart with them, Morris appears to announce that his man Faulkner 'has submitted him self to the mercy of a Barber' (Addition IV, lines 186–187) and is waiting outside 'to make a new vow befor your Lordshipp. heerafter to live Civell' (lines 187–188). Faulkner is brought in, and More, approving of his new appearance, orders him to be set free. More leaves the stage with a proverb (new to this version of the scene) which Dekker will allude to in *Satiromastix* (IV.iii.56):

> thy head is for thy shoulders now more fitt
> thou hast less haire vppon it but more witt
> *(Sir Thomas More*, Addition IV, lines 203–204).

Alone with his master, Faulkner in the revision is anything but repentant. 'Did not I tell thee allwaies of thes Locks', Master Morris chides; and Faulkner replies:

And the locks were on againe all the goldsmiths in cheapside should not pick them open. shart. if my haire stand not an end when I looke for my face in a glass. I am a polecatt. heers. a lowsie Iest. but if I notch not that rogue tom barbar that makes me looke thus like a Brownist. hange me. Ile be worss to the nitticall knave. then ten tooth drawings heers a head wth a pox

(Addition IV, lines 206–211).

Here the revised scene once ended, but Addition IV which to this point has been written in Hand C^{I} (the Scribe's), continues for thirty-one more lines in Hand E (Dekker's), and it is at this point that the passage reprinted in Professor Bowers' edition begins.

Dekker revised the original scene viii as a whole, and made it more dramatically effective by breaking the Faulkner episode into two parts, with the Erasmus scene at the centre. Where it is possible to compare the revision with the original, one finds a number of changes of word and phrase, none of great consequence. Dekker's presence in Addition IV can be genuinely felt only in the last fifty lines (the last twenty lines transcribed by C, and the thirty-one lines that follow in his own hand), where after the exit of More, he remodels the character of the shorn Faulkner, making him come to life in his truculence in a way that the original entirely misses.

[1] But Dekker added the words 'I am *ipse*' (unnoticed by Greg) to line 193. See Tannenbaum, '*Sir Thomas More*', p. 93.

The source of the Faulkner episode is Foxe's *Actes and Monuments*, where it is told not of More but of Sir Thomas Cromwell. In his 'story of the Lord Cromwell', Foxe relates how a serving man

who thinking to disceuer himselfe from the common vsage of all other men in strange newfanglenes of fashions by himselfe (as many there be whom nothing doth please, which is dailie seene and receiued) vsed to go with his haire hangyng about his eares downe vnto his shoulders, after a strange monstrous manner, counterfeiting belyke the wyld Irish men...

As this Ruffin ruffling thus with his locks was walkyng in the streetes, as chance was, who should meet him but the Lord Cromwell, who beholding the deforme and vnseemly manner of his disguised goyng, full of much vanitie and hurtfull example, called the man to question with him whose seruant he was, which being declared, then was demanded, whether his maister or any of his felows vsed so to go with such haire about their shoulders as he did, or no? which when he denied, and was not able to yeld any reason for refuge of that his monstruous disguising, at length he fell to this excuse that he had made a vow. To this the Lord Cromwell answered agayne, that for so much as he had made himself a votarie, he would not force him to breake his vowe, but vntill his vow should be expired, he should lye the meane tyme in prison, and so sente him immediately to the Marshalsey: where he endured, till at length this *intonsus Cato* beyng perswaded by hys maister to cut his haire, by sute and petition of freends, hee was brought agayne to the Lord Cromwell with his hed polled according to the accustomed sort of his other fellowes, and so was dismissed (*Actes and Monuments* (1583), II, 1188).

The name of Faulkner's master, Mr Morris, who appears at line 834 in the original scene, is the same as the name of Cromwell's secretary (Rafe Morice) who provided Foxe with the anecdote. The author of the original scene could have found him named in a marginal note on p. 1185 of the 1583 edition of the *Actes and Monuments*. Morris is one of the two speakers in the thirty-one-line passage that constitutes Dekker's autograph addition to the play. How the author of the original scene came to introduce an episode from the life of Cromwell into a play dealing with the life of More is a mystery.

As has already been noted, it is generally assumed that *Sir Thomas More* was never acted.[1] 'What seems to [have been] its first professional performance', as the critic in the London *Times* of

[1] For a critique of the opposite view of W. J. Lawrence, see Jenkins, 'Supplement', pp. 189–190.

11 June 1964 (p. 17) noted with appropriate caution, came on 10 June of that year at the Nottingham Playhouse. The producer was Frank Dunlop, and Ian McKellen acted the role of More in what the *Times* critic described as 'a beautifully modulated performance' that kept 'the jocularity within the bounds of character'.

COMMENTARY

3 *my Crowne is taken from mee.* Cf. *Sat.*, IV.i.69–73.

4 *Scowrd More ditch. G.H.*, B4–B4v: 'to purge it wil be a sorer labour then the clensing of *Augeaes* stable, or the scowring of Moore-ditch'.

5 *sheepe sharing. G.H.*, D1, 'in scorne of periwigs and sheep-shearing'.

8 *poll head. M.G.*, p. 115: 'this middle of *Powles* lookes strange and bare, like a long-hayrde Gentleman new powlde, washt and shaued'. *G.H.*, D1: 'this polling and shauing world'.

8 *make a Sarcen*, i.e. an inn sign displaying a grotesque head, like the one that advertised the Saracen's Head at Newgate. Cf. *S.H.*, V.i.14, n. and *Sat.*, I.ii.301, n.

18 *shavets.* The word does not occur in the *O.E.D.*, and Dyce's emendation 'shavers' (in his edition of the *Sir Thomas More* manuscript (London, 1844)) is certainly right. 'Shavers' is common, often with the meaning 'swindlers'; see *W.H.*, III.ii.32, n. The passage from *M.G.*, p. 115, quoted in the note on 'poll head' (line 8), continues: 'and I may fitly say shaued, for there was neuer a lusty Shauer walking here this halfe yeare'.

20 *Cutt.* 'A familiar name for an animal, generally a horse, properly one with a short or cut tail. Hence, a term of reproach' (Halliwell).

21 *march with bag & baggage. W.Y.*, p. 35: 'let vs therefore with bag & baggage march away from this dangerous sore Citie'. *S.D.S.*, B3v; *W.A.*, C4. *N.H.*, I.ii.72–73.

23 *poacht*, stamped down, trampled. 'Land is said to be *poached* when it is trodden with holes by heavy cattle' (Halliwell).

27 *tournd off...ladder. W.E.*, IV.ii.2.

29 *Spin...fyne thred.* Tilley, T252.

THE SHOEMAKERS' HOLIDAY

INTRODUCTION

DEKKER's source for *The Shoemakers' Holiday*, the first part of Thomas Deloney's *The Gentle Craft*, was entered in the Stationers' Register on 19 October 1597: '*Raphe Blore*. Entred for his copie vnder thandes of master *Dix* and master Man a booke called the *gentle crafte* intreatinge of Shoomakers. vj*d*.' As Deloney's editor, F. O. Mann, remarks: 'This entry certainly applies to the first part, which would not be distinguished as such until after the publication of the second.'[1] The book is specified as *The fyrste parte of the gentill Crafte* in the transfer to Thomas Pavyer on 14 August 1600, by which time, presumably, Part Two had appeared. The earliest extant edition of Part One is that of 1648; of Part Two, that of 1639. Dekker's debt to Deloney in *The Shoemakers' Holiday* is confined to Part One.

The first part of *The Gentle Craft* consists of three main stories: (1) St Winifred and St Hugh, (2) Crispin and Crispianus, (3) Sir Simon Eyre. The first (chapters 1–4) recounts the love of the young Sir Hugh for the fair virgin Winifred, who rejects his suit in favor of a life of Christian solitude. He goes into melancholy exile, passes through sundry adventures in Venice and elsewhere, and returns to his native Britain, the pangs of unrequited love still heavy upon him. He lands at Harwick, 'where for want of money he greatly lamented. And made much moan. But meeting with a merry Iourneyman-shoomaker dwelling in that town, and after some conference had together, they both agreed to trauell in the Countrey' (pp. 81–82). Meanwhile, Winifred has been imprisoned for her religious faith, a victim of the persecution of the Christians 'in the dayes of Diocletian... During which time, Sir *Hugh* wrought in a shoomakers shop, hauing learned that trade, through the

---

[1] *Deloney*, p. 521. Parenthetical page references in the text are to Mann's edition.

courteous directions of a kind Iourneyman, where he remained the space of one whole yeere, in which time he had gotten himselfe good apparell, and euerything comely and decent' (p. 82). But he has not forgotten Winifred. At length he returns to her, that 'he might sollicite his suit anew again', but learning of her imprison-ment, 'he so highly commended her faith and constancy, that at length he was clapt vp in prison by her, and in the end he was condemned to receiue equall torment, for a triall of his own truth' (p. 83). The shoemakers remain constant to the end. 'But during the time that they lay both in prison, the Iourneymen Shoomakers neuer left him, but yeelded him great reliefe continually, so that he wanted nothing that was necessarie for him, in requital of which kindnesse he called them Gentlemen of the *Gentle Craft*' (p. 83). The Lady Winifred and Sir Hugh, now united in a higher love, are executed, she by bleeding, he by drinking her blood which has been mixed with poison. With his dying breath, he pledges 'the kind Yeoman of the *Gentle Craft*':

I drink to you all (quoth he) but I cannot spare you one drop to pledge me. Had I any good thing to giue, you should soon receiue it: but my selfe the Tyrant doth take, and my flesh is bequeathed to the fowls, so that nothing is left but onely my bones to pleasure you withall; and those, if they will do you any good, take them: and so I humbly take my leaue, bidding you all farewell.

There with the last draught, he finished his life, whose dead carkasse after hanged vp where the fowls deuoured his flesh; and the young Princesse was contemptuously buried by the Well where she had so long liued. Then had he the title of St *Hugh* giuen him, and she of Saint *Winifred*, by which termes they are both so called to this day (p. 87).

Later, 'a company of Iourneymen Shoomakers passed along by the place where Saint *Hughs* dead body was hanging, and finding the flesh pickt cleane off from the bones' (p. 87), they remember their legacy and return by night to claim their own. They resolve to make 'diuers' of their tools from the bones of the saint, the better to profit from any virtue which the relics might possess (and also to avoid the suspicion of the tyrant who has ordered St Hugh's execution); and in consequence the tools of shoemakers 'euer since were called Saint *Hughes* bones' (p. 89).

In the story of Crispine and Crispianus (chapters 5–9), Britain is still oppressed by Roman tyranny. The Emperor Maximinus is seeking to destroy all the noble youth in the land, and 'the vertuous Queen of *Logria* (which now is called *Kent*) – dwelling in the city *Durouernum*, alias *Canterbury*', sends her young sons from her in disguise to 'seek some poore seruice' that will preserve them from mischance against the time when they are restored to 'dignitie and honour' (p. 90). At Feversham, the young princes hear 'certain shoomakers singing...as they sat at their businesse' in the early morning (p. 90); they are attracted by the merry sound, present themselves at the shoemaker's door, and declare themselves to be 'two poore boyes that want seruice', having been 'stript' from their friends by the fury of the wars (p. 92). They are received with favor by the shoemaker and his wife; they are bound apprentice for seven years to the shoemaker's service; and they take upon themselves the names of Crispianus and Crispine. Maximinus' officers make search for them, and they see their mother the Queen led to prison, but the secret of their identity is preserved. Four or five years pass while they serve their master, who grows wealthy as they grow 'cunning in their trade'; his house gains the reputation for breeding the best workmen in the country, with the result that their master is preferred to be the Emperor's shoemaker. Business brings Crispine to court, where he wins the love of the Emperor's daughter, Ursula. They are secretly married by an obliging – and conveniently blind – friar. Meanwhile, Crispianus has been 'prest to wars into the Countrey of *Gaul*, now called *France*' (p. 99), whither an army of Britons is sent to aid the Gauls against the invading power of '*Iphicratis* the Persian generall' (p. 100). In a vaunting speech before the battle, the general of the Gauls derides Iphicratis' low birth, the Persian general being the son of a shoemaker. To which Iphicratis replies: 'Indeed, my fathers trade is a reproach vnto me, but thou art a reproach to thy father: but thou shalt vnderstand that a Shoomakers son is a Prince born, his fortune made him so, and thou shalt find no lesse' (p. 100). The truth of this assertion is finely confirmed in the event, for it is Crispianus who distinguishes himself beyond all others in battle, and who rescues the French prince when the latter is being carried off prisoner by Iphicratis. So moved is Iphicratis to learn that his

9

heroic young adversary is a shoemaker by trade that he agrees to end the wars, and forever after to be a friend to the Gauls. The French King, writing his thanks to Maximinus for the Britons' help, recommends Crispianus to the Emperor's favor. Back in England, Crispianus visits his former master, only to discover that the Emperor's daughter, who has taken refuge in the shoemaker's house during her confinement, has borne a child to his brother. 'But after that he had in Princely manner saluted the new deliuered Lady, taking the infant in his arms, he kissed it, saying; Now I will say and swear (said he) that a Shoomakers Son is a Prince born, ioyning in the opinion of *Iphycratis*, and henceforth Shoomakers shall neuer let their terme die' (p. 106).

Crispianus then proceeds to court, delivers the French King's letter attesting to the honorable deeds he has so recently performed, is received with great favor, and – making known his true identity – secures the liberty of his mother, 'late Queen of *Logria*'. The Emperor would further reward him with the hand of his daughter, but she is not to be found. When eventually Ursula returns to court, accompanied by Crispine (still in his shoemaker's attire), her father promptly bids Crispianus take her to wife, but the daughter demurs:

Not so, dear Father (quoth she) this man hath best deserued my loue, that hath preserued my life, and his wife will I be.

Why *Vrsula* (said her Father) wilt thou darken the sun-shine of my ioy, with the clouds of foule obstinacy, and yoke thy selfe so vnequally? This man is a Prince.

And this mans son is another (quoth she).

That is strange (said the Emperour); can that child be a Prince, whose father is but a Shoomaker?

Then answeared *Vrsula*, My Royall Father, a Shoomakers son is a Prince born:

Most gracious Lord (quoth *Crispianus*) the very like sentence did I hear the renowned *Iphicrates* pronounce to the King of Gauls, when he vpbraided him with his birth (p. 107).

The child is then presented, its parentage is made known, Crispine is revealed as the brother of Crispianus, and his secret marriage to Ursula 'confirmed openly, with great ioy and triumph':

at which time the Shoomakers in the same town made Holiday: to whom *Crispine* and *Crispianus* sent most Princely gifts for to maintain their merriment. And euer after vpon that day at night, the Shoomakers make great cheare and feasting, in remembrance of these two Princely brethren: and because it might not be forgotten, they caused their names to be placed in the Kalender for a yeerly remembrance, which you shall find in the moneth of October, about three dayes before the feast of *Simon* and *Iude* (pp. 107–108).

The story of Simon Eyre (chapters 10–15) recounts how Eyre 'being brought young out of the North countrey, was bound 'prentice to a Shoomaker' (p. 109); how, as a young apprentice unable to pay his share of the shot, he promised his fellows that if ever he became Lord Mayor of London he would give a breakfast for all the 'prentices of London; how, having served his apprenticeship, he married, set up shop for himself, and needing a journeyman, hired a Frenchman named John Deneuale. It is Deneuale who learns of the ship of the Isle of Candy which, having sprung a leak and 'being vnable to sail any further', has been driven upon the English coast with its cargo of 'all kind of Lawns and Cambricks, and other linnen cloth: which commodities at that time were in London very scant, and exceeding dear' (p. 111). The cargo is for sale, the captain of the ship desiring to 'make what profit he could of his goods here'. Deneuale reports the matter to his master, who is interested, but cannot imagine how he can secure the necessary cash (£3,000 is the sum requested). He confides in his wife, who thinks upon the matter and devises a plan:

Now husband, I would haue you in the morning with Iohn the Frenchman to the Grecian Merchant, and with good discretion driue a sound bargain with him for the whole fraught of the ship, and thereupon giue him halfe a dozen Angels in earnest, and eight and twenty dayes after the deliuery of the goods, condition to deliuer him the rest of his money.

But woman (quoth he) dost thou imagine that he would take my word for so weighty a masse of money, and to deliuer his goods vpon no better security?

Good Lord (quoth she) haue you no wit in such a case to make shift? Ile tell you what you shall do: Be not known that you bargain for your own selfe, but tell him that you do it in the behalf of one of the cheif Aldermen in the City (p. 113).

In the morning, Eyre will present himself to the merchant in his own person, as a shoemaker; in the afternoon he will return in the dress of the alderman in whose behalf the shoemaker has acted.

The difference in Eyre's appearance from the humble journeyman of the morning to the grave alderman of the afternoon will, his wife is confident, be sufficient to prevent the merchant from recognizing the shoemaker in alderman's dress. Deloney does not describe either of Eyre's meetings with the merchant, but the ruse is successful, and we next find Eyre and his wife having supper at the home of the Lord Mayor; all the City is craving acquaintance with 'the Gentleman that bought all the goods that came in the black *Swan* of *Candy*' (p. 116), and is struck with wonder at the financial *coup* which this hitherto unknown shoemaker has brought off. As the Lord Mayor puts it to 'a graue, wealthy Cittizen, sitting at the Table' who has inquired Eyre's name:

This was a man that was neuer thought vpon, liuing obscure amongst vs, of none account in the eyes of the world, carrying the countenance but of a shoomaker, and none of the best sort neither, and is able to deal for a bargain of fiue thousand pounds at a clap.

We do want many such shoomakers (said the Citizen) (p. 116).

One of Deloney's best touches is his depiction of Eyre and his wife, back home that night, reliving the triumph of their admission into society. Mistress Eyre reflects with satisfaction on the sensation she and her husband have caused:

Of a truth (quoth she) although I sate closely by my Ladies side, I could eat nothing for very ioy, to heare and see that we were so much made of. And neuer giue me credit husband, if I did not hear the Officers whisper as they stood behind me, and all demanded one of another, what you were, and what I was: O (quoth one) do you see this man? mark him well, and marke his wife well, that simple woman that sits next my Ladie: what are they? What are they (quoth another)? Marry this is the rich Shoomaker that bought all the goods in the great Argozy (p. 117).

Not only has Eyre bought all the goods in the great ship, he is able to sell them at a substantial profit; his profits he invests in further successful enterprises, and his riches daily increase. The Lord Mayor and Aldermen choose him to be Sheriff of London; the cares incumbent upon this office cause him to 'put off his Shoomakers shop to one of his men' (p. 125); when, a few years later, he is chosen Lord Mayor of London, Eyre changes his copy and becomes 'one of the worshipfull Company of Drapers' (p. 131). It is now that he remembers his youthful promise to his fellow apprentices, and on a Shrove Tuesday morning he feasts all the 'prentices of London with a breakfast of pudding-pies and pancakes in his house and gardens. They are summoned thither by 'the ringing of a Bell in euery Parish', the signal that 'the Prentises should leaue work and shut vp their shops for that day, which being euer since yeerly obserued, it is called the Pancake Bell' (p. 132). Later, Sir Simon Eyre builds Leadenhall and establishes a market where shoemakers could buy leather on Mondays. He 'ended his life in *London* with great Honour' (p. 133).

Of the three stories which comprise Part One of *The Gentle Craft*, Dekker makes no use at all of the first, that of St Winifred and St Hugh,[1] though to be sure *The Shoemakers' Holiday* makes frequent allusion to the legend of St Hugh's bones and to the origin of the phrase 'Gentle Craft' in its application to the trade of shoe-makers.[2] The story of Crispine and Crispianus is the basis for the double romantic plot of Dekker's play. The two princely brothers, one of whom goes off to fight in his country's wars while the other remains at home to pursue a secret amour, become, respectively, the humble journeyman shoemaker, Rafe, who is pressed to the wars in France, and the highborn Rowland Lacy, who plays the truant from his colonelcy to stay in London and woo the Lord Mayor's daughter. It is one of Dekker's most effective strokes of dramatic conversion; what in Deloney is but a contrast of fraternal tempera-ments becomes in Dekker a matter of the different options that are available to two young men at opposite ends of the social scale.

---

[1] A few years later (*c.* 1608) it would be dramatized (with the story of Crispine and Crispianus) in William Rowley's *A Shoemaker a Gentleman*.

[2] As W. J. Halliday noted in his edition of *The Gentle Craft* (Oxford, 1928), p. 92, a different explanation of the origin of the phrase is given in Robert Greene's play, *George a Greene* (written *c.* 1590, printed in 1599):

'The shoemakers of Bradford have an altercation with King Edward of England and King James of Scotland who have come to the town disguised. During the altercation, George a Greene and Robin Hood come on the scene, also disguised, and beat the shoemakers away with staves. Peace is restored when the shoemakers recognize the valiant George a Greene, and all the party "fall a-drinking".'

The shoemakers are told:

'Mary, because you haue drunke with the King, and the king hath so graciously pledgd you, you shall be no more called Shoomakers; but you and yours, to the worlds ende, shall be called the trade of the gentle craft.' (Ed. J. C. Collins, lines 1135–1138)

Deloney's Crispianus, who has no beloved, can go off to the wars with an untroubled spirit; Dekker's Rafe is parted from his Jane. Crispianus returns from the wars a hero, his fortune made; Rafe returns as humbly undistinguished as he went, the only change in his condition being that he is now lame. In providing Rafe with a beloved whom he nearly loses while he is absent with the English armies in France, Dekker establishes an ironic parallel with the aristocratic Lacy who stays at home to further his suit to Rose. The irony carries its burden of implicit social commentary, but nowhere is Dekker's art more delicate than in the restraint employed here. There is no concern with pointing up the disparity between the courses that are open to the two young men; it is as much a social as it is a dramatic given, built into the class-structure of society even as it is built into the formal design of the play, which here may be observed quietly but poignantly mirroring the inequality of class privileges.

Dekker connected Deloney's stories of Crispine and Crispianus and of Simon Eyre by the simple device of making Eyre the shoemaker with whom the disguised Crispine/Lacy takes service; and he confirmed the connection by giving Lacy (disguised as the Dutchman Hans) the function of John Deneuale, Eyre's French journeyman in Deloney, who tells his master of the great ship from the Isle of Candy. In addition to John the Frenchman, Eyre's household in Deloney also includes a Dutchman, Hans, and an Englishman, Nicholas, and two chapters of *The Gentle Craft* (12 and 14) are given over to their rivalry for the love of one of Eyre's housemaids, Florence. Of all this Dekker makes no use, though it is possible that Deloney's night-time scene in which John, who has made Hans drunk and managed to have Nicholas put in jail, intercepts Florence at the Abbey of Grace where she has come to marry Hans, only to be suddenly confronted with his wife, newly arrived from France in search of him, may have provided a suggestion for the imbroglio engineered by Firke (V.ii) in the early-morning hours outside St Faith's Church under Paul's, when Jane's living husband is restored to her and she is delivered from Hammon.

Prior to Deloney, the name of Simon Eyre was to be encountered chiefly in the pages of chroniclers such as Grafton and Stow. He had served as Sheriff of London in 1434, and Mayor in 1445.[1] Apart from these civic distinctions, his chief claim to fame was his building of the Leadenhall.[2]

Since Stow's account of its history has been misread by editors of Deloney and Dekker, it had best be given in full.

Then in the yeare 1443. the 21. of *Henrie* the sixt, *Iohn Hatherley* Maior, purchased licence of the said King, to take vp 200. fodder of Leade, for the building of water Conduits, a common Granarie, and the crosse in west Cheape more richly for honour of the Citie. In the yeare next following, the Parson and parish of Saint *Dunston* in the east of London, seeing the famous and mightie man (for the wordes bee in the graunt: *cum nobilis & potens vir.*) *Simon Eyre*, Citizen of London, among other his workes of pietie, effectually determined to erect and build a certaine Granarie vpon the soile of the same Citie at Leaden hall of his owne charges, for the common vtilitie of the saide Citie, to the amplifying and inlarging of the sayde Granarie, graunted to *Henrie Frowicke* then Maior, the Aldermen, and Comminaltie and their successors for euer, all their Tenements, with the appurtenaunces, sometime called the Horsemill in Grasse streete, for the annuall rent of foure pound &c. Also certaine Euidences of an Alley and Tenements pertayning to the Horse-mill, adioyning to the sayd Leaden hall in Grasse streete, giuen by *William Kingstone* Fishmonger, vnto the parish church of S. *Peter* vpon Cornehill, doe specifie the sayd Granarie to be builded by the sayde honourable and famous Marchant *Symon Eyre*, sometime an Upholster, and then a Draper, in the yeare 1419. He builded it of squared stone, in forme as now it sheweth, with a fayre and large chappell in the East side of the Quadrant, ouer the porch of which hee caused to be written, *Dextra Domini exaltauit me*, The Lords right hand exalted me (*Survey*, I, 153–154).

Read in context, the year 1419 is presumably the year in which Eyre changed his copy from upholster to draper. It is certainly not the year in which he erected a public granary in the Leadenhall,

---

[1] For Eyre's terms of office as sheriff and mayor, see Stow, *Survey*, II, 173, 174. All references to the *Survey* are to Kingsford's edition.

[2] Though accounts of Eyre regularly credit him with building the Leadenhall (e.g. Stow, *A Summarie of Englyshe Chronicles* (1565), fol. 147v; Richard Grafton, *Chronicle of Briteyn* (1568), p. 595; Stow, *Survey*, I, 110), the edifice had been in existence at least since the end of the thirteenth century (see Kingsford's note in his edition of the *Survey*, II, 295). Stow himself traces its history from 1309 (*Survey*, I, 153). Originally a private estate, it passed into the hands of '*Richarde Whittington* and other Citizens of London' in 1408, and in 1411 'the said *Whittington* and other confirmed the same to the Maior and Comminaltie of London, whereby it came to the possession of the Citie' (*Survey*, I, 153).

but it has been taken to be so by all previous editors of *The Shoemakers' Holiday*.[1]

Stow gives Eyre's death as 18 September 1459.[2] According to the chroniclers, he was first an upholsterer and then a draper, never a shoemaker, and why he should have been connected with the gentle craft is not clear unless, as J. R. Sutherland has suggested,[3] it be because the Leadenhall with which Eyre was popularly associated had, 'since the fifth year of Elizabeth's reign,...been used as a leather market'.

How far the legend of Eyre had developed when Deloney took his story in hand we do not know. With his civic honors and his public benefactions,[4] he was a model for every London citizen. Deloney's depiction of him in *The Gentle Craft* is aimed at giving him the sort of background that the largest possible audience might identify with, and Eyre's career is cast in the mould of a Dick Whittington success story: the hard-working young apprentice whose steady application to his job brings him fame and fortune. Deloney's Eyre is a thoroughly sober citizen: serious in the conduct of his affairs and in the calculation of the risks he runs in the course of his advancement. He is a devoted, even a somewhat sentimental, husband;[5] he is modest and discreet in his behaviour at

[1] The error may be traceable to F. O. Mann who, in his edition of Deloney (p. 523) gives but an abbreviated version of the end of the Stow passage ('Certain Euidences ...doe specifie the sayd Granarie to be builded by the sayde honourable and famous Marchant, *Simon Eyre*, sometime an Vpholster, and then a Draper, in the Year 1419' plus the following sentence). But all the chronicles bear witness to the fact that the historical Eyre erected the public granary in Leadenhall in the year of his mayoralty, which extended from October 1445 to October 1446. This point is established in the first half of the passage quoted above from Stow. Hatherley and Frowicke, whom Stow names, were two of the three mayors who immediately preceded Eyre in the office (Hatherley in 1442, Frowicke in 1444, according to Stow's section on 'Temporall Gouernment' (*Survey*, II, 174)). It is clear that the granary was established in the mid-1440s, not in 1419. Stow's testimony elsewhere puts the matter beyond any doubt; in his *Englyshe Chronicles* (fol. 147v), Eyre's building of Leadenhall is recorded among the events of 1445, as it is in Grafton, *Chronicle of Briteyn*, p. 595. The date for the erection of Eyre's granary in Leadenhall is given as 1445 in Wheatley and Cunningham, II, 375; and as 1446 by H. A. Harben, *A Dictionary of London* (London, 1918), p. 344. [2] *Survey*, I, 154.

[3] J. R. Sutherland in his edition of *The Shoemakers' Holiday*, p. 8.

[4] The legacies provided for in Eyre's will are described in Stow, *Survey*, I, 154. Concerning these, see M. E. Lawlis, 'Another Look at Simon Eyre's Will', *Notes and Queries*, 199 (1954), 13–16.

[5] Witness the episode of the little table: Eyre is known to have 'a Table in his

all times. In short, the Simon Eyre of *The Gentle Craft* is an upstanding and altogether conventional member of the rising middle class. Dekker's transformation of this rather bourgeois figure into his madcap Sim Eyre is the most remarkable alteration he works on Deloney's material, though almost equally impressive is the metamorphosis of Deloney's modest and demure but exceedingly shrewd Mistress Eyre into Dekker's flighty Margery.

The transformational scheme that turns Deloney's Crispine into Dekker's Lacy inevitably turns Ursula, daughter of the Emperor Maximinus, into Rose, daughter of Sir Roger Otley, Lord Mayor of London. Dekker found the name of his heroine's father in the chronicles. Roger Otley was a London grocer who was sheriff in 1427 and mayor in 1434 (the year in which Eyre was sheriff).[1] In his role of the father who objects to his daughter's choice of husband, he has his opposite number in the Earl of Lincoln, uncle to Lacy,[2] who objects to his nephew's choice of wife. The Earl of Lincoln is a character of Dekker's creation, since Crispine in *The Gentle Craft* has neither father nor near relative serving as his guardian, and he contributes to the symmetry of Dekker's comic design. At bottom it is the familiar one which places young love in opposition to unsympathetic father-figures, and accordingly puts the lovers to their shifts if their romance is to win the day, but Dekker compounds the comedy of cross-purposes by making the father-figures themselves representative of sharply opposing social attitudes. Lincoln objects to the match because he does not want his nobly-born nephew to marry a citizen's daughter. Otley, equally opposed, does not want his daughter to marry an extravagant scion of the nobility. The opposition of both Otley and Lincoln

house whereon he breaks his fast euery day, that he will not giue for a thousand pounds' (*The Gentle Craft*, p. 123). The table is Mistress Eyre, whose habit it is to seat herself 'on a low stool' beside her husband's chair, lay 'a fair Napkin ouer her knees' and place her husband's plate thereupon (p. 124).

[1] Stow, *Survey*, II, 173.

[2] The name of Dekker's hero may have been suggested by Robert Greene's *Friar Bacon and Friar Bungay* (c. 1590), where Lacy, Earl of Lincoln, wins the love of Margaret, the fair maid of Fressingfield, in spite of the rival suit of the Prince of Wales. For a detailed study of connections between the names of characters in Dekker's play and the names of historical personages contemporary with Simon Eyre, see W. K. Chandler, 'The Sources of the Characters in *The Shoemakers' Holiday*,' *Modern Philology*, 27 (1929), 175–182.

to the match has the ironic effect of bringing them together in their efforts to frustrate it, though for very different reasons, which Dekker makes operative in the comedy of the play's opening scene.

The character of the King is another addition of Dekker's to the story of Eyre, whose breakfast for the apprentices at the end of *The Gentle Craft* is not graced by a royal presence. Chronology dictates that the only king who could have feasted with Simon Eyre during his adult life was Henry VI, but it has seemed to some critics that Dekker's king, with his easy camaraderie and his confident direction of the English war against the French, is conceived more in the image of Henry V than in that of his sorely tried son.[1]

On 15 July 1599, Henslowe advanced the sum of £3 'to bye A Boocke of thomas dickers Called the gentle Craft'.[2] The play's first recorded performance took place on the night of 1 January 1600, when it was acted at Court before Queen Elizabeth I by the Lord Admiral's Men. Thereafter, though the play was sufficiently popular to have six quarto editions printed between 1600 and 1657, its stage history is a blank until the early 1920s.

The first professional performance in modern times seems to have been the one produced by A. E. Filmer at the Birmingham Repertory Theatre in December 1922.[3] Though one reviewer termed it 'one of the most satisfying Elizabethan productions' in his memory,[4] its success seems to have been limited. 'Dekker's piece brought the airs of a timeless spring...Endearing; but audi-

[1] See, for example, L. M. Manheim, 'The King in Dekker's *The Shoemakers' Holiday*', *Notes and Queries*, 202 (1957), 432–433.

[2] *Henslowe's Diary*, p. 122.

[3] In his edition of *The Shoemakers' Holiday* for the Bankside Playbooks (London, n.d. [1924?]), C. M. Edmondston reported the play to have been

'recently produced at the Birkbeck Theatre, Chancery Lane, by the Graystoke Players before a large and appreciative audience, this being the first recorded performance of the play in London for over three hundred years. It had been played in Gloucestershire a year or two before that, and in both London and Oxford since then performances have been given' (p. 88).

I have been unable to trace these performances.

[4] Herbert Farjeon, 'Last Month in the Theatres', in *The Shakespeare Journal*, 3.9 (January 1923), 50.

ences preferred the uninhibited fun' of a new comedy, 'a satire on publicity-mongering' titled *Advertising April*.[1]

But at least twice in this century, *The Shoemakers' Holiday* has been staged with resounding critical and popular success. The first such occasion came in London with the Old Vic production in the spring of 1926. It was directed by Andrew Leigh, and the cast included Baliol Holloway as Simon Eyre, Edith Evans as Margery, Frank Vosper as Lacy, John Garside as Hodge, Horace Sequeira as Firke, Neil Porter as Rafe, Amy Nowell as Rose, Nell Carter as Jane, and William Monk as the King. We are told that 'It was entirely Leigh's idea to do the revival and he met with no little opposition.' Holloway was against it, and indeed is said to have 'hated it so much that he would frequently hurl the book of words angrily across the dressing-room'[2]. But he went on to triumph in the role of Simon Eyre, as did Edith Evans who, 'in her quaint make-up' transformed herself almost beyond recognition in the role of Margery ('only her laugh gave her away'[3]). James Agate has left a revealing glimpse of her performance:

'How shall I look in a hood?' asks the new-enriched dame, to be answered, 'Like a cat in the pillory.' Whereupon Margery has the astonishing, irrelevant, 'Indeed, all flesh is grass.' Hear Miss Evans say this, mark the relish with which she passes absurdity under your nose in the manner of a connoisseur extolling old brandy – note this, and you reflect, first, that Dekker was a good playwright, and, second, that the best wit in the world gains when it is delivered by a witty actress.[4]

The critic for *The Illustrated London News* acknowledged that 'In the moral of the play the modern mind would find something to cavil at': a 'hero who prefers cobbling to joining the army in France' and who arranges for another 'to take his place and become crippled, would not pass muster since 1914'. But he concludes exultingly: 'what sheer joy in the play! How well it is written!'

[1] J. C. Trewin, *The Birmingham Repertory Theatre, 1913–1963* (London, 1963), p. 67. Herbert Farjeon, the reviewer quoted above, was one of the authors of *Advertising April*.

[2] Harcourt Williams, *Old Vic Saga* (London, 1949), p. 71.

[3] J. T. Grein in *The Illustrated London News* (10 April 1926), 656.

[4] *The Contemporary Theatre, 1926* (London, 1927), p. 41.

The production was a 'triumphant success', both with the critics and at the box-office.[1]

In the summer of 1932, *The Shoemakers' Holiday* was adapted for performance as an open-air pageant by the Kidlington Historical Play Society at Kidlington. The reviewer in the London *Times* of 9 June 1932 (p. 10) termed it 'a spectacle well worth seeing', interspersed as it was 'with masques, dances, and special music'. Some 300 persons took part in the production.

The other great occasion in the modern stage history of *The Shoemakers' Holiday* took place six years later in New York when Orson Welles and John Houseman presented it at the Mercury Theatre on Saturday night, 1 January 1938. The play was adapted and staged by Welles, and it was severely cut. It was acted without intermission, and its playing time was 'one hour and nine minutes', according to Houseman, who acknowledges that it 'was one of the shortest shows ever to be presented on Broadway'.[2] The cast included Whitford Kane as Simon Eyre, Marian Warring-Manley as Margery, Hiram Sherman as Firke, Joseph Cotten as Lacy, Vincent Price as Hammon, Elliott Reid as Rafe, Alice Frost as Rose, Ruth Ford as Jane, and George Coulouris as the King. Music was by A. Lehman Engel: 'some impish instrumental jangles', according to Brooks Atkinson in his review of the production in the New York *Times* of Monday, 3 January 1938 (p. 17); he hailed it as 'an uproarious comic strip of Elizabethan fooling' and termed it 'the funniest jig of the season'. Atkinson returned to the subject a week later, in the New York *Times* of Sunday, 9 January 1938 (Section 10, p. 1), addressing himself specifically to the subject of Welles' adaptation. With its 'emphasis upon the journeymen shoemakers and apprentices who scramble through the scenes and the jolly shoemaker who becomes Lord Mayor of London and keeps open house for the members of the craft', the Mercury production of *The Shoemakers' Holiday* admittedly 'is only one aspect of Dekker', but for Atkinson the fact remains 'that this free-hand adaptation of a verbose old comedy is the funniest prank the season has yielded'. New York audiences took a particular

[1] Williams, *Old Vic Saga*, pp. 71, 78.
[2] John Houseman, *Run-Through, a Memoir* (New York, 1972), p. 332, note.

interest in seeing Dekker's comedy acted by the same company which, on alternate nights, was performing Welles' modern-dress production of *Julius Caesar* with its fascist overtones which had entered the Mercury repertory seven weeks earlier. According to Atkinson in the *Times* of 9 January, 'The young men who swarm through the terrifying scenes of *Julius Caesar* contribute the stoutest clowning to this dance of Elizabethan fools.' And he singles out for particular praise the performance of Hiram Sherman, 'a smiling, cynical ward-heeler of a Casca'[1] in *Julius Caesar*, who 'is so giddily comic in *Shoemaker* that the subordinate part of Firk becomes the core of Dekker's play'.[2] This, it seems, was what Welles had in mind. Houseman notes that, as Welles directed the play, 'it was no longer Simon Eyre, the happy Shoemaker, who was the star but his lewd journeyman, Firk'.[3] Not unreasonably, the English critic Ivor Brown, while admitting that he had enjoyed himself at the Mercury production, felt that 'in its preoccupation with boisterous fun' it had left out 'a kind of lyrical tenderness and a sweet opportunity for song and dance'.[4] The production ran in repertory with *Julius Caesar* for sixty-four performances, and was playing to standing room when it had to be closed to make way for the Mercury production of Shaw's *Heartbreak House*.[5]

Since the end of the Second World War there have been a number of English productions of *The Shoemakers' Holiday*. The play was staged in London at the Lyric, Hammersmith, in May 1944. The reviewer in the London *Times* (30 May 1944), 2, found Caven Wilson as Simon Eyre 'altogether too dry, too precise, too much buttoned-up to give the comedy the impetus it requires from this part', and considered that it was 'from the Cockney impishness' of Andrew Leigh as Firke 'that most of the impetus comes'. The cast also included Walter Hudd as Hammon and Patrick Barton as the King.

The Oxford University Dramatic Society produced *The Shoemakers' Holiday* at the Playhouse, Oxford, in March 1948.

[1] *Ibid.*, p. 299.
[2] Atkinson, New York *Times* (9 January 1938), Section 10, 1.
[3] Houseman, *Run-through*, p. 358.
[4] Quoted in *ibid.*, p. 333.
[5] *Ibid.*, p. 355.

The actors who, in the opinion of the *Times* reviewer, came 'nearest to what the play requires of them' were Robert Hardy as Firke, William Patrick as Rafe, John Schlesinger as Dodger, and Heather Cooper as Jane. Nevill Coghill appeared as the Dutch skipper.[1]

A performance of *The Shoemakers' Holiday* by the Tavistock Repertory Company at the Tower Theatre, Canonbury, directed by David Thompson in the spring of 1961 was adjudged by the *Times* reviewer (11 April 1961), 4, to be 'at least good enough to expose the quality of a work often clumsily revived'.

The Oxford University Dramatic Society returned to *The Shoemakers' Holiday* in the summer of 1961 with a production directed by David Webster and staged in the Cloister of Wadham College. The cast included Sam Walters as Eyre, John Watts as Lacy, Richard Sherrington as Hammon, and Nancy Lane as Rose.[2]

'The main effort' of a performance of *The Shoemakers' Holiday* by the Vic–Wells Association, presented at the Old Vic in February 1962, seemed 'to be directed towards filling in the spaces between lines rather than towards interpreting the lines themselves'.[3] The cast included Michael Turner as Eyre, Peter Ellis as Firke, Jane Downs as Margery, and Stephen Moore as Rafe.

In the summer of 1964, *The Shoemakers' Holiday* was presented at the Mermaid Theatre, London, in a production directed by David William in which there was 'a great deal of added business'.[4] Jeremy Rowe as the King was 'first seen coquettishly trying on a series of crowns and spraying himself liberally with an atomizer'. Robert Gillespie in a black cloak as Dodger flitted 'into dark corners with superfluous stealth'. Eyre's question to his wife at I.iv.32 ('wheres *Cisly Bumtrinket* your maide?') produced an addition to the *Dramatis Personae* in the person of a maid by that name. The wordless part was taken by Denise Coffey, who provided 'an abject spectre of resentment in the midst of gaiety'. John Woodvine was Eyre ('mountainously padded in slop breeches and twitching down to his finger-ends with benevolence and wild

---

[1] London *Times* (3 March 1948), 6.
[2] London *Times* (14 June 1961), 15.
[3] London *Times* (5 February 1962), 14.
[4] London *Times* (25 July 1964), 10.

caprice'). David Weston was Firke, and Hilda Fenemore was Margery. The production was revived in the spring of 1965, now directed by Robert Gillespie. The account by the *Times* critic gives a somewhat more restrained impression. John Woodvine, again in the role of Eyre, recreated the character 'with a marvellous ebullience'; the play's tone was 'perfectly caught' in the production as a whole: 'warm without sentimentality and its social and moral undertones...never more than indicated'.[1]

The Shoemakers' Holiday was produced by the Bristol Old Vic Theatre School, directed by Nat Brenner, at the Minack Theatre, Porthcurno, Penzance, Cornwall in the summer of 1968.[2]

The National Youth Theatre produced *The Shoemakers' Holiday*, directed by David Weston, at the Shaw Theatre in the summer of 1971 with George Irving as Eyre. According to Michael Billington in the London *Times* (26 August 1971), 6, the production's 'good fun' was 'often achieved at the expense of the characterization'.

In the summer of 1972, *The Shoemakers' Holiday* was produced in London at the Bankside Globe Playhouse by the Sheffield Crucible Company. The production was directed by Douglas Campbell, who also acted the role of Simon Eyre as 'a roaring nonentity', according to Irving Wardle in the London *Times* of 4 July 1972 (p. 9). 'Dekker's view of the London scene', said Wardle, was 'reduced to romantic lunacy'.

On 2 April 1970, *The Shoemakers' Holiday* was performed at the reopening of the newly overhauled quarters of the Habimah National Theatre of Israel in Tel Aviv.[3]

Reference is made in the Commentary to the work of the following editors of *The Shoemakers' Holiday*: C. F. Tucker Brooke and N. B. Paradise, in *English Drama, 1580–1642* (Boston, 1933); W. J. Halliday (London, 1927); J. Hampden (Edinburgh, n.d. [1932?]); A. Koszul (Paris, 1955); A. F. Lange, in vol. III of *Representative English Comedies*, General Editor, C. M. Gayley (New York, 1914); W. A. Neilson, in *Chief Elizabethan Dramatists*

---

[1] London *Times* (3 March 1965), 15.

[2] *The Minack Open-Air Theatre, A Symposium*, ed. Averil Demuth (Newton Abbot, Devon., 1968), p. 127.

[3] New York *Times* (29 March 1970), Section 2, 33.

(Boston, 1911); Ernest Rhys, in his Mermaid edition of five plays of Dekker (London, 1887); Hazelton Spencer, in his *Elizabethan Plays* (Boston, 1933); J. B. Steane (Cambridge, 1965); J. R. Sutherland (Oxford, 1928); Karl Warnke and Ludwig Proescholdt (Halle, 1886); C. B. Wheeler, in *Six Plays of Contemporaries of Shakespeare* (Oxford, [1915]); W. Tom Williams (London, 1927).

COMMENTARY

To all good Fellowes

16 *Three-mens songs.* 'A song for three voices; as a catch, glee, madrigal, etc.' (Nares). *The Winter's Tale*, IV.iii.41–42: 'the shearers (three-man song-men all, and very good ones)'.

18 *mirth lengthneth long life.* Sutherland compares Udall, *Roister Doister*, prologue, 8: 'For myrth prolongeth lyfe, and causeth health.' And cf. Old Merrythought's song at the end of Beaumont's *The Knight of the Burning Pestle*: 'Hey ho, 'tis nought but mirth, / That keepes the body from the earth.'

The first Three-mans Song

For the placement of the song in the text, see note on III.iii.24. Accounts of shoemakers regularly find them singing at their work. Among the accomplishments of the ideal journeyman, as listed in Deloney's *The Gentle Craft*, is the ability to 'bear his part in a three mans Song' (ed. Mann, p. 89).

4 *Summers Queene.* The queen of the May games or the midsummer festival. Cf. Robert Greene, *Greenes Mourning Garment*, IX, 143:

> Faire she was as faire might be,
> Like the Roses on the tree:
> Buxsame, blieth, and young, I weene,
> Beautious, like a Summers Queene

And Fletcher, *The Faithful Shepherdess*, I.i.18–19: 'How often have I sat crownd with fresh flowers / For summers queene.' S.D., III.ii.19.

5–8 *the Nightingale…sitteth, her breast against a brier.* Concerning this supposed habit of the nightingale, cf. Sir Thomas

Browne, *Pseudodoxia Epidemica*, III, 28 (*Works*, ed. G. L. Keynes (6 vols., London, 1928–1931), II, 268): 'Whether the Nightingale's setting with her breast against a thorn, be any more then that she placeth some prickles on the outside of her nest, or roosteth in thorny and prickly places, where Serpents may least approach her?' The idea is proverbial; Tilley, N183. *K.C.*, B1: 'whilst the Nightingale sate on the branches complaining against lust'. *R.A.*, C2: 'But shall I tel you at what signe the Spring dwelleth? cast vp your eies and behold, for by these marks shal you know her when she comes. When the nightingale sits singing with a brier at her brest, & the adulterer (that rauished *Philomell*) sits singing at the Thornes which pricke his conscience.'

11 *I do not like the Cuckoo*, on account of its traditional association with cuckoldry. Cf. *Love's Labour's Lost*, V.ii.900–902.

The second Three-mans Song

For a suggested tune for this song, see Chappell, I, 277–278 ('The Cobbler's Jigg').

5 *Trowle the boll*, i.e. pass (circulate) the bowl. Music for a round based on these words is given in Ravenscroft, *Pammelia*, no. 62 (1609), E2: 'Trole trole the bole to me, and I will trole the same again to thee.' The phrase occurs frequently in drinking-songs: e.g. W. Wager, *Enough is as Good as a Feast* (ed. R. M. Benbow (Lincoln, 1967)), line 293; Ulpian Fulwell, *Like Will to Like* (*The Dramatic Writings of Ulpian Fulwell*, ed. J. S. Farmer (London, 1906)), p. 25; Nashe, *Summer's Last Will and Testament* (III, 258). It provides one of the snatches of song that Old Merrythought sings in *The Knight of the Burning Pestle*, II.432.

8 *downe it*, with a quibble on the contents of the 'Nut-browne boll' and the refrain that follows.

9–10 *Downe a downe...Hey derie derie down*. For the refrain, cf. IV.i.1, and Old Merrythought's song in *The Knight of the Burning Pestle*, II.505–508:

> *Was never man for Ladies sake*,
> Downe, downe,

Tormented as I poore sir Guy!
De derry downe

10 S.D. *Close with the tenor boy*, 'i.e. chime in with the boy who is singing tenor' (Sutherland).

12 *Ring compasse gentle ioy*. 'Let joy reach its fullest range, let joy be unconfined' (Sutherland).

The Prologue

4 *wonder of all eyes*. O.F., I.i.111.

I.i

5 *cosen*, nephew (cf. I.i. lines 39, 72).

27 *imbezeld*, squandered. Beaumont, *The Knight of the Burning Pestle*, 1.302–305: 'thou art a wast-thrift, and art run away from thy maister, that lov'd thee well, and art come to me, and I have laid up a little for my yonger sonne *Michael*, and thou think'st to bezell that'.

46 *his grace*, i.e. the King; cf. V.ii.158.

58 *Mile end*. Then a common on the main eastern road out of London, used as a training-ground for the bands of citizen soldiers. Stow (*Survey*, 1, 103) records the 'great muster' of 8 May 1539 'made by the Cittizens, at the Miles end...to the number of 15000'. There had been another more recent one, on 27 August 1599 (the very period during which Dekker was presumably at work on this play), when according to Stow (*A Summarie of the Chronicles of England* (1604), p. 420) '3000 Citizens householders and subsidy men, shewed on the Miles end, where they trained all that day, and other vntill the fourth of September.' R.G., II.i.170.

59 *Tuttle fields*.

A large piece of open land in Westminster on the left bank of the Thames, south of Tothill St. Its exact boundaries are vague, but it extended as far as Vauxhall Bridge Road, and the actual Tot, or Toot, Hill seems to have been at the point where Horseferry Road forms an angle at its junction with Carey Street...Tournaments were held there, and wagers of battle decided...It was also a training ground for troops, and a practising place for archers (Sugden).

61 *Finsbury.* Then a swampy district to the north of London, and
another mustering-ground for the city train-bands. It was
especially noted for its archery ground. Cf. below, II.iii.55–
56, n.

63 *imprest,* advance pay of soldiers (*O.E.D.*, B.1, citing the present
passage). Cf. lines 65 and 145.

63 *furniture,* equipment. *1 Henry IV*, III.iii.199–202:

> Jack, meet me to-morrow in the Temple Hall
> At two a'clock in the afternoon;
> There shalt thou know thy charge, and there receive
> Money and order for their furniture.

85 *byas,* inclination, course (metaphor from the game of bowls).
O.F., IV.i.42, n.

90 *Portugues,* Portuguese gold coins, varying in value at different
times from £3 5s. to £4 10s. Harrison, II, xxv (ed. Furnivall,
I, 364): 'Of forren coines we haue...the portigue, a peece
verie solemnelie kept of diuerse, & yet oft times abased with
washing, or absolutelie counterfeited.' Cf. *S.H.*, II.iii.21.

116.2 *a peece.* Presumably a piece of leather, a cobbler's patch. Cf.
the story of the cobbler's wife in *W.Y.*, p. 47: 'vp she calles
her verie innocent and simple husband, out of his vertuous
shop, where like Iustice he sat distributing among the poore,
to some, halfe-penny pieces, penny-pieces to some, and two-
penny pieces to others, so long as they would last; his proui-
dent care being alwaies, that euery man and woman should
goe vpright'. And later (p. 48) where the cobbler is addressed
in a bawdy quibble: 'O thou that art trained vp in nothing
but to handle pieces'. Cf. Cotgrave, *s.v. Bobelin*: 'A patch,
botch, peece, set on a shooe, or garment'. But here the word
may also mean a gun; cf. *I.T.B.N.*, III.ii.0.1–2: '*Enter
Subprior with an earthen pot, and a lanthorne;* Scumbroath *with
him with a peice.*'

123–124 *pishery pasherie.* See line 157, and III.iii.40; V.iv.50.

127 *Towerstreete,* 'stretching from the Tower hill, west to S.
Margaret Pattens church Parsonage' (Stow, *Survey*, I, 130).

129 *firking,* fantastical. Cf. Nashe, *Have With You*, III, 80: 'the
concise and firking finicaldo fine School-master'.

130 *blubbered,* disfigured from weeping. Spenser, *The Faerie Queene,* II.i.13: 'her faire face with teares was fowly blubbered'.

135 *Midriffe,* 'Diaphragm; probably a slighting allusion to Margery's corpulence' (H. Spencer). *1 Henry IV,* III.iii.153–155: 'But, sirrah, there's no room for faith, truth, nor honesty in this bosom of thine; it is all fill'd up with guts and midriff.' Cf. *V.M.,* III.iii.23, and *S.H.,* I.iv.5.

136 *cormorant.* Firke's blunder for 'colonel', often spelled 'coronel', as at line 122, and in the prefatory epistle 'To all good Fellowes', line 10.

143 *occupied. Sat.,* IV.iii.266, n.

145 *The Londoners are prest.* Concerning Elizabethan methods of impressment, cf. Stow, *Annales* (edn. 1605), pp. 1281–1282):

The 9. of Aprill [1596] being good friday, in the afternoone, the lord maior and aldermen of London being in Powles churchyard, hearing the sermon at Paules crosse, were sodainelie called from thence, and foorthwith by a precept from her maiestie and counsell, pressed 1000. men, which was done by 8. of the clocke the same night, and before the next morning they were purueied of all manner of furniture for the wars, readie to haue gone towardes Douer, and so to the aide of the French in Caleis against the Spaniardes, but in the afternoone of the same Saturday they were all discharged: not withstanding on the 11. of Aprill being Easter daie, about tenne of the clocke before noone, came a newe charge, so that all men being in their parish Churches readie to haue receiued the Communion, the aldermen, their deputies, constables, and other officers, were faine to close vp the Church-doores, till they had pressed so manie men to be souldiers, that by twelue of the clocke, they had in the whole Cittie 1000. men, and those, forthwith furnished of armour, weapons and all thinges necessarie, were for the most part that night, and the rest on the next morrow sent awaie towards Douer, as the like out of other partes of the Realme: but about a weeke after they returned backe againe, for the French had lost Caleis.

The edition of 1615 (p. 770) adds: 'The Earle of Essex had the command of these men.'

149–150 *doe more then you can answere...day of his mariage.* Lange cites Deuteronomy 24: 5: 'When a man hath taken a new wife, he shall not go out to war, neither shall he be charged with any business: but he shall be free at home one year, and shall cheer up his wife which he hath taken.'

153 *wife...case.* 2 *H.W.*, IV.iii.76, n. And cf. *S.H.*, III.ii.87.

154 *but let that passe.* For this affectation, cf. Armado in *Love's Labour's Lost*, V.i.97–108; Fastidius Briske in Jonson's *Every Man out of his Humour*, III.iii.2–3, and later Shift in the same play, III.vi.53; Chapman, *All Fools*, V.ii.187; Chettle and Day, *The Blind Beggar of Bednal Green*, II.ii (ed. Bullen, *Works of Day*, p. 41). See *S.H.*, I.iv.50; II.iii.38–39, 112, 141; III.ii.19, 24 and *passim*.

157–158 *pols...edipolls.* Cf. Nashe, *Have With You*, III, 7: 'by *Poll* and *Aedipoll* I protest', and McKerrow's note (IV, 304–305): 'The not unusual collocation of these two interjections is probably a reminiscence of Lily's *Grammar*, where in the section "Of the Aduerbe" it is stated that "Some be of Swearing: as Pol, ædepol, hercle, medius fidius".' McKerrow, citing the present passage, concludes that 'The words seem sometimes to mean nonsensical talk.' For other examples, cf. *Every Woman in her Humour* (1609), H4: 'hee has his pols and his aedypols, his times and his tricks, his quirkes and his quilits'. And *Kemps Nine Daies Wonder* (1600), D4: 'One that hath not wit enough to make a ballet, that by *Pol* and *Aedipol*, would Pol his father, Derick his dad: doe anie thing how ill soeuer, to please his apish humor'.

158 *Cisly Bumtrincket.* Eyre uses the name indifferently both for his wife and, at I.iv.32, her maid. It seems to have been a humorously disparaging term for any female. When Tucca calls Mistress Miniver by it (*Sat.*, III.i.186–187) she reproaches him ('Why dost call mee such horrible vngodlie names then?'). Cf. Day, *Law Tricks*, Act V (ed. Bullen, p. 198): 'as for you, Sisley bumtrinkets, ile haue a bout with you at the single Stackado'. It occurs in the refrain of one of the canting songs in Brome, *A Jovial Crew*, II.ii.171–172: 'Now bowse a round health to the go-well and come-well / Of Cisley Bumtrinket that lies in the strummel.'

161 *Tawsoone* (Welsh *Taw són*) 'hold your tongue'. Cf. Jonson, *For the Honour of Wales*, 97: 'Aw, gadu i'n, tawson', which Herford and Simpson (x, 591) translate as 'Oh, leave us alone, shut up.' And William Rowley, *A Shoemaker a Gentle-*

man, I.ii.158–160: 'Peace Sisly, no problems, no figures, no womans Rhetorick, the tongue may undoe the whole body, *Tausume*, there is Greeke for yee wife.' The expression occurs, as Professor Bowers observed in his textual note on this passage (I, 90), in the Welsh dialect of *P.G.* (at III.ii.232; IV.iii.137; V.ii.87, 113), and Tucca uses it in addressing the Welshman Sir Vaughan in *Sat.*, V.ii.172. And cf. *N.H.*, IV.i.121; *W.E.*, IV.i.81.

164 *powder dankish.* *N.G.*, p. 72: 'the dankish powder of their apprehensions'. *M.M.L.*, II.i.16.

165 *Termagant*, the god of the Saracens in the Romances and Mystery plays. His Elizabethan reputation as a loud and violent personage is familiar from *Hamlet*, III.ii.13. And see Florio, *s.v.* *Termigisto*: 'a great boaster, quareller, killer, tamer or ruler of the Vniuerse, the child of the earth-quake and of the thunder, the brother of death'. With the chauvinism of the present passage, cf. *The History of the Tryall of Cheualry* (ed. Bullen, III, 343–344): 'Though wee have left our brave Generall, the Earle of Pembrooke, yet here's Cavaliero Bowyer, Core, and Nod, by Jesu, sound cards: and Mahound and Termagant come against us, weele fight with them. Couragio, my hearts! S. George for the honour of England!' Dekker speaks of 'the *Tartarian Tarmagant*' in *S.H.R.*, D4.

166 *the Lord of Ludgate.* Presumably a reference to the legendary King Lud, whose statue stood on the east side of Ludgate, which had been rebuilt in 1586 (Stow, *Survey*, I, 39). The phrase occurs again at line 216 in this scene and at I.iv.63; II.iii.33–34; V.i.36.

167 *tall*, valiant. *P.G.*, II.i.186. And *S.H.*, III.ii.57; V.iv.23.

167 *by the life of Pharo.* Genesis 42: 15–16. Cob the water-bearer uses the oath in the original version of Jonson's *Every Man in his Humour*, I.iii.70–77:

and the wenches, they doe so geere and tihe at him; well, should they do as much to me, Ild forsweare them all, by the life of Pharaoh, there's an oath: how many waterbearers shall you heare sweare such an oath? oh I haue a guest (he teacheth me) he doth sweare the best of any man christned: By Phoebus, By the life of Pharaoh, By the body of me, As I am a gentleman, and a soldier: such daintie oathes.

Jonson altered the phrase in the 1616 Folio to 'the foot of Pharaoh'. Cf. *The History of the Tryall of Cheualry* (ed. Bullen, III, 351): '*Bow.* Not we by this beard, not we by the life of Pharo.' *W.H.*, V.iii.34. And *S.H.*, II.iii.33; V.i.46.

181 *stirrop.* 'The shoemaker's strap, by which he keeps his last on his knee' (H. Spencer). Cf. the enumeration of the shoemaker's tools in Deloney, *The Gentle Craft*, p. 89: 'The Stirrop holding fast, while we sowe the Cow-hide'. *S.H.*, I.iv.34.

192 *pickethanke,* flattering, sycophantic. J. Phillip, *Patient Grissell* (M.S.R. (1909), prepared by R. B. McKerrow and W. W. Greg), line 312: 'Be no pickthanke, seke not the fruts of discensyon.' *1 Henry IV*, III.ii.25: 'smiling pick-thanks and base newsmongers'.

204 *crackt groates.* Coins were stamped with a ring inside which the sovereign's head was placed. A coin containing a crack extending inside the ring was unfit for currency. A groat was worth 4d. *W.H.*, II.i.178–179.

204 *mustard tokens,* like the 'crackt groates', a type of worthlessness. In the last decades of the sixteenth century, the need for small change 'led the shopkeepers of London and other large towns to issue halfpenny and farthing tokens of brass, tin, lead, or even leather, which they undertook to redeem or receive in payment for goods' (*Shakespeare's England*, I, 343). *V.M.*, II.iii.236.

207 *be doing with.* For the bawdy innuendo, cf. *Grim the Collier of Croydon,* Act IV (1662), p. 52: 'there is a tricksey Girle, / That three or four would fain be doing with'.

210 *bombast cotten-candle.* 'Candle with a cotton wick' (H. Spencer). Bombast was cotton-wool used as padding or stuffing for clothes. Here it may allude, as Spencer suggests, to Jane's plumpness. Eyre addresses the same term to Margery at II.iii.35–36. Cf. the reproach to the player in *Wily Beguiled* (M.S.R. (1912), prepared by W. W. Greg), prologue, 10–12: 'Why noble *Cerberus*, nothing but patch-pannell stuffe, olde gally-mawfreies and cotten-candle eloquence?'

213 *saint Martins.* Stow, noting that 'Men of trades and sellers

of wares in this City haue often times since chaunged their places, as they haue found their best aduantage', records how 'the Shoomakers and Curriors of Cordwayner streete, remoued the one to Saint *Martins Le Grand*, the other to London wall neare vnto Mooregate' (*Survey*, I, 81). *G.H.*, C3v: 'fetch thee [Q 1609: 'three'] bootes out of S. *Martens*'. *W.H.*, II.i.215, n.

215 *cracke me the crownes of the French knaues*. For the quibbles implicit in Eyre's words, see the notes on *P.G.*, II.i.219–220 and *I.T.B.N.*, II.ii.71.

219 *firke*, beat, trounce. Fletcher, *Women Pleased*, III.iii (1647), p. 36: 'I have paid her, / I have so ferk'd her face; here's the blood Gentlemen.' So too at *S.H.*, II.iii.37; IV.iv.98; V.ii.69; *W. of E.*, I.ii.101.

219 *Basa mon cues*, i.e. *baiseʒ mon cul*, 'kiss my backside'. Cf. Jack Cade in *2 Henry VI*, IV.vii.27–29: 'What canst thou answer to my Majesty for giving up of Normandy unto Mounsieur Basimecu, the Dolphin of France?' where for 'Basimecu' (the folio reading) Q 1594 reads 'bus mine cue'.

230 *pinckt*, perforated. *The Taming of the Shrew*, IV.i.133: 'Gabr'el's pumps were all unpinked i'th' heel.'

I.ii

1 *Here...banke.* Cf. *A Midsummer Night's Dream*, IV.i.1.

8–9 *starres...natiuity.* Cf. Marlowe, *Doctor Faustus* (Q 1604, ed. Greg, line 1474): 'You starres that raignd at my natiuitie'.

18 *Lady of the Haruest*, the Harvest Queen. Lyly, *Love's Metamorphosis*, I.ii.138–139: 'Ceres, the Lady of your haruest'. See Hazlitt, *Popular Antiquities*, II, 16.

22 *Doctors Commons.*

On the west side of this streete [Paul's Wharf Hill, Castle Baynard Ward], is one other great house builded of stone, which belongeth to Powles church, and was sometime letten to the *Blunts* Lordes *Mountioy*, but of latter time to a colledge in Cambridge, and from them to the Doctors of the Ciuill law and Arches, who keepe a Commons there, and many of them being there lodged, it is called the Doctors Commons (Stow, *Survey*, II, 17).

25 *out of cry*, beyond all measure. Deloney, *The Gentle Craft*, Part Two, p. 158: 'for I haue made them both beleeue that

you loue them out of all cry'. *P.G.*, II.i.82; *N.H.*, IV.i.31; *W.E.*, IV.i.2.

25–27 *here a wore a scarffe...iewells.* With this impression of Lacie in his martial finery, cf. the vision of Rafe, done up as lord of the May, in *The Knight of the Burning Pestle*, interlude after Act IV, lines 8–10: 'Let *Raph* come out on May-day in the morning and speake upon a Conduit with all his Scarfes about him, and his fethers and his rings and his knacks.' When, shortly after, he appears, the Citizen remarks (lines 23–24): 'hee's reasonable well in reparell, but hee has not rings enough'. Concerning scarves, see S. Rowlands, *The Knaves of Spades and Diamonds* (1613), A4v: 'Scarffes we doe want to hange our weapons by.'

28 *Old-ford.* 'A village near London, three and one half miles north east of St. Paul's, at the end of the Old Ford Road. It marks the sites of the old ford over the Lea by which the road from Essex entered London before the bridge at Stratford-at-Bow was built' (Sugden).

31 *mary gup*, a variant of 'mary gip'; both forms derived originally from the oath 'By St Mary of Egypt', as in Skelton, *The Garland of Laurel* (*Complete poems of John Skelton, Laureate*, ed. P. Henderson (London, 1931), p. 445): 'By Mary Gipsy, / Quod scripsi, scripsi.' This was confused with the exclamation 'gip' or 'gup', (1) 'a cry of anger or chiding addressed to a horse', (2) 'an exclamation of derision, remonstrance, or surprise' (*O.E.D.*). Lyly, *Midas*, V.ii.100–102:

Motto. I am as melancholy as a cat.
Licio. Melancholy? marie gup, is melancholy a word for a barbars mouth?
1 H.W., III.ii.67.

31 *with a wanion*, an imprecation, meaning 'with a vengeance', 'wanion' being an altered form of 'waniand', at the time of the waning moon, an unlucky hour (*O.E.D.*). Day, *The Isle of Gulls*, V.i (ed. Bullen, p. 308): 'is this your court custome with a wanion?'

32 *marry foh*, i.e. faugh, an exclamation of disgust. Dekker (and Middleton?), *Blurt, Master-Constable*, IV.ii.50–51: 'and you

will not believe me, marry foh! I have been believed of your
betters, marry, snick up!' *1 H.W.*, III.iii.116–117; *2 H.W.*,
V.ii.374.

37–38 *stampt crabs...veriuice*. Crab apples are stamped or pounded
to make verjuice; their sourness associates them with a wry
or wrinkled face. Lyly, *Mother Bombie*, III.iv.30–31: 'It was
crabbs she stampt, and stole away one to make her a face.'
Cf. *1 H.W.*, V.ii.206; *2 H.W.*, IV.iii.92.

38–39 *much in my gaskins, but nothing in my neatherstockes*. These
articles of male attire were used figuratively for degrees of
pride. The gaskins (or galligascons) were loose breeches of
knee length or shorter (often termed slops). Sometimes they
were bombasted, or stuffed (see note on I.i.210, above), and
this fashion, requiring more material than the simple loose
slops, created a more ostentatious appearance. The nether-
stocks, on the other hand, worn with the knee-length gaskins,
required very little material. 'Thus a person seemed great or
fine in bombasted clothes, but was small without such bombast' (Linthicum, p. 209, where the present passage is cited).
Sybil is saying simply that, so far as she is concerned, Lacy,
for all the fashionable elegance of his external appearance, is
but an ordinary mortal.

41 *go by Ieronimo. Sat.*, I.ii.372, n.

43–44 *olde debts...giblets*. Lange compares Harington's translation
of the *Orlando Furioso*, Book 43, stanza 136:

> But pardon thee, and thou shalt me forgive,
> And quite each other, all old debts and driblets,
> And set the hares head against the goose gyblets.

And he explains: 'Hence, according to Sybil's application –
"off with the old love, on with the new; an even exchange".'
For the proverbial expression: 'Set the Hare's head (foot)
against the goose giblets', see Tilley, H161. *W.H.*, V.iv.281–
282.

50 *goe snicke-vp*, go hang. *The Knight of the Burning Pestle*, III.174–
175: '*Raph* shall not bee beholding to him, give him his
money *George*, and let him go snick up.' And cf. the passage

from *Blurt, Master-Constable* quoted in the note on line 32, above.

54 *cambricke*. For the popularity of this material among Elizabethans, see Linthicum, pp. 95–96.

54 *romish gloues*. Dryden, *The Kind Keeper*, III.i (ed. Summers, IV, 307):

> *Trick*. I have been looking over the last Present of *Orange* Gloves you made me; and methinks I do not like the scent. – O Lord, Mr. *Woodall*, did you bring those you wear from *Paris*?
> *Wood*. Mine are *Roman*, Madam.
> *Trick*. The scent I love, of all the World. Pray let me see 'em.

And see the editor's note (IV, 552–553) for other references in Restoration drama, plus a recipe for 'The Roman and Milanese Perfume for Gloves'.

59 *sweat in purple*. Sybil's variant of the proverb 'Win purple and wear purple' (Tilley, P640).

61 *haue at vp tailes all*. 'Up tails all' is the refrain of an old song, the tune of which is in Queen Elizabeth's *Virginal Book* and in *The Dancing Master* from 1650 to 1690; see Chappell, I, 196. There are allusions in Beaumont and Fletcher, *The Coxcomb*, I.vi.42: 'Then set your foote to my foote, and up tails all'; in *Every Man in his Humour*, I.iv.92: 'vp-tailes all, and a louse for the hang-man'; in Sharpham, *The Fliere* (1607), FIv: 'she euerie day sings *Iohn for the King*, and at *Vp tailes all*, shees perfect'. *Sat.*, IV.iii.149. For the gambling expression 'have (throw) at all', see *2 H.W.*, III.ii.65, n.

61 *Iiggy, Ioggy*. *Sat.*, III.i.222. And *S.H.*, IV.i.29.

I.iii

1–2 *How many shapes haue gods and Kings deuisde, | Thereby to compasse their desired loues?* A renaissance commonplace: cf. Lyly, *Gallathea*, I.i.88: 'To gaine loue, the Gods haue taken shapes of beastes'; and Marlowe, *1 Tamburlaine*, V.i.184–187:

> That which hath stoopt the tempest of the Gods,
> Even from the fiery spangled vaile of heaven,
> To feele the lovely warmth of shepheards flames,
> And martch in cottages of strowed weeds.

I.iv

2–4 *brewisse...powder-beefe*, staples of Elizabethan diet. Brewis was broth, or bread soaked in broth; powder-beef was salt or pickled beef. *N.F.H.*, E3v–E4: 'bellies bumbasted with ale...and cheeks strutting out (like two footebals) being blowen vp with powder beefe & brewis'. And cf. Greene, *A Quippe for an Upstart Courtier*, XI, 264–265: 'wandring on further, *Mercury* espied where a company of shoomakers were at dinner with powdered beefe and brewesse: going to them, before hee could aske them any almes, they sayd, wellcome good fellow, what is thy stomack vp, wilt thou doe as wee doe, and tast of beefe?' For 'powder-beefe' as a term of abuse in the phrase 'powder-beefe-queanes', cf. *S.H.*, II.iii.63, and *Wily Beguiled* (M.S.R.), line 1605: 'my powderbeefe slaue'.

5 *Madge-mumble-crust.* Sat., III.i.139–140, n.

5 *Midriffe.* I.i.135.

5 *swag-belly.* Cf. *O.F.*, II.ii.56–57: 'swag-bellies, gluttons, and sweet mouth'd Epicures'. And *S.H.*, V.iv.21.

6 *kennels*, gutters. *S.D.S.*, D2v, of drunkards leaving a tavern: 'In which pickle if anye of them happen to be iustled downe by a post...and so reeles them into the kennell, who takes them vp or leades them home?' *Blurt, Master-Constable*, IV.iii.41–44: 'I beseech thee, dear Frisco, raise Blurt the constable, or some scavenger, to come and make clean these kennels of hell: for they stink so, that I shall cast away my precious self.' *1 H.W.*, I.i.63; *S.D.*, III.i.88; *M.M.L.*, I.ii.20.

9 *bandog.* Sat., I.ii.326, n.

16 *sowce wife*, a woman employed at preserving meat by steeping it in some kind of pickle, or souse. Greene, *A Quippe for an Upstart Courtier*, XI, 284, of a grazier: 'he knoweth as well as the Butcher by the feede of a Bullock how much Tallow he will yeelde, what his quarters will amount vnto: what the Tanner will giue for the Hide: nay, what the sowse wiues are able to make of the inwards'.

27 *trip and go.* Deloney, *Jack of Newberie* (ed. Mann, p. 57): 'your

old gossip, dame dainty, mistresse trip and goe'. Porter, *The Two Angry Women of Abingdon* (M.S.R.), lines 1977–1979:

Mis. Bar. Will ye not stand still?
Mal. No by Ladie no.
Mis. Bar. But I will make ye.
Mal.   Nay then trip and go.

And line 111 in this scene.

31 *yawling*, howling, bawling. *Blurt, Master-Constable*, II.ii.84–85: 'Who makes that yawling at door?'

32 *Cisly Bumtrinket*. I.i.158.

34 *swinge*, beat. *R.A.*, G4v: 'But as soone as he offers to strike thee, stand in defiance of him, and say thou hast praied vnto our Lady for helpe, and she hath promised to helpe thee, and to reuenge all thy iniuries...If then hee wil swinge thee, beare it patiently.'

34 *in*, with (Wheeler, citing Beaumont and Fletcher, *Philaster*, IV.ii.9: 'shoote in a stonebow').

34 *stirrop*. I.i.181.

35 *a drie beating*, one that draws no blood. *R.A.*, D2v: 'The dissention that hapned once at *Oxford*, betweene a Scholler and a Vintner, about a quart of paltry wine, was but a drie-beating, nay rather a flea-biting to this.' *V.M.*, IV.ii.113. And cf. *1 H.W.*, IV.ii.18; *R.G.*, III.iii.198.

37 *Frolick*. *R.G.*, V.i.97, n.

39 *Vpsolce*. Editors since Warnke and Proescholdt have assumed this to be some form of 'upsee' (from Dutch *op zijn*, in the fashion or manner of); it is often found in the literature of the period, in the drinking phrases 'upsie Dutch' and 'upsie freeze' (for which see *N.H.*, II.i.61, n.). Lange suggested that the form 'Vpsolce' very likely resulted from a misprint: 'i.e. "ol" = "al" was transposed or inserted by the compositor, who was doubtless not familiar with Dutch, into what was intended for "upsee." What Dekker wrote was probably: "Upsee al se byen".' Lange translated Lacy's song (lines 36–41) as follows:

> There was a boor from Gelderland,
>   Merry they are;

He was so drunk he could not stand,
   Dutch-full they all are –
Now drain the cannikin,
Drink, pretty mannikin!

43 *saint Hughes bones.* Deloney, *The Gentle Craft*, p. 89:

My friends, I pray you list to me,
And mark what S. *Hughes* bones shall be.

First a Drawer and a Dresser,
two wedges, a more and a lesser:
A pretty block three inches high,
in fashion squared like a Die,
Which shall be called by proper name,
a Heel-block, the very same.
A Hand-leather and a Thumb-leather likewise,
to pull out shoo-threed we must deuise;
The Needle and the Thimble,
   shall not be left alone,
The Pincers and the pricking Aule,
   and the rubbing stone.
The Aule steele and tackes,
   The Sow-haires beside,
The Stirrop holding fast,
   while we sowe the Cow-hide,
The whetstone, the stopping-stick,
   and the paring knife:
All this doth belong
   to a Iourneymans life,
Our Apron is the Shrine,
   to wrap these bones in:
Thus shrowded we Saint *Hugh*
   in gentle Lambs skin.

44 *vplandish,* inland, provincial.

50 *butter-boxe,* Dutchman. Regarding the Dutch appetite for butter, cf. Jonson, *Every Man in his Humour*, III.iv.42–44: 'they are of a *Flemmish* breed, I am sure on't, for they rauen vp more butter, then all the dayes of the weeke, beside.' And *S.H.*, II.iii.130–131. *W.H.*, II.iii.11; *N.H.*, IV.ii.12; *R.G.*, V.i.88.

64 *gallimafrie. P.G.*, II.i.96, n.

66 *Goeden dach meester, ende v vro oak.* 'Good day, master, and you, goodwife, too' (Lange). For 'vro', see below, III.ii.20, n.

71–73 *rubbing pinne...stopper...dresser...awles...paring knife
...hand and thumb-leathers.* See the passage from Deloney,
quoted in the note on line 43, above.

75 *be niet vorveard,* 'be not afraid' (Lange).

76 *groot and cleane,* 'large and small' (Lange).

81 *Ik weet niet...verstaw you niet.* 'I don't know what you say;
I do not understand you' (Lange).

82 *Why thus man.* Here Lange inserts stage direction: 'imitating
by gesture a shoemaker at work'.

84 *he speakes yawing like a Iacke daw.* Cf. *The Weakest Goeth to the
Wall* (M.S.R. (1912), prepared by W. W. Greg), lines 463–
464: 'learne to brall out butterbox, yaw, yaw, and yaune for
beare like a Iacke daw'. *P.G.,* IV.ii.46; *2 H.W.,* V.ii.94.

92 *Trullibubs,* tripe (the inwards of an animal); hence, trash, with
a quibble on trulls. Cf. Jonson, *Bartholomew Fair,* I.iii.64–66,
Quarlous to Win-wife: 'There cannot be an ancient *Tripe* or
Trillibub i'the Towne, but thou art straight nosing it.'

97 *Gargantua.* A book titled *Gargantua his prophesie* was entered in
the Stationers' Register 6 April 1592, and another, the *History
of Gargantua,* on 4 December 1594. There are earlier references in Edward Dering's letter prefixed to *A Briefe and
necessary Instruction* (1572), and in the account of Captain
Cox's Library in Robert Laneham's *Letter* describing Queen
Elizabeth's entertainment at Kenilworth, 1575.

The name of this giant was thus familiar in England in the
last decades of the sixteenth century, but allusions seem to
refer to the hero of the folk-tale rather than to Rabelais' novel.
The folk-tale was apparently known in an English translation
(now lost) of *Les croniques admirables du puissant Roy
Gargantua* of François Girault (*c.* 1534). For evidence that
an English version of this was in existence from some time
prior to 1572, see Huntington Brown's introduction to his
edition of Girault, *The Tale of Gargantua and King Arthur*
(Harvard University Press, 1932), pp. xxiv–xxxii. In England
in the 1590s 'the only Elizabethans who are known to have
begun to read [Rabelais] were a tiny handful of scholars'
(*ibid.,* p. xiii). Thus, 'since Gargantua was most frequently

mentioned merely as giant or symbol of the gigantic, or as the name of a popular tale, it seems safest, except where some exclusively Rabelaisian feature is given, to assume that the reference is to the popular chronicle' (*ibid.*, pp. xxx–xxxi). Brown cites a number of allusions to the name of Gargantua in Elizabethan drama – e.g. *As You Like It*, III.ii.225; *Every Man in his Humour* (quarto 1601), I.iv.130; the anonymous *Tryall of Cheualry*, IV.i (ed. Bullen, *Old Plays*, III, 328) – but not the present reference.

98–99 *heele-blocke.* Cf. Deloney, quoted in the note on line 43, above.

100–101 *O ich wersto...freelicke.* 'Oh, I understand you; I must pay for half a dozen cans; here boy, take this shilling; draw once freely' (H. Spencer).

102 *snipper snapper*, 'a young insignificant or conceited fellow' (*O.E.D.*, citing the present passage).

103 *my last of the fiues*, one of the smallest of the lasts, or wooden models of the foot on which shoemakers shape boots or shoes; the reference is to the boy's diminutive stature. Cf. Wither, 'A Love Sonnet' (*Poetry*, ed. F. Sidgwick (2 vols., London, 1902), I, 150): 'Her waist exceeding small, / The fives did fit her shoe'.

105 *mad Greeks...true Troians. J.M.M.*, H3–H3v: 'he that not an houre before had nothing but daggers in his mouth, leaps about their necks, cals them mad *Greekes*, true *Troians*, commands a gallon of sacke & suger to be burnt for the *Sergiants*'. Cf. *O.F.*, III.i.390: 'mad Troians'.

110 *clapper dudgeon.* Defined by Dekker in *O.P.*, N iv, as 'a Begger borne', but the word has never been satisfactorily explained. All that seems certain is that it refers to the attention-getting devices to which beggars resorted by means of the 'clapdishes' which they carried. Either they knocked on these with a 'dudgeon' or wooden dagger-hilt, or they made a clapping noise by opening and shutting the wooden cover; probably they did both. In any case the transference from beggar who makes a noise with a clapper to a noisy woman whose tongue is her clapper was obvious; this is the sense in which Eyre

uses the word in the present passage. Cf. the anonymous play of *The Fatal Marriage*, of uncertain date, but perhaps *c.* 1620, according to the Malone Society editors (M.S.R. (1959, for 1958), prepared by S. B. Younghughes and H. Jenkins, p. xi), lines 1216–1219, a servant to a lady:

> tut hee cannot find yee
> if you but take reciprocall advise
> to charme yoᵗ tongue as you bidd mee charme mine
> keepe in yoᵗ clapdish

111 *sowst cunger*, pickled conger eel. Cf. Doll to Falstaff, *2 Henry IV*, II.iv.53–54: 'Hang yourself, you muddy cunger, hang yourself.' And for like terms of opprobrium in Dekker, cf. *1 H.W.*, II.i.201: 'you sowcde gurnet'; *R.G.*, IV.ii.86: 'away soust Sturgion'.

112 *Hiperboreans*. 'They inhabite almost the *Pteropheron*, which wee heare saie lyeth beyond the North pole, a most blessed Nation... They knowe no debate, they are not troubled with diseases, all men haue one desire, which is to liue innocentlie' (*The excellent and pleasant worke of Iulius Solinus Polyhistor*, trans. Arthur Golding (1587), sigs. N3v–N4).

II.i

6 *take soile*. A hunting term for a stag taking to water when hard pressed. 'When an Hart or any Deare is forced to the water, we say he goeth to the Soyle' (Turberville, *The Noble Arte of Venerie* (1575), p. 241). *R.A.*, A2v: 'many of you will be hunted by Marshalls men, Bayliffes and Catch-poles: & that some will be driuen to take soile in the bottomeles riuers of the two Counters, they will so hardly be pursued either by Greyhounds of that breed, or else by Fleete-houndes, whose feet are as swift and sent as good'.

7 *embost*, exhausted; used of a hunted animal driven to extremity. Turberville, defining 'Other generall termes of the Hart and his properties' (p. 241), states: 'When he is foamy at the mouth, we saye that he is embost' (p. 242). Spenser, *The Faerie Queene*, III.xii.17: 'a dismayed Deare in chace embost'.

II.ii

2 *Vpon some no.* '*Upon some no* and *Upon some I* . . . seem to have been modish expressions of assertion, formed after *upon my word, upon my honour*' (Warnke and Proescholdt). Cf. lines 15–16.

8 *flead,* flayed. *V.M.*, II.i.141.

16 *Wounds,* by God's wounds.

26 *my suger-candie.* Cf. *Blurt, Master-Constable,* V.ii.102–103: 'no, no, no, my sugar-candy mistress, your goodman is not here'.

27 *honnisops.* A term of endearment (*O.E.D., s.v.* 'Honey', 7).

43 *Lucke had hornes.* In punning allusion to St Luke, whose emblem was the horned ox. See *W.H.*, IV.i.103, n.

46 *Gods pittikins,* God's little pity (diminutive of 'by God's pity'). Cf. *Cymbeline,* IV.ii.293: ' 'Od's pittikins! can it be six mile yet?' *W.H.*, V.iv.149.

II.iii

2 *wol,* full.

5 *copen,* bargain.

7–8 *den signe vn swannekin,* i.e., 'the sign of the Swan'. For the numerous London taverns of this name, see Sugden. The reference is presumably to one of the two named by Taylor the Water Poet in his account of 'foure Houses in *London* that doe sell Rhennish Wine, inhabited onely by *Dutchmen; namely,* The Stilliyard, The Swan in Thames street, The Swan in Crooked lane, The Sun at Saint Mary Hill' (*Taylors Travels and Circular Perambulation, through* . . . *the Famous Cities of London and Westminster* (1636), D7). In Deloney's *Gentle Craft* 'the merchant strangers' stay at 'the *George* in *Lumbard-street*' (p. 114), but the name of the ship from Candy is 'the black *Swan*' (p. 116).

17–18 *be an huge gainer himselfe.* Lange noted that 'The increasing demand for articles of luxury, as well as Elizabeth's protective policy, especially the granting of monopolistic privileges to trading-companies guaranteed ready sales and high prices', and he cited Harrison's complaint (*Description of England*, II, v, ed. Furnivall, I, 131–132) concerning the increasing prominence of merchants and the impact of their policies on English public life: their

number is so increased in these our daies, that their onelie maintenance is the cause of the exceeding prices of forreine wares, which otherwise when euerie nation was permitted to bring in hir owne commodities, were farre better cheape and more plentifullie to be had...I doo not denie but that the nauie of the land is in part mainteined by their traffike, and so are the high prices of wares kept vp, now they haue gotten the onelie sale of things, vpon pretense of better furtherance of the common-wealth into their owne hands: whereas in times past when the strange bottoms were suffered to come in, we had sugar for foure pence the pound, that now ...is well worth halfe a crowne, raisons or corints for a penie that now are holden at six pence, and sometime at eight pence and ten pence the pound: nutmegs at two pence halfe penie the ounce: ginger at a penie an ounce, prunes at halfe penie farding.

Lange comments further: 'Moreover, the abolition of the privileges of the Steelyard, followed by a warning to the resident Hanseatic traders to leave the kingdom before the end of Feb. 1598...must have compelled more than one German "marchant owner" to dispose of the cargoes of his argosies at great loss.' On 13 January 1598 the English government issued an order expelling the German merchants from the Steelyard, their headquarters in England since the thirteenth century. This was in retaliation for the decree issued by the Emperor in the previous August expelling the English Merchant Adventurers from the Empire as a company of monopolists. The Hanse merchants were ordered to depart the realm by 28 January but the date was extended first until the end of February and then until late July; the Lord Mayor of London was finally instructed to proceed to the seizing of the Steelyard on 25 July. See *S.P. Domestic*, 266: 14 (13 January 1598) and 266: 29 (26 January 1598), and *Acts of the Privy Council*, XXVIII, 613–614 (25 July 1598). See also *Studies in Economic History: the Collected Papers of George Unwin*, edited by R. H. Tawney (London, 1927), p. 217.

21 *Portegues.* I.i.90.

22 *saint Mary Oueries*, St Saviour's, Southwark. 'East from the Bishop of Winchesters house directly ouer against it, standeth a fayre church called saint *Mary* ouer the Rie, or Ouerie, that is ouer the water' (Stow, *Survey*, II, 56).

25 *Monday's our holyday.* 'In some parts of Yorkshire, any day devoted to idleness is called *Cobbler's Monday*, from the fact that members of that vocation seldom ply their trade till the Tuesday' (Hazlitt, *Popular Antiquities*, I, 304). *I.T.B.N.*, I.ii.80; *1 H.W.*, IV.i.2–3, n.

26 *sir sauce.* Deloney, *The Gentle Craft*, p. 124: 'What (quoth she) tell me sir sawce, is thy Master Sheriffe, or no?'

31–32 *take her...a button-hole lower.* Tilley, P181.

42 *prince am I none, yet am I noblie borne.* For the occurrence of this sentiment in *The Gentle Craft*, see introduction, pp. 9–10. For Dekker's wording of the sentiment, cf. *S.H.*, III.ii.138–139; III.iii.17 ('prince am I none, yet am I princely borne'), and Greene, *Orlando Furioso* (ed. Collins), line 93: 'I am no King, yet am I princely borne' (as suggested by Waldo F. McNeir, 'The Source of Simon Eyre's Catch-Phrase', *MLN*, 53 (1938), 275–276). But the source is inherent in Deloney. Eyre, dreaming of the gains that will make him 'a Gentleman foreuer' if only he can purchase the cargo of the ship from Candy, is told by his wife: 'Alas husband, that dignitie your Trade allows you already, being a squire of the *Gentle Craft*, then how can you be lesse than a Gentleman, seeing your sonne is a Prince borne?' (p. 112).

44 *kitchin stuffe*, the greasy refuse of the kitchen (cf. V.iv.21–22). *W.Y.*, p. 55: 'out of the house he wallowed presently, beeing followed with two or three doozen of napkins to drie vp the larde, that ranne so fast downe his heeles, that all the way hee went, was more greazie than a kitchin-stuffe-wifes basket'.

46 *sort*, company. Cf. Jonson, *Every Man in his Humour*, I.v.19–20: 'I was requested to supper, last night, by a sort of gallants.' And the passage from Chettle and Day's *Blind Beggar of Bednal Green*, quoted in the note on lines 71–72, below. *O.F.*, V.ii.37; *2 H.W.*, II.i.36; *V.M.*, III.iii.115.

47 *waile in woe. P.G.*, IV.ii.111, n.

51 *mo maides then mawkin*. Tilley, M39.

55–56 *turnd to a Turke, and set in Finsbury for boyes to shoot at*. Stow
(*Survey*, II, 76–77) records that 'In the yeare 1498. all the
Gardens which had continued time óut of mind, without
Moregate, to witte, aboute and beyond the Lordship of Fins-
bery, were destroyed. And of them was made a playne field for
Archers to shoote in.' Cf. Jonson, *Bartholomew Fair*, V.vi.93–
94: 'nay, Sir, stand not you fixt here, like a stake in *Finsbury* to
be shot at'. The figure of a Turk or Saracen was often used as
a butt in archery and tilting. *Sat.*, IV.ii.32, n.

59 *brown bread tannikin*. Cf. *Sat.*, I.ii.305: 'browne-bread-mouth
stinker', and note. For 'tannikin', see *P.G.*, III.ii.243, n.

60–61 *selling tripes in Eastcheape*. 'This Eastcheape is now a flesh
Market of Butchers there dwelling, on both sides of the streete,
it had sometime also Cookes mixed amongst the Butchers, and
such other as solde victuals readie dressed of all sorts' (Stow,
Survey, I, 216). Among the 'horrible vngodlie names' Tucca
calls Mistress Miniver is 'goody Tripe-wife' (*Sat.*, III.i.188).
Cf. *S.H.*, V.iv.23–24.

66–67 *the Bores head*. The tavern in Eastcheap was already famous on
the Elizabethan stage as the scene of the revels of Prince Hal and
Falstaff in *1 Henry IV*, II.iv and III.iii, and *2 Henry IV*, II.iv.

71–72 *Mesopotamians*. Cf. the description of a puppet show in
Chettle and Day's *Blind Beggar of Bednal Green*, IV.i (ed.
Bullen, p. 72): 'You shall likewise see the famous City of
Norwitch, and the stabbing of *Julius Caesar* in the *French
Capitol* by a sort of Dutch *Mesapotamians*.' Eyre's use of the
term in the present passage (and of such like terms as 'Phili-
stines', line 97, below; 'Babilonion' at III.ii.141; 'Greeks' and
'Troians' at I.iv.105; 'Cappidosians' at V.i.44; 'Assyrian' at
V.i.48) is typical of the popular Elizabethan practice of employ-
ing (with complete indifference to historical or geographical
appropriateness) vaguely Eastern-sounding names to imply
something in the nature of good fellow or good sport. Cf.
1 Henry IV, II.iv.11–12: 'tell me flatly I am no proud Jack like
Falstaff, but a Corinthian, a lad of mettle, a good boy'.

82 *yarke*, 'to draw stitches tight' (*O.E.D.*).

84 *from the bias*, off the course. *W.H.*, II.i.200.

91 *Skellum*, rogue (from Dutch *schelm*). Cf. *S.H.R.*, D4: 'for this
   last Cannon, shot *Schellum Wasserhand* through both his
   broad sides', with the marginal note: '*Schellum* in Dutch, a
   Theife'. The word is common on the Elizabethan stage, e.g.
   Haughton, *Englishmen for my Money* (M.S.R.), lines 1420,
   1700, 1794, 2145; *The Weakest Goeth to the Wall* (M.S.R.),
   line 444. *N.H.*, II.i.61; *I.T.B.N.*, V.iv.85; *R.G.*, V.i.93.

92 *Skanderbag. Sat.*, IV.ii.24, n.

93.1–2 *an Aldermans gowne*. In *The Gentle Craft*, Eyre, at the suggestion of his wife, represents himself as an alderman in order
   to gain credit from the merchant of Candy. See introduction,
   pp. 11–12.

95–100 *a seale ring . . . a garded gown . . . damask Casock . . . satten . . .
   veluet*. With these details of Eyre's apparel as he makes ready to
   meet the Skipper, cf. his wife's plans for sending him to the
   merchant of Candy dressed as an alderman in *The Gentle Craft*:

> Ile put thee on a very fair doublet of tawny sattin, ouer the which thou
> shalt haue a cassock of branched damask, furred round about the skirts
> with the finest foynes, thy breeches of black Veluet, and shooes and
> stockings fit for such array: a band about thy neck as white as the
> driuen snow, and for thy wrists a pretty pair of cuffs, and on thy head
> a cap of the finest black, then shalt thou put on a fair gown, welted
> about with Veluet, and ouerthwart the back thwart it shall be with rich
> foyne, with a pair of sweet gloues on thy hands, and on thy forefinger
> a great seale-ring of gold (p. 114).

Mann notes that 'the *ring* was emblematic of the London
alderman'.

95 *a garded gown*, one trimmed with guards (ornamental bands or
   borders of braid, lace, velvet, etc.).

97 *Philistines*. Cf. *J.M.M.*, H3v: 'they thankt him for his paines,
   and in requitall promist to deale with his *Philistines* (his
   creditors) that are now come vpon him'. *W.H.*, V.iv.173.

99 *as proud as a dogge in a dublet*. Tilley, D452, but 'also used for
   something particularly ridiculous, or out of keeping', as
   McKerrow noted in connection with Nashe, *Have With You*,
   III, 43: 'Tell mee (I pray you), was euer *Pegasus* a cow in a

cage, *Mercury* a mouse in a cheese, Dexteritie a dog in a dublet.' McKerrow's note, which cites the present passage, quotes Harrison, *Description of England*, II, vii (ed. Furnivall, I, 168): 'except it were a dog in a doublet, you shall not see anie so disguised, as are my countrie men of England'.

100 *beaten*, embroidered with metal. Cf. Marlowe, *Faustus* (Q 1604, ed. Greg, line 378): 'beaten silke'; and Beaumont, *The Knight of the Burning Pestle*, IV.33–34: 'let the King's daughter stand in her window all in beaten gold'.

101 *rearing*, 'ruffling up' (H. Spencer).

111–114 *I neuer likte thee so wel...apparell.* In *The Gentle Craft*, Eyre's wife anticipates her husband's fine appearance in his alderman's disguise: 'It doth my heart good, to see how trimly this apparell doth become you, in good faith, husband, me seems in my mind, I see you in it already, and how like an Alderman you will look, when you are in this costly array' (p. 115).

128–129 *thou shalt haue...Cittie.* Spoken from the height of Eyre's assumed dignity as an alderman.

II.iv

9–10 *no man of name, | But...Ardington.* Lange compares *Henry V*, IV.viii.104–105, where the King, reading a list of English dead at Agincourt, announces: 'Sir Richard Ketley, Davy Gam, esquire; | None else of name'. And cf. *Much Ado About Nothing*, I.i.5–7:

Leonato. How many gentlemen have you lost in this action?
Messenger. But few of any sort, and none of name.

III.i

20 *square*, fall out, quarrel.

24 *to fond*, i.e., to found; Neilson noted the pun on 'fond'.

51 *old change.* 'The kinges Exchaunge at London, was neare vnto the Cathedrall Church of Sainte *Paule*, and is to this daye commonlie called the olde Chaunge, but in Euidences the olde Exchaunge' (Stow, *Survey*, I, 54).

56 *mammet*, puppet. *Look About You* (M.S.R. (1913), prepared by

W. W. Greg), lines 3135–3136: 'Downe stubborne Queene, kneele to your wronged King, / Downe Mammet.' And Capulet to Juliet in *Romeo and Juliet*, III.v.183–185:

> to have a wretched puling fool,
> A whining mammet, in her fortune's tender,
> To answer, 'I'll not wed, I cannot love'.

94 *lurch*, 'to remain in or about a place furtively' (*O.E.D.*). *Merry Wives of Windsor*, II.ii.25: 'am fain to shuffle, to hedge, and to lurch'.

III.ii

3–5 *runne to Guild Hall . . . Shiriffe.* In *The Gentle Craft*, an officer comes to Eyre's house to report that the Lord Mayor and Aldermen have chosen him Sheriff of London, and to bid him come to them to signify whether or not he is willing to serve. His wife urges him to accept. 'So soon as he was gone out of sight, his wife sent one of his men after him to *Guild Hall*, to hearken and hear, whether her husband held his place or no: and if he do, bring me word with all possible speed' (p. 123).

8 *Nay when?* An exclamation of impatience. *Sat.*, I.ii.373.

20 *vro*, mistress (Dutch *vrouw*). So too at I.iv.66. *N.H.*, II.i.63.

24 *backe friend*, feigned friend. *V.M.*, II.i.83.

29 *corke.* The reference is to the soles of cork, worn on shoes for additional height. See Linthicum, pp. 247–248.

32–33 *fardingale . . . bumme.* What Mistress Eyre has in mind is a French farthingale, 'a roll resembling an automobile tire, stiffened by wire, or stuffed with cotton'. It 'was placed around the hips and the pleated skirt of the kirtle allowed to fall over it. A variation of this roll was used by 1580. Instead of a complete roll, a half roll, made by stuffing only part of it, was placed behind "like a rudder to the body", leaving the front straight' (Linthicum, p. 181). These rolls were commonly called 'bums' or 'bum-rolls'. Harrison (*Description of England*, II, vii) deplores such affectations in women's dress: 'What should I saie of . . . their galligascons to beare out their bums & make their attire to sit plum round (as they term it) about them? their fardingals, and diuerslie coloured nether stocks of

48

silke, ierdseie, and such like, whereby their bodies are rather
deformed than commended?' (ed. Furnivall, I, 170). Cf. *W.H.*,
II.ii.36.

33 *French-hoode*. It fitted closely about the head and ears, and though
once worn by fashionable ladies, it had come by the 1590s to be
worn principally by citizens' wives. *Sat.*, III.i.222, n.

39 *the poulterers in Gracious street*. Stow, writing of the Poultry,
reports that 'the Poulterers are but lately departed from thence
into other streets, as into Grasse street, and the ends of saint
Nicholas flesh shambles' (*Survey*, I, 186). Jonson, in *Neptunes
Triumph*, 299, refers to 'a plump Poultrers wife, in *Graces*
street'. *W.H.*, II.i.216.

41–44 *periwig...fan...maske*. All are among the items of women's
attire most often mentioned by the satirists. Cf. S. Rowlands,
Look to it, For, Ile Stabbe ye (1604), D2v:

> You with the Hood, the Falling-band, and Ruffe,
> The Moncky-wast, the breeching like a Beare:
> The Perriwig, the Maske, the Fanne, the Muffe,
> The Bodkin, and the Bussard in your heare.

And Jonson's Chloe who is off to court in *Poetaster*, IV.i.20–
21: 'O Cupid! giue me my fanne, and my masque too.'

45 *wicked*. In support of Professor Bowers' retention of the reading
of the quartos (see his textual note, I, 91) cf. *G.H.*, C4v: 'a
head al hid in haire, giues euen to a most wicked face a sweet
proportion, & lookes like a meddow newly marryed to the
Spring'. (The 1953 printing of Bowers' edition erroneously
read 'wrinkld', corrected to 'wicked' in an Errata slip.)

51 *drinke*. The use of the word to mean 'smoke' was due to a quibble
on 'pipe'. Cf. the interlude, *Wine, Beere, Ale, and Tobacco
Contending for Superiority* (1630), C4:

Tobaco.... What do yee stand at gaze – Tobacco is a drinke too.
Beere. A drinke?
Tobaco. Wine, you and I come both out of a pipe.

2 *H.W.*, IV.iii.21–22; *W.B.*, V.iii.46; *R.G.*, II.i.93; *M.M.L.*,
I.ii.58: 'Tobacco-drinkers'; *I.T.B.N.*, IV.ii.65.

52–54 *O fie vppon it...looke not like men that vse them*. So the

Citizen's Wife in Beaumont's *Knight of the Burning Pestle*,
1.202–205: 'fie, this stinking Tobacco kils men, would there
were none in *England*: now I pray Gentlemen, what good does
this stinking Tobacco do you? nothing, I warrant you; make
chimnies a your faces.' *W.H.*, V.i.119–125.

53 *slauering*. Cf. *G.H.*, B3: 'After thy [Tobacco's] pipe, shal ten
thousands be taught to daunce, if thou wilt but discouer to me
the sweetnesse of thy snuffes, with the manner of spawling,
slauering, spetting and driueling in all places, and before all
persons.'

57 *a tall souldier*. The phrase is common; e.g., Marlowe, *2 Tamburlaine*, IV.iii.70; Peele, *David and Bethsabe*, line 1562.
A Knack to Know an Honest Man (M.S.R. (1910), prepared
by H. de Vocht), lines 842–843: 'you are two good tall
youths, / And fit four souldiers.' For 'tall' meaning 'valiant',
cf. I.i.167.

82–83 *ka me, ka thee*. Cf. John Heywood's *Works* (1562), E1v:
'Ka me, Ka the, one good tourne asketh an other.' Tilley, K1.
W. of E., II.i.195.

87 *opened her case*. Cf. I.i.153, n.

103–112 *O mistres, ...salute you mistresse shrieue*. Cf. *The Gentle
Craft*, p. 124:

> The Assembly being then broken vp, the voice went Master *Eyer* is
> Sheriffe, Master *Eyer* is Sheriffe. Whereupon the fellow that Mistresse
> *Eyer* sent to obserue how things framed, ran home in all haste, and with
> leaping and reioycing said: Mistresse, God giue you ioy, for you are
> now a Gentlewoman.
>   What (quoth she) tell me sir sawce, is thy Master Sheriffe, or no?
> and doth he hold his place?
>   Yes Mistresse, he holds it now as fast as the stirrop doth the shooes
> while we sow it.
>   Why then (quoth she) I haue my hearts desire, and that I so long
> looked for, and so away she went.

104 *smugge vp*, to smarten up one's appearance; to make trim or
gay (*O.E.D.*). Deloney, *The Gentle Craft*, p. 95: 'But tell me
Crispine, art thou not in loue, that thou doest smug up thy selfe
so finely.'

111 *grieue*, a governor of a province or town, a sheriff (*O.E.D.*).

120–121 *yes, tis three pence, I smel the Rose.* 'Confusion between coins of the same type so near in value was very easy, and a rose was accordingly placed behind the Queen's head on the sixpence, threepence, three halfpence, and three farthings to distinguish them from the groat, the two-penny piece, the penny, and the halfpenny' (*Shakespeare's England*, I, 342–343). But the joke would seem better if the threepence and three-halfpence pieces did not *both* have the rose; the point seems to be that Firke gets a coin – a threepence – that to his surprise has a rose on it, while he is expecting a coin – three-halfpence – that does not. Perhaps when he says 'Tis but three halfe pence' he is expecting Margery to give him three half-penny pieces, which did not have the rose; but this does not exactly square with her statement (line 118): 'heer's a three-peny peece'; she would seem to be offering a single coin, not three separate ones. Lange says that the threepenny silver piece was not in general circulation. 'It was maundy money, and Mrs. Eyre is here affecting the attitude of almoner of the sovereign.'

126 *with a full mouth.* Some editions place the phrase in quotation marks, as one of Margery's characteristic utterances ('Hodge, with a full mouth'), but it is descriptive, not attributive. 'Speake mee in the olde key, ...with a full mouth' and not 'pulingly', is what the apprentices would have her do, rather in the way that Hotspur would have his Lady 'Swear me... A good mouth-filling oath' (*1 Henry IV*, III.i.253–254). Cf. *O.F.*, II.ii.64.

127 *crie twang.* Cf. Nashe, *Have With You*, III, 69: 'and afterward, in the yeare when the earth-quake was, he fell to be a familiar Epistler, & made *Powles Church-yard* resound or crie twang againe with foure notable famous Letters'. Porter, *The Two Angry Women of Abingdon* (M.S.R.), lines 1331–1333: 'I had a sword, I the flower of smithfield, for a sword, a right fox I faith, with that and a man had come ouer with a smooth and a sharp stroke, it would haue cried twang.' *W.E.*, III.ii.90.

127.1 *a gold chaine.* Sat., III.i.115, n.

134–135 *Roger, Ile make ouer my shop and tooles to thee.* Cf. *The*

Gentle Craft, p. 125: 'But you must now imagine, that a thousand cares combred the Sheriffe, in prouiding all things necessary for his office: at what time he put off his Shoomakers shop to one of his men.'

136 *thou shalt haue an hundred for twentie*, i.e. in return for the loan of the twenty 'Portegues'; see II.iii.19–21.

140 *mistris*. Spencer, noting that Q6 and modern editions read 'master', observes that 'this speech may well be taken as a response to Margery's donning the French hood'.

III.iii

16 *flip flap*. Presumably an allusion to the flapping side pieces of Margery's French hood. Cf. III.ii.133, and V.i.15; *Sat.*, III.i.222. But perhaps a reference to her fan; cf. *O.F.*, I.ii.162.

21–22 *a pound of care paies not a dram of debt*. Tilley, P518.

23 *sacke and sugar*. For its association with old age, cf. *The London Prodigal* (ed. Brooke, *Shakespeare Apocrypha*), I.ii.102–103: 'Drawer, let me haue sacke for vs old men: / For these girles and knaues small wine are best.' And *1 Henry IV*, II.iv.470–472: 'If sack and sugar be a fault, God help the wicked! If to be old and merry be a sin, then many an old host that I know is damn'd.' *R.A.*, B3v, of winter: 'the vnconscionable binder vp of Vintners Faggots and the onely consumer of burnt Sacke and Suger: This Cousen to death, further [Grosart: 'father'] to sicknes, and brother to olde age'. Cf. *N.H.*, V.i.112–113; *M.M.L.*, II.i.83; *2 H.W.*, I.iii.84–85.

24 *Its wel done*. Lange took this to be 'The lord Mayor's approving comment on the first three-men's song, which has just been rendered', and a number of editors (e.g., Rhys, Williams, Neilson, H. Spencer, Brooke and Paradise) insert the song following line 23. But if so it would have to be sung either by Eyre and two anonymous servants, or by three anonymous servants, and in a play dealing with jolly shoemakers who were famous for singing at their work, the song must surely have been sung by the apprentices, who do not enter until line 51. It seems better to assume (with such editors as Halliday, Hampden,

Koszul, Steane) that the song was performed just before the dancing exit, following line 71. In such a view of the stage business at this point, the Lord Mayor's comment 'Its wel done' would be taken as an approving pronouncement on the *carpe diem* views that Eyre has just given voice to.

35 *cockney*, a cockered or pampered child. Lyly, *Euphues*, I, 244 (Ferardo to his daughter Lucilla): 'But why cast I the effect of this vnnaturalnesse in thy teeth, seeing I my selfe was the cause? I made thee a wanton and thou hast made mee a foole, I brought thee vpp lyke a cockney, and thou hast handled mee lyke a cockescombe.' *N.F.H.*, C4: 'our cockering mothers, who for their labour make vs to be cald Cockneys'. *G.H.*, F4: 'I could make Cockneies, whose fathers haue left them well, acknowledge themselues infinitely beholden to me for teaching them...how to spend their patrimony.'

40 *wash*. The word is here used as an adjective, meaning 'washy, weak' (*O.E.D.*). As a term for effeminacy, cf. Fletcher, *Bonduca*, IV.i (1647), p. 61, of 'great Ladies':

> they're onely made for handsome view, not handling;
> their bodies of so weak and wash a temper,
> a rough pac'd bed will shake 'em all to pieces.

And Fletcher's *Rule a Wife and Have a Wife*, III.i (1640), D3v: 'Tis a wash knave, he will not keep his flesh well.'

40 *pisherie pasherie*. I.i.123–124.

41–42 *outsides...linings*. Lange compares *W.K.*, IV.ii.206–207: 'I regard no mans out-side, 'tis the lineings / Which I take care for.'

42 *mouse*. As a term of endearment, cf. Deloney, *2 The Gentle Craft*, p. 143: 'speake my prettie mouse'; Lyly, *Mother Bombie*, IV.ii.62: 'God saue you, pretty mouse.' And Beaumont, *The Knight of the Burning Pestle*, III.134–135: 'Come, hugge in mine arms sweet mouse, hee shall not fright thee any more.' *W.H.*, II.i.130; III.i.11; *R.G.*, II.i.145.

47.1 *a Taber and a Pipe*. The regular accompaniments to the morris dance. Cf. the opening scene of Marston's *Jack Drum's Entertainment* (ed. Wood, III, 181): 'Enter *Jacke Drum*, and

Timothy Twedle, with a Taber and a Pipe.' And later (III, 182):
'The Taber and Pipe strike vp a Morrice.' *W. of E.*, II.i.37. For
morris-dancers, see Hazlitt, *Popular Antiquities*, I, 139–151. A
morris is danced in *W. of E.*, III.iv.49.1, and *S.D.*, II.i.82.S.D.

61 *frister*, sweetheart (Dutch *vrijster*, from *vrijen*, to woo or court).
The earliest example in *O.E.D.* is from 1640. See *S.H.*, IV.i.52.

68 *Stratford Boe.* This suburb, 4½ miles north-east of St Paul's,
'was a convenient distance for an afternoon's outing for the
Londoners' (Sugden).

70 *tickle it.* Cf. the song sung by the morris dancers in *Jack Drum's
Entertainment*, Act I (ed. Wood, III, 183): 'Skip it, & trip it,
nimbly, nimbly, tickle it, tickle it lustily.' The first three-man's
song is presumably sung at this point.

III.iv

0.2 *muffled.* A common form of disguise on the Elizabethan stage.
Cf. *Measure for Measure*, V.i.486, where the Duke asks concerning Claudio who has just entered: 'What muffled fellow's
that?'

21–22 *what ist you buy? | What ist you lacke sir?* The city trades-
man's regular greeting to a customer. Cf. Jonson, Chapman,
and Marston, *Eastward Ho*, I.i.66–67: 'What doe yee lacke
Sir? What ist you'le buye Sir?' *W.A.*, G3v: 'The Armies
hereupon brake vp, the Siege raised, the Citty gates set wide
open. Shop-keepers fell to their old, *What doe you lacke.*'
1 H.W., I.v.9; *2 H.W.*, II.ii.1; *W.H.*, V.iv.99; *R.G.*, II.i.1;
M.M.L., II.i.11.

46–47 *a womans fray, | That means, come to me, when she cries, away.*
Cf. the proverb: 'A Woman says nay (no) and means aye'
(Tilley, W660). *P.G.*, I.i.49.

IV.i

3 *pell mel. P.G.*, IV.ii.167.

10 *licoring. R.G.*, IV.ii.70.

11 *Forware*, 'indeed' (Spencer). And IV.iii.29, 35.

11 *hort I*, 'hark 'ee' (Spencer).

12 *vampies*, the forepart or upper leather of a boot or shoe. Thus

Greene, in *A Quippe for an Upstart Courtier* (XI, 263), speaking of the abuses of shoemakers: 'Beside, you will ioin a neates leather vampy to a calues leather heele: is not heere good stuffe maister shoomaker?'

17 *counterfeits*. 'The word "vamps"... was sometimes used in the sense of "counterfeits", because to furnish with a new vamp was "to patch" and so serve up something old as new. Hence, Firk's pun on coins' (Williams).

20 *coosin...one of your auntes*. *1 H.W.*, I.ii.119–121, n.

24 *do...doing*. For the sexual quibble, cf. *N.H.*, IV.i.200, n. And *S.H.*, I.i.207.

26 *yearkt and firkt*. 'Yerk' is a term in shoemaking: 'To draw stitches tight, to twitch, as a shoemaker in sewing' (*O.E.D.*, 1). Cf. II.iii.82. It also means 'to strike smartly, esp. with a rod or whip' (*O.E.D.*, 2), in which sense Dekker uses it in *S.D.S.*, D4v: '*Candle-lights* Coach is...drawne...by two *Rats*: the *Coachman* is a *Chaundler*, who so sweats with yearking them, that he drops tallowe.' And it can mean simply to push or pull suddenly, to jerk (*O.E.D.*, 4). In which latter sense it is very near to what is here the principal meaning of 'firk': 'to urge, press hard; to drive' (*O.E.D.*, 2, a). The words occur again in combination at IV.iv.98.

29 *Iiggy ioggy*. I.ii.61.

30 *Oatemeale*, a cant term for a swaggerer or profligate. Cf. Lyly, *Mother Bombie*, V.iii.185–190:

Pris.....Wast thou priuie to this practise?
Lucio. In a manner.
Pris. Ile pay thee after a manner.
Spe. And you, oatemeale groate! you were acquainted with this plot.

And Folly's song in *S.D.*, I.i.98–99: '*do mad pranck with | Roaring boies and oatmeals*'.

31 *bagpuddings*. *1 H.W.*, I.i.142, n.

39 *Whoop*. *P.G.*, IV.ii.22, n. And *S.H.*, V.ii.195.

52 *Vat begaie you*, 'What do you want?' (Lange).

53–54 *pull on her shooes*. Cf. *1 H.W.*, V.ii.258–259: 'Gaffer shoomaker, you puld on my wiues pumps, and then crept into her pantofles.' For the comparable quibble on 'draw on', see *N.H.*, V.i.34, and *M.M.L.*, IV.iii.6.

55 *edle*, noble (Lange).

56 *Cornewalle*, the old name for Cornhill (cf. I.ii.30), as Professor Bowers, following the suggestion of J. George in *Notes and Queries*, 194 (1949), 192, observed in his textual note (1, 92). Dekker used the old name again in *M.G.*, p. 117: 'thus they ran through *Cornewell* iust in the middle of the street'. The identification with Cornhill was made (long before George) by F. P. Wilson in his note on the *M.G.* passage (*Plague Pamphlets* (Oxford, 1925), p. 240), where other examples of the older form (in each case given as 'Cornewell') are cited.

60 *budget*, pouch. Cf. Haughton, *Englishmen for my Money* (M.S.R.), lines 1244–1245: 'who would thinke my Maister had so much witte in his old rotten budget'. *W.Y.*, p. 37: 'in such strange, and such changeable shapes did this Cameleon-like sicknes appeare, that they could not (with all the cunning in their budgets) make pursenets to take him napping'. Cf. Tilley, F187 and K118.

62 *meete yo gane*, 'with you go' (Lange).

IV.ii

20 *Watlingstreete*. Stow records 'that at this present, the inhabitants thereof are wealthy Drapers, retailors of wollen cloathes both broad and narrow, of all sorts, more then in any one streete of this citie' (*Survey*, 1, 346).

28 *Saint Faiths Church vnder Paules*. 'At the West ende of this Iesus Chappell, vnder the Quire of Paules, also was a parrish Church of Saint Faith, commonly called S. Faith vnder Pauls, which serued for the Stacioners and others dwelling in Paules Churchyard, *Pater noster row*, and the places neare adioyning' (Stow, *Survey*, 1, 329). Cf. Nashe, *Have With You*, III, 25: 'What, *Tom*, thou art very welcome. Where hast thou bin this long time; walking in Saint *Faiths* Church vnder ground, that wee neuer could see thee?' And Beaumont, *The Knight of the Burning Pestle*, v.47–50, where Master Humphrey, the rejected lover of Luce, says:

> Since my true-love is gone, I nevermore,
> Whilst I do live, upon the sky will pore;
> But in the darke will weare out my shooe-soles
> In passion, in Saint *Faiths* Church under *Paules*.

48 *murren*, plague, pestilence (especially of cattle); used in exclamation of anger. *1 H.W.*, I.v.95; *W.H.*, IV.i.212; V.iv.108; *W.E.*,
IV.ii.58.

65–66 *Cripplegates*. Cf. the similar quibble in *S.D.S.*, E3v: 'This
Signior Ioculento...comes prawncing in at *Cripplegate*, and he
may well doe it, for indeede all the parts hee playes are but
con'd speeches stolne from others, whose voices and actions
hee counterfeites: but so lamely, that all the Cripples in tenne
Spittle-houses, shewe not more halting.'

67–68 *wedding and hanging goes by destiny*. *Merchant of Venice*,
II.ix.82–83: 'The ancient saying is no heresy, / Hanging and
wiving goes by destiny.' Tilley, W232.

IV.iii

15–16 *now...Is Maior of London*. 'There bee in this Citie, according to the number of Wardes 26. Aldermen, whereof yearely,
on the feast day of Saint *Michael* the Archangell, one of them is
elected to be Mayor, for the yeare following, to begin on the
28. of October' (Stow, *Survey*, II, 187).

27 *Pull on my shooe*. Lange notes the recurrence of the dramatic
device in *M.M.L.*, IV.iv and Rowley, *A Shoemaker a Gentleman*, II.iii. The source of the incident is in *The Gentle Craft*.

29 *Forware*. IV.i.11.

36 *neits leither*. *S.T.W.*, IV.ii.71, n.

IV.iv

36 *scud*. Porter, *The Two Angry Women of Abingdon* (M.S.R.), line
1418: 'runne from death and nimbly scud for feare'. *M.G.*,
p. 126: 'at last with much adoe he fell flounce into the Saddle,
and away he scudded out at townes end'. *L.C.*, I4v: 'he gallops
away as if the Deuill had hired him of some Hackney-man, and
scuds through thicke and thinne, as if crackers had hung at his
heeles'. *W.H.*, III.ii.21.

45 *honnikin*, i.e., 'hunnican', an uncultured fellow (*O.E.D.*, *s.v.* 'Hun', 3).

52 *lubber*. Used of another Dutch suitor, Vandalle, in Haughton's *Englishmen for my Money* (M.S.R.), lines 1726–1727: 'Well, what shall we doe with this Lubber? / (Louer I should say.)'.

62 *sir knaue*. Rowley, *A Shoemaker a Gentleman*, IV.i.70–72: 'Mistris! gods me; I am a Madam sir knave, though I am a Nurse, I can tell you: Goe too, learne your duty.'

70 *bob*, cheat, deceive. *W. of E.*, III.iii.101.

76 *the tune of Rogero*. This ballad tune gets its name from the *Aria di Ruggiero*, itself named from Ariosto's *Orlando Furioso*, Canto 44, stanza 61, beginning 'Ruggier, qual sempre fui, tal esser voglio'. It was a popular Italian ground bass on which a singer could extemporize a descant when chanting epic poetry; the ballad tune is not the original ground bass, but a descant erected upon it. See Simpson, pp. 612–614, and Chappell, I, 93–95. It is mentioned by Nashe in *Have With You*, III, 122; and Heywood in *A Woman Killed With Kindness*, II, 30.

82 *dance the shaking of the sheetes*. A ballad titled 'The Daunce & songe of Deathe' (beginning 'Can you dance *The shaking of the sheets?* – / A dance that every one must do') was entered to John Awdelay in the Stationers' Register in 1568–1569. Thenceforth the ballad's opening line, with an inevitable quibble, was much repeated by Elizabethan writers. Dekker alludes to the dance tune elsewhere in *M.G.*, p. 125; *Sat.*, II.i.131; *W.H.*, V.iii.28–29; and again in the present play at V.v.28. See Simpson, pp. 651–653.

83 *diggers*, delvers into secrets (Spencer).

86 *in sadnesse*, seriously, in earnest. *M.M.L.*, III.i.35; *W.K.*, II.i.33.

91 *feeling*, slang for a bribe, or a tip. Cf. Jonson, Chapman, and Marston, *Eastward Ho*, V.iii.73–75: 'But if you haue a Friend to deliuer your tale sensibly to some Iustice o'the Towne, that hee may haue feeling of it, (doe you see?) you may be bayl'd.' And Day, *The Isle of Gulls*, I.iv (ed. Bullen, p. 229):

Lisan. . . . .and doost thou take after thy maister?

Ma. No, madam, I take commonly afore my maister; for where he takes
he takes all and leaues nothing for me to take.
Lisan. Oh, I feele your meaning.
Ma. Let my Maister haue some feeling of yours and heele prefer your
sute.

92 *aurium tenus . . . genuum tenus. Aurium tenus* = 'up to the ears';
genuum tenus = 'up to the knees'. But in Firke's translation,
the Latin renders up other meanings: *tenus* is made to mean
'ten'; *aurium* is Firke's version of *aurum* (gold); *genuum* is his
fumbling stab at *argentum* (silver). He is demanding a bribe, a
'feeling' (see note on preceding line). In William Lily's
Grammar (1567), C3v, 'Aurium tenus, Up to the eares' is
given as an example of the use of the genitive case with *tenus.*

93 *strechers*, with a quibble on the double meaning (1) an instru-
ment for easing the fit of boots or shoes, (2) lies.

96 *No point.* A bit of stage French that has entered Firke's speech.
Cf. *The Wisdom of Doctor Dodypoll* (M.S.R. (1965, for 1964),
prepared by M. N. Matson), lines 541–545:

Hans. . . . Well I shall haue your good word, I see M. Doctor.
Doct. I sayt.
Hans. But not a rag of money.
Doct. No by wy trot: no point money; me gieue de beggra de money:
no point de braue man.

O.F., V.i.100; *M.M.L.*, II.i.15; *N.S.S.*, IV.ii.115.

98 *firkt and yerkt.* IV.i.26.

103 *Pitchers haue eares.* Tilley, P363.

110–111 *London stone . . . the pissing conduit leakes nothing but*
[*misprinted 'put' in text*] *pure mother Bunch.* Cf. Jack Cade in
2 Henry VI, IV.vi.1–4: 'And here, sitting upon London Stone,
I charge and command that, of the city's cost, the pissing-
conduit run nothing but claret wine this first year of our reign.'
'London stone' stood in Candelwick Street. Stow writes of it:

On the south side of this high streete, neare vnto the channell is pitched
vpright a great stone called London stone, fixed in the ground verie
deepe, fastned with bars of iron, and otherwise so strongly set, that if
Cartes do run against it through negligence, the wheeles be broken, and
the stone it selfe vnshaken . . . Some haue said this stone to be set, as

a marke in the middle of the Citie within the walles: but in truth it standeth farre nearer vnto the riuer of Thames, then to the wall of the Citie (*Survey*, I, 224–225; see Kingsford's note, II, 316).

The stone is now encased in the wall of St Swithin's Church, Cannon Street, opposite to its original site. Concerning the 'pissing conduit', cf. Stow: 'Some distance west is the Royall Exchaunge,...and so downe to the little Conduit, called the pissing Conduit, by the Stockes Market, and this is the south-side of Three needle streete' (*Survey*, I, 183).

The fullest account of 'mother Bunch' is found in the jest book titled *Pasquils Jests, mixed with Mother Bunches Merriments*, published in 1604 (reprinted by W. C. Hazlitt, *Shakespeare Jest-Books* (London, 1864), vol. III). There she is described as the 'most delightful Hostesse of *England*' (p. 7). She is said to have dwelt

in Cornehill (neere the Exchange) and sold strong Ale, whose health to this day all joviall drunkards never do forget; the many vertues of her Ale is impossible for one penne to write...Mother *Bunch* lived an hundreth, seventy and five yeares, two dayes and a quarter, and halfe a minute, and died in the prime of her charity (pp. 9–10).

Nashe, in *Pierce Penilesse*, I, 173–174, speaks of 'Mother *Bunches* slimie ale, that hath made her and some other of her fil-pot facultie so wealthie'. There are other allusions to her in E.S., *The Discouerie of the Knights of the Poste* (1597), B1–B1v: 'as well knowne for his profession, as mother Bunches ale to nipitaty'; and *The Weakest Goeth to the Wall* (M.S.R.), lines 246–247: 'O for one pot of mother *Bunches* Ale, my owne mothers Ale, to wash my throat this mistie morning'. Dekker mentions her again in *Sat.*, III.i.162.

118 *in conie*, or 'incony', a cant word meaning 'rare', 'fine', 'delicate', 'pretty', 'nice'. Cf. Jonson, *A Tale of a Tub*, IV.i.104–108, where another secret marriage is being discussed:

> For (by this meanes) *Miles* I may say't to thee,
> Thy Master must to *Awdrey* married be.
> But not a word but mum: goe get thee gone;
> Be warie of thy charge, and keep it close.
> *Met.* O super-dainty Chanon! Vicar in coney.

Porter, *The Two Angry Women of Abingdon* (M.S.R.), line 2200: 'O I haue sport in cony Ifaith.' And *Blurt, Master-Constable*, II.ii.23–24, of a woman's gown: 'it makes you have, O, a most incony body'.

133 *hey passe, and repasse. O.F.*, V.ii.10, n.

133 *pindy pandy.* Cf. Middleton and Rowley, *The Spanish Gipsy*, III.i.115: 'Pindy-pandy rascal toys'.

149 *chop vp.* Deloney, *The Gentle Craft*, p. 97: 'And at this time there was in *Canterbury* a blind Frier that in many yeers had neuer seen the Sun; to this man did *Crispine* go, thinking him the fittest Chaplain to chop vp such a marriage.' *1 H.W.*, V.ii.14.

149 *the Sauoy.* The Savoy Hospital was founded by Henry VII, suppressed by Edward VI, and newly founded by Queen Mary in 1556. It contained a chapel which, according to Stow, 'serueth now as a Parish church to the Tenements thereof neare adioyning and others' (*Survey*, II, 95), and which was something of a byword for the irregular marriages celebrated therein. Cf. Middleton, *Your Five Gallants*, II.i.42–43: 'I have had two [knights' heirs] stolen away at once, / And married at Savoy.' Since the precincts of the chapel were a sanctuary, the whole district had a dubious reputation. Cf. Barry, *Ram-Alley*, Act II (1611), D2v:

> Foote wench we will be married to night,
> Weele sup at th'Myter, and from thence
> My brother and we three will to the Sauoy.

R.G., III.i.28.

153–155 *a messe of shoomakers meate...to co\zen my gentleman of lame Rafes wife*, arranged for at IV.ii.57–61. A messe is, strictly, a set of four (originally one of the groups into which the company at a banquet were divided), as at *W.E.*, II.i.58; but the 'messe of shoomakers' here seems merely to correspond to the 'lustie crue of honest shoomakers' at IV.ii.58, and elsewhere Dekker uses the word simply to signify a numerous company, as at *R.G.*, I.ii.62: 'a messe of friends'; *M.E.*, 58: 'the whole messe of the Poets'.

154 *the wooll sack in Ivie lane.* A tavern in Faringdon Ward within.

Jonson mentions it in *The Alchemist*, V.iv.41, and *The Devil is an Ass*, I.i.66.

158 *iumbling*. The word had bawdy implications. Cf. Barry, *Ram-Alley*, Act IV (1611), F2: 'your iumblings / In horslitters, coatches or caroatches'. Field, *Amends for Ladies*, II.i.41–44: 'I haue seene a woman looke as modestly as you, and speake as sinceerely, and follow the Fryars as zealously, and shee has been as sound a jumbler as e're paid for 't'; and later in the same play, IV.ii.51–53:

> *Bould.* Z'oones, would you had beene in my place.
> *Welt.* Z'oones, I would I had, I would haue so jumbl'd her honestie.

In *N.S.S.*, IV.ii.110–111, Medina in his disguise as a French doctor says: 'me know you ha jumbla de fine vench and fill her belly wid a Garsoone'.

V.i

9 *dainty come thou to me*. A popular ballad tune; allusions to it are in *Shirburn Ballads*, ed. Andrew Clark (Oxford, 1907), pp. 84, 297; *Pepys Ballads*, ed. Hyder E. Rollins (Cambridge, Mass., 1929), II, 33. The tune is lost. See Simpson, p. 577, and Chappell, II, 517.

14 *Saracens head*. The allusion is to the ferocious face displayed on the sign of an inn bearing this name, such as the one outside Newgate. See *Sat.*, I.ii.301, n.

16–17 *a redde petticoate*, the Lord Mayor's scarlet gown.

22 *buffe-ierkin varlets*, sergeants. *W.H.*, III.ii.92–94.

24 *my browne Queene of Perriwigs*. Spencer thought this alluded to the fact that Margery 'now has wigged flunkies to attend her', but 'buffe-ierkin varlets' would hardly be wearing periwigs. The expression refers to Margery herself, who has mentioned getting a periwig at III.ii.37–41, just as she has there mentioned getting a farthingale and a French hood (lines 32–33); in the course of the present scene (lines 14–15 and here), Eyre makes it clear that she now has them all. For the use of 'browne' as suggestive of sexual lustiness, cf. Lyly, *Mother Bombie*, III.iv.15: 'I loue a nutbrowne lasse, tis good to recreate.' And

Shakespeare, *Henry VIII*, III.ii.295–296: 'when the brown wench / Lay kissing in your arms'.

27 *Hamborow*, Hamburg (which is to say, German, in vague reference to Lacie's Dutch disguise).

29 *marchpane*, marzipan. *S.D.*, IV.i.271.

40 *to see my new buildings*. The reference is to the granary which the historical Simon Eyre caused to be erected in the Leadenhall. See Introduction, pp. 15–16, and V.v.154.

43–49 *I promised...clap vp their shop windows, and away*. Cf. *The Gentle Craft*, pp. 131–132:

> Within a few yeers after, Alderman *Eyer* being chosen Lord Maior of *London*, changing his copy, he became one of the worshipfull Company of Drapers, and for this yeer he kept a most bountifull house. At this time it came into his mind what a promise once he made to the Prentises, being at breakfast with them at their going to the Conduit, speaking to his Lady in this wise: Good Lord (quoth he) what a change haue we had within these thirty yeers? And how greatly hath the Lord blessed vs since that? blessed be his Name for it.
>
> I do remember, when I was a young Prentise what a match I made vpon a Shroue tuesday morning, being at the Conduit, among other of my companions; trust me wife (quoth he) tis worth the hearing, and Ile tell thee how it fell out.
>
> After we had filled our Tankards with water, there was some would needs haue me set down my Tankard, and go with them to breakfast (as many times before I had done) to which I consented: and it was a breakfast of Pudding-pies. I shall neuer forget it. But to make short, when the shot came to be paid, each one drew out his money but I had not one peny in my purse, and credit I had none in the place; which when I beheld, being abashed, I said; Well my Masters, do you giue me my breakfast this time; and in requitall thereof, if euer I be Maior of *London*, Ile bestow a breakfast one all the Prentises of the City: these were the words, little thinking, (God wot) that euer it should come to passe: but such was the great goodnesse of our God, who setteth vp the humble, and pulleth down the proud, to bring whom he pleaseth to the seat of Honour. For as the scripture witnesseth, Promotion cometh neither from the East nor from the West, but from him that is the giuer of all good things, the mighty Lord of heauen and earth. Wherefore wife, seeing God hath bestowed that vpon me that I neuer looked for; it is reason that I should perform my promise: and being able now, Ile pay that which then I was not able to do: for I would not haue men say that I am like the Ebon-tree, that neither beares leafes nor fruit. Wherefore wife, seeing that Shroue tuesday is

so neer at hand, I will vpon that day fulfill my promise, which vpon that day I made.

Truly (my Lord) (quoth she) I will be right willing thereunto.

Then answered my Lord, as thou dost loue me, let them want neither Pudding-pies nor Pancakes, and look what other good chear is to be had, I will referre all to your discretion.

Hereupon great prouision was made for the Prentises breakfast: and Shroue tuesday being come, the Lord Maior send word to the Aldermen, that in their seuerall Wards they should signifie his mind to the Citizens, to craue their fauours that their Prentises might come to his house to breakfast, and that for his sake they might play all the day after. Hereupon it was ordered that at the ringing of a Bell in euery Parish, the Prentises should leaue work and shut vp their shops for that day, which being euer since yeerly obserued, it is called the Pancake Bell.

V.ii

17 *neither Hamon nor Hangman.* Steane suggests 'A double pun: (1) the similar sound; (2) the Hammon in the play and the Haman in the Book of Esther, who having prepared a gallows fifty cubits high for his enemy was strung up on it himself.'

28 *cry clubs for prentises.* The apprentices' usual call for help from their fellows in effecting a rescue. *P.G.*, IV.ii.166.

31 *bird spittes.* Used contemptuously for a small dagger; cf. Porter, *Two Angry Women of Abingdon* (M.S.R.), lines 1804–1805: 'giue me good words, or by Gods dines Ile buckle yee, for all your bird-spit'.

62 *buske point.* The 'buske' was 'a strip of wood, whalebone, steel, or other rigid material passed down the front of a corset, and used to stiffen and support it' (*O.E.D.*). The 'buske point' was the ribbon or lace tag which tied the busk in place.

67 *Blew coate.* The characteristic dress of servants. *2 H.W.*, I.ii.196, n.

67–68 *giue you a new liuerie...Saint Georges day.* Servants were traditionally permitted to change masters (and so livery) on St George's Day. Blue was the usual color of servants' livery. The servant here, however, is promised a livery of black and blue and red, from the bloody beating Firke threatens to administer.

118 *Lie downe...and laugh. O.F.*, V.ii.41, n.

144 *lacde mutton*, a cant term for prostitute. Deloney, *Thomas of Reading* (ed. Mann, p. 218): 'no meat pleased him so well as mutton, such as was laced in a red petticoate'. But the term is often employed, as here, merely for the sake of a quibble (in this case on '*Lacie*', line 143), and Firke's use of it no more reflects on Jane's character than Speed's use of it does on Julia's in *The Two Gentlemen of Verona*, I.i.96–98: 'I (a lost mutton) gave your letter to her (a lac'd mutton), and she (a lac'd mutton) gave me (a lost mutton) nothing for my labor.'

167 (wrongly numbered 166 in the text) *codpeece point. Sat.*, IV.i.171, n.

178 (177) *tri-lill. P.G.*, IV.iii.44, n.

188 (187) *feede and be fat. Sat.*, IV.i.150, n.

191–192 (190–191) *drie fattes*, tubs used to hold dry things, as opposed to liquids. *I.T.B.N.*, V.ii.6.

193 (192) *colloppes*, slices of meat.

210 (209) *march faire. Sat.*, I.ii.399, n.

V.iii

10 *huffe cap*, roisterer, swaggerer. Marston, *What You Will*, III.ii.72: 'a huff-cap swaggering sir'. Dryden, *The Spanish Friar*, Act IV (ed. Summers, v, 172): 'As for you, Colonel Huff-cap, we shall trie before a Civil Magistrate who's the greater Plotter of us two.'

V.iv

0.2 *with napkins on their shoulders*. They are waiting on table; see opening S.D. of *R.G.*: '*Enter...*Neatfoot *a seruingman...with a napkin on his shoulder, and a trencher in his hand as from table*.' And Chapman, *An Humourous Day's Mirth*, opening S.D. for scene viii, which is set in Verone's ordinary: 'Enter *Verone* with his napkin upon his shoulder, and his man *Jacques* with another, and his *Son* bringing in cloth and napkins.'

2 *these Caniballes, these varlets my officers*, the sergeants who attend on Eyre in his office as mayor, whom he has labelled 'piecrust eaters' and 'buffe-ierkin varlets' at V.i.21–22, and two or three of whom he has assigned to accompany Margery. Cf. *N.H.*, I.ii.11; II.i.255; *S.D.*, I.i.115.

9–10 *cramme wealth in innocent lamb skinnes.* The reference is to the
leather purses made from the skin of lambs. Cf. *O.F.*, I.i.334,
where the wondrous purse is called 'an Indian mine in a Lambs
skinne', and I.ii.77–81: 'And gold, which ryseth like the sunne
out of the *East Indies*, to shine vpon euery one, is like a Conie
taken napping in a Pursenet, and suffers his glistring yellow
face deitie to be lapt vp in Lambskins, as if the innocencie of
those leather prisons, should dispence with the Cheuerill
consciences of the Iron harted Iaylers.'

11–16 *we are at our wits end for roome, . . . do they drink liuely.* Cf.
The Gentle Craft, pp. 132–133:

> The Prentises being all assembled, my Lord Maiors house was not able
> to hold them, they were such a multitude, so that besides the great Hall,
> all the Gardens were set with Tables, and in the backside Tables were
> set, and euery other spare place was also furnish'd: so that at length they
> were al placed and while meat was bringing in, to delight their eares,
> as well as to feed their bodies, and to drown the noise of their pratlings,
> Drums and Trumpets were pleasantly sounded: that being ended, the
> waits of the City, with diuers other sorts of Musick played also to
> beguile the time, and to put off all discontent.
>
> After the first seruice, were all the Tables plentifully furnished with
> Pudding-pies and Pancakes, in very plentifull manner; and the rest
> that remained was giuen to the poore. Wine and Ale in very great
> measure they had giuen, insomuch that they had no lack, nor excesse
> to cause them to be disordered. And in the midst of this their merriment,
> the Lord Maior, in his Scarlet gown, and his Lady in like manner went
> in amongst them; bidding them all most heartily welcome, saying
> vnto them, that his promise so long ago made, he hath at length per-
> formed.

21 *swag-belly.* I.iv.5.

22 *kitchinstuffe.* II.iii.44.

23 *tall.* I.i.167.

24 *East-Cheape.* II.iii.61.

following line 29] Most editors (e.g., Rhys, Hampden, Halliday,
Neilson, H. Spencer, Brooke and Paradise, Koszul) insert 'The
second Three-mans Song' at this point. Since there is nothing
in the text to suggest that it comes here, it seems preferable to
take literally the directive printed at the head of the song (1, 21):
'*This is to be sung at the latter end*', and assume that it provided

a musical finale for the close of the play. Williams places it at the end.

46 *Islington whitepot*. *O.E.D.* defines 'whitepot' as 'a dish made (chiefly in Devonshire) of milk or cream boiled with eggs, flour, spices, etc.' For its identification with Islington – a rural suburb to which Londoners were fond of making excursions to eat various cream dishes – cf. Brome, *The New Academy*, III.ii (ed. Shepherd, II, 61): 'white-pots, pudding-pies, stew'd prunes, and Tansies [,] / To feast their Titts at *Islington* or *Hogsden*'.

46 *happerarse*. (*O.E.D.*, citing *Dictionary of the Canting Crew*): '*Hopper-arst*, when the Breech sticks out'.

47 *carbonado*, meat or fish scored across and grilled. *N.G.*, p. 76: 'much mutton hast thou to answer for, which thou hast made away (being sluttishly fryed out in steakes, or in burnt Carbonadoes)'. *N.F.H.*, B4: 'the *Vniuersall Region* is built altogether vpon Stoues and *Hotte-houses*, you cannot set foote into it, . . . the bonefiers that are kept there, neuer goe out; insomuch that all the Inhabitants are almost broylde like *Carbonadoes* with the sweating sicknes'.

48 *auoide Mephostophilus*. With this jocular allusion to Marlowe's *Doctor Faustus*, cf. Jonson, *The Case is Altered*, II.vii.134–135: 'thou art not lunatike, art thou? and thou bee'st, auoide *Mephistophiles*'.

49 *Miniuer cap*. Miniver was a kind of fur: plain white, according to R. Holme, *Academie of Armorie* (1688), which seems to have been the English signification notwithstanding Cotgrave's divergent explanation of miniver as 'the furre of Ermines mixed, or spotted, with the furre of the Weesell' (*O.E.D.*). Linthicum (p. 226), on the evidence of a passage in the 1631 edition of Stow's *Annals* (p. 1039), says that miniver caps 'were old-fashioned in the twelfth year of Elizabeth's reign. They were tri-cornered and three or four inches high. They seem not to have been worn by persons above the rank of gentlewoman.' *Sat.*, II.i.129.

50 *partlets*, neckerchiefs. Cunnington writes of women's gowns in the second half of the sixteenth century: 'The neck was high or

low; but if low, was usually filled in with a partlet and ruff'
(Phillis Cunnington, *Costume in Pictures* (London and New
York, 1964), p. 48). Linthicum (p. 163) states that 'partlets
went out of fashion' about 1580.

51 *flewes*. Skeat and Mayhew thought this a reference to 'flapping
skirts', H. Spencer to 'the flaps of the French hood'. The word
is ordinarily used of 'the large chaps of a deep-mouthed
hound' (*O.E.D.*) as in Lyly, *Midas*, IV.iii.6–7: 'when a hound
is fleet, faire flewde, and well hangd'; and Shakespeare, *A Midsummer Night's Dream*, IV.i.119–120: 'My hounds are bred out
of the Spartan kind; / So flew'd, so sanded.' 'Flewes' are then
a reference to Margery's dewlaps.

51 *whirligigs*. Cf. 2 *H.W.*, V.ii.157–158: 'your Rems, and your rees,
and your whirligigs, and deuices'. And *W.E.*, III.i.115–116:
'when the whirligiggs of theire braines haue don spininge
the'ile stand still'. *Sat.*, V.ii.181.

51 *go, rub, out of mine alley*. The metaphor is from the game of
bowls, a 'rub' being an impediment which diverts a bowl from
its proper course. It is a favorite of Dekker's; cf. 2 *H.W.*,
V.ii.100; *W.B.*, III.ii.57; III.iii.50; *R.G.*, IV.ii.215.

52 *Sultan Soliman*, Süleyman I the Magnificent, sultan of the
Ottoman Empire from 1520 until his death in 1566. His
military exploits in eastern Europe, Asia Minor and northern
Africa made him an awesome figure in the eyes of Christian
Europe, and this impression was confirmed by the notoriety
surrounding the execution, on Süleyman's own orders, of his
son Mustafa in 1553. The story is told – among many other
places – in the thirty-fourth novel of volume II of Painter's
Palace of Pleasure (*c.* 1580). It is the subject of Fulke Greville's
Mustapha (original version *c.* 1594–1596). Sultan Soliman
appears in Kyd's *Soliman and Perseda* (*c.* 1590).

Cf. Tucca's address to the King in *Sat.*, V.ii.163–165: 'all hats
and caps are thine, and therefore I vaile: for but to thee great
Sultane Soliman, I scorne to be thus put off'. Marston, *What
You Will*, I.i.134–135: 'one [who] was even a prince, / A Sultan Solyman'.

53 *Tamburlaine. Sat.,* IV.iii.169–170.

55 *free-booters,* roving pirates, as in *G.H.,* B4v: 'set vpon (as it were by free-booters) and tane in his owne purse-nets by fencers and cony-catchers'. But in the present passage, the word is used simply for the sake of the quibble on 'boots'. *W. of E.,* IV.ii.100.

V.v

1 *fact,* crime. *V.M.,* IV.ii.67.

15 *Dioclesian,* i.e., emperor. The first part of Deloney's *Gentle Craft* takes place during his reign; Crispianus, one of the princes disguised as a shoemaker, marries his daughter. He appears in *V.M.*

15 *hump,* here, as at line 26, below, one of Eyre's exclamations of exuberance.

19 *yonker,* young man. *3 Henry VI,* II.i.24: 'Trimm'd like a younker prancing to his love'. *P.G.,* II.i.47; *N.H.,* IV.i.131.

22 *Tamar Chams beard.* Cf. *Much Ado About Nothing,* II.i.268–269: 'fetch you a hair off the great Cham's beard'. *Sat.,* V.ii.182, n.

23 *shaue it off, and stuffe tennis balls with it. G.H.,* C4v:

> a head al hid in haire, giues euen to a most wicked face a sweet propor-
> tion,...which beauty in men the Turkes enuying, they no sooner lay
> hold on a Christian, but the first marke they set vpon him, to make him
> know hees a slaue, is to shaue off all his haire close to the scull. A
> *Mahumetan* cruelty therefore is it, to stuffe breeches and tennis balles
> with that, which when tis once lost, all the hare-hunters in the world
> may sweat their hearts out and yet hardly catch it again.

> *W.A.,* D3v, of Covetousness: 'He kept not so much as a Bar-
> ber, but shaued his owne head and beard himselfe, and when it
> came to wey a pound, hee sold it to a *Frenchman* to stuffe
> tennis balles.' Similar allusions are common. Cf. *Much Ado
> About Nothing,* III.ii.46–47: 'the old ornament of his cheek
> hath already stuff'd tennis-balls'. And Barry, *Ram-Alley,* Act
> III (1611), D4:

>> If you come there,
>> Thy beard shall serue to stuffe, those balls by which
>> I get me heat at Tenice.

28 *the shaking of the sheetes.* IV.iv.82.

45 *degenerous*, degenerate (Latin *degener*). *W.H.*, V.i.96.

115 *a ladie and bryde?* The text should read 'a ladie and a bryde' (Q 1600, sig. K3v).

154–158 *my new Leden hall... Mondayes and Fridayes.* Cf. *The Gentle Craft*, p. 133: 'Then after this, Sir *Simon Eyer* builded *Leaden-Hall*, appointing that in the midst thereof, there should be a Market place kept euery Munday for Leather, where the Shoomakers of *London*, for their more ease, might buy of the Tanners without seeking any further.'

172–180 *I promist... feast al the prentises.* Cf. V.i.43–49, n.

173–177 *For andt... as tis now*,] A textual note, which should be equipped with an (*) to direct attention to Professor Bowers' discussion of this passage on p. 93 of vol. 1, is missing from p. 89. In the discussion on p. 93, for 'at the head of sig. K4' read: 'at the head of sig. K4v.'

OLD FORTUNATUS

INTRODUCTION

During the first months of 1596, a play which Henslowe refers to as
the first part of *Fortunatus* was being acted in London at the Rose
Theatre by the Admiral's Men. Henslowe records six performances
between 3 February and 24 May.[1] No mention is made of a second
part. But three-and-a-half years later a second part had either been
written or was being anticipated when, on 9 November 1599,
Henslowe paid Dekker £2 'in earnest of abooke cald the hole hys-
tory of ffortunatus'.[2] A further payment of £3 followed on 24
November, and Dekker received £1 'in full payment of his booke of
fortunatus' on 30 November.[3] Presumably, Dekker was revising
the old play, but there is a good deal of uncertainty about just what
this implies. Was the old play his, or the work of another dramatist?
Was the old play in fact a two-part play which Dekker was now
condensing into one? Or was he now providing the hitherto missing
Part Two and in the process joining it with an abridged version of
the old Part One into a single play? While, as critics have noted,
reference to a first part 'presupposes a second',[4] it is significant that
in Henslowe's record of performances of a *Fortunatus* play in the
early months of 1596, the designation of a first part occurs but once,
in connection with the earliest recorded performance, that of
3 February. Thereafter, in recording performances of the play in the
months that followed (10, 20 February, 14 April, 11, 24 May) he
refers to it simply as *Fortunatus*. Can this mean that, initially, a
second part had been planned, but that plans for it were dropped?
In that case, Dekker's work in November 1599 would consist of
revising and condensing the already existing Part One, and supply-
ing a second part. This would be consistent with Henslowe's

---

[1] *Henslowe's Diary*, pp. 34–37.
[2] *Ibid.*, p. 126.
[3] *Ibid.*, p. 127.
[4] Hunt, p. 30; see also Price, p. 43.

emphatic references (on 9 and 24 November) to Dekker's work on 'the whole history of Fortunatus', and would explain why Dekker received for this work the large sum of £6, Henslowe's usual fee for a new play.[1]

This seems the most likely interpretation of the existing evidence, but it is offered with appropriate diffidence since the existing evidence is so incomplete;[2] and speculation from it is complicated by the fact that the work Dekker had brought to completion by the end of November had itself to be revised during the first two weeks of December. The day after Dekker had received final payment for the play, we find Henslowe (under date of what he terms 31 November) advancing the dramatist the sum of £1 'for the altrenge of the boocke of the wholl history of fortewnatus'.[3] The reason for this is contained in Henslowe's entry of 12 December, where a further sum of £2 has been paid to Dekker 'for the eande of fortewnatus for the corte'.[4] The play was being adapted for court performance, where it was duly played before the Queen on 27 December.[5]

---

[1] Chambers, I, 373. Hunt's explanation of the amount paid to Dekker (p. 30, n. 9) is not satisfactory: 'The question of pay need not disturb us, for Dekker was then the brightest star in Henslowe's firmament, and his task [of revising two old plays] was perhaps as difficult as writing a new play.'

[2] The interpretation has the support, however, of C. H. Herford, *Studies in the Literary Relations of England and Germany in the Sixteenth Century* (Cambridge University Press, 1886), pp. 210–211:

'In Feb. 1596, a play called the *First part of Fortunatus* began to run with great success at Henslowe's theatre. It probably dealt with only the first half of the story, – the history of Fortunatus the father. Its attraction however, like that of most marvellous stories, rapidly wore off; and it ceased to appear. Three years later, an attempt was made to revive it by adding the second half, – the history of Andelosia; and the task was put into the hands of a young playwright, Thomas Decker.'

As evidence for his statement that the attraction of the 1596 play 'rapidly wore off', Herford cites Henslowe's Diary: 'The takings were at first unusually large (£3 and more); but by May 24, they had fallen to 14s. and the play was withdrawn' (p. 210, note 4).

[3] *Diary*, p. 127.

[4] *Ibid.*, p. 128.

[5] Professor Bowers (I, 107) thought 'there is perhaps no bar to the conjecture that the November conflation of two old plays could have been done with court performance as the objective'. But if this were so, then there would have been no need for Henslowe to have paid Dekker for 'altering' his book on 31 November when he had already paid the dramatist 'in full' for it on the day before.

Scholars have never failed to remark that Henslowe must have gotten something more for the £3 paid to Dekker in December than the prologue at Court with the two old men, and their closing epilogue. The allegory of Virtue and Vice, which is not to be found in the story of Fortunatus in the German *Volksbuch* on which the play is based, and the closing compliment to the Queen, when Fortune falls before her, must equally have been a part of the new material that Dekker provided when it became known that the play would have a royal audience.[1]

The text of *Old Fortunatus* as we have it represents, then, Dekker's December 1599 alteration of the work of revision and adaptation which he had done during the previous month on one or more plays that dated back at least to the beginning of 1596. Whether or not Dekker was the author of the *Fortunatus* play (or plays) of 1596 is impossible to know.[2] If he were not, then his revision was thorough, for the play as we have it is his.[3]

[1] The new ending of the play, with its compliment to the Queen, which Dekker provided for the Court performance presumably begins at V.ii.260.1. For the view that the play originally ended at V.ii.260, see below, introduction, pp. 86–87.

[2] He could have been. Henslowe did not record the names of playwrights before 1598, and Dekker's name appears in the *Diary* for the first time on 8 January of that year, but by then he was clearly no novice and his career as a dramatist must have begun several years before. There is no evidence for a pre-1596 version of *Fortunatus*, though Fleay, I, 126, taking the proverbial phrase 'an Almond for Parrat' at I.i.53 to be an allusion to the Marprelate tract published with that title *c.* 1590, considered the play's original version to date from that period, and Chambers (III, 291) surprisingly acceded to this conjecture, even adding: 'I should not wonder if Greene, who called his son Fortunatus, were the original author.'

[3] W. L. Halstead ('Surviving Original Materials in Dekker's *Old Fortunatus*', *Notes and Queries*, 182 (1942), 30–31) attempts to show that three passages of Dekker's play contain either material taken over from the earlier version (which he assumes to be not by Dekker), or 'old material that was rewritten less by Dekker than was the remaining material'. These are: (1) the opening of the play to the beginning of the Kings–Fortune scene, (2) Fortunatus' speech after the exit of Fortune and the subjected kings, (3) the scene in which Agripyne makes her first appearance. Halstead finds in these scenes 'a particular type of prose', one that is 'heavily laden with Euphuism plus a touch of Arcadianism'. He finds them exhibiting such stylistic elements as 'parallelism and balance, repetition of words or of root-forms of the words, antithesis of idea, parisonic antithesis, animation of inanimate objects, alliteration regular and transverse, fabulous naturalism, play on words, and exaggerated comparisons'. He gives no specific examples to illustrate any of these qualities, and his impression of these scenes seems to have been strongly influenced by Fleay's notion that the prose parts of *Old Fortunatus* are full of Lylian reminiscence.

The German *Volksbuch* of Fortunatus, which is the play's source, exists in two versions: the first published at Augsburg in 1509, another published at Frankfurt am Main in 1550.[1] The tale was dramatized by Hans Sachs in 1553.[2] No English version of the story seems to have been available in the sixteenth century. The earliest recorded English translation was entered in the Stationers' Register as *The History of Fortunatus* on 22 June 1615,[3] but of this no copy is known. What is apparently the earliest extant English translation is undated but is placed conjecturally in 1650 by the British Library Catalogue.[4] A later translation appeared in 1676.[5] Both translations are based on the Frankfurt edition of 1550.[6]

The story as given in the *Volksbuch* goes thus: born in Famagosta, in Cyprus, of an improvident father who runs through his inherited wealth, Fortunatus (age eighteen) leaves his by then impoverished home to make his fortune. He takes service with the Earl of Flanders, who has stopped off in Cyprus *en route* home from Jerusalem, and accompanies the Earl back through Venice to his home. Fortunatus gains the Earl's favor, but arouses the envy of his fellow-servants. They plot to get rid of him; one tells him that the Earl, newly married, plans to have his four chamberlains (of whom Fortunatus will be one) gelded out of jealousy for his wife and her ladies; Fortunatus flees. He goes to London, lives riotously for a brief while, then takes service with a Florentine merchant (Jeroni-

---

[1] Herford (*Studies in Literary Relations*, p. 205, n. 1) summarizes the differences between the two versions thus: 'The Augsburg texts, written in a Bavarian dialect, are in many places ampler in detail and circumstance: they use Romance forms more readily; the woodcuts also are wholly different, and on the whole superior, though less elaborate.'

[2] Hans Scherer in the introduction to his edition of *Old Fortunatus*, p. 22.

[3] Arber, III, 568. J. O. Halliwell (in *Descriptive Notices of Popular English Histories* (London: Percy Society, 1848), XXIII, 40–41) noted a reference to the *Fortunatus* tale in the epistle dedicatory to Meredith Hammer's translation of Eusebius, 1577.

[4] Shelf-mark 12410.bb.8.

[5] The full title reads: *The Right Pleasant, and Variable Tragical History of Fortunatus. Whereby a Young-man may learn how to behave himself in all Worldly Affairs and Casual Chances. First Penned in the Dutch Tongue: There-hence Abstracted, and now first of all Published in English; By T.C.* (London, 1676) (British Library Shelf-mark C.38.a.21). A second edition was printed in 1682. A Dutch translation (Amsterdam, 1631) states on its titlepage that it is *De achte mal herdruckt*; see Scherer, p. 13, n. 1.

[6] Herford, *Studies in Literary Relations*, p. 405.

mus Roberti) in Lombard Street; but a murder being committed in Roberti's house (by one Andrew on a rich merchant), Roberti's household is wrongfully accused and hanged, and Fortunatus but narrowly escapes execution. He flees to Picardy, and finding no service there, goes on to Brittany, where wandering in a forest he loses his way. He takes refuge in a tree, is pursued by a bear which he kills and whose blood he drinks, having had no food for two days, and falls asleep. Awakening on the third day in the forest, he sees 'standing before him a Fair and Beautiful Woman, mufled over the eyes'.[1] She announces herself to be Lady Fortune, and gives him the choice of her six gifts: 'Wisdom, Riches, and Strength, Health, Beauty, and long Life' (p. 44).

Fortunatus took no long deliberation of the matter, but said, then I desire of Riches such plenty, that I may not lack so long as I live. With that, forthwith she gave unto him a Purse, and said, Receive this same of me, and in what Country soever thou art, as often as thou puttst thy hand into it, thou shalt draw forth ten pieces of Gold of the same nations coyn. And this Purse shall retain this vertue, during the life of thee, and of thine own Children, whosoever shall possess it, either thou, thy children, or any other; but no longer after your death: therefore esteem it accordingly, and take special care thereof. Then said *Fortunatus*, Right courteous and beautiful Lady, Forasmuch as you have freely bestowed such an incomparable Iewel on me, reason would that I also be bound to do something for your sake, lest that this worthy benefit in time slip out of my Remembrance. She answered him demurely, saying: If thou hadst chosen Wisdom instead of Riches, thou wouldst not have been so careful to yield recompence where it is not deserved: For knowest thou not, that I am guided by the finger of the omnipotent God? And perceivest thou not that mine eyes are mufled not regarding whom I pleasure, nor seeing where I bestow? render thanks therefore only where it is due unto the Giver of all good Gifts; to whom thou canst yield no better recompence, than of thy riches freely received, to bestow on the poor and needy, where, when, and to whom it is expedient' (pp. 44–45).

Fortunatus makes a vow

that this day he would evermore keep holy; and in what Country soever he were, he would bestow on the same day four hundred pieces of Gold of that Nations Coyn, upon some marriable virgin, in perpetual remembrance how he first obtained his riches. Then said the Lady, follow me, and she led him by chance (as the blindman casteth his staff) overthwart the Wood into a beaten

[1] *The History of Fortunatus* (1676), p. 43. Parenthetical page-references are to this edition.

way, willing him to follow that path without turning on the left hand or the right, and that he should not look where she become, neither any more trust unto her (pp. 45–46).

Fortunatus buys horses and incurs the wrath of an Earl; he is imprisoned and questioned regarding the source of his wealth; he is finally released 'but bereft...of all his goods' (p. 51). At an inn in Angiers he meets a much-travelled Irishman named Leopoldus whom Fortunatus hires to travel with him. They go to Ireland together to visit Leopoldus' family, and proceed on to St Patrick's Purgatory in 'the City Vernecks' (p. 59) which they explore (it is a labyrinthine cave) and nearly get lost, but are brought out by an old man who goes in after them. Fortunatus and company go to Constantinople. Their host (in an inn) several times tries to rob them, and in one attempt is killed by Leopoldus; they leave town quickly (but not before Fortunatus has bestowed 400 duckets towards the marriage of a poor virgin, in fulfillment of his vow, when the anniversary of his gift from Fortune occurs). After extensive travels in the Balkans and northern Europe, they return to Cyprus, sixteen years after Fortunatus' departure from there. His parents are dead now. He hires a large house and sets up a splendid household; later he buys the house his father had once owned and lost, and there and on adjoining land (having plucked down all houses thereon) he 'builded a goodly large Palace after the bravest manner' (p. 80), and 'by the house also he founded a sumptuous Church, and twelve more houses for twelve Priests to continue in divine service of God'; he endows all the establishment with 1400 duckets yearly. The King of Cyprus arranges his marriage with Cassandra, youngest daughter of a local Earl. Leopoldus, now aged, is settled in a nearby house of his own, but shortly dies. Fortunatus and Cassandra have two sons, Ampedo (the elder) and Andolocia.

After twelve years of marriage, Fortunatus goes forth to visit the Heathen nations. He goes to Alexandria and gives a gift of 'costly Iewels' to the Souldan (p. 102), who rewards him, thereby arousing the envy of other merchants. Fortunatus sends his ship on to trade with other countries with instructions to pick him up in Alexandria two years later. Meanwhile, he will visit 'many strange Countries' (p. 104). He goes first to Persia; 'from thence he passed through the dominions of the great *Cham* of *Cathay*, and so through the desart, came to the Court of *Prester John*, who had under him, both of the Iles and firm Land lxxii Kings, every one of the which Countries is full of People, fair Cities, and strong holds' (p. 105). Fortunatus returns to Alexandria through Jerusalem. He dines with the Souldan the night before his departure for Famagosta, and the Souldan shows him his 'wishing Hat' ('a plain Felt hat, base and simple to behold' (p. 109)). He tells Fortunatus of its virtues.

Then demanded *Fortunatus*, if he that made that Hat were yet alive: The King said, of that I am uncertain. Then thought *Fortunatus* in his mind: How well would this Hat agree with the Purse? and said unto the King: Methinks, sithence that Hat hath such great vertue, that it would seem very heavy on his head that weareth it. Then answered the King, that it was no heavier than another Hat, and therewith bid him to essay it on his head, asking him whether he felt it otherwise. *Fortunatus* answered, saying: Verily I did not think it had been so light, neither supposed I that your Grace would be so unadvised to set it on my head: with that he suddenly wished himself into his ship, willing speedily to hoise the sail, and having a fresh gale of wind, they sailed swiftly away: when the Souldan saw he was thus deceived of such an incomparable Iewel, perceived also at the window that the ship was under sail, he in great rage commanded his men to set after *Fortunatus*, and to bring him back prisoner, threatning to him a cruel death. But ere they could be scantly appointed, the ship was clean passed out of sight; so that the Messengers returned again in vain, whereof the King was exceeding sorry (pp. 110–111).

The Souldan sends a Venetian named Marcholandus as ambassador to Fortunatus to get back the hat, but Fortunatus refuses to return it. He provides for the instruction of his children, and lives happily for some years with his family. Cassandra dies. Fortunatus languishes (p. 117). On his death-bed, he tells his sons of the virtues of purse and hat.

He commanded moreover that they should not part the Iewels, but use them in common friendly together, neither that they should make any person privy to the vertue of the purse, were she or he never so well beloved unto them: for so said he, have I concealed it this xl. years, and never uttered it save now to you only: with that he ceased speaking, and gave up the Ghost; whom his Sons caused to be honourably buried in the minster which he had erected (p. 118).

After mourning for twelve months for Fortunatus' death, Andolocia proposes that he and his brother should travel, but

Ampedo refuses. They finally agree that Andolocia will travel with the purse for six years, and Ampedo will remain at home with two coffers full of gold plus the hat. At the end of six years, Andolocia will return and Ampedo will have the purse. Andolocia visits the court of the King of France, and has an amour with a lady who deceives him with a substitute in bed. He goes on to the King of Spain's court, where he is knighted for valor and chivalry (p. 125). He leaves after 'certain years' and goes to London, where he becomes noted for the splendid house he sets up, and where he serves valiantly in England's wars with Scotland. He falls in love with Agrippina, the King's daughter, and lavishly entertains her and her mother at his house. He entertains as well the King and his lords, all of whom are impressed with his magnificence.

Then thought the King, it were good to abate the pride of *Andolocia*, and to make him ashamed; wherefore he appointed the next day also to take his recreation with *Andolocia* again, and forthwith sent privy commandment, that no Wood-seller should upon pain of his grievous displeasure, sell or give one stick of Wood, or any kind of fuel unto *Andolocia*, or any of his retinue, during the space of two days. Howbeit *Andolocia* was glad of it, and had prepared all the Delicatest Victuals that was to be had for money: but when he could by no means get any Wood or other fuel, he was sore afraid lest he should be utterly shamed, not knowing how the Cooks should dress the meat; but when he saw no other remedy, he sent speedily to the Merchants Ships, and to all the Grocers in *London* to buy an huge quantity of Canes, Cloves, Nutmegs, Liquorish, Ginger, and Cinamon, which were used in the Chimneys and Ovens, to burn instead of Wood, to dress the Meat. About dinner time, though the King supposed that Andolocia's Kitchin was but simply provided for lack of Fire, yet would he and other Lords that were with him before, ride unto Andolocia's Lodging, where they smelt such an exceeding strong and sweet savour, that they mused whereof it should be. Then the King demanded whether Dinner was ready? it was answered, that all Things were Prepared, and that with sweet Spices instead of Fuel, whereat the King and all the Lords marvelled greatly (p. 129).

The King wonders about the source of Andolocia's wealth; he confers with the Queen, who suggests that Agrippina can best discover the secret. She instructs her daughter, when next Andolocia visits her, 'to try whether you can obtain to understand of him, whence he getteth such abundance of goods: *Agrippina* promised to do her utmost endeavour in that behalf' (p. 131).

At their next meeting, Agrippina asks the source of his wealth, and Andolocia demonstrates the virtue of the purse by counting out 1000 crowns in her lap. She agrees to lie with him that night. She reports to the Queen, and they arrange for the preparation of a duplicate purse and a 'somnoriferous potion'. Andolocia comes to Agrippina that night, drinks the potion, falls asleep, and she robs him of the purse, replacing it with the counterfeit one. She reports to the Queen, and both carry the news to the King. Andolocia awakens, furious at having missed his night's pleasure with Agrippina from oversleeping; he returns home to prepare for a dinner for the King on the morrow, and discovers the loss of his purse. 'Then was he in a great perplexity, and almost dismayed with bitter anguish and sorrow: calling to mind, how for the contempt of his Fathers advice (that willed him to utter the secrets of the Purse to no creature) he was in this manner plagued' (p. 138). He dismisses his household and returns to Ampedo in Cyprus. The latter is glad to see him return, 'hoping to enjoy the purse again, and that he should be no more careful to spare as he had done these ten years' (p. 139). After dinner, Andolocia reports the loss of the purse. Ampedo upbraids him: 'if we had observed our Fathers will, our Iewels had not been separated, but you will needs aduenture in dangerous travel to work your own mischief whereof I sufficiently forewarned you' (p. 140). Later, seeing how hard Andolocia takes the loss, Ampedo comforts him; 'let the purse go with all ill luck and mischief with it', he says (p. 141). Andolocia steals the wishing-hat, and wishes himself back to England (via stop-overs in Genoa, Florence, and Venice, where he picks up jewels). He gains access to Agrippina's chamber as a jeweller, and when she gets the purse to pay him for what she will buy, he seizes her and wishes them both off in some wilderness.

With that they were carried through the Air in a small space unto a desart place in an Isle that bordereth upon *Ireland*, and were set there under a tree, whereon were growing fair Apples. As *Agrippina* was thus suddenly under the tree, having the Iewels in her Lap, and the Purse at her Girdle, she said to the Merchant: Lord, for thy mercy where are we now, or how came we hither? I am exceeding faint and hot; therefore I pray reach me some of those Apples to refresh me. The Iewels that he had left poured he into her lap also, and set the hat on her head to shadow her from the parching heat of the Sun, lest it should trouble him in Climbing. As he was thus on the top of the tree, looking for the fairest Apples, she sitting under full heavily, began to say, would God I were in my Chamber again. With that she was presently in her Chamber. The King, the Queen, and the Courtiers asked where she had been, and where the Marchant was become that carried her away? She said: God bless me from such Merchants; I suppose it was the Devil himself, or some of his Angels; Howbeit I left him on the top of a tree: but I pray you trouble me with no more questions, for I am exceeding faint and weary, and must needs rest me a while (p. 145).

Left alone in the desert, Andolocia curses his lot and himself. He wanders lost; in his hunger he eats of the 'very fair red Apples' (p. 146) he finds growing on a tree,

whereof as soon as he had eaten a couple, there sprang out of his head two horns, like as it were of a Goat, which he could by no means get off. Then began he more inwardly to feel the vengeance of God, for his theft and whoredom before time committed, and asked mercy for his sins, saying: O wretch that I am, O unhappiest of all other men; thus monstrously disfigured like a beast, for that I have beastly lived, and have not taken small correction therefore patiently: Wherefore, O God Almighty, sithence I am deprived of all mens help and succour, forgive me my offences, take from me this deformity, and assist me in this extream calamity (pp. 146–147).

He meets a Hermit who gives him two apples to eat of another tree.

So soon as he had clean swallowed the two Apples, his Horns were vanished away. *Andolocia* thereof was exceeding glad, and demanded of the Hermit how it came to pass that he had so soon gotten Horns, and was so soon rid of them again: The Hermit said: The Creator of all things hath given this secret nature to these two trees; neither be there their like on earth, but in this desart only. Then desired *Andolocia* that he might carry some of these Apples with him. The Hermit willed him to take as many as he list: But (saith he) I perceive thy mind is greatly cumbred with temporal and transitory estates, but it were far better to content thee with a competent life, and not to bring thy soul in danger, for a small pleasure. But these perswasions could not now sink very deep into Andolocia's heart, who was now wholly bent to recover again his Purse and his Hat, and to be revenged of *Agrippina* (pp. 148–149).

Equipped with apples of both sorts, he returns to London and goes to Court disguised as an apple-vendor:

when he knew *Agrippina* should pass, [he] laid abroad his Apples very handsomly upon a fine cloath and wrapped them in Sarcenet, whereby they should seem more precious, and called them Apples of *Damasco*. When many did require the price of them, he held them at three Crowns every Apple: so that none would buy of them, whereof he was glad, not meaning to sell of them but only to *Agrippina*. At the last when *Agrippina* with her Ladies passed by, he asked if it would please her grace to buy any precious Apples of *Damasco*. *Agrippina* asked what was the price of one of them? He said: Three Crownes. Then asked she what vertue was in them more than in other to be so dear? *Andolocia* answered, that they would cause excellent beauty, and make a sharp wit in them which should eat of them. *Agrippina* then willed one of her Gentlewomen to buy two of them. *Andolocia* then having accomplished his purpose, put up his wares, and conveyed himself speedily away (pp. 149–150).

Agrippina goes to her chamber and after eating the apples finds two horns sprung out of her head. Her 'Old Chamberlain' ('a Witty Gentlewoman') secretly seeks physicians to cure her; Andolocia, disguised, presents himself to the old woman and is taken secretly to Agrippina's chamber (no one else at court, neither her parents nor the courtiers, knows of her disfigurement). In her chamber, Andolocia recovers the wishing-hat; he treats the horns, which diminish, but he does not allow them to disappear altogether until he has the purse.

And whereas *Andolocia* meant to have rough and sharp Communion with *Agrippina*, he was now somewhat pacified when he hath the Hat, and in Courteous manner said unto her: Gracious Lady, you see that your malady is now well diminished, the chiefest cure that resteth behind, is to drive the root of the Horns out of the skul, to the which must be used very costly medicines, which if I cannot find in this Realm, I must needs either go my self, or send some other Doctor to fetch such things whereof I shall inform him, in other Countries; which will ask great charges. Besides this, would I know what certain sum of money you will give me, when you shall be clean rid of your Horns, and that your forehead shall be as smooth as ever it was. The Princess answered, I have certainly found that your science is excellent and true, therefore I beseech you to do your best to help me, and spare no money. The Physitian said: You bid me not to spare, but I have no money, whereof I should be liberal...she went to her Coffer and brought out the Purse, hanging it at her girdle,...and went to the Window, where she counted out three hundred Crowns. When *Andolocia* perceived she had the Purse and Iewels about her, he groped under his Gown, as though he sought for a Purse to put his money in, cast off his Cap, set on his Hat, clasped *Agrippina* fast about the middle, and wished himself in a solitary Desart, which was presently accomplished by the vertue of the Hat (pp. 158–159).

The old chamberlain reports to the Queen that Agrippina has vanished again, this time with the physician as before with the merchant. The King, when he hears of this, suspects the physician to be Andolocia,

whom you [the women] have falsely deceived. For it is no other like but he that gave unto him such a Purse, hath given him such Wisdom also, when he should lose it, to recover it again. It is the will of God that he only should enjoy the Purse, and none else; like as his pleasure is that I should be only King of this Realm: would God therefore that we had but our Daughter again, and with the Purse well might he speed that hath most Right thereto (p. 160).

In the desert, Andolocia reveals himself to Agrippina, reviles her for her unkindness to him, and refuses to remove her horns. With them, she does not wish to return to her parents, so he agrees to place her in a 'Nunnery of Noble Women' ('near unto St. Patricks Purgatory' (p. 163)); he pays the Lady Abbess 600 crowns (thrice the usual entrance fee) to have her admitted. After various travels around Europe, he returns to Ampedo in Cyprus, 'who received him gladly, and liked well that he came home so stately' (p. 166). Andolocia tells him what he has been doing while away.

Ampedo marvelled at his strange adventures, and yet greatly rejoyced that he was now safe come home with the purse and the hat, both which *Andolocia* offered to his Brother; but *Ampedo* said: I will not have the Purse at all, it bringeth him that hath it to such care and danger, as I have read of our Father, and now heard the like of thee (p. 166).

Andolocia is glad to keep it. He goes with his men to Court, and learns from the King of Cyprus that he would like to marry his son to Agrippina, but he has recently learned that she has disappeared. Has she as yet been found? he asks Andolocia. Andolocia says it is true that she has disappeared, but he knows of her whereabouts in a religious house in Ireland, and will see that she is reunited with her father for the sake of the marriage. With the aid of the wishing-hat, he wishes himself first into 'the wilderness, where the Apples were that would procure and take away horns' (p. 168), and after experimenting on himself to find which is which, he took 'of both sorts with him, and from thence conveyed himself unto the Abbey in *Ireland*' (p. 169). First he removes Agrippina's horns, and then takes her to England, and himself returns to Famagosta. Ambassadors from Cyprus arrive at the English court 'to entreat of a marriage between *Agrippina* and the young Prince of *Cyprus*' (p.

171). They supply a picture of the prince, which pleases the Queen and Agrippina, and the marriage is agreed to. She goes to Cyprus, where the wedding is performed. Andolocia distinguishes himself in the jousting that takes place during the revels following the wedding ceremony, and thereby gains the envy of two nobles: 'the Earl *Theodorus* of England, who came over with the Queen [i.e. Agrippina]' (p. 174), and 'the Earl *Limose* (who had his House in an Isle not far from *Famagosta*' (p. 174). On his return to his home from the wedding festivities, Andolocia is ambushed by the Earls, who kill all his men and make him prisoner in the Castle of Limose.

Ampedo imagining with himself that his Brother was come into some distress by occasion of his Purse, and that by racking and torments he might be forced to confess of the Hat also, whereby he might in like manner come into the like danger; in a great fury he cast the Hat into the fire, and stood by it till it was burned to ashes. And when he could by no means hear tell what was become of his Brother, he conceived thereby such an inward grief, that for thought he fell sick, and shortly after ended his life (p. 176).

Limose tortures Andolocia, who finally reveals the secret of the purse. Limose shares the secret with Theodorus. Andolocia remains imprisoned, but Theodorus, not feeling safe so long as he is alive, strangles him. He goes to Limose to report what he has done, and to get the purse for his half year (according to their bargain), but when Limose brings it forth, it is found to yield no money. Theodorus accuses Limose of deception; they fall to blows; Limose is 'deadly wounded' (p. 182). Word of their quarrel comes to the King of Cyprus and he examines Theodorus (Limose being too badly wounded to talk); he extracts a full confession from Theodorus concerning Andolocia's death. Both Earls are executed. Andolocia's corpse, which had been cast into a ditch, is recovered and buried in the Chantry Church which his father had founded at Famagosta. The Court mourns for him. Ampedo and Andolocia having no heirs, their costly palace and all the rich things therein are taken over by the King; here 'the young King and Queen held their Court, until his Father departed out of this life; and then began they to reign and govern the whole Realm of Cyprus' (p. 184).

It will be readily acknowledged that there is sufficient material in this rambling narrative not only for a two- but for a three- or even a four-part play. So far as a two-part play is concerned, the narrative of the *Volksbuch* falls readily enough into two sections, one dealing with the career of Fortunatus and ending with his death, the other with the careers of his sons, particularly Andolocia. This division is evident in Dekker's play, which breaks off sharply at the end of Act II with Fortunatus' death; with the beginning of Act III, the scene has shifted to England and from there to the end the concern is with Andelocia and Ampedo and the use they make of their father's gifts of the miraculous purse and hat.

How much of the work of dramatic compression had been done by the time Dekker took the story in hand can never be known in the absence of the old play. The extant play begins at a properly strategic point: Fortunatus wandering lost in the woods, just before his encounter with Fortune. The encounter itself has been interestingly embellished, with the train of dethroned kings and newly raised monarchs who accompany the goddess and who are not found in the *Volksbuch*. The cause of dramatic economy is aided by the Chorus, which can summarize Fortunatus' travels with as much dispatch as Marlowe's Chorus can summarize Faustus'.[1] In the second half of the play, the travels of Andelocia are also aided by a Chorus (at the beginning of Act IV). His involvement with the Princess Agripyne follows essentially the narrative line laid down in the *Volksbuch*. An effort has been made to prune the *Volksbuch*'s copiousness: Agripyne's mother has been eliminated from the play, and her suitor, the Cyprian prince, is incorporated into the action at a much earlier point as a love-sick suitor, even as the lords who eventually murder the brothers are introduced earlier as noblemen at the English court. The love interest between Agripyne and her suitors, Orleans and the Prince of Cyprus, is the chief addition to this second part. It is developed mainly in the first half of III.i, before the appearance of Andelocia, and it is tempting to see in the scene, which is an interpolation in the Fortunatus story, a distinctly Dekkerean touch. The plot concerning the witty and flirtatious Agripyne, the French prisoner who dotes on her, and the Cyprian prince who woos her but eventually gives her over, seems like a first

[1] Herford, *Studies in Literary Relations*, pp. 213–214, who notes the probable influence of the *Henry V* choruses as well (p. 214, n. 1).

84

version of the plot concerning Violetta and her French prisoner
Fontinelle and her other suitor Camillo who eventually gives up his
claim to her in *Blurt, Master-Constable* of some two years later, a
play in which Dekker had a hand, and which probably is entirely his.

The principal difference to be noted between the Fortunatus
story as told in the *Volksbuch* and in Dekker's play is the insistent
morality of the play. This is evident in the treatment of the goddess
Fortune, whose traditional capriciousness is defined at length in the
play. It is also evident in the treatment of the two sons of Fortunatus. In the *Volksbuch*, they are chiefly differentiated by the fact
that Andelocia, like his father, is a notorious gadabout while
Ampedo prefers to stay at home. The *Volksbuch* finds no moral
implications in these respective preferences. In the play the brothers
continue to be characterized by their contrasting tastes, but it is now
clear that Andelocia's restless spirit is the very badge of his incon-
stancy, while Ampedo's contentment with his own quiet life and his
distrust of the gifts of Fortune would seem to bear witness to a
humbler, more modest, in a word a more virtuous, spirit. Thus it is
surprising to hear Virtue denounce him at the close of the play as
one who

> made no vse of me, but like a miser,
> Lockt vp his wealth in rustie barres of sloth:
> His face was beautifull, but wore a maske,
> And in the worlds eyes seemd a Blackamore.
> So perish they that so keepe vertue poore.
> (V.ii.275–279)

What, to judge from this, Dekker seems to have intended in the
contrasted depiction of the two brothers was a demonstration of
two kinds of intemperance, an excess and a deficiency, two ways of
violating the mean where virtue lies: a demonstration in the manner
of Book II of *The Faerie Queene*. Andelocia is the prodigal, squan-
dering his gifts, and Ampedo is the niggard who makes no use of
his. Something of this contrast between Ampedo on the one hand,
and Fortunatus and Andelocia (who is very much his father's son)
on the other, is evident as early as II.ii.157ff., when Ampedo would
label as 'vanities' the experiences which his globe-trotting father is
relating and to which his brother is raptly listening. To the word
'vanities', Fortunatus replies: '*Ampedo*, thy soule is made of lead,

too dull, too ponderous to mount vp to the incomprehensible glorie, that trauell lifts men to.' The servant Shadow thereupon defines the other extreme: 'My olde masters soule is Corke and feathers, and being so light doth easily mount vp.' The moral scheme of the play, then, would seem to juxtapose the trivial inconsequence of Fortunatus' – and later Andelocia's – aimless journeying and pointless expenditure with the stolid humorlessness of Ampedo's equally inconsequent sobriety. If Andelocia is too giddy to manage any meaningful use of his gifts, Ampedo is too unimaginative to conceive of any worthy use for his.

The story of Fortunatus has certain Faustian overtones, as has often been noted,[1] and the model afforded by Marlowe's tragedy was not lost on Dekker when he addressed himself to the adaptation of the story to the stage. In both Marlowe's *Dr. Faustus* and Dekker's *Old Fortunatus*, the protagonist's character is promptly revealed by an act of choice that has a decisive effect on all that follows. Riches are to Fortunatus what knowledge is to Faustus, and Fortune, in the words of Herford,[2] is as 'inexorable [an] exacter' as Mephostophilis. But as Herford and all scholars since have recognized, the introduction of the figures of Virtue and Vice does not altogether accord with the moral scheme of the play as Dekker seems to have conceived it before alteration for court performance was decreed. The identification of the fruit of the respective trees of Vice and Virtue with that which provides and takes off horns, while it may have served to help incorporate the allegorical figures into the dramatic action, is also troublesome by any standards of moral signification, because as Herford says: 'those who taste the apple of Virtue are also the malefactors who murder Andelosia for the purse'.[3] And it is disconcerting to find the figure of Fortune, as exhibited in the play's first scene – in the words of Herford, 'the supreme arbiter of the world, bringing the destinies in her train, and overthrowing greatness at her good pleasure' – suddenly falling 'into the position of one of a Triumvirate'.[4] The play as originally conceived was a triumph of Fortune, and it must (as Herford suggests) have originally closed with Fortune's words:

[1] *Ibid.*, pp. 213ff.   [2] *Ibid.*, p. 217.
[3] *Ibid.*, p. 217.   [4] *Ibid.*, p. 216.

England shall ne're be poore, if *England* striue,
Rather by vertue, then by wealth to thriue.
(V.ii.259–260)

But the rules of courtly compliment required a tribute to the Queen,
and the allegorical scheme which Dekker adopted for the manage-
ment of this required a triumph of Virtue over Fortune.[1]

The performance at Court for which Dekker altered *Old Fortunatus*
took place apparently on 27 December 1599.[2] Earlier in December,
Henslowe had loaned £10 to the players 'to by thinges for ffortunatus',[3] presumably in preparation for the Court production.
Whether or not the play was staged in the public theatre is uncertain.
If so, it seems not to have been in the Admiral's repertory for long
because on 20 February 1600 it was entered for publication in the
Stationers' Register.[4] The quarto of 1600 duly appeared, the only
printed edition the play would receive in English during the next

[1] The compliment offered the Queen by referring the moral and dramatic issues
that have arisen in a play to her for solution had a famous precedent in the close of
Peele's *Arraignment of Paris* (printed in 1584). The relation of *Old Fortunatus* to
the tradition of allegorical and theatrical 'triumphs' is noted by Herford (*Studies in
Literary Relations*, pp. 215–216). The tradition in its popular form is well illustrated
by the anonymous *Rare Triumphes of Love and Fortune*, printed in 1589 and –
according to the titlepage of that edition – 'Plaide before the Queenes most excellent
Maiestie'. The date of its performance at Court was apparently 30 December 1582
(W. W. Greg in his introductory note to the edition of the play in the Malone
Society Reprints (1930), p. vi).
[2] During the Christmas season 1599–1600, the Admiral's Company performed at
Court on 27 December and 1 January. *The Shoemakers' Holiday* was acted on the
latter date. [3] *Diary*, p. 128.
[4] One month later, on 18 March 1600, Henslowe on behalf of the Admiral's men
paid 40s. 'to staye the printinge' of *Patient Grissil* (*ibid.*, p. 132). That no such action
was taken in behalf of *Old Fortunatus*, and that the play was allowed to go so promptly
into print, may indicate that its life in the public theatre was over. Hunt (p. 31) notes
that the opening line of the prologue presumably intended for use in the public
theatre ('Of *Loues* sweete war, our timerous Muse doth sing') is meaningless as the
play now stands, 'since "Love's sweet war" is assuredly not the theme' of the play
as we have it. It presumably accompanied either the 1596 *Fortunatus*, or the November
1599 revision before it was altered for Court performance. W. L. Halstead, in 'A
Note on *Old Fortunatus*' (*Modern Language Notes*, 54 (1939), 351–352), thinks it
unlikely that the play was publicly staged after its alteration for Court: the alterations
'show deliberate appeal to the Queen and virtually insured success at the Court, but
the play was outmoded for the London theatre audience, and so it was relegated to
the printshop'.

200 years. It was doubtless the publication of the quarto which brought the play so forcibly to the attention of Robert Allot while he was compiling his dictionary of quotations, *Englands Parnassus* (entered in the Stationers' Register on 2 October 1600). Allot quotes thirteen passages from *Old Fortunatus* in his collection (see Commentary).[1] There are occasional contemporary references to Fortunatus and his purse and hat, but they are as likely to refer to the tale as to Dekker's play, which did not hold the stage in England.[2]

It had a greater vogue, not surprisingly, in Germany, the land of the story's birth, whither it was carried in dramatic form by English actors. A Fortunatus play was acted in Graz in February 1608,[3] and in Dresden on 11 July 1626.[4] A German text of the play is preserved in the collection of *Englischer Komödien und Tragödien* published in 1620, where it bears the title *Comoedia von Fortunato und seinem Seckel und Wünschhütlein, darinnen erstlich drei verstorbenen Seelen als Geister, darnach die Tugend und Schande eingeführet werden.*[5] Act I, which is clearly modeled on Dekker, opens with Fortunatus and Echo; Fortune appears to him, offers her gifts, and he makes his choice. Fortunatus is with the Soldan at the beginning of Act II; he steals the hat and departs, but is shortly confronted with Fortune, who announces his end. He counsels Andolosia and Ampedo, and dies. In Act III, the brothers separate the hat and the purse, and

---

[1] Allot does not name the play, but signs the passages simply with Dekker's name. References to *Englands Parnassus* in the Commentary are to Crawford's edition.

[2] The allusion to '*Fortunatus* hat' in Jonson's *The Case is Altered* (I.ix.24) is either to the tale or to the 1596 version of the play, for Jonson's comedy seems to date from 1597–1598. In Marston's *Antonio's Revenge* (a play which, like Dekker's, seems to date from 1599) a character announces (II.i.143–144): 'I have old Fortunatus' wishing-cap, / And can be where I list, even in a trice.' There is a reference to '*Fortunatus* his pouch' in Field's *A Woman is a Weather-cocke*, III.iv.22 (acted in 1609). And in Fletcher, Massinger and Field's *The Honest Man's Fortune* (1613) a character declares: 'Oh *Fortunatus*, I envie thee not / For cap, or pouch, this day Ile prove my Fortune' (Beaumont and Fletcher folio of 1647, 166). Halliwell noted that 'the tale is mentioned' by Henry Crope in *Vertues Commonwealth or the Highway to Honour* (1602).

[3] Scherer, p. 19.   [4] *Ibid.*, p. 20, note 1.

[5] British Library Shelf-mark: C 95.b.36. The relation of the German text to Dekker's play is examined by Paul Harms, *Die deutschen Fortunatus-Dramen und ein Kasseler Dichter des 17. Jahrhunderts*, Theatergeschichtliche Forschungen, v (Hamburg and Leipzig, 1892).

88

Andolosia goes to England; his use of spices to supply the lack of firewood is depicted. The King confers with Agrippina, and she causes Andolosia to show her the purse; an assignation is arranged for the coming night. She reports to her father, and when she meets with Andolosia, gives him a sleeping-potion in a drink and takes the purse, leaving another in its place. Andolosia, with his servant, discovers the theft, and returns to his brother in Famagosta. The King suggests that Agrippina should give the purse to him, but she refuses. Back in Famagosta, Andolosia reports the theft to Ampedo, who first upbraids, then comforts his brother. Andolosia takes the hat and returns to England. Act IV opens with a debate between Virtue and Vice, the former wearing 'ein Narrenhütlein' (sig. O2). Andolosia appears disguised as a jeweler and is admitted to Agrippina's chamber. When she brings forth the purse to pay for the jewels that she has purchased, he says: 'Nun wünsche ich mich in einen wilden Wald da keine Leute innen sind' (sig. O4); in the next scene they are in the desert place. Andolosia climbs the tree for apples for Agrippina; he leaves the hat with her, and when she wishes herself back home again, she is promptly conveyed thither. Andolosia bewails her disappearance; he tastes one of the apples and sprouts horns; Fortune appears, removes his horns with the other variety of apple, and leads him out of the forest. In Act V, Andolosia is found hawking his 'Epffelchen von Damasco'. First one Count, then another, and then Agrippina appears in turn to ask about the virtues of the apples, and to buy of them. Andolosia and his serving-man then take their leave, and the two Counts and Agrippina appear successively with horns. Andolosia comes on in his doctor's disguise; the first Count takes him to Agrippina and her father. He removes the Count's horns by way of demonstrating his curative powers; then he addresses himself to Agrippina, by which time he has spied his 'Wünschhütlein' and by its powers wishes himself into a wilderness with her. There he denounces her, then takes her to a cloister in Ireland where he leaves her and wishes himself to Famagosta. But he is soon off again to retrieve Agrippina. *En route* to Ireland he stops in the wilderness and takes fruit first from the 'Baum der Schande' but quickly discovers his mistake ('ich fühle etwas auff meinem Häupte'), and taking fruit from the 'Bawm der Tugend' (sig. Q7) proceeds to Agrippina's cloister and removes her horns. He restores her to her father's London palace and returns to Famagosta. The two Counts appear (the second of whom still bears his horns), both bent on vengeance. They come upon Andolosia and his serving-man, who taunts them ('Gnädiger Herr wen sehren wir da? Es seind die beiden Herrn, den wir am nechsten zu Lunden Epffel verkaufften, vnd zwar der eine hat noch Hörner, Epffelchen von Damasco. Epffelchen' (sig. R2)). The Counts kill the servant, and seize and bind Andolosia, demanding to know the source of his wealth. They take him away. Ampedo, distraught at the death of his brother's servant and the disappearance of his brother, burns the hat, and dies. The two Counts gain the purse from Andolosia and kill him; then they find the purse empty and fall to quarreling. The King and Agrippina come upon them; the first Count confesses all and the King condemns them both. Fortune appears and the King and Agrippina kneel before her. The King prays for her continued favor to his kingdom, and Fortune promises that it will flourish like the laurel tree.

The first two-and-a-half acts of the German *Comoedia* are clearly a redaction of Dekker's play. But in the manner of reported texts (which is what the German *Fortunatus* is), this one was at the mercy of the memory of the reporter, and as the reporter found his memory failing as he proceeded in his attempt to reconstruct the stage action, he was forced to turn to other sources for help. The obvious available source was the *Volksbuch*. Beginning with the account of Agrippina's theft of the purse, the German *Comoedia* tends to draw more and more heavily on the *Volksbuch*. To be sure, it never to the end loses sight of Dekker's model. The presence of Virtue and Vice in Act IV of the German play bears witness to the Dekker source; there are no such figures in the *Volksbuch*; and the German text has followed Dekker in having Fortune (not a Hermit, as in the *Volksbuch*) instruct Andolosia in the knowledge of the fruit that has the power to remove horns. The identification of the horn-giving fruit and the horn-removing fruit with, respectively, the trees of vice and virtue is of course derived from Dekker. Increasingly, however, in Act IV and especially in Act V, the German *Comoedia* turns at least as often to the *Volksbuch* for its material as to Dekker. Andelocia's disguise as a jeweler and his first abduction of Agripyne are described by Dekker in eight lines (24–31) of the Chorus to Act IV. It forms a whole scene of Act IV of the German play. Just as Dekker at IV.i.91ff. gives Andelocia a soliloquy following Agripyne's abrupt departure by means of the hat, so too does the German text, but this, in a way that is typical of the later scenes of the *Comoedia*, is taken not from Dekker but from the 1551 Frankfurt edition of the *Volksbuch*:

Comoedia	*Volksbuch*
Agrippina, O Agrippina wo seid ihr? O Agrippina hast du dich vnwissend mit meinem Wünschhut auch weg gewünschet, O weh, O mordio, verfluchet sei dieser Bawm, verfluchet sei auch die Frucht darauff, unnd der welcher ihn gepflantzet, verfluchet sei die Stunde darin ich gebohren war, der Tag und die Stunde die ich je erlebet, O du bleicher Todt, warumb erwürgtestn mich nicht, ehe ich in diese Hellen-Angst und Noth gekomen bin? Verfluchet sei der Tag unnd die Stunde, worin ich Agrippinan zum erstenmal ansahe, verfluchet sei auch meine Hand, womit ich ihr den Wunschhut auffsetzet. Nun wolt ich nichts mehr wünschen, als das mein Bruder in diesen Waldt bei mir wehre, so wolt ich in erwürgen, uñ mich darnach an diesen Bawm hencken: (sigs. O4v–O5)	*Als nu Andolosia auff dem Baun sasz, unnd sahe das Agrippina hinweg was mit dem Hütlin, darzu mit alle den Kletnoten so er in dreien großen und mechtigen Stedten auffbracht het, Verfluchet er den Baum, die Frucht darauff, und der den daher gepflantzt het, sprach auch wetter, Verfluchet sey die stund darinn ich geboren ward, die Tag und Stund die ich jhe gelebt hab. O grimmiger Todt, warumb hast du mich nicht, erwürget, eh das ich in diese angst und Not kommen bin? Verfluchet sey der Tag und Stund, darinn ich Agrippinam zu dem ersten mal ansahe, Nu wolte Gott das mein Bruder in dieser Wildenuss bey mir wer, so wolt ich ihn erwürgen, unnd mich selber an ein Baum hencken, (sig. K8)*

The latter half of the Fortunatus story (Andelocia's dealings with Agripyne) has an analogue in the tale 'of the magic ring, brooch and cloth, which an emperor left to his son; how he lost them and how they were recovered' in the *Gesta Romanorum* (ed. S. Herrtage (London, 1879), pp. 180–193).

Dekker's *Old Fortunatus* was produced at Covent Garden on 12 April 1819, and acted eleven times during that season.[1]

Reference is made in the Commentary to the work of the following editors of *Old Fortunatus*: C. W. Dilke, in vol. III of *Old English Plays* (London, 1814); Ernest Rhys, in his Mermaid edition of five plays of Dekker (London, 1887); H. Scherer (Erlangen, 1901).

[1] John Genest, *Some Account of the English Stage* (Bath, 1832), VIII, 702.

COMMENTARY

Persons

The name of the Priest of Fortune, who speaks at I.iii.20ff., and appears again at IV.i.111.2, should be added to Professor Bowers' list of *Dramatis Personae* in I, 112.

The Prologue at Court

3–4 *Pandora... Gloriana... Cynthia... Belphœbe... Astræa.* For Pandora ('the all-endowed', or 'all-accomplished': Hesiod, *Works and Days*, 80–82) and Astræa as names for Queen Elizabeth I, see Peele, *Descensus Astreae. The Device of a Pageant, borne before M. William Web, Lord Maior of the Citie of London, on the day he tooke his oath, being the 29 of October, 1591* (*Harleian Miscellany* (London, 1813), x, 69): 'Our faire Astraea, our Pandora faire,/Our faire Eliza, or Zabeta faire'. Spenser, in the letter to Raleigh which prefaces *The Faerie Queene*, announced his intention of representing Elizabeth not only as Gloriana but in the person of Belphœbe as well, therein following the example of Raleigh, who had celebrated the Queen as Cynthia – 'Phoebe and Cynthia being both names of Diana' – in his *The Ocean to Cynthia*, of which only a fragment (the eleventh book and part of the twelfth) is extant. For a full account of compliments to the Queen as Cynthia, Gloriana, and Belphœbe, see Elkin Calhoun Wilson, *England's Eliza* (Cambridge, Mass., 1939). For the praise of the Queen as Astraea, see Frances Yates, 'Queen Elizabeth as Astraea' (which takes the present passage as its point of departure) in the *Journal of the Warburg and Courtauld Institutes*, 10 (1947), 27–82.

4 *seuerall names to expresse seuerall loues.* Dekker echoed the phrasing and the cadence of this years later (1630), in *B.R.W.R.*, p. 204, in the midst of a passage descriptive of the epidemics of plague that attended on the deaths of both Queen Elizabeth and King James: 'He [Jehovah] hath seuerall sorts of weapons; seuerall Punishments, for seuerall Offences.'

9–10 *Eliza...Elizium.* Cf. Peele, *The Arraignment of Paris*, lines 1150–1151: 'The place Elizium hight, and of the place, / Her name that governes there Eliza is.'

30 *Panthæon.* Cf. Spenser, *The Faerie Queene*, I.x.58 (Redcrosse concerning Gloriana's palace): 'that bright towre all built of christall cleene, / *Panthea*'.

47 *still one.* In allusion to the Queen's motto, *Semper Eadem.*

The Prologue

9 *circle...eye.* Jonson, *Every Man out of his Humour*, induction, 216–217: 'We hope to make the circles of your eyes / Flow with distilled laughter.' *S.D.*, I.i.200–202.

18–20 *our muse intreats...Chorus.* Cf. *Henry V*, prologue, 23–34.

I.i

1 *So, ho, ho, ho, ho.* Originally, a hunting-call used to direct attention of the dogs or other hunters to a hare which has been started; but by extension, used generally as a call to secure attention. Cf. Porter, *The Two Angry Women of Abingdon* (M.S.R.), lines 2041–2043, where a character is lost in the woods at night:

> Shall I stand gaping here all night till day?
> And then be nere the neere, so ho, so ho.
> *Will.* So ho, I come, where are ye? where art thou? here.

And Dekker (and Middleton?), *Blurt, Master-Constable*, IV.ii.39–40: 'Ho, ho, Frisco, madonna! I am in hell, but here is no fire; hell-fire is all put out. What ho, so ho, ho!' Cf. *R.G.*, II.ii.68; *I.T.B.N.*, III.ii.69; *W.H.*, II.iii.25; *P.G.*, II.i.155; IV.ii.22–23; *M.M.L.*, I.i.34; *S.D.*, III.iv.33; *L.D.*, IV.iv.2. And *O.F.*, II.ii.332.

2 S.P. *Eccho.* For a list of echo-scenes 'from Euripides to Thomas Hardy' see Lucas, *Webster*, II, 195–196, and Herford and Simpson, *Jonson*, IX, 494.

15 *I am so full of chinckes.* Terence, *Eunuchus*, 105: 'plenus rimarum sum'. In Fortunatus' quibble, 'chinckes' means money in line 14, and holes in his dress in the present passage. For 'chinks' as a term for money, cf. *Romeo and Juliet*, I.v.116–117.

18–19 *still daunce in this coniuring circle.* *Blurt, Master-Constable*,
II.ii.250: 'I am conjured, and will keep my circle.'

21 *laugh and bee leane.* A variant of the proverb 'laugh and be fat';
cf. V.ii.39.

41 *Wagtailes*, small birds.

44 *a woman, . . . kind of cattell.* Lodge, *Euphues his Shadowe* (1592),
I2v: 'for whether it were femenine feare, or dissembled
affection, or some such folly or fancie, that haunteth that
sweete kind of cattel, no sooner did she heare of *Philamis*
departure, but. . .she sodainly filled the whole house with her
fond complaints'. Beaumont and Fletcher, *The Scornful Lady*,
III.i.5: 'these woemen are a proud kinde of cattell'.

49 *Snip snap.* Used of a 'smart remark or reply; sharp repartee'
(*O.E.D.*), or of one who indulges in such repartee, though for
the term as used of persons, *O.E.D.* gives no example earlier
than 1785. Cf. Nashe, *Have With You*, III, 10: 'deal as *snip snap*
snappishly with him as euer he was delt withall'. And *Blurt,
Master-Constable*, II.i.126–127, of a pert page-boy: 'O, here's
a sure pocket dag! and my sister shoots him off snip-snap.'
P.G., V.ii.236.

53 *an Almond for Parrat.* The phrase apparently goes back to
Skelton's *Speke Parrot*, 8, 9: 'when sent to great ladies, "Then
Parot must haue an almon or a date."' Haughton, *Englishmen
for my Money* (M.S.R.), lines 1769–1773:

> Ah sirra now weele bragge with Mistres Moore,
> To haue as fine a Parret as she hath,
> Looke sisters what a pretty foole it is:
> What a greene greasie shyning Coate he hath,
> An Almonde for Parret, a Rope for Parret.

One of the tracts in the Martin Marprelate Controversy
(undated, but published apparently in 1590) is titled *An Almond
for a Parrat.* McKerrow reprinted it among 'Doubtful Works'
in vol. III of his edition of Nashe, and noted (IV, 461) that the
phrase 'seems to mean an answer for a fool'. See Tilley, A220.
1 H.W., V.ii.279; *W.H.*, V.iv.129.

54 *cracke me this Nut.* Another parrot phrase, like the preceding;

see Tilley, N359. Between 5 September 1595 and 23 June 1596, Henslowe records sixteen performances by the Admiral's men of a play (now lost) of this title (*Diary*, pp. 30–34, 36, 37). It seems to have been revived during the season 1601–1602 (*ibid.*, pp. 185, 187).

55–56 *wilde man...throw Squibs.* Pageants were regularly accompanied by a 'wild-man' or 'green-man', dressed in leaves and flowers, whose duty it was to clear the way for the procession by throwing fireworks among the crowd. See Robert Withington, *English Pageantry* (Cambridge, Mass., 1918), I, 72–77.

62 *Noddie.* W.H., IV.i.31, n.

63 *downe great heart.* Scherer notes the occurrence of the phrase in *Misogonus*, II.iii.65 (ed. Bond).

63.3–4 *broken Crownes and Scepters.* In Drayton's *Robert, Duke of Normandy* (1596), lines 106–107, Fortune wears about her neck a chain made of 'Princes crownes & broken scepters' (*Works*, I, 257). For traditional descriptions of Fortune, see H. R. Patch, *The Goddess Fortuna in Medieval Literature* (Cambridge, Mass., 1927), and his *Tradition of Boethius* (1935).

63.6 *shee treading...goes vp.* Cf. the S.D. in *1 Tamburlaine*, IV.ii.29.1, whereby Tamburlaine mounts his throne using the captive Bajazeth as a footstool: '*He gets up upon him to his chaire.*' A similar scene occurs in the 1616 edition of *Faustus*, III.i, where the Pope enters with the command 'Cast downe our Foot-stoole' and proceeds to mount his throne on the back of Saxon Bruno, the imperial nominee for the papacy, who is led in in chains (ed. Greg, lines 895ff.).

81 *Phaetons.* Used again as an image of fallen pride in *D.D.*, E3:

> These *Dames*, who each day in French *Chariots* sat
> Glistring like *Angels*, a prowd-bounding *Trot*
> From foure faire *Steedes* drawing all on them to wonder,
> That the Clowdes eccho'd, and the *Earth* shooke vnder:
> But when their *Coursers* tooke their full *Cariere*,
> It look'd like that *Day*, when the *Thunderer*
> Struck with his *Triple-fire Heauens Rider* downe;
> For (from their horses nostrils) *Breath* was throwne
> Hot-quick as lightning, and their Hoofs vp-hurld
> Such Clowdes of *Smoake*, as when he fir'd the world.

To this passage, Dekker provides the marginal note: '*Phae-
tont. Fab. | Ouid. | Metam. lib.* 2.' Henslowe records payments
to Dekker for a play titled *Phaeton* in January 1598; Dekker
was paid to alter it for Court performance in December 1600
(*Diary*, pp. 86, 137). The play is lost. Cf. *O.F.*, II.i.49.

84 *Weau'd wanton loue-nets in our curled hayre.* An adaptation of a
Petrarchan commonplace. Cf. Lodge, *Euphues his Shadowe*
(1592), B4v: 'I saw on earth a Fowler heauenly faire, / That
made hir nets the trammels of hir haire.' *The Pilgrimage to
Parnassus* (ed. Leishman), lines 388–389: 'Of my Corinnaes
haire loue makes his nett / To captiuate poore mortall wand-
ringe hartes.'

93 *your cries to me are Musicke. L.D.*, II.iii.86.

94 *roundure,* 'rounded form or space' (*O.E.D.*). *D.D.*, D3: 'Were
all the *Rowndure* betwixt *Hell* and *Heauen* / *One Clowd*
condensd'.

105 *wild beast multitude. L.D.*, III.iv.20–22, n.

108 *tread on neckes. L.T.*, 70.

111 *wonder of all eyes. S.H.*, prologue, 4; and cf. *M.E.*, 89, n.

156 *rustie.* The word is regularly associated with the coach of
Night. Cf. Marlowe, *1 Tamburlaine*, V.i.294: 'ugly darknesse
with her rusty coach'; and *Edward II*, IV.iii.44: 'duskie night,
in rustie iron carre'. Marston, *Antonio and Mellida*, IV.i.11:
'the rusty coach of night'. The steeds which draw the coach of
Night are found champing 'on their rustie bits' in Spenser,
Faerie Queene, I.v.20.

158 *Negro paramour. . .night.* Cf. *L.D.*, III.i.5–7.

159 *this circle.* Cf. lines 18–19.

172 *Tartarian.* In its Elizabethan usage, it is not always clear
whether this refers to the region of central Asia (Tartary) or to
the infernal regions of Greek and Roman mythology (Tartarus). In *1 Tamburlaine*, the word is used of the natives of
Tartary, as in references to 'that Tartarian rout' (I.i.71) and
'Tartarian thieves' (II.ii.16) and to Tamburlaine himself as
'the great Tartarian thiefe' (III.iii.171); but the allusion in
Part Two (II.iii.18–19) to one who 'scaldes his soule in the
Tartarian streames, / And feeds upon the banefull tree of hell'

clearly has reference to Hades, and this is its usual signification
in Dekker. In *D.D.*, D2, he alludes to Lucifer's 'Tartarean
Pallace', and to Lucifer himself as 'the Crim Tartar' (D2v). So
in *L.C.*, D1v, with the reference to 'the *Tartarian* their Lord
and Maister' and the 'lowe Countries in Hell'. There are references to 'beggerly *Tartarians*' in *W.A.*, E4, and to 'the
Tartarian Tarmagant' in *S.H.R.*, D4, where both are associated with allegories of hell. Tartary as a place of heathen
rogues and Tartarus as a place of pagan devils fuse in a term of
general opprobrium, as in *1 Return from Parnassus* (ed.
Leishman), lines 511–512: 'he cald me Pagan, Tartarian,
heathen man, base Plebeian'. Cf. *I.T.B.N.*, V.iv.80, n.

173–208 *These I created... Fortunes grace.* Of the eight examples of
Fortune's victims and favorites cited here, five are mentioned
in Chapter 44 ('Of Fortune') of La Primaudaye's *The French
Academy* (1589), pp. 447–448:

Gregory the 7. from a poore monke was lift up to the dignitie of chiefe
bishop of Rome: and *Henry* the 4. Emperor, was brought to that extreme
miserie by wars, that he asked the said *Gregory* forgivenes, and cast
him selfe down at his feete. And yet before this miserable monarch
could speake with him, he stood three daies fasting and barefoote at the
popes palace gate, as a poore suppliant waiting when he might have
entrance and accesse to his holines. *Lewes* the Meeke emperor, & king
of France, was constrained to give over his estate, & to shut himselfe
up in a monasterie, through the conspiracie of his own children... But
was not that a wonderfull effect of fortune, which hapned not long
since in Munster, principal town in the country of Westphalia, wherin
a silly botcher of Holland, being retired as a poore banished man
from his country, called *Iohn* of Leiden, was proclaimed king, was
served & obeid of all the people a long time, even untill the taking and
subversion of the said towne after he had borne out the siege for the
space of three yeeres... Will you see a most wonderful effect of
Fortune? Look upon the proceedings of that great *Tamburlane*, who
being a pesants son & keeping cattell, corrupted 500. sheepheards his
companions. These men selling their cattel, betooke them to armes,
robbed the merchants of that country, & watched the high waies.
Which when the king of Persia understood of, he sent a captain with
a 1000. horse to discomfit them. But *Tamburlane* delt so with him, that
joining both togither they wrought many incredible feats of armes.
And when civil war grew betwixt the king and his brother, *Tamburlane*
entred into the brothers pay, who obtained the victory by his means,

& thereupon made him his lieutenant generall. But he not long after spoiled the new king, weakened & subdued the whole kingdome of Persia. And when he saw himselfe captain of an army of 400000. horsmen, and 600000. footemen, he made war with *Baja{et* emperor of the Turkes, overcame him in battell, and tooke him prisoner. He obtained also a great victorie against the Souldan of Egypt, and the king of Arabia. This good successe (which is most to be marvelled at and very rare) accompanied him alwaies untill his death, in so much that he ended his daies amongst his children, as a peaceable governour of innumerable countries. From him descended the great *Sophy* who raigneth at this day, and is greatly feared and redoubted of the Turke. But that miserable *Baja{et* who had conquered before so many peoples, and subdued innumerable cities, ended his daies in an iron cage, wherein being prisoner, and overcome with griefe to see his wife shamefully handled, in waiting at *Tamburlanes* table with hir gowne cut downe to hir Navell, so that hir secrete parts were seene, this unfortunate Turke beate his head so often against the Cage, that he ended his life.

176 *Henry the fift.* Dekker's error for Henry IV of Germany, as Rhys (followed by Scherer) suggested. His forced submission to Pope Gregory VII is recounted by Foxe (*Actes and Monuments* (1563), pp. 24–26) as an example of the Roman Church's tendency to subvert the power of princes; a woodcut depicting 'Henricus the Emperoure with his wyfe and child, barefote and barelegd, wayting on the Pope iii. dayes and iii. nightes at the gates of Canossus' is on p. 25.

179 *Frederick Barbarossa.* Another often-cited Reformation example of the Papal abuse of power. Foxe includes his story in *Actes and Monuments* (1563), p. 41, where a woodcut depicting 'Pope Alexander treading on the neck of Frederick the Emperoure' is to be found on p. 40. A year earlier John Jewell, Bishop of Salisbury, in *An apologie or aunswer in defence of the Church of England* (1562), had asked rhetorically concerning Pope Alexander III:

Who so ill-favouredly and monstrously put the emperor Frederic's neck under his feet, and, as though that were not sufficient, added further this text out of the Psalms [91 : 13]: 'Thou shalt go upon the adder and cockatrice, and shalt tread the lion and dragon under thy feet?' Such an example of scorning and contemning a prince's majesty, as never before this was heard tell of in any remembrance; except, I ween, either of Tamerlanes the king of Scythia, a wild and barbarous creature, or else of Sapor king of the Persians (*Works*, Parker Society (Cambridge, 1848), III, 76).

The incident is alluded to in the 1616 text of Marlowe's *Doctor Faustus*, III.i (ed. Greg, lines 945–951).

184 *Lewes the meeke*. 'Lodouicus, the first of that name, and sone of Charles ye great, began his reigne ouer ye realme of Fraunce, & also his empyre ouer ye Romaynes, in ye yere of grace. DCCC. and. xv... This for his mekenes was callyd Lewys the mylde, or meke' (Fabyan, *Chronicles* (London, 1811), cap. c.lix, p. 148). His dissensions with his three sons – Lothair, Pepin, and Louis, who at one stage force his deposition and his retirement to a monastery, whence he is eventually restored to the throne – are recorded by Fabyan, cap. c.lx and cap. c.lxi. He died in 840.

187 *Baiazet*. In addition to La Primaudaye's account of his story, there was an earlier English version of it in *The Foreste or Collection of Histories* (1571), translated by Thomas Fortescue from Claude Gruget's French translation of Pedro Mexia. Dekker must have known the volume. Viriat and Primislaus appear in it (see notes on lines 200 and 201, below), and in what follows the detail about 'the croomes' seems to have found its way into line 190:

Baiaceth [in battle with Tamburlaine]...resisted in person valiantly the furous rage of the enimie. How be it, he therby gained such, and so many knokes, that as he was in the end, in deede vnhorste, so was he for lake of reskewe presented to the greate *Tamburlaine*, who incontinently closed hym vppe, in a Kaege of yron, carriynge hym still with hym, whither soeuer he after wente, pasturyng him with the croomes, that fell from hys table, and with other badde morselles, as he had been a dogge: whence assuredly we may learne not so much to affie in riches, or in the pompe of this world: for as much as he that yesterdaie was Prince and Lorde, of all the worlde almost, is this daie fallen into suche extreame miserie, that he liueth worse then a dogge, fellowe to theim in companie, and that by the means of him that was some tymes a poore Sheaperde or if you rather will, as some reporte, a meane souldiour, who after as we see aspired to such honour, that in hys time none was found that durst, or could abide hym: the other that descended of noble race or linage, constrained, to liue an abiecte, in most lothsum, and vile seruitude. This tragidie might suffice, to withdrawe men, from this transitorie pompe, and honour, acquaintying theimselues with Heauen and with heauenly thinges onely (*The Foreste* (1571), fols. 85–85v).

As a stage figure Bajazeth would of course have been familiar
from Marlowe's *Tamburlaine*, Part One (*c.* 1587), where his
defeat, his incarceration in a cage and his suicide are represented.

200 *Viriat.*

Wherefore, the better to animate men, to asspire to great matters, I will
remember the examples of some in perticuler, issuying out of meane,
and simple parentage, whiche in the ende, excelled in honour, and
vertue. And in the firste place, *Viriat* a Portugale, so muche renoumed
emong the historiens, especially *Romaines*, on whom he eftsones did
cruell, and bloodie reuenge. This man was the soonne of a poore
Shepherde, and in his youth aided his father in his charge: but hauyng
his harte inclined to matters more high, and of greater importaunce,
lefte to keepe Shepe, and other tamed beastes, followyng more busily
the chase of the wilde, and sauage, where in he excelled in courage all
others. After this the *Romaines*, inuadyng the Spaniardes, he gathered,
and assembled certaine his companions, by whose helpe he skirmishte,
at tymes, with the enemie, at tymes also againe, for practise with his
friendes, where he so valiaunte was, so noble, and couragious, that in
fewe daies he had gathered an armie sufficiente, with which being
entered the field, he gaue battaile to the *Romaines*, in defence of that
countrie: whiche warres, or rather enmmitie continued fowertene yeres,
duryng whiche tyme, he obtained againste theim, sundrie greate, and
honourable victories. By meanes whereof, he grewe in honour, and
aucthoritie, dreade, and faired for his prowes continually of his enemie:
but in fine, vnkindly by treason was slaine, to the greate discomforte,
and sorrowe of all his armie, by whiche he was (as duetie would)
most pompously buried (*The Foreste*, fols. 99–99v).

He died *c.* 139 B.C. Lydgate mentions him in *The Fall of Princes*,
VI, 841–861, ed. Henry Bergen (Washington, 1923), Part
Three, pp. 697–698.

201 *Primislaus.*

An other matter like straunge to this, happened in *Bohemia*, where as
one *Primislas* the soonne of a Plough manne, was then chosen kyng,
when he moste busily, was labouryng the soile in the fielde. For at that
tyme the *Bohemians*, not knowyng whom thei might chuse for their
kyng, did to passe out a horse vnbridled into the fieldes, lettyng hym
to go, whether it best liked him, hauing all determined, with moste
assured purpose, to make him their king, before whom this horse
arrested, so came it them to passe, that the horse first staied hym before
this *Primislas*, busied then in turnyng the gleabe, a simple Carter:
so beyng forthwith confirmed (as is before) their soueraigne, he ordered

hym self, and his kyngdome very wisely. He ordained many good and profitable lawes, he compassed the citie of *Prage* with walles, besides many other thynges, merityng perpetuall laude, and commendation (*The Foreste*, fol. 101v).

202 *Monke Gregorie*. Known as Hildebrand, he became Pope Gregory VII (*c.* 1020–1085). Not long before Dekker's play, he had been beatified by Gregory XIII in 1584. He would be canonized by Paul V in 1606.

207 *Iohn Leyden*, originally Jan Beuckelson, Bockelson, or Bockold (*c.* 1509–1536), journeyman tailor and Dutch Anabaptist who led a Protestant rebellion in the north German city of Münster (1534) and ruled as king. He did not enjoy '*Fortunes* grace' for long. The local prince–bishop regained control of the city in 1535; John was subsequently tortured and put to death. An account of events in Münster is given in the tenth book of the work of Joannes Philippson, known as Sleidanus, which was translated by J. Daus and published in 1560 as *A Famouse Cronicle of oure time, called Sleidanes Commentaries*. Not long before Dekker's play, Nashe in 1593 had given a lively account of John of Leyden and the seige of Münster in *The Unfortunate Traveller* (II, 232–241). In 1605 Samuel Rowlands, in *Hell's Broke Loose*, makes John of Leyden ask, by way of invoking a precedent for his rise to power from humble origins: 'Haue you not heard that *Scythian Tamberlaine* / Was earst a Sheep-heard ere he play'd the King?' (sig. D3v). When his rebellion has been crushed, Rowlands comments:

> *Ambitions* wheele, which Traytors do aspire,
> Hath brought the Rebels to their altitude:
> And now declining, downe-ward they retire,
> By iust Reuenge a downe-fall to conclude,
> From top of Treason, thus they turne about:
> For now behold, their cursed date run out.   (Sig. E3)

208 *Emperie*. L.D., I.ii.14, n.

217–293 *Before thy soule...make me rich*. Quoted by Lamb, I, 192–194, omitting lines 254–258.

220–221 *the lawes of Fate...inuiolate*. Quoted under the heading 'Fate' and attributed to Dekker in *Englands Parnassus* (Crawford, no. 451).

222–223 *Daughters of Ioue and...night,* | *Most righteous Parce.*
Hesiod, *Theogony,* 211ff.: 'And Night bare...the Destinies
and ruthless avenging Fates, Clotho and Lachesis and Atropos,
who give men at their birth both evil and good to have, and
they pursue the transgressions of men and of gods: and these
goddesses never cease from their dread anger until they punish
the sinner with a sore penalty.' But elsewhere in the *Theogony*
(901ff.) they are said to be the daughters of Zeus and Themis.
Cf. *O.F.,* II.ii.253.

242 *Ioue...Ganimede. 2 H.W.,* I.i.7.

248 *Golds sacred hunger.* A translation of Virgil, *Aeneid,* III.57:
'Auri sacra fames'. Dekker cites the Latin in a marginal note
in *D.D.,* F1v, beside the following passage: 'Gods holy hunger
though it oft did kill me, | Gods holy Banquet *yet did neuer fill
me.*' A fuller version of the quotation from the *Aeneid* (III.56–
57) is cited in a marginal note to *W.A.,* B4v ('*Auri sacra fames* |
quid non morta- | *lia cogis Pectora*'), beside a passage describing
Money and her army:

> yet is the Empresse, vnder whose collours they fight, full of riches
> (which are the sinews of Warre) of great commaund, feared and loued,
> yea adored as a Diety, of a *Maiesticall* presence of incomparable bewty;
> Such a one, that euen the very sight of her is a Charme strong enough
> to make men venture their liues in the quarrell of her right.

An emblem in Whitney's *A Choice of Emblemes* (1586), p. 179,
is headed 'Auri sacra fames quid non?' The verses appended to
it read in part as follows: 'Oh, thirste of goulde, what not? but
thou canst do: | And make mens hartes for to consent there-
to.' Cf. Lyly, *Midas,* I.i.62, for the use of the Virgilian quotation in a context similar to Fortunatus' present moment of
choice.

263 *a wiseman poore.* Dilke (III, 117) cites Ecclesiastes 9: 14ff.

263–267 *a wiseman poore...schoole.* Quoted under the heading
'Wisedome' and attributed to Dekker in *Englands Parnassus*
(where the 'a' is omitted from line 267; Crawford, no. 1706).
For the use of the lines (in altered form) at the conclusion of
Love's Garland, or Posies for Rings, &c., published in 1624, see
Crawford's note, p. 491.

277–278 *The fairest cheeke...foule.* Quoted under the heading
   'Beautie' and attributed to Dekker in *Englands Parnassus*
   (where 'fairest' reads 'fairer'; Crawford, no. 95).

288 *Midas.* Cf. *G.H.*, Biv: 'You *ordinary Gulles*, that through a
   poore and silly ambition to be thought you inherit the reuenues
   of extraordinary wit, will spend your shallow censure vpon the
   most elaborate Poeme, so lauishly that all the painted table-
   men about you, take you to be heires apparant to rich *Midasse.*'

295 *famisht in his store.* Cf. Whitney, *A Choice of Emblemes* (1586),
   p. 18, 'In auaros':

> Septitivs ritche, a miser moste of all,
> Whose liuinges large, and treasure did exceede:
> Yet to his goodes, he was so much in thrall,
> That still he vsd on beetes, and rapes to feede:
>   So of his stoare, the sweete he neuer knew,
>   And longe did robbe, his bellie of his due.

303 *dribble out the Sea by drops.* Tilley, S183.

310 *Wisedomes diuine embrace.* 'I think it is evident that many of the
   sentiments in this Scene were drawn by our poet from the
   choice made by Solomon in the beginning of his reign, of
   wisdom in preference to riches, or honour, or power over his
   enemies, or length of life, as recorded in the First Book of
   Kings' (Dilke, III, 119).

330 *Musicke with her siluer sound.* From the song 'In commendation
   of Musick' in Richard Edwards, *The Paradise of Dainty
   Devices* (1576), ed. H. E. Rollins (Cambridge, Mass., 1927),
   p. 63. It is quoted at greater length by Peter in *Romeo and
   Juliet*, IV.v.126ff. Cf. *Sat.*, II.i.71.

331 *ho God be here.* Once a pious salutation, the phrase, as McKerrow comments in a note on Nashe, *Pierce Penilesse* (I, 181),
   'seems to have been commonly used without any very definite
   meaning'. *Blurt, Master-Constable*, II.ii.214. *1 H.W.*, V.ii.347.

334 *Lambs skinne. S.H.*, V.iv.9–10, n.

336 *tawnie face.* Cf. Jonson, *Bartholomew Fair*, II.vi.21–22: 'that
   tawney weede, tabacco'. *B.L.*, C4: 'my braue *Tawny-faces*'.
   L.C., H1–H1v: 'A man that sees them would sweare they had
   all the yellow Iawndis, or that they were Tawny Moores

bastardes, for no Red-oaker man caries a face of a more filthy complexion.' *Blurt, Master-Constable*, II.ii.294: 'roaring, tawney-faced rascal'. Cf. *O.F.*, I.ii.187, and *L.D.*, I.i.154.

336 *Tobacconist. N.F.H.*, A4v: 'that great *Tobaconist* the Prince of Smoake & darknes, *Don Pluto*'.

I.ii

1 *knights of the post*, men who gained a living by giving false evidence in law courts. *B.L.*, G4: 'olde knights of the post, that will periure themselues for pots of Ale'. *D.T.*, A4v (the city of Westminster, of the sins that flourish in its confines): 'Thou art held to be (*O London*) the lowdest swearer in the kingdome, . . . yet I feare, I haue those about me that for filthy mouthing wil put thee down, for I am haunted with some that are called *Knights* onely for their swearing'; the margin contains the notation: 'Knights of / the Post'. *A Knack to Know a Knave* (1594) (M.S.R. (1964, for 1963), prepared by G. R. Proudfoot), lines 795–796: 'Why, I haue bene a poste knight in *Westminster* this xii. year, / And sworne to that which no one els would venture on.' *Sat.*, I.ii.284; *I.T.B.N.*, II.ii.180.

Their practices are disclosed at length in *The Discouerie of the Knights of the Poste* . . . By E.S. (1597).

3 *it was not corporall*, i.e. not a corporal oath (one 'ratified by corporally touching a sacred object', as distinguished from a verbal oath (*O.E.D.*)).

17–18 *a leane dyet makes a fat wit.* Tilley, D329.

23 *sweare like puritans at one bare word.* Referring to the Puritan disinclination to take oaths, to swear by anything. Cf. *Every Man in his Humour* (ed. 1601), III.i.77–80:

> He will not sweare: he has some meaning sure,
> Else (being vrg'd so much) how should he choose,
> But lend an oath to all this protestation?
> He is no puritane, that I am certaine of.

And Tourneur, *The Atheist's Tragedy*, I.ii.181–183:

> *D'am*. . . . . By – You will make mee sweare.
> *Lan.* O! by no meanes. Prophane not your lippes with the foulnesse of that sinne.

24 *like good bowlers, we are able to rub out and shift in euery place.*
A rub in the game of bowls is an impediment by which a bowl
is diverted from its proper course; 'to rub out' is, figuratively,
'to continue in a certain course with more or less difficulty or
restraint; to contrive, or make shift' (*O.E.D., v.*¹ III.15). Cf.
N.F.H., B4v: 'very fewe Poets can be suffred to liue there,...
yet some pittifull fellowes...not Poets indeede, but ballad-
makers, rub out there, and write Infernals'. 'Shift' in the present
line means simply to make shift. In the following line, Shadow
puns on 'shifted' meaning to have changed clothes (*O.E.D.,
v.* II.9). The verbal quibbles in both lines are the basis for the
twenty-fourth jest in *J.M.M.*, B4v: 'Two Brothers meeting
together, sayd the welthier of them, to the other: And how
goes the world Brother? what, you rub out, make shift to liue[.]
Yes faith replyed the second, I thank God, and liue without
shifting too.' The pun was common. Cf. Lodge, 'The Deafe
mans Dialogue' appended to *Euphues his Shadowe* (1592),
M1v: 'but for the rest [of poets] I would they might shift more
and shift lesse. *Philam.* How meane you this shift, me thinks it
needs some syfting? *Celio.* I would they had more shift in
shirts, and lesse shift in subtiltie.'

29 *logger-headed*, used of a heavy-headed animal; see *W.E.*, III.i.20,
n. Cf. *The Rare Triumphs of Love and Fortune* (M.S.R. (1931,
for 1930), prepared by W. W. Greg), line 642: 'a logger
headed foole', and line 981: 'thou loggerheadded iacke'.

35 *Angel.* One of many quibbles on the gold coin (the noble, valued
at 10s.), commonly called an angel from the design of St
Michael killing the dragon that was stamped on it. Cf. *Sat.*,
I.ii.109; III.i.94; *1 H.W.*, II.i.68. And *O.F.*, I.ii.89.

35–36 *this broad brim fashions.* One of the signs of a dejected lover;
cf. *Blurt, Master-Constable*, II.i.24ff., where Truepenny explains to Fontinelle why he can see none of love's tokens upon
him: 'your hat nor head are not of the true heigh-ho block, for
it should be broad-brimmed, limber like the skin of a white
pudding when the meat is out, the facing fatty, the felt dusty,
and not entered into any band'. And later Hippolito to Camillo,
who is in fact a dejected lover: 'Now, my fool in fashion, my

sage idiot, up with these brims, down with this devil, Melancholy' (III.i.608).

51 *baits...golden hookes*. A favorite Dekker image; cf. *1 H.W.*, II.i.296; *W.H.*, II.ii.118; *W.B.*, II.i.201; III.i.229; *W. of E.*, IV.i.139; *W.E.*, II.i.7. And *P.G.*, IV.ii.200: 'golden baites'.

52 *Cynthian*, moon-like, used for the sake of 'siluer' in the following line.

54 *squinteide*. A favorite Dekker epithet; cf. *L.D.*, II.iii.119: 'The squint ey'd multitude'; *S.H.R.*, F1v: 'some squint-eyd Asse'; *N.G.*, p. 65: 'Vnsquint-eyde Surueyor of Heroicall Poems'; and *I.T.B.N.*, prologue, 22: 'Squint-Eyes'. In the present play, the term occurs again in the Chorus to Act II, line 24. *W.K.*, prologue, 4.

62 *crab-tree fac'd*, i.e. sour-faced. Nashe, *Lenten Stuffe*, III, 183: 'frost-bitten crab-tree fac't lads'. *2 H.W.*, IV.i.211.

66–67 *trees in September...beare neither fruit nor leaues*. Cf. *D.T.*, C1: 'The vnwholesome breath of Autumne, who is so full of diseases, that his very blowing vppon trees, makes theyr leaus to fal off'.

68–69 *flourish...Auncient bearers*. An 'auncient' is a flag or banner. For the quibble with 'flourish', cf. *W.H.*, I.i.160; II.i.7–8. 'Auncient bearers' are standard or ensign-bearers, here used with a bawdy quibble on 'bearers'.

76 *lime twigges*, snares (twigs smeared with bird-lime for catching birds). *S.T.W.*, IV.i.50; *2 H.W.*, III.ii.28.

78 *Pursenet*. *2 H.W.*, IV.ii.31, n.

79–80 *Lamb-skins*. I.i.334.

81 *Cheuerill*, of kid's leather, and so yielding, stretching. *S.D.S.*, F2: 'The *Shauing* of poore Clients especially by the Atturneyes Clearkes of your Courts, and thats done by writing their Billes of costs vpon *Cheuerell*.' A 'cheverel conscience' is a proverbial phrase (Tilley, C608).

82 *Snudges*, misers. Nashe, *The Unfortunate Traveller*, II, 215: 'the King saies flatly, you are a myser and a snudge, and he neuer hoped better of you'. And *Summers Last Will and Testament*, III, 287:

> Christmas, I tell thee plaine, thou art a snudge,
> And wert not that we loue thy father well,
> Thou shouldst haue felt what longs to Auarice.

W.A., G IV: 'Issue therefore forth amongst good fellows, that will sooner fight for thee, then those snudges & miserable cormorants that now feede vpon thee.' And *O.F.*, II.ii.351.

90–91 *weare on his thumbe, . . . a seale Ring.* Cf. Brome, *The Northern Lasse*, II.i (ed. Shepherd, III, 23): 'one that is good only in Riches, and wears nothing rich about him, but the Gout, or a thumb-Ring with his Grandsirs Sheep-mark, or Grannams butter-print on't, to seal Baggs, Acquittances, and Counterpanes'. *S.H.*, II.iii.95.

97–98 *an Asse laden with riches . . . must leaue his burthen to some other beast.* Cf. the proverbs 'An Ass is but an ass though laden with gold' (Tilley, A352), and 'The Ass though laden with gold still eats thistles' (Tilley, A360).

103–104 *silkes and veluets . . . in Mercers shops, as in prisons.* Cf. *W.A.*, C4v–D1, where in the war against Money, impecunious younger brothers are given 'the charge of the most resolute troopes that were to scale the Cittie . . . and to ransacke all the Mercers and Gold-smiths shops, not so much to set free the silkes, veluets, plate and iewels imprisond most cruelly in them, as to vndoe the old Cittizens, & then to marry their yong wiues'.

104 *for feare of the smell of waxe*, i.e. for fear of the bonds, with their legal waxen seals, that would-be but needy gallants like Andelocia would enter into in order to buy the mercer's wares now and pay for them later if only the mercers were agreeable.

105 *a man made out of waxe*, 'used as a term of emphatic commendation' (*O.E.D.*) which notes that the origin of the expression is not clear and suggests 'as faultless as if modelled in wax'). The phrase is proverbial; Tilley, D453. With Dekker's use of it in the present passage, cf. *S.D.S.*, B3v: 'is now a new man made out of wax, thats to say, out of those bonds, whose seales he most dishonestly hath canceld'. Cf. *Sat.*, IV.iii.236–237, and *W.H.*, II.i.204–205:

Mist. Hony. Hees a Knight made out of waxe.
Iust. He tooke vp Silkes vppon his bond I confesse.

108 *Counters,* used with a quibble (prompted by the reference to
'prisons' in line 104) on the two City gaols, each under the
control of a sheriff; one was in Wood Street, Cheapside, the
other near St Mildred's Church in the Poultry.

114 *who's the foole now?* The refrain of a ballad titled 'Martyn said to
his man, whoe is the foole nowe', licensed 9 November 1588.
Rollins, no. 1681, and see Simpson, pp. 776–777. See *O.F.*,
IV.i.124, 130.

119 *horne-mad,* enraged. *1 H.W.*, I.ii.91, n.

133 *Camelion. S.D.S.,* B2v: 'For you must vnderstand, that the
Politick Bankrupt is a *Harpy* that lookes smoothly, a *Hyena*
that enchants subtilly, a Mermaid that sings sweetly, and a
Cameleon, that can put himselfe into all colours.' *L.D.*, III.iv.22.

153–154 *foote-clothes,* cloths – often richly ornamented – spread
over the back of a horse and hanging down at the sides. They
are frequently referred to as signs of wealth. *W.Y.*, p. 34:
'Sextons gaue out [during the plague], if they might (as they
hoped) continue these doings but a tweluemoneth longer, they
and their posteritie would all ryde vpon foote-cloathes to the
ende of the worlde.' *2 H.W.*, IV.i.95; *Sat.*, III.i.221; *W. of E.*,
V.ii.182.

162 *a flip-flap,* a fan, a fly-flopper (*O.E.D.*, citing this example).

164 *three blew Beanes...rattle bladder.* Cf. Jonson, *Bartholomew
Fair,* I.iv.75–76: 'he has learn'd nothing, but to sing catches,
and repeat *rattle bladder rattle*'. Greene, *Orlando Furioso* (the
Alleyn manuscript, ed. Collins, I, 269): 'lett him put his arme
into my bagg thus deep: yf he will eate, go...he shall haue it.
thre blew beans...a blewe bladder; rattle, bladder rattle'.
Tilley, B124.

173 *a Fig,* Italian *fico;* 'A contemptuous gesture which consisted in
thrusting the thumb between two of the closed fingers or into
the mouth' (*O.E.D.*). *E.V.*, I4v: 'on them, they looke as at
their vndervassails, and crying a *Fico,* for their Creditors,
because there they liue safe, to spend other mens moneys'.
S.T.W., IV.ii.72; *W. of E.*, II.i.87. Tilley, F210.

187 *tawnie cheekes.* Cf. I.i.336, and *M.E.*, 1147.

196–199 *Turkish Emperour . . . Souldan.* Cf. *N.G.*, pp. 66–67:

> could haue gone to the great Turkes *Serraglio* . . . as tollerably and farre
> more welcome, than if I had beene one of his Eunuches. *Prester Iohn*,
> and the *Sophy*, were neuer out of mine eye . . . The Soldan of *Egipt* I
> had with a wet finger: from whence I trauailed as boldly to the Courts
> of all the Kings in Christendome, as if I had bin an Embassadour (his
> pomp only excepted).

197 *Prester Iohn.*

> In the Inland of *Africa*, lyeth a very large countrie: extending it selfe
> on the East, to some part of the red sea: on the South, to the kingdome
> of *Melinde*, and a great way farther: on the North, vnto *Egipt*: on the
> West, vnto *Manicongo*, the people whereof are called *Abisini*: and it
> selfe, the dominion of him, whome wee commonly call in English,
> Prester Iohn: but in Latine some tearme him, *Praeciosus Iohannes*,
> because of his ritches: but the most part *Presbiter Iohannes:* writing of
> him, that as he is a prince absolute: so he hath also a priestlike, or
> patriarchall function & iurisdiction among them. This is a verie mightie
> prince, & reputed to be one of the greatest Emperors of the world
> (George Abbott, *A Briefe Description of the whole world* (1599), C8).

P.G., V.i.18.

198 *great Cham of Tartarie.*

> *M. Paule Venetus* writeth, that this people [the Tartars] once inhabited
> Ciurga & Barge, prouinces scituated vpon the Scythick Ocean, without
> citie, castle or house, wandering like the Arabians from place to place,
> according to the season of the yeere. They acknowledged *Vncham*
> (whom some interprete *Prester Iohn*) for their soueraigne Lord, to
> whom they gaue the tenth of their cattell. In processe of time they
> multiplied to such numbers, that *Vncham* being iealous of their neigh-
> bourhood, began to lessen their number and forces, by sending them,
> now hither, now thither, vpon most long and desperate voiages, as
> occasion offered. Which when they perceiued, they assembled them-
> selues, resoluing to leaue their naturall soile, and to remooue so far
> from the borders of *Vncham*, that neuer after he should haue cause to
> suspect their numbers: this they performed. After certaine yeeres they
> elected amongst them a king, called *Changis*, to whom for the greatnes
> of his glorie and victories, they added the sirname of *Great*. This
> *Changis*, departing from his owne territories in the yeere of our Lord
> 1162. with a most fearefull armie, subdued partly by force, partly by
> the terror of his name, nine prouinces . . .

The circuit of this Empire in the times aboue spoken of, stretched from the vtmost bounds of Asia to Armenia, and from Bengala to Volga, yea their incursions pierced euen to Nilus and Danubius. The Macedonian and Roman Empires were neuer so large. But bicause they were rather runnagates then men of warre, wanting politike gouernment and militarie discipline, sometime ruling one prouince, sometime another, they rather wrought spoile and terror to the conquered nations, then feare of bondage or subiection, and at last seated themselues beyond the mountaine Caucasus. After, it became diuided into manie principalities, yet so that the title and maiestie of the Empire, remained alwaies to the great Cham, who (as we said before) tooke the originall of this name from the great *Changis*. At this day, this Empire reacheth from the desert Lop on the one side, and the lake Kitauia on the other, to that famous wall of China scituate betweene 43. and 45. degrees, which leadeth from mountaine to mountaine, till it end at the Ocean, and diuideth the Tartars from the Chinois: and from the Scythian Ocean, to the confines of Tipura and the bordering regions (Giovanni Botero, *The Worlde, or An historicall description of the most famous kingdomes and common-weales therein* (1601), pp. 143–145).

Later (p. 170), Botero notes that 'The King of China feareth no neighbour but the great Cham of Tartaria.' Cf. *O.F.*, II.i.12. *S.T.W.*, III.i.87.

199 *the Souldan.* 'The supreme ruler of a Mohammedan country' (Skeat and Mayhew). The term is variously used, e.g. for the King of Egypt (as in *1 Tamburlaine*, I.ii.6, and in the passage from Dekker's *N.G.* cited in the note on lines 196–199, above), and the King of Persia, as in the anonymous *King Leir* (M.S.R. (1907), prepared by W. W. Greg), lines 425–426: 'I thought as much to haue met with the Souldan of Persia, / As to haue met you in this place.' Here it is used of the ruler of Persia (see the Chorus to Act II, lines 35–39), for 'The chiefe citty of Persia, was Babilon' (Abbott, *A Briefe Description of the whole world* (1599), B4v).

I.iii

0.2–3 *siluer halfe moones, increasing by litle and litle, till they come to the full.* This description of Vice's garments sounds like Pliny's account of the skin of panthers: 'Some report, that they have one marke on their shoulder resembling the moone, growing and decreasing as she doth, sometime shewing a full compasse, and other-whiles hollowed and pointed with tips like hornes' (*Naturall Historie* (edn. 1601), VIII.17, p. 204).

0.4. *CRESCIT EVNDO. S.D.S.*, C3v:

How quickly after the Art of *Lying* was once publiquely profest, were false *Weights* and false *Measures* inuented! and they haue since done as much hurt to the inhabitants of Cities, as the inuention of *Gunnes* hath done to their walles: for though a *Lye* haue but short legs (like a Dwarfes) yet it goes farre in a little time, *Et crescit eundo*, and at last prooues a tall fellow: the reason is, that *Truth* had euer but one *Father*, but *Lyes* are a thousand mens *Bastards*, and are begotten euery where.

0.8 *Vertue, a coxecombe on her head.* I.i.120.

3 *bosome sticke.* Cf. the passage attributed to Dekker in *Englands Parnassus* (under the heading 'Groaue'; Crawford, no. 2232): 'that greene meade, / Whose bosome stucke with purple Violets'. Five lines of the *Parnassus* passage are reproduced in Heywood's *Love's Mistress*, II.i (first printed in 1636). For the suggestion that Heywood took them 'from the lost play on Cupid and Psyche, which was written jointly by Dekker, Chettle, and Day, and paid for by Henslowe on May 14, 1600', see Crawford's note, p. 529. Cf. *O.F.*, III.i.341.

13–14 *wood-bind...embrace.* Cf. *Englands Parnassus*, 'Groaue' (Crawford, no. 2232): 'About whose waste the amorous woodbind twines, / Whilst they seeme maidens in a louers armes.'

23 *Cedar.* II.ii.230, n.

48–49 *Autumnes haire...rotten browes.* Cf. the passage from *D.T.*, quoted in the note on I.ii.66–67, above.

57 *Vertue is fairest in a poore aray.* Misquoted in a passage attributed to Dekker under the heading 'Vertue' in *Englands Parnassus* (Crawford, no. 1622), where 'poore aray' reads 'poore art aye'.

74 *Vertue abhorres to weare a borrowed face.* Quoted under the heading 'Vertue' and attributed to Dekker in *Englands Parnassus* (Crawford, no. 1623).

II. Chorus

1–4 *The world...made.* Quoted under the heading 'World' and attributed to Dekker in *Englands Parnassus* (Crawford, no. 1806).

21 *folded armes,* the familiar sign of grief. With the whole of the present passage, cf. *J.M.M.,* G3–G3v:

> The thing that complained, was a man: that for age, would haue seemed *Reuerend,* but that *Care*...made his countenance appeare miserable...: In his face were the *Ruines* of youth, In his garments, of *Time:* In both, the *Triumphs* of pouerty, His Armes were seuentimes folded together, like a withered garland of willow, worne carelessly by a forsaken Louer: Sometimes did he vnwinde them, but then did his handes claspe each other so harde, that betweene them they embraced many witnesses, for now his eyes stood (like floating Islands[)] compassed rownde with waters: his cheekes like Bankes to Riuers, eaten hollow by cruell torrents. Had Aduersity...not giuen him any one of these scarres to be knowne by, it might easily be iudged hee was a Wretch, for he was a Prisoner.

24 *squint-eide.* I.ii.54.

28–29 *like a lustie Eagle, | Cuts...through the skie.* Cf. II.ii.128.

35–39 *Babylon...Soldan.* I.ii.199, n.

II.i

6 *Ioue...shower of gold.* 2 *H.W.,* V.ii.177, n.

10 *the Turkish Soliman. S.H.,* V.iv.52, n.

15 *christall Charriots. S.D.,* II.i.151.

49 *Phaeton.* I.i.81.

52 *clap...wings.* Cf. *T.T.,* 121.

56–57 *Orpheus,...Euridice, S.D.,* II.i.298–300.

94 *Aluarado. W.B.,* III.i.264, n.

101 *No does?* i.e. does it not? Scherer compares *King John,* IV.ii. 207: 'No had, my lord?'

106 *peise,* estimate the weight, by poising in the hand. *1 H.W.,* III.i.168.

II.ii

18 *Cuckoo, bald once a yeere.* Cf. *Sat.*, III.i.128, n.

20–21 *all haile...a ratling salutation.* For the pun, cf. *Love's Labour's Lost*, V.ii.339–340:

> *King.* All hail, sweet madam, and fair time of day!
> *Princess.* 'Fair' in 'all hail' is foul, as I conceive.

The Two Noble Kinsmen, III.v.100–101:

> *Schoolmaster.* Thou doughty Duke, all hail! All hail, sweet ladies!
> *Theseus.* This is a cold beginning.

The anonymous *Claudius Tiberius Nero* (M.S.R. (1914), prepared by W. W. Greg) lines 2298–2299:

> *Pis.* Haile Mother Rome.
> *Sol.* I, stormes of vengeance on thy curssed head

For a like piece of wit, cf. *W.E.*, III.ii.37–39:

> *Penda.* Awle the showers aboue vs, power downe vppon your mighty heads –
> *Voltimar.* Wee shalbee sure to haue rayne enough then.

25–26 *fantasticke...outlandish feathers.* Cf. lines 210–211, and *P.G.*, II.i.62–63.

26–27 *leade the world in a string.* Tilley, W886. *W. of E.*, II.ii.20.

27 *hot shot. I.T.B.N.*, II.i.104.

33 *Hay any ends of Gold or Siluer*, a street vender's cry. *W.E.*, I.iii.35.

46–47 *the seuen wise Masters.* The reference is to the popular Middle English romance, also known as *The Seven Sages of Rome.* A prose version of it was published by Wynkyn de Worde *c.* 1520, and reprinted by William Copland *c.* 1550. There were numerous chapbook versions of the story. Not long after writing *Old Fortunatus*, Dekker was to be engaged in a dramatization of it. Henslowe records payments totaling £6 to Chettle, Dekker, Haughton and Day between 1 and 8 March 1600 for a play titled *The Seven Wise Masters* (*Diary*, p. 131). Later in the month, the *Diary* (p. 132) records expenditures amounting to £38 in connection with the pro-

duction of the play. Dekker refers to the title elsewhere. Cf.
N.G., pp. 67–68:

What woodcocks then are these seauen wise maisters [of 'the seauen
poore Liberall Sciences'] to answere to that worme-eaten name of
Liberall, seeing it has vndone them?...My seauen lattin-sellers, haue bin
liberall so long to others, that now they haue not a rag...left for
themselues: Yea and into such pitifull predicaments are they fallen,
that most of our Gentry...takes them for the Seauen Deadly Sinnes.

And *Blurt, Master-Constable*, IV.ii.1–3: 'Saint Jacques and
the Seven deadly Sins (that is, the Seven Wise Masters of
the world), pardon me, for this night I will kill the devil!'

56 *swag-bellies*. Professor Bowers' emendation of Q 'sway-bellies'.
The phrase occurs in *S.H.*, I.iv.5 and V.iv.21 (but not at
II.iii.5, as Professor Bowers' textual note (1, 201) states).

57 *Paradox*. Cf. *Sat.*, IV.iii.68.1, n.

60 *Crusado*, a Portuguese coin bearing the figure of the cross.
1 H.W., III.i.205, n.

64 *with a full mouth*. *S.H.*, III.ii.126.

72 *a hungrie Dogge eates durtie puddings*. Tilley, D538. *V.M.*,
II.i.76–77

82–84 *hunger...eate through stone walles*. Tilley, H811.

87 *sawce being lickerish*. Cf. *N.H.*, II.i.177: 'sawcie and lickerish'.

92–95 *the seuen liberall sciences...few care for her sixe sisters*. *N.G.*,
p. 67: 'neither in any one of those Kingdomes...could I
either find or heare...nor read of any...that caryed such an
honest mind to the Common-wealth of the *Castalians* as to
keepe openhouse for the seauen poore Liberall Sciences'.
M.E. 1103–1109.

94 *make a man leape at a crust*. Tilley, H820.

95 *daunce after her pipe*. 'Dance after my pipe' is an alternate title
of the ballad generally known as 'The Shaking of the Sheets,
or The Dance of Death'. It is reprinted in *Roxburghe Ballads*,
III, 184. See Chappell, 1, 84–85, and Simpson, pp. 652–653.
The phrase was a popular expression. Cf. Jonson, *Every Man
out of his Humour*, III.ix.114: 'Nay, I cannot stay to dance
after your pipe.' And the invocation to tobacco in *G.H.*, B3:
'After thy pipe, shal ten thousands be taught to daunce.'

Blurt, Master-Constable, II.ii.157–159: 'souls are things to be trodden under our feet when we dance after love's pipe'; and IV.ii.30–33: 'The Spanish pavin? I thought the devil could not understand Spanish: but since thou art my countryman, O thou tawny Satan, I will dance after thy pipe.' *W.H.*, II.i.157.

98–99 *dagger*...*pies. Sat.*, I.ii.304–305, n.

104–213 *Touch mee not*...*Italianate.* Quoted by Lamb, I, 194–196, omitting lines 106–109, 111–115, 118–122, 127, 130, 132, 136–137, 154, 161–162, 170–171, 192–196, 206–208.

104 *I am nothing but ayre.* Cf. Fletcher, *Women Pleased*, II.iv (1647), p. 29: 'I am all Ayre, nothing of earth within me.' And the anonymous *The Distracted Emperor* (ed. Bullen, III, 170): 'My earthe to ayre; these twoe base elements / Can challengde nothing in my composition.'

113 *planet strucken. W.H.*, V.i.205–206.

115 *fetching fegaries.* Cf. *Sat.*, IV.ii.121, n.

118 *age is like loue, it cannot be hid.* Tilley, L500.

126 *trauellers must lie.* Tilley, T476.

128 *cut through the ayre like a Falcon.* Cf. Act II, Chorus, 28–29.

146–147 *walking your stations,* going your rounds, the meaning suggested by McKerrow for the phrase in a note (wherein the present passage is cited) on Nashe's *Lenten Stuffe*, III, 192: 'throughout Belgia, high Germanie, Fraunce, Spaine, and Italy hee flyes, and vp into Greece and Africa, South and Southwest, Estritch-like, walkes his stations'.

155–156 *Phenix*...*fires. F.B.N.A.*, p. 222: 'When the *Phoenix* knoweth shee must die, shee buildeth a nest of al the sweetest spices, and there looking stedfastly on the Sunne: shee beateth her wings in his hottest beames, and betweene them kindleth a fire amongst those sweet spices, & so burneth her selfe to death.' *M.E.*, 859–860.

158–159 *soule*...*lead*...*mount.* III.i.452–453.

161 *Corke and feathers.* Cf. Lyly, *Campaspe*, IV.i.17–21: 'Why, hee hath eaten nothing this seuennight but corke and feathers... He is so light, that he can scarse keepe him from flying at midnight.'

183 *Heroes.* Trisyllabic.

184 *Iouiall. W.E.*, I.ii.114, n.

195 *a dog has his day.* Tilley, D464.

200–205 *In some...destruction.* Quoted under the heading 'Ambition' and attributed to Dekker in *Englands Parnassus* (Crawford, no. 19).

201 *Dedalus old waxen wings.* Cf. the anonymous *King Leir* (M.S.R.), lines 416–417: 'I would he had old Dedalus waxen wings, / That he might flye, so I might stay behind.'

206–208 *since...hands.* Quoted under the heading 'Kings' and attributed to Dekker in *Englands Parnassus* (where 'their' reads 'the', and 'hands' reads 'hand'; Crawford, no. 854). *L.D.*, II.ii.14–15.

213 *Italianate.* Cf. Lyly, *Euphues and his England*, II, 88: 'if any English-man be infected with any mysdemeanour, they say with one mouth, hee is Italionated; so odious is that nation to this, that the very man is no lesse hated for the name, then the countrey for the manners'.

213.1 *working.* The three Destinies are presumably passing from one to another the thread of Fortunatus' life, which they will shortly terminate. Cf. lines 242–243, 253–254.

230 *Cedar*, the familiar emblem of ambitious pride. Cf. Spenser, *The Faerie Queene*, I.i.8; Marlowe, *Edward II*, II.ii.16; Shakespeare, *Richard III*, I.iii.263; Lyly, *Endimion*, II.i.93–95; Drayton, *Englands Heroicall Epistles*, 'Queene Margaret', lines 75–80:

> Whilst on his knees this wretched King is downe,
> To save them labour, reaching at his Crowne,
> Where like a mounting Cedar, he should beare
> His plumed Top aloft into the ayre;
> And let these Shrubs sit underneath his Shrowds,
> Whilst in his armes he doth imbrace the Clowds.

B.L., B3: 'The fall of *Cedars* that tumble from the tops of Kingdomes'. *W.K.*, I.iv.20. And *O.F.*, I.iii.23.

234 *plum'd thee like an Estrich.* Cf. *1 Henry IV*, IV.i.98. *N.G.*, pp. 91–92:

> Like to plumde Estridges they ride,
> Or like Sea-pageants, all in pride
>
> So from th'infected citie fly
> These Swallowes in their Gallantry,

116

Feather of Pride, how are thou tost?
How soone are all thy beauties lost?
How easely golden hopes vn-winde?

S.H.R., C1v: 'The *Vices* are Gallant Fellowes, they are Mounted, and haue no small Fooles to their Followers: they haue Plumes, like *Estridges*, and Perfumes like Muske-cats.' *W.A.*, F4v: 'behold the rich-plumde estridges, who had most fethers on their backes, and least cause to murmure, began to mutinie amongst themselues, the imprisoning of *Money*'. *W.E.*, II.i.17.

234–235 *Estrich...eaten Metals.* Cf. *Batman vppon Bartholome* (1582), p. 187, XII.33, 'Of the Estridge', which is said to be 'so hot, that he swalloweth and defieth [i.e. digests] and wasteth yron'. The notion is much alluded to; cf. Marston, *Histriomastix*, Act V (ed. Wood, III, 287):

> *Phil.* Swallow those words, or thou shalt eate my sword.
> *Lar.* He is no Estrich sir, he loves no yron.

The allusion is a favorite of Dekker's. Cf. *W.Y.*, p. 35: 'disarmde I may wel say, for fiue Rapiers were not stirring all this time, and those that were worne had neuer bin seene, if any money could haue bene lent vpon them, so hungry is this Estridge disease, that it will deuoure euen Iron'. *L.C.*, E1v: 'If my yong Estrich gape to swallow downe this mettall ...then is the gold powred on the board'; and K2, of the cheater known as Jack-in-a-box: 'It hath the head of a *man*... the eyes of a *Hawke*, the tongue of a *Lap-wing*, ... the stomacke of an *Estrich*, and can digest siluer as easily, as that Bird dooth Yron.' Cf. *N.S.S.*, IV.i.32–33; and *L.T.*, 139–140, where 'The third show is an Estridge, cut out of timber to the life, biting a horse-shoe.' Tilley, 197.

243 *faster...don*, addressed to the Destinies. Cf. line 253.

253 *Ioues daughters.* I.i.222.

267 *Don Dego*, i.e. Don Diego ('James'), a name for a Spaniard. Cf. *N.F.H.*, C1: 'the very bowels of these Infernall Antipodes, shall be ript vp, and pulld out, before that great Dego of

Diuels his owne face'. And *Blurt, Master-Constable*, II.ii.292–294 (Hippolito to the Spaniard Lazarillo who has just greeted the 'sanguine-cheeked ladies'): 'how now, Don Dego? sanguine-cheeked? dost think their faces have been at cutler's? out, you roaring, tawney-faced rascal!' *S.T.W.*, IV.ii.52.

300 *a bald fashion*. Cf. line 219.

302 *blocke*, the wooden shape on which the hat was moulded, and hence the fashion of the hat. Cf. *2 H.W.*, I.iii.15–17: 'Mine is as tall a felt as any is this day in *Millan*, and therefore I loue it, for the blocke was cleft out for my head, and fits me to a haire.' *S.D.S.*, E4v: 'the blocke for his heade alters faster then the Feltmaker can fitte him, and thereupon we are called in scorne *Blockheades*'. *G.H.*, D1v: 'fit his head for an excellent blocke'. *W.A.*, D4v: 'his hatte is like his head, of the old blocke'. *Sat.*, I.ii.120–121; *1 H.W.*, V.ii.144.

308 *Sounds his third sommons*. A theatrical allusion; the reference is to the three flourishes of trumpets which warned the audience to assemble in the Elizabethan theatre. The third flourish was followed by the prologue and the beginning of the play. Cf. Jonson, *Every Man Out of his Humour*, induction, 292; *Poetaster*, induction, 61; *Cynthia's Revels*, III.iv.58. *G.H.*, E4: 'Before the Play begins, fall to cardes,...to gul the *Ragga-muffins* that stand a loofe gaping at you, throw the cards...round about the Stage, iust vpon the third sound, as though you had lost.' And Dekker's address to the reader that prefaces his list of errata in the quarto text of *Satiromastix* (reprinted in 1, 306 of the present edition): 'In steed of the Trumpets sounding thrice, before the Play begin: it shall not be amisse (for him that will read) first to beholde this short Comedy of Errors.'

322–323 *drop my soule out at mine eyes*. Cf. III.i.85–86.

331 *a Dor-mouse skin*. In allusion to the proverb: 'As dull as (To sleep like) a Dormouse' (Tilley, D568).

345 *lattin*, i.e. 'latten', a mixed metal of yellow color, either identical with, or very like, brass (*O.E.D.*).

351 *Snudge*. I.ii.82.

363 *Alablaster*. *P.G.*, IV.i.124.

367–368 *stept to agree with Charon for his boate hyre.* Cf. *N.F.H.*, D4v:

> In a fewe¯minutes therefore is he come to the banck-side of *Acheron*, where you are not bayted by whole kennels of yelping watermen, as you are at Westminster-bridge, and ready to be torne in peeces to haue two pence rowed out of your purse: no, Shipwrights there could hardly liue, there's but one boat, & in that one, *Charon* is the onely Ferri-man.

D.D., C4–C4v:

> I hollowed to the *Ferriman* (me thought)
> And with a stretch'd voyce, cry'd a *Boate*, a *boate*:
> *Hee* came at first call, and when neere he drew,
> That of his *Face* and *Forme*, I had full view,
> My bloud congeal'd to ice with a cold feare,
> To see a *Shape* so horribly appeare:
> ...I heard his name was *Charon*.

I.T.B.N., I.i.7–8; *L.D.*, V.iii.151–152.

383 *cap you.* Not, of course, to be taken literally, since according to the terms Andelocia has just proposed, he would be taking the cap, or hat, from Ampedo (in exchange for the purse), not presenting him with it. He is making a joke on the meaning 'arrest' (from the Latin *capias* as in the term 'writ of capias', a writ of arrest). Cf. Beaumont, *The Knight of the Burning Pestle*, III.172: 'Twelve shillings you must pay, or I must cap you.'

392 *fadge*, fit, suit.

392 *because I cannot lie*, as travellers are reputed to do. Cf. lines 126–127.

396–397 *Fashions...a beastly disease.* It was a disease of horses. *G.H.*, B4: 'Fashions then was counted a disease, and horses dyed of it: But now (thankes to folly) it is held the onely rare phisicke, and the purest golden Asses liue vpon it.'

407 *whilst you kisse your hand...poyson you.* *S.H.R.*, E3: 'After this hee trauelled into *Italy*, and there learned to embrace with one arme, and stabbe with another: to smile in your face, yet to wish a ponyard in your bosome: to protest, and yet lye: to sweare loue, yet hate mortally.'

III.i

5–79 *This musicke...graue.* Quoted by Lamb, 1, 197–198.

17–18 *loues voice doth sing | As sweetely in a begger as a king.* Cf. the proverb: 'Love lives in cottages as well as in courts' (Tilley, L519).

29–30 *eye... | Wrinckled with Idiot laughter.* Cf. prologue, 9–11.

38 *Iron fist.* II.ii.228.

61 *Idea,* in the Platonic sense of 'archetype' or 'perfect pattern'. *P.W.,* B3: 'In fashioning her *Idæa,* or the figure of her body in his phantacy, her eyes through the windowes of his soule, presented themselues to him like a paire of starres.' *Blurt, Master-Constable,* II.i.103–104: 'in the darkest hell on earth I'll find | Her fair idea to content my mind'. *L.D.,* II.iii.99.

85–86 *soule...eyes drop into her hands.* II.ii.322–323.

89 *encountred. N.H.,* I.iii.55, n.

115 *a Spruce silken face Courtier.* For 'Spruce Courtier', cf. *2 H.W.,* I.iii.29. For 'silken face', cf. *S.T.W.,* IV.i.77; and Marston, *Certaine Satyres,* II.62–63: 'then with his silken face | Smiles on the holy crue'. The phrase 'silken Courtiers' occurs in *L.D.,* I.i.153.

123 *smile in our sleeues.* A common expression; cf. Nashe, *Anatomie of Absurditie,* 1, 21; Greene, *Third Part of Conny-Catching,* X, 179; and Tilley, S535.

184 *The Ruby-colourd portals of her speech.* Shakespeare, *Venus and Adonis,* 451–452: 'Once more the ruby-color'd portal open'd, | Which to his speech did honey passage yield.'

188–191 *shee disdaines...loues fire.* Cf. *Blurt, Master-Constable,* III.ii.15–17:

> Shall I profane
> This temple with an idol of strange love?
> When I do so, let me dissolve in fire.

211 *bard,* 'a covering of armour for the breast and flanks of a war-horse' *(O.E.D.).*

257–259 *eye...circles...cheekes.* Cf. lines 28–30, and prologue, 9–11.

284–286 *My Corocon... Tierra Inglesa.* 'My heart is very heavy, my soul much tormented. No, by heaven. The Spanish foot has no music in England.'

289–290 *Verdad Signor...humilde.* 'True, Sir, the Spanish dance is very lofty, majestic, and is for monarchs. Your English [dance is] low, fantastic and very humble.'

292 *sworne...crosse of his pure Toledo.* W.A., D1–D1v: 'such like, who had all vowed by the crosse of their swords, and by the honour of a souldier'. 'Toledo' refers to the Spanish city, famous for the fine steel of its swords. Cf. *Blurt, Master-Constable*, II.ii.287–288, where the Spaniard Lazarillo says: 'Mars armipotent with his court of guard, give sharpness to my toledo.' *P.G.*, III.ii.31.

296–300 *No lo quiero... Mas alta.* 'I will not contradict. Your eye makes your prisoner captive. Listen, let the Spanish pavane be your music and [with] solemnity and majesty. Page, give me tobacco, take my cloak and my sword. Louder, louder! Stand aside, stand aside, friends, louder, louder!'

297 *Oyes*, i.e. 'oyez', hear ye, 'a call by the public crier or by a court officer...to command silence and attention for the reading of a proclamation' (*O.E.D.*). For its use to signal a song or a dance, cf. Lyly, *Gallathea*, IV.ii.1; and Shakespeare, *Merry Wives of Windsor*, V.v.41: 'Crier Hobgoblin, make the fairy Oyes.' *B.L.*, C1v: 'This *Ceremony* being set abroach, an *O-yes* was made.' And cf. *S.D.*, II.i.205–206:

> *Humor.* No more of this, dances! awake the musick.
> *Folly.* Oyes! Musick!

I.T.B.N., V.iv.122.

297 *la pauyne Hispanola.* N.F.H., C2: 'If I can but harp vpon thy string, hee shall now for my pleasure tickle vp the *Spanish Pauin.*' The 'pavin' or 'pavan' was a stately dance (Spanish *pavana*). The Spaniard Lazarillo dances it in *Blurt, Master-Constable*, IV.ii.30–33.

339–342 *Marble bosome...melt.* Cf. *W.Y.*, pp. 26–27: 'raine downe your gummy teares into mine Incke, that euen marble bosomes may be shaken with terrour, and hearts of Adamant melt into compassion'.

341 *stucke the earth.* I.iii.2–3.

363 *gilded beames. P.G.,* I.i.9.

379 *Musicke with her siluer tongue.* I.i.330.

390 *occupiers,* tradesmen. *N.G.,* p. 68: 'How much happier had it
bin for them, to haue changed their copies, & from Sciences
bin bound to good Occupations, considering that one *London-
occupier* (dealing vprightly with all men) puts vp more in a
weeke, than seuen Bachilers of Art (that euery day goe barely
a wooing to them) do in a yeare.' *N.F.H.,* B2: 'Bawdes, that
now sit no longer vpon the skirtes of the Cittie, but iett vp
and downe, euen in the cloake of the Cittie, and giue more
rent for a house, then the proudest *London* occupier of them
all.' The word had bawdy implications; cf. *Sat.,* IV.iii.266, n.

390 *mad Troians.* Cf. *S.H.,* I.iv.105, n.

391 *give...the bag,* i.e. cheat him. *W.H.,* IV.ii.203, n.

401 *billets,* pieces of wood cut to a proper length for fuel (*O.E.D.*).

417 *Caterpillers to the Commonwelth. B.L.,* C1v: 'the idle drones
of a Countrie, the *Caterpillers* of a commonwealth, and the
Ægiptian lice of a Kingdome'. The phrase is common; cf.
Greene, *A Disputation Betweene a Hee Conny-catcher and a
Shee Conny-catcher,* X, 201; and Shakespeare, *Richard II,*
II.iii.166.

419 *bauins,* bundles of brushwood (*O.E.D.*). *J.M.M.,* B1: 'A
Iest...is a Bauin which beeing well kindled maintaines for
a short time the heate of laughter.'

452–453 *leaden soule...mount.* II.ii.158–159.

IV.i

27 *set vp my rest,* a gambling term from primero, meaning 'to
stake one's all'. Cf. Gascoigne, *Supposes,* III.ii.1–13 (ed. J. Q.
Adams, *Chief Pre-Shakespearan Dramas* (Cambridge, Mass.,
1924):

> This amorous cause that hangeth in controuersie betwene Domine
> Doctor and me may be compared to them that play at primero: of
> whom some one, peraduenture, shal leese a great sum of money before he
> win one stake, and at last, halfe in anger, shal set vp his rest, win it, and
> after that another, another, and another, till at last he draw the most part

of the money to his heape, the other, by litle and litle, stil diminishing his rest, til at last he be come as neere the brinke as earst the other was.

N.G., p. 70: 'Yet remembring what a notable good fellow thou wert...I set vp my rest, and vowde to consecrate all my blotting-papers onely to thee.'

31 *pepper*, do for, make an end of, with the added implication of infect with venereal disease. *2 H.W.*, IV.iii.61, n.

42 *your old byas*. The image is from the game of bowls, the bias being the construction or form of the bowl which causes it to swerve when rolled, or the curved course in which it runs. *R.A.*, B3: 'The Moone (like a Bowle) will keep her olde byas'. *R.G.*, III.ii.167–168.

42 *cogging*, playing tricks, cheating. The word also carries the sense of 'fawning', as in *W.Y.*, p. 5: 'intreate (as Players do in a cogging *Epilogue* at the end of a filthie Comedy) that, be it neuer such wicked stuffe, they would forbeare to hisse'. *W.H.*, II.i.112; II.ii.21.

79 *Sugred delicious*. *2 H.W.*, I.i.55–56.

106 *wildnesse*. Dilke's emendation of Quarto 'wildernesse', which Professor Bowers has here received into the text, is unnecessary. 'Wilderness', meaning 'wildness of character, licentiousness', is an acknowledged form in *O.E.D.* (5.b.fig.), which cites *Measure for Measure*, III.i.141: 'such a warped slip of wilderness'.

106 *tottred*. A unique instance in Dekker of the form as a verb. It is a favorite adjectival form of his; see *I.T.B.N.*, I.ii.139, n.

124 *Who's the foole?* I.ii.114, n.

180 *read this ha, ha, he.* I.iii.0.6.

190 *Arete. M.E.*, 770, n.

193 *Sibi sapit.* I.iii.0.9.

208–212 *The path...ascend*. Quoted under the heading 'Vertue' and attributed to Dekker in *Englands Parnassus* (where 'pearle' reads 'pearles'; Crawford, no. 1621).

IV.ii

9 *curld her lockes*. Cf. Marston, *Sophonisba*, V.i.12–13: 'make enraged Neptune toss / His huge curl'd locks'. *Sat.*, IV.i.87–88, n.

15 *wherryed*, driven. A wherry is a coach or a small boat (cf. *W.H.*,
V.i.155). The verb is a favorite of Dekker's. Cf. *S.H.R.*, B4:
'how the *Queene of the night* (the *Moone*) is, (with a swifter
whirling then the *Sunne* her brother) whiried vp and downe in
a coach of siluer'; *D.D.*, D4v, of the Hyperborean wind: 'out
he whorries, and 'fore him driues / (In whirlewindes,) *Haile*,
Frosts, *Sleete*, and *Stormes*'. *W.W.W.*, B5v: 'Ten thousand
Bullets from iron wombes deliuer'd, / Flye whurrying in the
Ayre.' *M.M.L.*, II.iv.117, n.; *2 H.W.*, I.i.49; *Sat.*, IV.ii.23.

28.1-2 *Irish Coster-mongers*. They are frequently mentioned in the
drama of the period. Cf. Jonson, *The Alchemist*, IV.i.57;
The Irish Masque at Court, 4–6; *Christmas his Masque*, 218–
221. *2 H.W.*, I.i.36: 'there [in England] all Costermongers are
Irishmen'; and *W.H.*, II.ii.199–201: 'as Frenchmen loue to
be bold, Flemings to be drunke, Welchmen to be cald *Brittons*,
and Irishmen to be Costermongers'.

30 *peepins: peeps feene*, i.e. pippins. *S.D.*, IV.i.59–60: 'he means
to turn *Costermonger*, and is projecting how to forestall the
market; I shall crie Pippins rarely'. Marston, *Jack Drum's
Entertainment*, Act I (ed. Wood, p. 191): 'he whose throat
squeakes like a treble Organ, and speakes as small and shrill,
as the Irish-men crie Pip, fine Pip'. Guilpin, *Skialetheia*,
Ep. 68 (1598), B6:

> As *Caius* walks the streets, if he but heare
> A blackman grunt his note, he cries *oh rare*!
> He cries *oh rare*, to heare the *Irishmen*
> Cry pippe, fine pippe, with a shrill accent

33-34 *peeps . . . Pome water*. Cf Jonson, *The Irish Masque at Court*,
4–6: 'I sherue ti mayesties owne cashter-monger, bee mee
trote: ant cry peep'sh, ant pomwater'sh i' ty mayesties sheruice,
'tis fiue yeere now.'

34 *Pome water*, 'a large juicy kind of apple' (*O.E.D.*). *W.E.*,
III.ii.155.

34-35 *apple Iohn*, 'a kind of apple said to keep two years, and to be
in perfection when shrivelled and withered'; so called,
presumably, because it is ripe about St John's Day (*O.E.D.*).
Cf. Shakespeare, *2 Henry IV*, II.iv.1–8. *S.D.*, IV.i.241.

45 *as Cree*ᶻ*e saue me.* For this familiar bit of stage Irish, cf. *2 H.W.*, I.i.15; *W.E.*, III.ii.151.

60–61 *Irish man...cut di countrie-mans throate.* The reference is to the proverbial savagery of the wild Irish kern. Cf. V.i.66, and *W.B.*, V.vi.97.

96 *Saint Patrickes Purgatorie,* on Lough Derg in Ulster. Stanyhurst describes the place and the traditions associated with it at the beginning of the fourth chapter ('Of the strange and woonderfull *places in Ireland*') of his *Description of Ireland* (printed in Holinshed's *Chronicles* (1587), II, 28). St Patrick, seeking to convert the people of Ulster, found them unimpressed by the torments of hell which he depicted as the punishment awaiting sinners. They thus address him: 'You sermon to vs of a dungeon appointed for offendors and miscredents. In deed if we could find that to be true, we would the sooner be weaned from the sweet napple of our libertie, and frame our selues pliant to the will of that God, that you reueale vnto vs.' St Patrick appeals to God

> to giue out some euident or glimsing token of the matter they importunatlie required. Finallie by the especiall direction of God, he found in the north edge of Ulster a desolate corner hemmed in round, and in the middle thereof a pit, where he reared a church, called Reglis or Reglasse. At the east end of the churchyard a doore leadeth into a closet of stone like a long ouen, which they call S. Patricke his purgatorie, for that the people resort thither euen at this daie for penance, and haue reported at their returne estrange visions of paine and blisse appearing vnto them.

For the mediaeval legend, see F. W. Locke, 'A New Date for the Composition of the *Tractatus de Purgatorio Sancti Patricii*', *Speculum*, 40 (1965), 641–646. For other references to it in the drama of the period, cf. *Hamlet*, I.v.136, and Middleton, *Anything for a Quiet Life* (ed. Lucas, *Webster*, vol. IV), IV.i.176. Dekker alludes to it elsewhere in *2 H.W.*, I.i.42–43, and *W.E.*, IV.ii.83–84.

105 *Doctor Dodipoll. Sat.*, V.ii.323, n.

105 *fat. I.T.B.N.*, I.ii.112, n.

131 *circles...eyes.* Cf. prologue, 9, and *M.E.*, 6–7.

V.i

60 *speckled soule.* Cf. *P.G.*, I.ii.71: 'Before my soule looke black with speckled sinne'.

66 *Irish kerne. 2 H.W.*, III.i.148, n.

83 *Those that would seeme most wise, doe turne most fooles.* Cf. the proverb, 'Who weens himself wise, Wisdom wots him a fool' (Tilley, W522).

85.1 *like a French Doctor. W.K.*, II.iii.44.1, n.

100 *no point. S.H.*, IV.iv.96, n. And cf. *Blurt, Master-Constable*, II.i.132–133: 'No, *point, par ma foi*: you see I have many tongues speak for me.'

101 *bul-beggera*, a terrifying thing or person. Nashe, *Strange Newes*, I, 319: 'Whether I seeke to bee counted a terrible bulbegger or no, Ile baite thee worse than a bull.'

109 *Laroone*, 'A felon, theefe, robber, purloyner, stealer, imbeazeler, pilferer, filcher, nimmer' (Cotgrave, *s.v. Larron*). *W.E.*, V.iii.101.

181 *Ware the horne. Sat.*, V.ii.281.

V.ii

6 *Stand and deliuer. B.L.*, Hiv: 'For the *High Law* is nothing else but taking a pursse by the High-way-side, so that to bee a good practitioner in this *Law*, a man needes no more but a bold stern look, a good heart, and a good sword: the cases that hee is to pleade vpon, is onely Stand and deliuer.'

10 *crie hey-passe...repasse*, a juggling term, used as 'Hey presto!' Marston, *What You Will*, III.ii.279–280: 'The world's turn'd juggler! / Casts mists before our eyes. Hey-pass re-pass!' *N.G.*, p. 76: 'You talke of a Plague in *London*, & red Crosses set vpon dores, but ten plagues cannot melt so many crosses of siluer out of Lawyers purses, as the *Winchesterians* (with a hey-pas, re-pas) iugled out of theirs to put into their owne.' *S.H.*, IV.iv.133. *S.T.W.*, IV.i.45.

15 *trudge. N.G.*, p. 78: 'if any guest did but once bite his lip, or grumble, he was cashierd the company for a mutinous fellow, the place was not for him, let him trudge'. The word is

common, but is a particular favorite of Dekker's. *P.G.*,
V.i.59; *Sat.*, II.ii.46; *2 H.W.*, IV.i.195; *N.H.*, I.iii.16; *M.M.L.*,
I.ii.47; *W.E.*, V.i.37. For his prose pamphlets, cf. *O.P.*, N4;
L.C., F4v; *R.A.*, C3v; *W.Y.*, p. 32.

16–17 *the little Welshwoman in Cyprus, that had but one horne in her
head.* Probably an allusion to Margaret Griffith, wife of David
Owen, of Llan Gaduain, in Montgomeryshire, whose picture
is prefixed to a pamphlet entered in the Stationers' Register
on 28 October 1588 and titled 'A miraculous and monstrouse
but most true and certen discourse of a woman (nowe to be
seene in London) of thage of lx. yeres in the middest of whose
forehead by the wonderfull woorke of God, there groweth
out a Croked horne of 4 ynches long' (Arber, II, 504). There
are other allusions to this woman in Nashe, *Have With You*,
III, 77: 'the foulest vgly gentlewoman or fury that might
be,... thrice more deformed than the woman with the horne
in her head'; and Marston, *The Malcontent*, I.viii.18–21: 'the
horn of a cuckold is as tender as his eye, or as that growing in
the woman's forehead twelve years since that could not endure
to be touch'd'.

32 *mad Herogliphickes.* Cf. Jonson, *The Case is Altered*, I.iv.6–10:

> *Iuni*...ha, you mad *Hierogliphick*, when shal we swagger?
> *Valen. Hieroglyphick*, what meanest thou by that?
> *Iuni.* Meane? Gods so, ist not a good word man? what? stand vpon
> meaning with your freinds?

G.H., B2v: 'lay open all thy secrets & the mystical *Hiero-
gliphick* of *Rashers* ath coales, *Modicums & Shooing hornes*.'

34 *Gammoth ares,* i.e. 'gamut are', or 'gam-ut a-re'; they are
the first two notes of Guido d'Arezzo's musical scale. Cf.
Shakespeare, *The Taming of the Shrew*, III.i.73–74, and Nashe,
Have With You, III, 23: 'the melodious God of *Gam vt are*'.
G.H., B1v: 'You Courtiers that do nothing but sing the
Gamuth Are of complementall courtesie'.

37 *sort*, company. *S.H.*, II.iii.46, n.

39 *laugh and be fat. Blurt, Master-Constable*, I.ii.201–203: 'our
haste is as great as thine; yet, to endear ourselves into thy lean
acquaintance, cry, rivo hoh! laugh and be fat'. Tilley, L91.

Cf. *O.F.*, I.i.21: 'laugh and bee leane'. And cf. *N.H.*, I.iii.34–35; *W.B.*, II.ii.15.

41 *laugh and lie downe*, a quibble on the name of an obsolete card game, 'laugh and lay down'. *Blurt, Master-Constable*, III.i.96: 'Come, wilt thou go laugh and lie down?' Tilley, L92. *N.G.*, p. 76; *S.H.*, V.ii.118; *N.S.S.*, I.ii.23.

70 *Good gifts...turne*. Quoted under the heading 'Gifts' and attributed to Dekker in *Englands Parnassus* (Crawford, no. 580). Cf. *M.M.L.*, III.i.176–177.

118 *spurne*, kick. *Blurt, Master-Constable*, I.i.23–24: 'men's heads spurned up and down like foot-balls'. *G.H.*, B2: 'with your feete spurne open the doore and enter'. And cf. *O.F.*, V.ii.207. *M.M.L.*, III.ii.198–200; *V.M.*, IV.i.183; *L.D.*, II.i.6, n.

135 *with a mischiefe*, with a vengeance. *R.G.*, II.i.203; *I.T.B.N.*, I.i.49.

152 *deaths frozen hand*. *L.D.*, I.i.167.

154 *No man...blest*. Quoted under the heading 'Man' and attributed to Dekker in *Englands Parnassus* (Crawford, no. 1095). Tilley, M333.

217 *Those...forgoe*. Quoted under the heading 'Auarice' and attributed to Dekker in *Englands Parnassus* (Crawford, no. 58).

275–276 *like a miser, | Lockt vp his wealth*. Cf. I.i.295, n.

331–333 *All that they had...alone liues still*. Quoted under the heading 'Vertue' and attributed to Dekker in *Englands Parnassus* (where 'they' (line 331) reads 'wee'; 'Sends' (line 332) reads 'Seemes'; and 'but' (line 332) is misprinted 'hut'; Crawford, no. 1635).

337–338. *All these...|Are shaddowes*. Cf. *A Midsummer Night's Dream*, V.i.423–424.

The Epilogue at Court

17 *Arithmetician*. Cf. the prayer for Charles I in *B.R.W.R.*, p. 204: 'our most gracious Soueraigne King *Charles*, whose yeares the great Arithmetician of Heauen, multiply, and blesse the numbers, till they bee all golden ones'.

19 *fortie two*. In 1599/1600, Queen Elizabeth I was in the forty-second year of her reign.

PATIENT GRISSIL

INTRODUCTION

Dekker, Chettle and Haughton's *Patient Grissil* was the fifth play on which Dekker and Chettle collaborated during 1599. Earlier in the year had come their *Troilus and Cressida* (payments recorded in Henslowe's *Diary* between 7 and 16 April),[1] *Agamemnon* (payments recorded by Henslowe on 26 and 30 May;[2] the play is probably the same as the *Orestes' Furies*, in earnest of which Henslowe had loaned 5s. to Dekker on 2 May),[3] and *The Stepmother's Tragedy* (payments recorded between 24 July and 14 October).[4] During this last period the pair were also working with Jonson and an 'other gentleman' (perhaps Marston) on the tragedy of *Robert II, King of Scots* (payments recorded between 3 and 27 September),[5] Dekker and Jonson themselves having just completed another tragedy, *Page of Plymouth* (payments between 10 August and 2 September).[6] All of these plays are lost.

Neither Dekker nor Chettle had previously collaborated with Haughton. His *Englishmen for my Money, or A Woman Will Have her Will*, had been produced by the Admiral's Company the year before (payments recorded by Henslowe between 18 February and early May 1598),[7] but thereafter for the next eighteen months he is mentioned only twice in Henslowe's *Diary*, on 20 and 25 August 1599 when a total of 30s. was loaned him in earnest of *The Poor Man's Paradise*;[8] the small amount and the lack of further reference to the play suggest that it may never have been finished. Haughton was plainly a less experienced dramatist than either of his two collaborators; Henslowe refers to him as 'younge' the

---

[1] *Henslowe's Diary*, pp. 106, 107.   [2] *Ibid.*, p. 121.
[3] *Ibid.*, p. 119.   [4] *Ibid.*, pp. 123, 125.
[5] *Ibid.*, p. 124.   [6] *Ibid.*, pp. 123, 124.
[7] *Ibid.*, pp. 87, 89.   [8] *Ibid.*, p. 123.

first time he mentions him in the *Diary* (5 November 1597),[1] and his career with the Admiral's Company, which was to extend over the next two years, was still getting under way in the fall of 1599, when plans for *Patient Grissil* were launched.

The play is first mentioned sometime between 16 October and 1 November, when Henslowe loaned Chettle 20s in earnest of it.[2] But two months followed before the play was finally completed and the bulk of payments to the dramatists was made: £3 to all three on 19 December[3] and £6 to all three on 26 December;[4] 5s. to Dekker on the 28th;[5] and 5s. to Haughton on the 29th.[6] On 26 January 1600, Henslowe paid 20s. 'to buy a grey gowne for gryssell'[7] and the play was presumably on the stage shortly thereafter. It was evidently successful; at any rate, the Admiral's Company took steps to keep it out of print when Henslowe, on 18 March 1600, paid 40s. to stay its printing.[8] By this time, the trio of dramatists who had written it had joined forces again and with John Day added to their number had composed a new play, *The Seven Wise Masters* (payments from Henslowe recorded between 1 and 8 March 1600).[9] During the previous month, Dekker, Haughton and Day were at work on *The Spanish Moor's Tragedy* (partial payment on 13 February 1600),[10] the play that is almost certainly preserved under the title *Lust's Dominion*.

The entries in Henslowe's *Diary* make it clear that between late October when work on *Patient Grissil* presumably began and mid-December when it was finished, no one of the three collaborators was giving the play his undivided attention. From the beginning of November through the first week of December, Haughton was engaged in two collaborations with John Day: the tragedy of *Cox of Collumpton* (payments recorded on 1, 8 or 9, and 14 November),[11] and the tragedy of *Thomas Merry*, or *Beech's Tragedy* (payments on 21 and 27 November, and 5 and 6 December).[12] Throughout November, Dekker was working on *Old Fortunatus* (payments recorded on 9, 24 and 30 November),[13] and upon

---

[1] *Ibid.*, p. 72.   [2] *Ibid.*, p. 125.   [3] *Ibid.*, p. 128.
[4] *Ibid.*, p. 129.   [5] *Ibid.*, p. 129.   [6] *Ibid.*, p. 129.
[7] *Ibid.*, p. 130.   [8] *Ibid.*, p. 132.   [9] *Ibid.*, p. 131.
[10] *Ibid.*, p. 131.   [11] *Ibid.*, pp. 125, 126.   [12] *Ibid.*, pp. 127, 128.
[13] *Ibid.*, pp. 126, 127.

completing it proceeded immediately to the job of altering it for performance at Court (payments on 31 [*sic*] November and 12 December).[1] Chettle also seems to have been otherwise engaged for at least part of this time. Henslowe loaned him 10s. on 10 November in earnest of an unnamed play,[2] and another 10s. on 27 November in earnest of *The Orphans' Tragedy*[3] (a play that was left incomplete at this time and was still incomplete on 24 September 1601 when Henslowe loaned Chettle a further 10s. in partial payment for it).[4] Before final payments were received for *Patient Grissil*, Chettle and Haughton were devising a new play, *The Arcadian Virgin*, in earnest of which they received a total of 15s. from Henslowe on 13 and 17 December.[5] From *Patient Grissil*, Dekker turned to writing a play by himself, *Truth's Supplication to Candlelight* (payments from Henslowe on 18 and 30 January 1600).[6]

Whatever may be the origins of the Griselda story in myth and folklore, it enters European literature at a definite point in time, in 1353 with the publication of Boccaccio's *Decameron*, where it appears as the closing tale. Twenty years later Petrarch found himself so moved by Boccaccio's story that he prepared a Latin paraphrase of it (*de Insigni Obedientia et Fide Uxoris*), and this according to the testimony of Chaucer's Clerk was the source of the story as it is told in *The Canterbury Tales*.[7] The tale seems to have been dramatized first in France; a play called *Le Mystère de Grisélidis* was performed in Paris in 1395.[8] Hans Sachs dramatized it in 1556, and around the same time the story seems to have received its first dramatic treatment in England when a Latin dramatization (*De patientia Grisilidis*) was devised by Ralph Radcliff for perform-

[1] *Ibid.*, pp. 127, 128.   [2] *Ibid.*, p. 126.   [3] *Ibid.*, p. 127.
[4] *Ibid.*, p. 182.   [5] *Ibid.*, p. 128.   [6] *Ibid.*, p. 130.
[7] 'The Clerk's Prologue', 26–38, in *The Complete Works of Geoffrey Chaucer*, ed. F. N. Robinson, 2nd ed. (Oxford University Press, 1957). For the sources of the story, see Dudley David Griffith, *The Origin of the Griselda Story* (Seattle, 1931), which explores the story's relation to the Cupid and Psyche tales; and J. Burke Severs, *The Literary Relationships of Chaucer's Clerkes Tale* (New Haven, 1942), which contains a text of Plutarch's Latin translation of the Boccaccio story.
[8] J. J. Jusserand, *A Literary History of the English People* (London, 1894), I, 332, n. 3.

ance by the boys of his grammar school in the dissolved friary of the Carmelites at Hitchin in Hertfordshire.[1] The repertoire of Radcliff's plays, as described by Bale, suggests the moral implications which the Griselda story and its heroine held for the period. *De patientia Grisilidis* occurs in a list which also includes plays dealing with Chaucer's Melibeus, the martyr Jan Hus, and such biblical figures as Jonah, Lazarus, Job, Judith, and Susanna: examples all, as Herford has noted, 'of steadfast endurance, of patient suffering'.[2] When, not long after Radcliff's play, the story was dramatized for professional actors by John Phillip,[3] the sense of its value as a moral exemplum is evident. The titlepage of the undated quarto edition of Phillip's play reads: 'The Commodye of / pacient and meeke Grissill, / Whearin is declared, the good example, of her pacience towardes her Hus=/band: and lykewise, the / due obedience of Children, toward their Parentes.'[4]

During the last half of the 1560s, five entries in the Stationers' Register refer to the Griselda story. Two record payment of licensing fees by Thomas Colwell, one for the year extending from July 1565 ('for prynting of an history of meke and pacyent gresell'), the other for the year extending from July 1568 ('for pryntinge of the history of payciente gresell').[5] Both must refer to Phillip's

---

[1] Radcliff's play is lost. We know of it from John Bale's account of Radcliff and his school in *Scriptorum Illustrium Maioris Brytanniae* (Basle, 1557–1559), I, 700. Some of the plays at Radcliff's school may have been in English, but the *De patientia Grisilidis* was almost certainly in Latin for the opening words which Bale quotes ('Exemplar ut sim muliebris pa[tientiae]') are part of a verse. C. H. Herford suggests that they 'are the opening words of Griselis, who must have been prologue as well as heroine' (*Studies in the Literary Relations of England and Germany in the Sixteenth Century* (Cambridge University Press, 1886) p. 113, note). The limits suggested by Harbage and Schoenbaum (*Annals*, p. 28) for the date of Radcliff's play are 1546(?)–1556.

[2] *Studies in Literary Relations*, p. 111.

[3] The date of Phillip's play is uncertain. Chambers (III, 466) suggested that the reference (at line 51 of the Malone Society Reprint) 'to the "wethercocke of Paules" perhaps dates before its destruction in 1561'; accordingly, Harbage and Schoenbaum suggest 1558–1561 as limits (*Annals*, p. 34). G. K. Hunter in his bibliography to F. P. Wilson's *English Drama, 1485–1585* (Oxford, 1969), p. 223) suggests that the play was written *c.* 1566, as does *The New Cambridge Bibliography of English Literature* (1974), col. 1417.

[4] The titlepage continues with the assurance that 'Eight persons maye easely play this Commody' and lists the way in which roles can be doubled.

[5] Arber, I, 309, 385.

play, the titlepage of which names Colwell as printer. The other three entries all occur during the year extending from July 1565: (1) 'a ballett intituled the sonnge of pacyente Gressell vnto hyr make' (Arber, I, 296; Rollins, no. 2486, who suggests the song is probably preserved in Phillip's play); (2) 'ij ballettes to the Tune of pacyente Gressell' (Arber, I, 301; Rollins, no. 137); (3) 'Danderly Dyscaffe' (Arber, I, 302; Rollins, no. 482, who identifies this entry with Grissell's song in Phillip's play beginning 'God by his prouidence deuine' and containing the refrain 'Singe danderlie Distaffe, & danderlie / Ye Virgins all come learne of mee').

Thus at least one and perhaps more of these entries in the Stationers' Register are to be identified with songs in Phillip's play, but if a distinct ballad on the subject of Patient Grissil was not in existence then, one came into being in the course of the next thirty-odd years. The earliest extant copy of 'A most pleasant Ballad of patient Grissell. To the tune of the Brides good morrow', is preserved in the Huth Collection in the British Library and dated [1600?]. The ballad is included in the second part of Deloney's *The Garland of Good Will*;[1] of this, the earliest extant edition is dated 1631, but Deloney's collection was apparently entered in the Stationers' Register on 5 March 1593 (Arber, II, 627, as 'The garden of good will' to John Wolf; it was signed over to Edward White on 27 August 1596).

In 1619 a chapbook containing a prose narrative of the Griselda story was published with the following titlepage (wherein the story's value as exemplum is directed to more pragmatic ends than those invoked on the titlepage of Phillip's play): 'The / Ancient True and Admirable / History of / Patient Grisel, / A Poore Mans Daughter in France: / Shewing / How Maides, By Her Example, In Their Good Behaviour / May Marrie Rich Husbands; / And Likewise Wives By Their Patience And Obedience / May Gaine Much Glorie.'[2]

---

[1] *Works*, pp. 346–350. The ballad is reprinted as well in *Roxburghe Ballads*, ed. W. Chappell (London, 1874), II, 269–274; in Joseph Lilly, *A Collection of Seventy-Nine Black-Letter Ballads and Broadsides, Printed in the Reign of Queen Elizabeth, Between the years 1559 and 1597*, second issue (London, 1870), pp. 17–23; and in *Bishop Percy's Folio*, ed. J. W. Hales and F. J. Furnivall (London, 1868), III, 423–430. For music for 'The Bride's Good-Morrow', see Simpson, pp. 66–67.

[2] The 1619 narrative has been edited by J. P. Collier (Percy Society (London, 1842), vol. III), and H. B. Wheatley (Villon Society (London, 1885)).

Though this chapbook cannot be traced before 1619, it is generally held to be a reprint of an earlier original, and to have been composed some years before, apparently 'towards the end of the sixteenth century'.[1] It almost certainly pre-dates Dekker, Chettle and Haughton's play, and they may have been acquainted with it. It contains the main ingredients of the story which they dramatize, but it has had no discernible influence on their treatment of a tale which was also available to them in Phillip's play and in the Ballad (which has clearly left its mark on the play; see below, p.142).

Finally, mention should be made of another version of the Griselda story, printed *c.* 1630 and titled: 'The Pleasant / and Sweet History / of patient Grissell. / Shewing how she from a poore mans / Daughter, came to be a great Lady in *France*, / being a patterne for all vertuous / Women.' This combination of verse and prose in eleven chapters is nothing more than a reprint of the Ballad (divided into what are termed Chapters 3–9) flanked by two brief prose chapters setting the scene at the beginning, and two further chapters that dilate on Grissil's happiness and the moral value of patience at the end.[2] This, like the chapbook of 1619, may be a late reprint of an earlier original. Its prose expansions of the Ballad have no connection with the play of 1599.

As a full-scale dramatization of the Griselda story, Phillip's play deserves more attention than it usually receives in accounts of Dekker, Chettle and Haughton's later version.[3] It is a late morality of the type wherein ethical abstractions mingle with human figures. After a prologue spoken by the Vice, Politic Persuasion, the Marquess Gautier enters with his train (which includes Fidence, Reason, and Sobriety) from a day of hunting. The counsellors voice their

[1] Harold Jenkins, *The Life and Work of Henry Chettle* (London, 1934), p. 159.

[2] The *c.* 1630 combination of Ballad *cum* prose chapters has been edited by J. P. Collier (Percy Society (London, 1842), vol. III). The prose chapters are reprinted in Deloney, pp. 493–495.

[3] Phillip's play was unknown until 1907, when a copy was discovered in the library of Lord Mostyn. It is now in the possession of the Elizabethan Club, Yale University. A type facsimile of the text, prepared by R. B. McKerrow and W. W. Greg, was published by the Malone Society Reprints in 1909. Quotations from the play in the account that follows are based on this edition, to which the parenthetical line-numbers have reference.

appeal that he should marry and beget an heir, and Gautier agrees, assuring them that he will shortly make his choice. Grissil is introduced, singing and spinning, with her father, Janicle, and her mother, who is dying. Gautier directs his attendants to prepare for his wedding day, for he will bring home his bride on the morrow. Grissil, whose mother has now died, enters and sings another song; there follows a comic scene between two pages whose masters are *en route* to the 'Marquis place' (529); Grissil appears again, and now the Marquess enters with his lords; he greets her and confesses his love, assuring Janicle, who has by now appeared, that his intentions are honorable; Janicle consents, and Grissil modestly complies. While the court ladies take her off to dress her for the wedding, Janicle solicits Gautier to bring up any children they may have in godly obedience, and Gautier promises. Grissil appears in rich robes (822) and she and Gautier sing a song and depart. Politic Persuasion, alone, describes his intentions to sow strife:

> I tell you I haue found out such an inuension,
> As among the common sort, shall kindle discencion:
> A *Marquis* maried to a beggerlye Grissill,
> Her father an olde foole, and an impotent criple,
> His store and substaunce in value not worth twentie pence,
> This geare cannot chuse but breed inconuenience,
> I will not cease priuely her confusion to worke.
>
> (891–897)

He seeks to suggest to Reason and Sobriety that it is unfit that Grissil's 'seed should rule or haue dignitie' (927), but they tell him his talk is vain, and Diligence enters to announce that Grissil has given birth to 'a bewtifull Childe amyable to behould' (948).

Alone again, Politic Persuasion, undaunted, determines to cast another scheme to effect Grissil's ruin, and when Gautier enters, singing of his love, the Vice goes to work. Gautier has just completed a catalogue of Grissil's virtues:

> A *Dido* for her Chastitie, *Penellope* for truth,
> A *Thisbe* for her ardent loue, and *Pyramus* insueth:
> *Cassandra* shee for pacyence, full aptly maye be namde,
> Amonge the rout of chasted Dames, my Matrone may bee famde:

135

Whose vertues farre abound, and sandie shores excell,
From Courtlie Dames for counsell graue, my spouse doth beare
  yᵉ bell.

(986–991)

Politic Persuasion, hearing this, goes straight to the point, in the
manner and in the accents of Satan:

God ge [*sic*] goddeauen my Lorde wyth all my hart,
If your wyfe be so vertuous as nowe ye import,
Surelie, surely shee is worthy commendacion,
Shee may be made a saynte for her good conuersacion:
But harke my Lorde nay nowe harken in your eare,
Try hir that waye and by myne honestie I sweare,
You shall see hir decline from Vertues so rife,
And alter topsie turuie hir saintish lyfe:
Hir pacyence quicklye shall chaunged bee,
I warrant your honor will say it is not shee.

(992–1001)

Gautier promptly assents, calls in Diligence and orders him to
take Grissil's infant daughter from her and pretend, on the commandment of the Marquess, to murder it; in fact, he is instructed
to take it to 'Bullin Lagras' (Bologna) to the Countess of Pango,
Gautier's sister. This is done over the impassioned appeals of the
Nurse, Gautier explaining that his nobles 'disdaine' his wedded
state, and will force him into exile if he does not sacrifice Grissil's
child. Grissil prays for patience:

My Child alas in swadlinge clouts, bereft and slaine with sword.
Lord help, Lord ayd, my wofull plight on me take some remord,
Albeit such dirfull hap haue chauncst, graunt pacience to my paine
That I maye seme this crosse of thine, with ioye for to sustaine

(1205–1208)

The child is brought to the Countess of Pango, who agrees to
take it.

Grissil gives birth again; Politic Persuasion goes for the mid-
wife; a son is born, and there is rejoicing by all but Politic
Persuasion, who does his work offstage this time. After the nurse
has finished singing a lullaby to the baby, Diligence enters with
drawn sword to kill the infant; again passionate appeals from the
nurse, to no avail. Diligence takes the child, and it too is sent to
Bullin Lagras and the Countess of Pango. Politic Persuasion, in

soliloquy, reflects on the blows he has given Grissil, but acknowledges that her patience is yet unmoved. New schemes are called for.

> But sith that nether of these attempts hir pacience can moue,
> I am minded ageinst hir a new assault to proue,
> Which shall exempt hir from the top of fortunat prosperitie,
> And plounge hir deepe in the floods of aduersytie
>
> (1482–1485)

After a whispered conversation between the Vice and Gautier,
Gautier addresses Grissil, telling her that the death of both their
children is not enough to 'appease the blooddie mynde, / Of nobles
al, nor staunch the raige of commons moast vnkind' (1504–1505);
Grissil is still the 'roote' of all his grief, anguish and care. Hearing
this, Grissil is prepared to die:

> Let thousand gasshes scortch this flesh, let them their raige displaye,
> Let thousand woundes by stroake of kniues, take *Grissills* life away
>
> (1516–1517)

Politic Persuasion, on the sidelines, is amazed ('Howe manie such
wiues maye a man fynde'). But Gautier assures her that her life
need not be threatened; all that is required is that she be sent back
naked to her father's house, for he will wed another. To this she
assents, and Gautier for a moment is touched and ready to give over
the trial (1568–1569); he is only kept firm by the urgent injunctions
of the Vice:

> Procead forward faint not, your purpose prosequte,
> Be not reputed a coward, the fackt excequte,
> Let your countenaunce be sterne, like a gentillman looke byg,
> Els for this drift ile not giue a fyg.
>
> (1584–1587)

Grissil asks only for a smock to cover her nakedness, and this is
granted. She takes her leave, and Politic Persuasion shortly thereafter takes his, for the last time ('Fare ye well all, I will bee packing, /
Tush ther wants a man, where Pollicie is lacking' (1669–1670)).

Rumor enters, announcing Grissil's fall 'from the top of pros-
perytie' and her return to 'suffer paynfull pouertie' with her old
father (1684–1685). And the Common People (*Vulgus*) now enter,
stirred up by what Rumor has reported of Grissil's state, with

which they sympathize. So too do Reason and Sobriety. All greet
her as she returns to her father's house. When they are alone
together, Janicle curses Fortune for her woe (1761), but she will
not have it so:

> Blame not Fortune for my ouerthroe,
> It was the will of God, that it should be so:
> And what creature liuing, can withstand his prouidence,
> This Crosse is to trye vs, as hee doth his elect
>
> (1766–1770)

Patience and Constancy appear, and Grissil greets them as sent
from God (1809), and embraces them, and Janicle does likewise.
They exit, and Diligence appears to announce that the Marquess
has journeyed to Bullin Lagras to fetch his new spouse; Diligence
is to bring Grissil to court to make all ready for the new bride. To
this she readily consents.

At the court are now the Marquess, his sister, and his son and
daughter; Grissil comes into their presence. To Gautier's question:
'is not my spouse beautifull and faire' (1923), she replies that
'Ther can not in the world bee a fayrer' (1932), but then continues:

> But harke my Lord, what I saye to thee agayne,
> Take heed thou pricke her not, with the Needles of disdayne:
> As thou hast done the other, for shee hath bin brought vp
> dayntelie,
> And peraduenture, can not take the matter so pacientlie.[1]
>
> (1933–1936)

And now Gautier commends her virtues with the announcement:

> Thou onely art my Spouse, and beloued mate,
> Thee onely I fancye, all other Spousalls I hate:

[1] This poignant touch has its origin in Boccaccio, where Griselda says: 'But with
all my heart I beg you not to inflict those same wounds upon her that you imposed
upon her predecessor, for I doubt whether she could withstand them, not only
because she is younger, but also because she has had a refined upbringing, whereas
the other had to face continual hardship from her infancy' (*Decameron*, translated by
G. H. McWilliam (Penguin Books), p. 822). It is regularly included in redactions of
the tale. Cf. Chaucer, *The Clerk's Tale*, 1037–1043; and Dekker, Chettle and
Haughton's *Patient Grissil*, V.ii.147–150. In the 1619 chapbook, Grissil says: 'only,
gracious lord, take heed of one thing; that you trie not this new bride as you have
done your ould wife; for she is yong, and peradventure of another straine, and so
may want of that patience and government, which I, poore I, have endured' (ed.
Wheatley, p. 43).

And this Virgin which thou deemest, my Spouse shall bee,
Is thy Daughter and mine, this is the veritie,
And this young man, which thou seeist in sight,
Is thy sonne and mine, my loue and Ladie bright

(1943–1948)

The children pay tribute to their mother's sufferings, and her patience, as do Reason and Sobriety; the two counsellors solemnly affirm the propriety of Grissil's children inheriting the rule of their father's nation. Janicle appears, and Gautier calls on his nobility to clothe Grissil's father in robes of honor (2024). Grissil's one remaining wish is now satisfied; her son and daughter are presented to their grandfather, and all go off 'with ioyfullnes' (2090).

Past scholars have been emphatic in their denial that Dekker, Chettle and Haughton's play owes anything to Phillip's comedy,[1] and this may be true so far as direct indebtedness is concerned. Nonetheless, the play ought not to be ignored for it is a unique witness to what the preceding generation had found in the story, and to the conventions available to a dramatist of that generation for putting the story on the stage. Its personified Virtues and its swaggering Vice and the jogging metres of its accentual verses must have seemed as quaintly old-fashioned by the end of the 1590s as they seem today. But Phillip's play represents a stage in the development of the Griselda story, specifically as concerns the Marquess' motivation, that ought not to be overlooked, for it points in the way that both the Ballad and the play of 1599 will take in their attempts to account for Griselda's treatment at the hands of her noble husband.

In neither Boccaccio's story nor Chaucer's redaction of it is there a hint that the Marquess' subjects repine at his marriage with a woman of such humble birth as Griselda. On the contrary, we are told that they are inclined to look upon their ruler with a new respect, since only an uncommonly wise man 'could ever have perceived the noble qualities that lay concealed beneath her ragged and rustic attire'.[2] Chaucer makes the same point (*The Clerk's Tale*, 425–427). The Griselda of both Boccaccio and Chaucer wins all hearts, and her husband's subjects bitterly resent his treatment of

[1] E.g., Hunt, p. 59, n. 35; Jenkins, *Henry Chettle*, p. 161.
[2] *Decameron*, p. 817.

her. As one after another her two children disappear (in Boccaccio and Chaucer there is a six-year difference in their ages), the people condemn the Marquess for a murderer and a cruel tyrant (*Decameron*, p. 819; cf. *Clerk's Tale*, 722–728). When she is sent back to her father's house clad only in her shift, she goes 'amid the weeping and the wailing of all who set eyes upon her' (*Decameron*, p. 820; cf. *Clerk's Tale*, 897–898). In both Boccaccio and Chaucer we have the pretext which the Marquess offers Griselda, to the effect that it is the resentment of his subjects which causes him to cast off both her children and eventually her. But in both Boccaccio and Chaucer, the pretext is only that, invoked by the Marquess to account for the trials to which he is bent on putting his wife. It has no substance in these early versions of the story, and properly so, for the impulse to subject the wife to humiliation and grief comes from within the husband; there is a principal source of the story's dark fascination. To attempt to account for the impulse by rational explanation is to dissipate the story's mystery and drastically to over-simplify the character of the Marquess; and this is what one sees happening in the later English versions: Phillip's play, the Ballad, and the play of 1599.

In the character of the Vice, the sixteenth-century morality made ready to the playwright's hand an all-too-convenient dramatic means for giving mysterious human impulses a local habitation and a name. Phillip gave to the particular impulse which motivates so much of the action of his *Patient Grissil* the name 'Politic Persuasion' and set it the dramatic function of externalizing and rationalizing the Marquess' obscure desire to test his wife. The important thing, so far as the dramatic treatment of the story is concerned, is that the presence of Politic Persuasion tends to give a certain rational objectivity to what in Boccaccio and Chaucer has been but subjective pretense: the Marquess' explanation to his wife and perhaps to himself that public pressures force him to treat her as he does. There is no such public pressure in the world of the story as shown in Boccaccio and Chaucer, but in Phillip's play it has been given an objective identity and a voice. Phillip's play occupies the psychologically ambiguous ground shared by so many Tudor moralities; there is a sense in which the Vice, Politic

Persuasion, is the external voice of an inner evil, the overt manifesta-
tion of all the Marquess' efforts to deceive himself with specious
arguments for Griselda's disgrace. But to the extent that Politic
Persuasion moves independently in the world of Phillip's play (as
we see him doing, for example, in his conversation with Reason
and Sobriety at lines 918ff.), and does not exist simply as a dimen-
sion of the Marquess' imagination, an aspect of his spiritual and
psychological nature, he represents a force in the world that gives
credence to what in Boccaccio and Chaucer have been but pretexts
concerning voices in society that grumble at Griselda's rise. It is
interesting to see this point developed in the Ballad, where the
voices of the dissenting nobles are very real:

> When that the Marques did see that they were bent thus
>   against his faithfull wife,
> Whom most dearley, tenderly, and entirely,
>   he loued as his life:
> Minding in secret for to proue her patient heart
>   therby her foes to disgrace:
> Thinking to play a hard discourteous part,
>   that men might pitty her case... [1]

According to the Ballad, the Marquess' ill-treatment of his wife is
part of a calculated campaign to win sympathy for her.

While in the play of 1599, the determination to test his wife
seems to have sprung full blown from the head of the Marquess
(we first hear of it at II.ii.20–21), and is not occasioned by any felt
need to win for her the hearts of his people, the dramatists have
nonetheless provided a courtly faction hostile to Grissil, thereby
continuing in the way charted by both Phillip's play and the
Ballad. The anti-Grissil faction is heard, for example, at I.ii.275–
280, in the voices of the courtiers, Mario and Lepido, and Pavia
(brother to the Marquess), and thereafter Mario and Lepido are
regularly heard disparaging Grissil because (sycophants that they
are) they are brought to believe that the Marquess has indeed
turned against her. His test of her is also a test of his courtiers, and
these two 'flatterers' are in the end revealed for what they are and
expelled (V.ii.209). But if two have been found false, the Marquess

---

[1] Lines 57–64 (Deloney, p. 347). See also Commentary on I.ii.270–280.

has found one courtier true, Furio, who despite his name and his role as the unwilling agent of the Marquess' sundry trials of his wife, reveals a genuine if gruff sympathy for her.[1]

That the Marquess has occasion in the course of the play to test others besides his wife may be intended to make his testing of his wife seem less egregious. In this as in other ways the dramatically inflexible quality of his character is compromised by the dramatists' efforts to suggest rational motives for behavior that is essentially irrational. For example, the notion (expressed at III.i.162–165, and again at IV.i.210–211) that the Marquess' trial of Grissil is aimed at bestowing on her a high fame is a bit of sentimentality that ill accords with his mad persistence in devising trials for his wife: a persistence which provides, after all, the propelling force of the action. In view of the uncertainty which marks the handling of his character through so much of the play, it was a superior dramatic instinct which gave him at the end a moment of truth, when after charging the courtiers with the wrongs they have done to Grissil, he is heard to acknowledge: 'My selfe haue done most wrong, for I did try / To breake the temper of true constancie' (V.ii.204–205).

In Boccaccio and Chaucer, and in Phillip's play, Grissil's trials proceed in three stages: first a daughter is born and taken from the mother; time passes and a son is born and the mother is deprived of this child too; then the Marquess renounces her as his wife and sends her back to her father's house. In the Ballad 'Of patient Grissel and a Noble Marquesse', Grissil's children are twins ('two goodly children at one birth she had. / A sonne and daughter God had sent'),[2] and the dramatists of 1599 avail themselves of this detail, serving as it does to compress the span of time covered by the play's action.[3] Nonetheless, the threefold nature of Grissil's trial is retained in Dekker, Chettle and Haughton's play: the first

---

[1] The hint for this character may have come from Chaucer's 'ugly sergeant' (*Clerk's Tale*, 673) who goes at the Marquess' bidding to take away (presumably for execution) each of Grissil's children in turn.

[2] Lines 67–68 (Deloney, p. 348).

[3] A formidable problem of time remains, however, and this concerns the lapse of years (twelve in Boccaccio) that must be assumed to pass between the birth of Grissil's daughter and her return as the supposed bride-to-be of the Marquess. Grissil's children are taken from her at IV.ii.189. At IV.iii.250 ff., the Marquess announces the impending visit of his new bride. See Jenkins, *Henry Chettle*, pp. 175–176.

humiliation to be visited on her is the dismissal of her father and brother, who have accompanied her to court upon her marriage (III.i); then Grissil herself, with her two children, is sent back to her father's house (IV.i); Furio comes to her there and takes both children from her (IV.ii). The trials in the play, though addressed to Grissil, extend to her family, and this brings us to the most notable additions that have been made to the original story: the new characters of Grissil's brother Laureo, and the clownish servingman, Babulo. Together with the poignantly drawn character of Janicola, Grissil's father, they provide a richly human trio of voices – tender, bitter, humorous – which serves as accompaniment to, and commentary on, Grissil's trials, and which represents the play's finest poetic and dramatic achievement.

The story of Grissil is combined in the 1599 play with two subplots, one dealing with the Marquess' Welsh kinswoman Gwenthyan and Sir Owen, the Welsh knight who woos and wins her; the other with the Marquess' sister Julia and her suitors. Each contributes its share to the play's central topic of marriage and the question of male or female dominance. Sir Owen's unavailing efforts to tame the redoubtable Gwenthyan amount to a parody of the Marquess' tactics with the yielding Grissil; and looking on at both couples is Julia, who – understandably in the circumstances – is not attracted by anything she can observe in the married state. Consideration of the play's three plots (Grissil and the Marquess, Gwenthyan and Sir Owen, Julia and her suitors) leads to consideration of the authorial shares of the play's three authors. It would be convenient to suppose that each plot was the work of a single author, but the matter is not that simple.

It was once held that, because Welsh characters appear in *Satiromastix* and *Northward Ho*, Dekker must have had a fondness for the type, and so the scenes in *Patient Grissil* involving Sir Owen and Gwenthyan must be his.[1] Jenkins registered a faint demur at this,[2] but it remained for W. L. Halstead to point out that there is an essential difference between the handling of Welsh dialect in *Patient Grissil* and its usage in the other two plays, and the differ-

---

[1] Cf. Hunt, p. 60.   [2] *Henry Chettle*, p. 173.

ence turns on the fact that 'the dramatist in *Patient Grissil* shows more mastery of the Welsh language than Dekker exhibited in either' *Satiromastix* or *Northward Ho*.[1] Halstead concluded that Dekker was not the author of the Welsh dialect scenes in *Patient Grissil*, and the same conclusion was reached independently some years later by D. M. Greene.[2] Greene has demonstrated that *Patient Grissil* contains – as *Satiromastix* and *Northward Ho* do not – 'a large quantity of actual Welsh (phonetically spelled), which sometimes runs to whole exchanges of several lines' (p. 173). All in all, the treatment of Welsh in the Sir Owen–Gwenthyan scenes represents what Greene terms 'a serious attempt either to imitate fairly exactly a real spoken dialect, or to create a synthetic one on sound linguistic principles' (p. 173). And he concludes regarding the three plays with which Dekker is associated and which contain Welsh characters: 'Only in *Patient Grissil* is there a use of the Welsh language beyond what any Londoner of the period might pick up on the streets' (p. 177).

If Dekker did not write the Welsh dialect scenes in *Patient Grissil*, then who did? Greene acknowledges that the lost works of Chettle might have exhibited fluency in dialect comparable with that on exhibit here; of that we can never know. But among extant works by the dramatists of *Patient Grissil*, there is Haughton's *Englishmen for my Money*, with its three speakers of dialect (an Italian, a Frenchman, and a Dutchman): their speeches, says Greene, 'suggest that their author, like Sir Owen's creator, was making a serious attempt to reproduce the broken English of actual national types' (p. 179). Greene attributes the scenes featuring Sir Owen and Gwenthyan to Haughton, and the attribution is as secure as such things can ever be. They are certainly not Dekker's, and nobody but Fleay has ever regarded them as Chettle's. The scenes featuring Julia and her suitors have always been regarded as Haughton's, so that his share of the play emerges with some clarity: II.i, III.ii, IV.iii, and the end of V.ii.

The most difficult authorial problem which the play poses is to

---

[1] 'Collaboration on *Patient Grissil*', *Philological Quarterly*, 18 (1939), 384.
[2] 'The Welsh Characters in *Patient Grissil*', *Boston University Studies in English* 4 (1960), 171–180.

distinguish Chettle's work from Dekker's. The problem might be less formidable if more of Chettle's work survived, or if what did survive shed more light on *Patient Grissil*.[1] It is hard to find many traces of the author of *The Tragedy of Hoffman* or of such non-dramatic pamphlets as *Kind-Heart's Dream* or *Piers Plainness' Seven Years' Prenticeship* or *England's Mourning Garment* in *Patient Grissil*. That being so, one is more or less reduced to giving what is clearly not Dekker's to Chettle, and Chettle does not suffer by the practice. The chief responsibility for the conduct of the main action seems to have been Chettle's. Both Dekker and Chettle worked on the Grissil story, Chettle's concern apparently being those sections of the plot dealing directly with Grissil and the Marquess, while Dekker was responsible for the scenes of Grissil with her family. This division inevitably involved some overlap in individual scenes where Grissil's affairs with the Marquess impinge upon her family. An example is I.ii, which Dekker begins with a 172-line scene depicting Janicola, Grissil and Babulo at their work of basket-making, and the return of Janicola's son, Laureo, forced to return home because he has no more money to continue at the university. But with the entrance of the Marquess and his train at 172.1, Dekker disappears, and his presence is not evident again until after the re-entrance of Babulo at 285.1. The intervening section of the scene, where the Marquess makes known his choice of Grissil as his bride, is presumably the work of Chettle. In III.i, Dekker dramatizes the expulsion from court of Janicola, Laureo and Babulo, and his share in the scene ends with the exit of Babulo at 119.1. Chettle handles the closing portion, an exchange between the Marquess and Grissil, and a somewhat longer passage between the Marquess and the courtiers Mario and Lepido. Then IV.ii opens with a scene that is clearly the work of Dekker: Janicola and Laureo, now back home, shortly joined by Babulo who has come upon Grissil and her children. Furio and the Marquess (disguised) enter at 108.1, and while Dekker is almost certainly present throughout the whole of the scene (Janicola, Laureo and

---

[1] The uncertainty concerning Chettle's share in the play is demonstrated in the assignment of I.i and II.ii; these are usually regarded as Chettle's, but such a recent scholar as George Price (p. 90) has assigned them to Dekker.

Babulo are on stage to the end), Chettle may have a hand in the speeches of Grissil and the Marquess in this latter section. The main lines of the authorial division then seem to be as follows:

I.i: Chettle
I.ii.1–172: Dekker
I.ii.173–285: Chettle
I.ii.286–337: Dekker
II.i: Haughton
II.ii: Chettle
III.i.1–119: Dekker
III.i.120–165: Chettle
III.ii: Haughton
IV.i: Chettle
IV.ii.1–108: Dekker
IV.ii.109–230: Dekker (and Chettle?)
IV.iii: Haughton
V.i: Dekker and Chettle
V.ii: Chettle and Haughton (and Dekker?)

The shares are reasonably clear-cut for most of the play, though it would be foolish to suppose that no one of the three dramatists ever contributed a touch to the work of one of his fellows. The last act, however, presents an example of dramatic collaboration of unusual closeness and harmony. Thus, V.i seems an exhibit of Chettle and Dekker's styles at their least distinguishable. The scene may be Chettle's, it may be Dekker's, it may be the work of both.[1] Dekker's presence in V.ii seems slight, but one hesitates to deny his presence there. Mainly, however, it seems to be Chettle and Haughton who conduct the play to its finale.

[1] See Jenkins, *Henry Chettle*, p. 177, concerning the changes that have overtaken the character of Babulo (elsewhere the creation of Dekker) in V.i:

'Yet Babulo here seems slightly different from the Babulo we have previously delighted in. The strain of the philosopher in him, without being deepened, is yet made more obvious to the cruder imagination. The characterisation is somewhat less subtle, and his speeches are not pervaded with the same deft touches of light but pregnant wit. Some of his delightful humour is recaptured, but he is in the main merely a partner in the dialogue.'

Reference is made in the Commentary to the work of the following editors of *Patient Grissil*: J. P. Collier (London, 1841); A. B. Grosart (in vol. v of his edition of Dekker's *Non-Dramatic Works* (London, 1886): Grosart included the play in this edition because it had been omitted from the Pearson reprint (1873) of Dekker's *Dramatic Works* and so – in 1886 – was 'not readily accessible'); G. Hübsch (Erlangen, 1893).

COMMENTARY

I.i

6 *wagoner. Romeo and Juliet*, III.ii.2; *S.D.*, V.i.110.

9 *gilt beames.* Cf. the verses headed 'Of Apollo' and attributed to Dekker in *Englands Parnassus* (Crawford, no. 1988):

> *Ioues* faire haird sonne, whose yellow tresses shine,
> Like curled flames; hurling a most diuine
> And dazeling splendour, in these lesser fires
> Which from thy guilt beames (when thy Car retires,)
> Kindle those Tapers that lend eyes to night. . .

The entire passage in *Englands Parnassus* consists of eighteen lines, of which all but two are repeated in Heywood's *Love's Mistress*, first printed in 1636. For the suggestion that Heywood found them in the now-lost play on Cupid and Psyche for which Chettle, Dekker and Day were paid in full by Henslowe on 14 May 1600, see Crawford's note, pp. 509–510. Cf. *P.G.*, III.i.132. *O.F.* III.i.363.

9 *Alchimy. W.K.*, III.i.188–189.

12 *sally.* For the relevance of this occurrence of the form to the 'sallied flesh' passage in the first and second quarto texts of *Hamlet*, I.ii.129, see F. T. Bowers, 'Hamlet's "Sullied" or "Solid" Flesh. A Bibliographical Case-History', *Shakespeare Survey*, 9 (1956), 44.

14 *hunting is a sport for Emperors.* Cf. George Gascoigne's verses 'in the commendation of the noble Arte of Venerie', prefixed to Turberville's *The Noble Arte of Venerie or Hunting* (1575):

> it is a *Noble sport,*
> *To recreate the mindes of Men, in good and godly sort.*
> *A sport for Noble peeres, a sport for gentle bloods,*
> The paine I leaue for servants such, as beate the bushie woods,
> To make their masters sport. . .
> *Hunting was ordeyned first, for Men of Noble kinde.*

16 *a contracted brow.* M.M.L., IV.iv.57–58. And cf. P.G., II.ii.95–96.

17 *Bias,* inclination, course (metaphor from the game of bowls). O.F., IV.i.42, n.

49 *though our tongues speake no, our hearts sound yea.* Cf. the proverbs, 'A Woman says nay and means aye' (Tilley, W660), and 'A Woman's heart and her tongue are not relatives' (Tilley, W672). S.H., III.iv.46–47.

I.ii

1–2 *tooth and naile.* Tilley, T422. S.H.R., DIV: '*Pride* got still before him, and he followed her at an ench like a mad-man, tooth and nayle.' The phrase occurs in Chettle's *Hoffman* (M.S.R. (1951), prepared by H. Jenkins), line 1153: 'stand to it tooth and nayle'. *Sat.*, V.ii.320.

2–3 *plaid boe peep.* Porter, *The Two Angry Women of Abingdon* (M.S.R.), lines 1950–1951: 'Nay then all hid, I faith she shall not see me, / Ile play bo peepe with her behind this tree.' And cf. *Sat.*, V.ii.153–154: 'our vnhansome-fac'd Poet does play at bo-peepes with your Grace, and cryes all-hidde as boyes doe'. Cf. P.G., IV.iii.249.

5 *don is the mouse.* W.H., V.iv.3, n.

7 *snug.* Cf. Dekker (and Middleton?), *Blurt, Master-Constable,* IV.iii.23: 'I will snug close; out goes my candle's eye.'

15–16 *I thinke I shall not eate a pecke of salt: I shall not liue long sure.* Cf. the proverb, 'Every Man must eat a peck of dirt (ashes, salt) before he dies' (Tilley, M135).

48 *russets.* J.M.M., F2: 'vpon the market daies these two come to towne, she attired like a comely country woman in cleanly white linnen with a mufler on her face, and in russet clothes outward signes of the countries honest simplicity'.

60 *shipwracke.* L.D., III.ii.74.

61–62 *tailors to take measure | Of Grissils bodie. W.E.*, V.iii.114–115.

65 *sins blacke face. L.D.*, II.ii.89–90.

71 *soule...black...speckled sinne. O.F.*, V.i.60; *N.S.S.*, V.iv.64.

72 *vnderling. L.D.*, I.ii.230, n. And *P.G.*, IV.ii.143.

80 *by hooke or by crooke*, i.e. by any means, fair or foul. 'The phrase derives its origin from the custom of certain manors, where tenants were allowed to take fire-bote "by hook or by crook", that is, so much of the underwood as could be cut by a crook, and as much loose timber as could be pulled from the trees by a hook.' (E. H. Blakeney on *The Faerie Queene*, V.ii.27, Spenser Variorum, V, 174–175). Tilley, H588. *M.G.*, p. 128.

88 *tread their shooes a wrie*. The phrase is often applied to erring wives. Cf. *W.Y.*, p. 47: 'An honest Cobler...had a wife, who in the time of health treading her shooe often awry, determined in the agony of a sicknesse...to fall to mending'; and *W.A.*, F3v:

> There was one little dwarfish Cobler...who tooke bread and salt, and praid God it might be his last, if he ran not ouer all the fine dames that withstoode him, in blacke reuenge that hee neuer had their custome in his shop, because it could neuer be found out or seene, that any of them did euer treade her shooe awry.

Blurt, Master-Constable, III.iii.149–151: 'Let these be the rules to square out your life by, though you ne'er go level, but tread you[r] shoes awry.' Tilley, S373. Cf. *M.M.L.*, IV.iv.16–17; *V.M.*, III.iii.35.

93 *golden Slumbers. B.H.*, 137. And *P.G.*, IV.ii.99.

94 *sweet content*. Perhaps suggested, as Harold Jenkins has remarked (*Henry Chettle*, p. 163), by the ballad 'Of Patient Grissel and a Noble Marquesse', line 14 (concerning Grissel's bower): 'where loue & vertue liues with sweet content' (Deloney, p. 346).

104 *Crisped*, closely curled. The phrase occurs again at IV.ii.80. For its application to water, cf. Shakespeare, *1 Henry IV*, I.iii.106, where the river Severn is said to have 'hid his crisp head in the hollow bank'; Jonson, *The Vision of Delight*, 186–187: 'The Rivers runne as smoothed by his hand; | Onely

their heads are crisped by his stroke'; and Milton, *Paradise Lost*, IV, 237: 'crisped Brooks'. Cf. *M.E.*, 1153: 'crisped forlocks'.

120 *Muses...the seauen deadly sins.* Cf. the similar confusion regarding the seven liberal sciences in *N.G.*, p. 68: 'into such pitifull predicaments are they fallen, that most of our Gentry ...takes them for the Seauen Deadly Sinnes, and hate them worse than they hate whores'.

122 *muses...beggers.* The condition of beggary to which the muses are reduced is a principal theme of 'The Epistle Dedicatory' to *N.G.* Cf. p. 69:

> Let them be sent into the courts of Princes, there they are so lordly, that...euery one lookes ouer them, or if they giue them any thing, it's nothing but good lookes. As for the Citie, thats so full of Crafts-men, there is no dealing with their misteries: the nine *Muses* stand in a brown study, when they come within their liberties...And for those (whom in English we call poore snakes) Alas! they are barde (by the Statute against Beggers) from giuing a dandiprat or a *Bawbee*.

127 *poore Iohn*, dried and salted hake, often referred to as a type of poor food. *W.W.W.*, D2v: 'But, when *Pay* slackes; and *health* with *Victuals* gon, / *Souldiers* being forc'd to liue on dry poore *Iohn*'. *S.T.W.*, IV.ii.53.

128-129 *a Cue of breade*, literally, a half-farthing worth of bread. Cf. Minsheu, *Ductor in Linguas* (1617): 'Cue, halfe a farthing, so called because they set down in the Battling or Butterie Bookes in Oxford and Cambridge the letter q. for halfe a farthing' (quoted by Leishman (ed.), *The Three Parnassus Plays*, where Luxurio thus takes leave of academic life in *1 Return*, 420–423: 'Adew single beare and three qus of breade, if I conuerse with you anie longer, some Sexton must toll the bell for the Death of my witt').

136 *deuill...angell of golde.* A familiar pun, based on the two senses of angel: (1) the spiritual being, and (2) the gold coin (the noble) stamped with the image of St Michael killing the dragon. Cf. Webster, *The Duchess of Malfi*, I.i.285–286: 'Take your Divels / Which Hell calls Angels.' The pun recurs in *V.D.*, I2: 'Euery *Angell* of gold that flyes into thy Coffers

with such stollen wings, will be turned into a Diuell, and stand
round about thy death-bed to torment thee.'

262 *conferre*, compare (Halliwell).

270–280 *Ile gild that pouertie. . .a beggers name.* With this passage
wherein the Marquess justifies his choice of Grissil and his
nobles voice their resentment at it, compare the Ballad 'Of
Patient Grissel and a Noble Marquesse', lines 33–50 (Deloney,
p. 347):

And when that she was trimly tired in the same ['silke & Veluet']
    her beauty shined most bright:
Far staining euery other braue & comely Dame
    that did appeare in her sight,
Many enuied her therefore,
Because she was of parents poore,
    and twixt her Lord & she great strife did raise:
Some saide this and some said that,
Some did call her beggars brat,
    and to her Lord they would her oft dispraise.
O, noble Marques (qd. they) why do you wrong vs
    thus basely for to wed:
That might haue gotten an honourable Lady
    into your Princely bed:
Who will not now your noble issue still deride
    which shall be hereafter borne,
That are of bloud so base by their mothers side,
    the which will bring them to scorn:

275 *distaine*, defile. Shakespeare, *The Rape of Lucrece*, 786.

281–282 *a squint. . .purblind.* Cf. *L.D.*, II.ii.33: 'Squint purblind
glances'.

286 *sirha. 1 H. W.*, II.i.198, n.

299 *scillicet*, i.e. scilicet, namely. *N.G.*, p. 70: 'made an Encomiasti-
call Oration in praise of *Nobody*, (*scilicet* your proper selfe)'.

322 *cogging*, cheating, deceiving. *O.F.*, IV.i.42.

323 *giue her the belles, let her flye. N.H.*, IV.ii.23–24, n.

II.i

2 *teeth water. 2 H. W.*, IV.ii.12.

8–9 *court of Conscience*, 'conscience as a moral tribunal' (*O.E.D.*,
*sb.*¹ 11.c, citing this example). The phrase was derived from

the mediaeval conception of the Chancellor as the keeper of
the King's conscience and of the Court of Chancery as a Court
of Conscience, correcting the injustices perpetrated by the
Common Law in particular cases. Cf. *I.T.B.N.*, II.ii.131.

20 *spangled babie. Sat.*, II.ii.34.

20–23 *come into a Stationers shop...tongue.* Like Clove in Jonson's
Every Man out of his Humour, III.i.29–31: 'he will sit you a
whole afternoone sometimes, in a booke-sellers shop, reading
the *Greeke, Italian,* and *Spanish*; when he vnderstands not
a word of either'. So too the Page of his master (Amoretto)
in *The Return from Parnassus*, Part Two (ed. Leishman,
1277–1290):

> Why, presently this great linguist my master will march through Paules
> Church-yard, come to a booke binders shop, and with a big Italian
> looke and a Spanish face aske for these bookes in Spanish
> and Italian; then turning, through his ignorance, the wrong end of the
> booke vpward, vse action on this vnknowne tong after this sort: first
> looke on the title and wrinckle his browe; next make as though he red
> the first page and bite the lippe; then with his nayle score the margent,
> as though there were some notable conceit; and lastly, when he thinkes
> hee hath gulld the standers by sufficiently, throwe the booke away in
> a rage, swearing that hee could neuer finde bookes of a true printe
> since he was last in Padua, enquire after the next marte, and so
> departe.

24 *its greeke to him.* Tilley, G439.

27 *neuer be saued by his book*, because unable to read the 'neck-
verse' and so escape hanging by pleading benefit of clergy.
Cf. *Sat.*, I.ii.117, n.

31–32 *house keeping you know is out of fashion.* A common complaint; cf. Jonson, *Every Man out of his Humour*, I.ii.37–42:
'First (to be an accomplisht gentleman, that is, a gentleman of
the time) you must giue o're house-keeping in the countrey,
and liue altogether in the city amongst gallants; where, at your
first apparance, 'twere good you turn'd foure or fiue hundred
acres of your best land into two or three trunks of apparel.'
And cf. Hall, *Virgidemiarum*, V.ii (ed. Davenport), beginning
'Housekeeping's dead, *Saturio*', with the editor's notes on
lines 1ff. (pp. 238–239) and 67ff. (pp. 242–243). In *W.A.*,

Parsimonie in an oration to the Empress Money advises her to 'giue ouer your needlesse expences and open housekeeping in the Country,...and betake yourself to the close safetie of the Cittie' (E1–E1v). Cf. *P.G.*, III.i.109–110.

32 *kisse the post*, be shut out. Heywood, *A Woman Killed with Kindness*, viii.161–162: 'my good host, / When he comes late home, he must kiss the post'. *N.F.H.*, G4v: 'looking as hungrily, as if he had kist the post'. And *P.G.*, IV.iii.246. Tilley, P494.

32–33 *in a worde. L.D.*, II.iii.15. And *P.G.*, II.ii.16.

40 *long coate*, the usual dress of an idiot, or fool. Nashe, *Have With You*, III, 17: 'fooles, ye know, alwaies for the most part (especiallie if they bee natural fooles) are suted in long coates'. Marston, in *The Scourge of Villanie*, XI, 174, refers to 'The long fooles coat'. *R.G.*, II.ii.74.

43 *guarde*, with a quibble on the ornamental trimming of the fool's long coat. Cf. *Henry VIII*, prologue, 15–16: 'a fellow / In a long motley coat guarded with yellow'. Beaumont and Fletcher, *The Noble Gentleman*, V.i.93–94 (of the Duke, who has been acting foolishly): 'According to his merits he should weare, / A guarded coate, and a great wooden dagger.' *2 H.W.*, V.ii.313.

44 *set...vpon thy skirts. W.H.*, IV.ii.211, n.

47 *yonker. S.H.*, V.v.19, n.

47 *right Trinidado*, the best kind of tobacco. Cf. Bobadill in *Every Man in his Humour*, III.v.72–88:

'Tis your right *Trinidado*! did you neuer take any, master Stephen?
Step. No truely sir; but I'le learne to take it now, since you commend it, so.
Bob. Sir, beleeue me (vpon my relation) for what I tell you, the world shal not reproue. I have been in the *Indies* (where this herb growes) where neither my selfe, nor a dozen gentlemen more...haue receiued the tast of any other nutriment, in the world, for the space of one and twentie weekes, but the fume of this simple onely. Therefore, it cannot be, but 'tis most diuine! Further, take it in the nature, in the true kind so, it makes an *antidote*, that (had you taken the most deadly poysonous plant in all *Italy*) it should expell it, and clarifie

you, with as much ease, as I speake. And, for your greene wound,
your *Balsamum*, and your St. Iohn's *woort* are all mere gulleries, and
trash to it, especially your *Trinidado.*

52–53 *leaden...braines. I.T.B.N.*, II.i.199.
54 *changeable Silke. N.F.H.*, D4: 'Religion goes all in changeable
silkes, and weares as many maskes as she do's colours.'
58 *complement.* For its use, cf. Chapman, *An Humourous Day's
Mirth*, II.30–32: 'there is no better sport than to obserue the
compliment, for that's their word, compliment – do you
mark, sir?' Marston, *Jack Drum's Entertainment*, Act III (ed.
Wood, p. 209)

> *Bra. Ju.* What shall we observe you for?
> *Bra. Sig.* Oh for our complement.
> *Pla.* Complement, whats that?
> *Bra. Sig.* Complement, is as much as (what call you it) tis derived of
> the Greeke worde, a pox ont.

And Planet later, after having witnessed Brabant Senior's
encounter with Puffe: 'By the Lord fustian, now I understand
it: complement is as much as fustian.' And cf. Jonson,
Discoveries, lines 2274–2277: 'You are not to cast a Ring for
the perfumed termes of the time, as *Accomodation, Complement,
Spirit, &c.* But use them properly in their place, as others.'
58 *Fastidious.* Fastidious Briske in Jonson's *Every Man out of his
Humour* is much given to such affected words.
58–59 *Caprichious.* The word was apparently introduced into
English by Gabriel Harvey who, in *Pierces Supererogation*
(1593), labelled Nashe 'Signior Capricio' (*The Works of
Gabriel Harvey*, ed. A. B. Grosart (3 vols., London, 1884–
1885), II, 109), denoting 'a fantastic person'. See H. C. Hart,
'Ben Jonson and Gabriel Harvey', *Notes and Queries*, 9th
series, 12 (1903), 161–162, where numerous occurrences of
the word in Harvey's works are given. It soon caught on. Cf.
Jonson, *The Case is Altered*, II.vii.63–79, where Valentine
distinguishes between 'two sorts of persons that most commonly are infectious to a whole auditory'. One 'is the rude
barbarous crue', the other 'a few *Caprichious* gallants'.

Iunip. Caprichious? stay, that word's for me.
Valen. And they haue taken such a habit of dislike in all things, that
they will approue nothing, be it neuer so conceited or elaborate, but
sit disperst, making faces, and spitting, wagging their vpright eares,
and cry filthy, filthy.

Guilpin speaks of a 'Capritcious humor' in *Skialetheia* (1598),
B8v; and Fastidious Briske uses the word in *Every Man out
of his Humour*, II.i.119: 'Nay, thou art so capriciously conceited now.' And cf. *Cynthia's Revels*, II.i.7–10: 'act freely,
carelessly, and capriciously, as if our veines ranne with quicksiluer, and not vtter a phrase, but what shall come forth
steept in the verie brine of conceipt, and sparkle like salt in
fire'. But the word quickly became commonplace; Chapman's
gentleman usher is using it by *c.* 1602 (*The Gentleman Usher*,
V.i.16–17: 'What, a plague! / Shall a man fear capriches?').
And cf. Dekker's reference, in *S.H.R.*, D1v, to 'a terse, spruise,
neatified Capricious *Taylor*'.

59 *Misprizian*, misunderstanding. Moria, one of the affected court
ladies, uses the word in *Cynthia's Revels*, IV.iv.31–32: 'I must
confesse, shee is apt to misprision.'

59 *Sintheresis.* Clove uses the word while talking fustian with
Orange in *Every Man out of his Humour*, III.iv.21–22 ('Now,
sir, whereas the *Ingenuitie* of the time, and the soules *Synderisis*
are but *Embrions* in nature') where it seems to function as
part of a parody of Marston's vocabulary. The word occurs
twice in *The Scourge of Villanie*, at VIII, 211 ('Returne, returne,
sacred *Synderesis*'), and XI, 236–238 ('So cold and dead
is his *Synderisis*, / That shadowes by odde chaunce somtimes
are got, / But ô the substance is respected not'). *P.G.*, III.ii.
56.

67 *to spit well.* Cf. the address to Tobacco in *G.H.*, B3: 'After thy
pipe, shal ten thousands be taught to daunce, if thou wilt but
discouer to me the sweetnesse of thy snuffes, with the manner
of spawling, slauering, spetting and driueling in all places,
and before all persons.' *W.H.*, V.i.194–195: 'peace I heare
them spitting after their Tobacco'.

74 *so they can crie wighee.* In allusion to the proverb 'It is an ill

Horse that can neither whinny nor wag his tail' (Tilley, H671). Cf. *W.K.*, I.i.47–48, n.

78–79 *daunce a morrice…hung with belles. L.C.*, H2: 'the men weare scarfes of Callico, or any other base stuffe, hanging their bodies like Morris-dancers, with bels, & other toyes, to intice the countrey people to flocke about them, and to wounder at their fooleries or rather rancke knaueryes'. *R.G.*, I.ii.222–223; *W. of E.*, II.i.38.

82 *out a crie. S.H.*, I.ii.25, n.

89 *By Cods vdge me*, God judge me. So Dav Jenkin in Jonson's *For the Honour of Wales*, 22: 'by got 'utch me'. *N.H.*, IV.i.42.

91 *shentleman. N.H.*, V.i.474, n.

96 *gallimaufrie*, a dish made by hashing up odds and ends of food; a ridiculous medley. As applied to language, cf. Nashe, *Have With You*, III, 42: 'hauing…musterd together, in one galimafrie or short Oration, most of the ridiculous senseles sentences, finicall flaunting phrases, and termagant inkhorne tearmes throughout his Booke'. Chettle, *Kind-Hartes Dreame* (ed. G. B. Harrison (London, 1923)), p. 32: 'hee put me downe with such a galliemafrey of latine ends, that I was glad to make an end'. And *W.H.*, II.i.24–25: 'lattin whole-meates are now minc'd, and serude in for English Gallimafries'. Cf. *S.H.*, I.iv.64.

102–103 *Caprichious…misprize.* Cf. lines 58–59.

114 *Diogenicall*, churlish. Nashe, *Christs Teares*, II, 109: 'Diogenicall and dogged'. See *Sat.*, I.ii.290, n.

119 *out Athlassed.* Nashe, *Christs Teares*, II, 117: 'ouer-Atlassing myne inuention'. *S.D.*, IV.i.52–54:

> lay
> A bountie of more sovereigntie and amazement,
> Then the Atlas of mortalitie can support.

133 *shenglier*, presumably 'gainlier' (handsomer).

136–137 *spanish leather*, the expensive Cordovan. Cf. Marston, *Scourge of Villanie*, XI, 157–161:

> What strange disguise, what new deformed shape
> Doth hold thy thoughts in contemplation?
> Faith say, what fashion art thou thinking on?

A stitch'd Taffata cloake, a payre of slops
Of Spanish leather?

And Davenport's note (p. 366) suggesting that Marston 'is probably thinking of the wide thigh-boots with elaborately decorated turned-down tops, made of Cordovan leather, and fashionable at this time'. Cf. T.M., *The Ant and the Nightingale, or Father Hubburds Tales* (1604), of a lavishly dressed gallant:

casting mine eyes lower, I beheld a curious pair of boots of king Philip's leather, in such artificial wrinkles, sets, and plaits, as if they had been starched lately and came new from the laundress's, such was my ignorance and simple acquaintance with the fashion... But that which struck us most into admiration, upon those fantastical boots stood such huge and wide tops, which so swallowed up his thighs, that had he sworn, as other gallants did, this common oath, Would I might sink as I stand! all his body might very well have sunk down and been damned in his boots (Middleton's *Works*, ed. Bullen, VIII, 70–71).

G.H., C3v: 'Or if thy quicksiluer can runne so farre on thy errant as to fetch thee [Q three] bootes out of S. Martens, let it be thy prudence to haue the tops of them wide as ye mouth of a wallet, and those with fringed boote-hose ouer them to hang down to thy ankles.' The term is synonymous with affectations of dress. Cf. Haughton, *Englishmen for my Money* (M.S.R.), line 1887: 'That   *Spanish*-leather spruce companion'. *Blurt, Master-Constable*, III.iii.30: 'Spannish-leather learning'. *1 H.W.*, I.ii.33, n.

138 *proiects*. Cf. line 58.

139 *bias*, course. *P.G.*, I.i.17.

140 *complement*. Cf. line 58.

147 *dahoma*, i.e. *dewch yma*, Welsh for 'come hither'.

153 *obloquie*. Marston, *Antonio's Revenge*, IV.i.215–216: 'revenge / Upon the author of thy obloquies'.

155 *so ho*. *O.F.*, I.i.1, n. And *P.G.*, IV.ii.22–23.

158 *Fastidious*. Cf. line 58.

165–168. *Belly the ruddo whee: wrage witho, Manda gen y Mon du ac whelloch en wea awh. / Sir Owen gramarcye whee: Gwenthyan Manda gen y, ac welloch en Thlawen en ryn mogh*, i.e. *Ble 'roeddech chwi, wraig weddw?; mae'n dda gen i, myn Duw, eich gweld chwi yn wir iawn,* Welsh for 'Where were you, widow woman?; I'm glad, by God, to see you indeed', and *Syr Owen,* gramercy *i chwi: Gwenllïan, mae'n dda gen i (genni hi) eich gweld yn llawen yr un modd,* 'Sir Owen, many thanks to you: Gwenllïan, I'm glad (she's glad) to see you content in the same way.'

173 *Welshe tongue is finer as greeke tongue.* Cf. *1 H.W.,* I.iii.88: 'Ile speake Welch, which is harder then Greek.' And on the score of the language in general, cf. Drayton, *Englands Heroicall Epistles,* 'Queene Katherine to Owen Tudor', 125–130:

> The *British* Language, which our Vowels wants,
> And jarres so much upon harsh Consonants,
> Comes with such grace from thy mellifluous Tongue,
> As doe the sweet Notes of a well-set Song,
> And runs as smoothly from those Lips of thine,
> As the pure *Tuskan* from the *Florentine*

In *L.C.,* B2, Dekker speaks of 'the Voluble significant *Welch*' language. Cf. *W.E.,* III.ii.117–118.

174 *Neates tongue.* For the quibble, cf. *W.H.,* II.i.25–27: 'Let vs therefore cut out our vplandish Neates tongues, and talk like regenerate Brittains.' And *N.H.,* II.i.200–201: 'teach mee to speake some welch, mee thinkes a Welchmans tongue is the neatest tongue!'

180–181 *King Tauie... Sir Owens countrieman.* Sir Owen's conflation of the biblical King David with Saint David (*c.* 520–*c.* 600) patron saint of Wales.

183 *welsh-harpe.* *N.H.,* II.i.222–223, n.

184 *Persabe,* i.e. Bersabe, Bathsheba.

186 *tall,* valiant. *W.H.,* III.ii.55.

189 *pribles & prables,* petty disputes, quarrels. *The Merry Wives of Windsor,* I.i.54–55: 'It were a goot motion if we leave our pribbles and prabbles.'

193 *pundall.* Possibly a corruption of 'punctual', as J. P. Collier suggested in his edition of the play, p. 93. If it is Welsh, it could possibly be an attempt to render *bodlon,* 'willing'.

203 *diggon,* enough. *N.H.* II.i.222, n.

206–207 *wag to the coward,* move on to the coward, the coward being Emulo (cf. line 34). Sir Owen and Gwenthyan will proceed on to him now so that, presumably, Sir Owen can exult in Emulo's recent humiliation in the matter of the laths and the boots, and in Emulo's defeat as a rival for the hand of Gwenthyan. For 'wag' meaning 'go, depart, be off', cf. *The Merry Wives of Windsor,* I.iii.5–6: 'let them wag; trot, trot'.

213–214 *Vn loddis Glan e Gwenthyan mondu. | Gramercie wheeh, Am a Mock honnoh,* i.e. '*Yn lodes lân i, Gwenllïan, myn Duw,* Welsh for 'My fair lass, Gwenllïan, by God', and Gramercy *i chwi am 'y moddhau ('y mharchu) ohonoch,* 'Many thanks to you for pleasing me (respecting me).'

216 *Io...hey ho,* i.e. from an exclamation of joy to one of weary disappointment.

217–218 *fire made of bay leaues...noise. V.M.,* II.ii.31–33, n.

219–220 *crowne...crackking...passe currant.* Coins were stamped with a ring inside which the sovereign's head was placed. If a coin contained a crack extending inside the ring, it was unfit for currency; thus the basis for a familiar quibble. Shakespeare, *1 Henry IV,* II.iii.93–94: 'We must have bloody noses and crack'd crowns, / And pass them current too.' *N.G.,* p. 76: 'Patient they were..., for they would pocket vp any thing, came it neuer so wrongfully, insomuch that very good substantiall householders haue oftentimes gone away with crackt crownes, & neuer complained of them that gaue them. If euer mony were current...now was the time.' Cf. *1 H.W.,* III.i.26; *W.H.,* II.i.176–179; *S.T.W.,* IV.i.9. On the practice of soldering, cf. Lodge, *Wits Miserie* (1599), E2v, where the demon of Usury buys up 'crackt angels at nine shillings the piece' and makes bargains with them, while the borrower 'ventures on the crackt angels, some of which can not flie for soldering'.

257 *leade apes in hell. The London Prodigal* (ed. Brooke), I.ii.28–29: 'But tis an old prouerbe, and you know it well, / That women dying maides lead apes in hell.' Haughton, *Englishmen for my Money,* line 1310: 'I may lead Apes in Hell, and die a Mayde.'

Sat., I.i.39; II.i.140. The phrase occurs again in the present play at V.ii.282. Tilley, M37.

259–260 *hell...barlibreake. 1 H.W.*, V.ii.317–318, n.

261–262 *wedlocke, your Iacke an Apes clog.* Cf. Jonson, *Poetaster*, IV.ii.54–57: 'could they not possibly leaue out my husband? me thinkes, a bodies husband do's not so well at Court: A bodies friend, or so – but husband, 'tis like your clog to your *marmaset*'. Cf. the proverb 'Can Jacknapes (an ape) be merry when his clog is at his heel?' (Tilley, J10).

263–264 *virginitie...turns vs into Angells.* Cf. the proverb 'Virgins are angel-like creatures' (Tilley, V69, where the earliest example is from 1616).

266 *in heauen are no weddings.* Matthew 22: 30; Mark 12: 25.

276 *as some Indians doe the Sunne, adore it. L.D.*, III.ii.245: 'heavens great Star, which Indians do adore'.

292–294 *time...a bald friend. G.H.*, C2v: 'Truth (because the bald-pate her father *Time*, has no haire to couer his head) goes (when she goes best) starke naked.' *W.A.*, B2v: 'the backe of Time...was bare and made bald by mens abusing it'. Cf. *1 H.W.*, V.ii.71, n.

II.ii

22 *A wrinckled forehead. D.D.*, C3: '*Iustice* and *Wrath* in wrinckles knit his forhead.' *W.Y.*, p. 11: 'The Element...scowled on the earth, and filling her hie forehead full of blacke wrinckles ...at length she...was deliuered of a pale, meagre, weake childe, named *Sicknesse*.' *W.H.*, I.ii.118–119; *M.M.L.*, III.ii.93–94; IV.v.18–19.

22–23 *both...eyes...balles of fire. L.D.*, I.i.73–74.

50–52 *poyson...infected...Exhald...Sunne.* Cf. *The Death of Robert Earle of Huntingdon* (M.S.R. (1967, for 1965), prepared by J. C. Meagher), lines 2728–2732 (the sun is being addressed):

> Then surfet with thy exhalations speedily:
> For all earths venemous infecting wormes
> Haue belcht their seuerall poysons on the fields,
> Mixing their simples in thy compound draught.
> Well *Phoebus* well, drinke on.

54 *screech-owle.* *L.D.*, I.ii.1.

92 *Grissills bones,* with a quibble on gristle.

96 *Contract...forehead.* Cf. I.i.16.

122 *High Cedars...lowe shrubs safe remaine.* *1 H.W.*, IV.i.109, n.

129–130 *eyes | Looke red with hate or scorne.* *2 Henry VI*, III.i.154: 'Beaufort's red sparkling eyes blab his heart's malice.' *V.M.*, III.ii.68, n.

159 *beggers brat.* Jenkins (*Henry Chettle*, p. 163) has suggested that the phrase may have been borrowed from the Ballad 'Of patient Grissel', where it occurs in a passage (quoted in the note on I.ii.270–280, above) describing the resentment Grissel occasions among the nobles at the Marquess' court. Jenkins' statement that the phrase when used in Phillip's comedy (line 911) refers to Grissel's children, and not to the heroine, is wrong. At that point in Phillip's play, her children are not yet born. The phrase is used of Grissel at line 911 and again at line 923.

III.i

5–6 *necessary member...wicked members.* Cf. Nashe, *Have With You*, III, 106, of an intelligencer: 'a necessary member in a State to bee vsde to cut off vnnecessarie members'. *W.H.*, II.i.59–60.

14 *in decimo sexto.* A metaphor from the book in which the size of a page is a sixteenth of a sheet. It is frequently used to mean small; cf. Lyly, *Mother Bombie*, II.i.44–46: 'looke where *Halfepenie, Sperantus* boy, cometh; though bound vp in *decimo sexto* for carriage, yet a wit in *folio* for coosnage'. *W.Y.*, p. 20: 'like *Stowes* Chronicle in *Decimo sexto* to huge Hollinshead'.

29 *a cloke for the raine.* *W.H.*, V.iv.262, n.

32 *ship of fooles,* the title of Alexander Barclay's translation (1509) of Sebastian Brandt's *Narrenschiff* (1494). Dekker alludes to it elsewhere in *N.G.*, p. 70; *G.H.*, B2; *S.H.R.*, D2; *W.B.*, II.i.89.

32 *hoyst sayle.* *R.G.*, IV.i.116, n.

50 *when?* An exclamation of impatience. *Sat.*, I.ii.373, n.

67 *Little said is soone amended.* Tilley, L358.

108 *hit vs ith teeth. Sat.*, I.ii.188, n.
109–110 *giue ouer houskeeping, tis the fashion.* II.i.31–32, n.
119 *Stultorum plena sunt omnia.* Cicero, *Ad Familiares*, IX.22.4.
     The quotation also appears on the titlepage of *G.H.* It is
     a favorite tag. Marston places it at the head of Satire x of
     The Scourge of Villanie, p. 163, and quotes it in *The Malcontent*,
     V.iii.43. Tilley, W896.
132 *gilt beames.* I.i.9.
147 *beast...multitude. L.D.*, III.iv.22. And *P.G.*, V.ii.201–202.

III.ii

2 *purchase*, winning, acquisition.
8 *curuet.* For the application of the term to prancing courtiers, cf.
     Harvey, *The Trimming of Thomas Nashe*, III, 35: 'coruettest
     and shewest thy Crankes among a company of valorous famous
     captaines, whose stirrop thou art not worthy to hold'. Marston,
     The Scourge of Villanie, XI, 99–103:

> Roome for *Torquatus*, that nere op'd his lip
> But in prate of *pummado reuersa*,
> Of the nimble tumbling *Angelica*.
> Now on my soule, his very intelect
> Is naught but a curuetting *Sommerset*.

     Cf. *V.M.*, II.i.11, n.
18 *sa, sa, sa. R.G.*, III.iii.155, n.
19–61 *Fleay*, I, 361, noted the similarity between the duel here
     described and the one reported by Fastidious Briske in Jonson's
     Every Man out of his Humour, IV.vi.66–122:

> *Fast.* Good faith, signior, (now you speake of a quarrell) I'le acquaint
> you with a difference, that happened betweene a gallant, and my
> selfe – sir Pvntarvolo, you know him if I should name him, signior
> Lvcvlento.
> *Pvnt.* Lvcvlento! what in-auspicious chance interpos'd it selfe to your
> two loues?
> *Fast.* Faith, sir, the same that sundred Agamemnon, and great Thetis
> sonne; but let the cause escape, sir: Hee sent mee a challenge (mixt
> with some few braues) which I restor'd, and in fine we met. Now
> indeed, sir, (I must tell you) he did offer at first very desperately, but
> without iudgement: for looke you, sir. I cast my selfe into this figure:

now he, comes violently on, and withall aduancing his rapier to
strike, I thought to haue tooke his arme (for he had left his whole
body to my election, and I was sure he could not recouer his guard)
Sir, I mist my purpose in his arme, rasht his doublet sleeue, ran him
close by the left cheek, and through his haire. He againe, lights me
here (I had on, a gold cable hatband, then new come vp, which I
wore about a murrey *French* hat I had) cuts my hatband (and yet
it was massie, gold-smithes worke) cuts my brimmes, which by
good fortune (being thicke embrodered with gold-twist, and
spangles) disappointed the force of the blow: Neuerthelesse, it
graz'd on my shoulder, takes me away six purles of an *Italian* cut-
worke band I wore (cost me three pound in the exchange, but three
daies before.)

Pvnt. This was a strange encounter!

Fast. Nay, you shall heare, sir: with this wee both fell out, and breath'd.
Now (vpon the second signe of his assault) I betooke me to the
former manner of my defence; he (on the other side) abandon'd his
body to the same danger, as before, and followes me still with
blowes: But I (being loth to take the deadly aduantage that lay before
mee of his left side) made a kind of *stramazoun*, ranne him vp to the
hilts, through the doublet, through the shirt, and yet mist the skin.
Hee (making a reuerse blow) falls vpon my emboss'd girdle (I had
throwne off the hangers a little before) strikes off a skirt of a thick-
lac't sattin doublet I had (lin'd with some foure taffataes) cuts off
two panes, embrodered with pearle, rends through the drawings out
of tissew, enters the linings, and skips the flesh.

Carl. I wonder he speakes not of his wrought shirt!

Fast. Here (in the opinion of mutuall dammage) wee paus'd: but
(ere I proceed) I must tell you, signior, that (in this last encounter)
not hauing leisure to put off my siluer spurres, one of the rowels
catcht hold of the ruffle of my boot, and (being *Spanish* leather, and
subiect to teare) ouerthrowes me, rends me two paire of silke stock-
ings (that I put on, being somewhat a raw morning, a peach colour
and another) and strikes me some halfe inch deepe into the side of
the calfe; Hee (seeing the bloud come) presently takes horse, and
away. I (hauing bound vp my wound with a peece of my wrought
shirt) –

Carl. O! comes it in there?

Fast. Rid after him, and (lighting at the court-gate, both together)
embrac'd, and marcht hand in hand vp into the presence: was not
this businesse well carried?

Every Man Out was acted in 1599; *P.G.* in the early months
of 1600. Herford and Simpson (IX, 369), while acknowledging

that Dekker and Chettle may have copied Jonson, also think
it possible (with Chambers, *Elizabethan Stage*, III, 292) 'that
there had been a courtiers' duel in which no damage was done
to anything but their clothes'.

27 *retorted*. Another of Emulo's fashionable words. Cf. Marston,
Antonio's Revenge, I.ii.85–86:

> *Matzagente*. I scorn to retort the obtuse jest of a fool.
> *Balurdo draws out his writing tables and writes.*
> *Balurdo*. 'Retort' and 'obtuse'; good words, very good words.

31 *a pure Toledo siluered*. Cf. Jonson, *Every Man in his Humour*,
II.iv.80–83:

> *Bray*...nay, 'tis a most pure *Toledo*.
> *Step*. I had rather it were a *Spaniard*! but tell me, what shall I giue you
> for it? An' it had a siluer hilt –

O.F., III.i.292.

43 *vapulating*, beating.

45 *cannon*, i.e. canion, 'ornamental rolls, laid like sausages round
the ends of the legs of breeches' (*O.E.D.*). *N.H.*, II.i.22, n.

49 *signe I* (   ), *this legge*. Professor Bowers thought 'The
round brackets apparently signify an indecent movement of
the legs, which Emulo makes ingenuously here' (I, 292). It
may be so. But empty brackets are found again at IV.ii.167
where no indecency seems to be implied. The text surrounding
the brackets in both passages seems corrupt, and I suspect that
in both cases the round brackets signify the printer's inability
to deal with indecipherable copy. Cf. *The Family of Love*,
I.iii.49, and Dyce's note (reprinted in Bullen's edition of
Middleton's *Works*, III, 24) suggesting that empty brackets
indicate the author has 'used some expression which the
printer was afraid to insert'.

49 *carnation silke stocking*. *1 H.W.*, III.ii.28–29.

50 *imprision*. A compositor's misreading of 'misprision'? Cf.
II.i.59.

51 *ingenious*. For the affected use of the word, cf. the account of
'*Signieur word-monger the Ape of* Eloquence' in Samuel
Rowlands, *The Knave of Clubbes* (1609), E3:

As on the way I *It[e]nerated,*
A *Rurall* person I *Obuiated,*
Interogating times *Transitation,*
And of the passage *Demonstration,*
My aprehension did *Ingenious-scan,*
That he was meerely a *Simplitian*

53   *vulnerated,* wounded.

56   *the Syntheresis of my soule.* II.i.59.

59   *&c.* A sign meaning that the player could go on speaking extemporaneously. It occurs frequently in the drama of the period. Cf. Greene, *Orlando Furioso* (ed. Collins), line 1133 (and the editor's note, I, 318); Marlowe, *Dr. Faustus* (ed. Greg), Quarto 1604, line 996 (and the editor's note, p. 359). To the examples cited there may be added Chapman, *May-Day,* IV.ii.80; Marston, *Histriomastix* (p. 282); Middleton, *The Family of Love,* II.iii.99; *Blurt, Master-Constable,* IV.iii.30; *W.H.,* IV.i.198; *W. of E.,* V.i.154. And *P.G.,* IV.ii.22, 23, 28.

74   *larded. W.E.,* II.i.16, n.

88   *Abram.* Used of an impostor, as in the canting phrase 'Abraham-man' meaning a rogue who disguised his body with counterfeit sores and feigned madness for purposes of begging. The phrase is particularly ironic as applied to the elaborately dressed Emulo, for Abraham-men are regularly described as going about half-naked, according to *O.P.,* M1, 'not for want of cloathes, but to stirre up men to pittie, and in that pittie to coozen their deuotion'.

90–91   *Italy . . . that nutriment, which I suckt from thee,* i.e. lies. Cf. *S.H.R.,* E3: 'After this hee trauelled into *Italy,* and there learned to embrace with one arme, and stabbe with another: to smile in your face, yet to wish a ponyard in your bosome: to protest, and yet lye: to sweare loue, yet hate mortally [Quarto 1613 reads 'mortality'].'

115   *scalde,* scurvy. *Sat.,* IV.i.103.

122   *wifes case.* 2 *H.W.,* IV.iii.76, n.

132   *smug,* trim, spruce. Haughton, *Englishmen for my Money* (M.S.R.), line 2263: 'Now afore God she is a sweete smugge Girle.' Lyly, *Midas,* IV.i.109–110: 'Dairie girles, / With faces

smug, and round as Pearles'. *Sat.*, III.i.131; *I.T.B.N.*, IV.ii.119; *2 H.W.*, III.ii.84.

181–182 *Terdawgh . . . Terdawgh whee*, i.e. *Dydd da iwch*, Welsh for 'Good day to you', and *Dydd da i chwi*, 'Good day to *you*.'

232 *Tawsone*, i.e. *Taw sôn*, Welsh for 'hold your tongue'. *S.H.*, I.i.161, n.

233–235 *O mon Iago, mon due . . . /Adologo whee Gwenthyan, bethogh en Thlonigh, er moyen due./Ne vetho en Thlonigh, Gna wathe gethla Tee*, i.e. *O myn Iago, myn Duw*, Welsh for 'O by [Saint] James, by God', and *Atolwg i chwi, Gwenllïan, byddwch yn llonydd er mwyn Duw*, 'Prithee, Gwenllïan, be quiet for God's sake', and *Ni fydda yn llonydd gwna waetha gelli di*, 'I shan't be quiet, do the worst thou canst.'

238 *plew coates*, i.e. servants, so termed from the blue coats in which they were characteristically dressed. *S.H.*, V.ii.67.

243 *Tannekin the Froe.* 'Tannekin' is a diminutive form of Anne, specifically used for a German or Dutch girl. 'Froe' is a Dutch woman (from Dutch *vrouw*). Marston, *The Dutch Courtesan*, I.i.140–142: 'a pretty, nimble-ey'd Dutch Tanakin; an honest soft-hearted impropriation; a soft, plump, round-cheek'd froe'. In *The London Prodigal* (ed. Brooke), IV.iii.8–9, Luce, who has entered 'like a Dutch Frow', announces, 'my name, forsooth, be called *Tanikin*'. For the use of the word as a term of abuse, cf. *S.H.*, II.iii.59. For 'froe', cf. *M.E.*, 588; *W.H.*, V.i.166; *B.H.*, 261.

243 *Rebato. Sat.*, I.i.48, n.

261 *prade your neaces*, break your necks? But earlier in the line, 'prade' means 'prate', as in Gwenthyan's line at IV.iii.7.

269 *ile haue her willes.* Cf. II.i.194. The subtitle of Haughton's *Englishmen for my Money* is 'A Woman will haue her Will' (Quarto 1616, titlepage). The phrase is often repeated in the text of that play, e.g. lines 372–373, 1389, 2181, 2229, 2239, 2673. Tilley, W723.

270–272 *Catho crogge, Ne vetho, en Thlonigh gna wathee Gethla tee./ A breath vawer or no Tee*, i.e. *Gato (Gad hi) (Cerdd i) grogi; ni fydda yn llonydd, gwna waetha gelli di*, Welsh for 'May she

(Let her) (Go thou) hang; I shan't be quiet, do the worst thou canst', and *Y frech fawr arnat ti*, 'The great pox on thee.'

IV.i

8–9 *A great Romaine Lord,/ Taught his young Sonne to ride a Hobby-horse.* Aelianus, *A registre of Hystories*, Book XII, contains an account 'Of certaine notable men, that made themselues playfellowes with children' which includes the following:

> *Agesilaus* riding vpon a reede, on cockhorse as they terme it, played with his sonne being but a boy: and when a certayne man passing by, sawe him so doe, and laughed therewithall, *Agesilaus* sayde thus. *Nunc tace, cum vero & ipse pater euaseris, tunc etiam patres imitaberis.* Now hold thy peace and say nothing: but when thou art a father, I doubt not, thou wilt doe as fathers should doe with their children. *Architas Tarentinus*, being both in authoritie in the common wealth, that is to say a magestrat, and also a Philosopher, not of the obscurest sorte, but a precise louer of wisdom: at what time he was a housband, a houskeeper, and mainteined many seruants, he was greatly delighted with their younglinges, vsed to play oftentimes with his seruauntes children, and was wonte when he was at dinner and supper, to reioyce in the sight and presence of them: yet was *Tarentinus* (as all men knowe) a man of famous memorie and noble name (trans. Abraham Fleming (1576), fols. 124v–125).

19 *curioust.* This unusual superlative form has been cited by Collins in comparison with Greene, *Alphonsus*, lines 1830–1831: 'no curioser Ile bee / Then doth become a maide of my degree'; and by McKerrow in illustration of Nashe, *Have With You*, III, 124: 'The victorioust Captaines and Warriours, the inuinciblest *Caesars* and Conquerours, the satyricallest confuters...he trowles vp.' Chettle uses comparable forms twice in *Piers Plainness* (ed. J. Winny in *The Descent of Euphues* (Cambridge, 1957)): 'the desperatest associates' (p. 127), and 'the excellentst I ever knewe' (p. 128). And cf. *Hoffman*, IV.ii. (M.S.R.), line 1873: 'miserablest men'.

61 *speckled shame.* Cf. I.ii.71: 'speckled sinne'; and II.ii.53: 'speckled infamie'.

75 *wrawle*, bawl. *W.E.*, IV.ii.78–79: 'wrawlinge bastards'.

124 *theis.* In the 1970 reprint of vol. 1, Bowers has unnecessarily
replaced Q 'this' with 'theis'. For the use of 'this' as a plural
demonstrative instead of 'these', cf. what may be Haughton's
Grim the Collier of Croydon, Act V (1662), p. 66: 'This two
hours', and Dekker's *I.T.B.N.,* V.i.88: 'this hot broiles'.

124 *Alablaster. W.E.,* V.i.148; *O.F.,* II.ii.363.

147 *melt...waxe.* Cf. *L.D.,* V.i.279–280.

IV.ii

12–14 *the earth may euen as well | Challenge the potter to be partiall, |
For forming it to sundry offices.* Cf. Romans 9: 20–21.

19 *mell,* 'to concern or busy oneself' (*O.E.D.*).

22 *whoop.* For this cry of excitement, cf. *Look About You* (M.S.R.
(1913), prepared by W. W. Greg), line 1754: 'whoop heer's
another Client'. Beaumont and Fletcher, *The Coxcomb,*
I.vi.109: 'Lead valiantly sweet Constable, whoop! ha Boyes!'
Haughton, *Englishmen for my Money,* 906: 'hee cride whoope
holly-day'. *S.H.,* IV.i.39; V.ii.195; *1 H.W.,* V.i.85; *V.M.,*
II.i.166.

22–23 *so ho ho. O.F.,* I.i.1, n.

23–25 *heere's sixteene pence a weeke, and sixteene pence a weeke,
eight groates, sope and candle.* Alluding to the weekly cost of
maintaining each child. A groat = 4d. Cf. 114–115: 'there's
foure groates, and heere's foure more'.

41 *Pope Innocent.* Cf. the pun occasioned by the little daughter of
Sir William Pope when King James I visited her father: 'A
female Pope, you'll say; a second Joan? / No, sure; she is
Pope Innocent, or none.' (Quoted by Mann, in Deloney's *Works,*
p. 537).

45 *a deare yeare,* a year of dearth. *W.B.,* I.ii.247, n.

46 *Iacke dawe. S.H.,* I.iv.84.

76 *russet gowne.* It is prominent in the Ballad 'Of patient Grissel
and a Noble Marquesse'. Upon her consent to marry him,
'Her country russet was chang'd to silke & veluet' (line 31),
and when she is sent back home:

> Her veluet gowne most patiently she slipt off,
> her kirtle of silke with the same:

> Her russet gowne was brought again with many a scoffe,
> to heare them all her selfe she did frame.   (Lines 131–134)

80 *crisped spring.* I.ii.104.

99 *Golden slumbers.* I.ii.93. What follows is the most famous lyric in the Dekker canon. Chappell, who seems not to have known of the song's appearance in *Patient Grissil*, referred to it as 'an old lullaby' and adapted the words of lines 99–102 to the tune of 'May Fair' (II, 587). Hence the designation ('Chappell. Tune *May Fair*.') which sometimes accompanies the song in collections that make no mention of Dekker or the present play (e.g. in John Hullah's *The Song Book* (London, 1866), p. 99). The words continue to be heard. In the late 1960s, the Beatles introduced them into their *Abbey Road*.

110 *alla mire,* i.e. alamire, the lowest tone but one in Guido d'Arezzo's scale (*O.E.D.*), thus continuing the musical idiom from earlier in the line. 'Fa' and 'sol' are, respectively, the names of the fourth and fifth notes of d'Arezzo's hexachords.

111 *and he we waile in woe.* A punctuation problem; Grosart places a comma after 'we' (v, 193).

111 *waile in woe.* A quotation from *A woefull ballade made by master George Mannyngton an houre before he suffered at Cambridge castell,* beginning 'I waile in wo, I plunge in pain.' It was entered in the Stationers' Register on 7 November 1576, and printed in Clement Robinson's *A Handefull of pleasant delites* (1584) (ed. Hyder E. Rollins (Harvard University Press, 1924), p. 65). Another version is printed in Joseph Ritson, *Ancient Songs and Ballads,* ed. W. C. Hazlitt (London, 1877), pp. 188–191. Quicksilver sings an imitation of it from his prison cell in the last act of Jonson, Chapman, and Marston's *Eastward Ho.* The tune ('Labandale Shot') to which the ballad was sung is given in Simpson, p. 418. *S.H.*, II.iii.47.

114–115 *there's foure groates, and heere's foure more.* Cf. lines 23–24.

142 *must is for Kings.* Cf. *Sat.*, V.i.24.

143 *vnderlings.* I.ii.72.

147 *the little hop a my thombes.* Deloney, *The Gentle Craft,* Part Two (ed. Mann), p. 145: 'he is but a dwarfe in respect of a man, a shrimpe, a Wren, a hop of my thumbe'.

166 *cry prentises and clubs.* Greene, *A Disputation Between a Hee
Conny-catcher, and a Shee Conny-Catcher* (x, 215), of the
altercation that follows when a sheriff's officer tries to make
an arrest: 'another tooke the man and haled him away, the
Officer he stooke hard to him, and sayd hee was his true
prisoner, and cried Clubbes: the Prentises arose, and there
was a great hurly burly, for they tooke the Officers part'.
J.M.M., H1v–H2: 'the Citie had beene in an vprore, for you
might heare the clashing of swords, the hacking of bils, and
such a confused noise, as if all the Diuels in hell had fallen
together by ye eares. Some cald for more lights, others to put
out, some cryed clubs, others to strike him downe.' *S.H.*,
V.ii.28.

166–167 *the corporation cannot be (   ) sirra.* For the blank
parenthesis, cf. III.ii.49, n.

167 *pell mell.* 'Of combatants: Without keeping ranks; hence, at
close quarters, hand to hand' (*O.E.D.*). *R.A.*, C4v: 'to the
skirmish fall they pell mell'. *S.H.*, IV.i.3; *L.D.*, IV.ii.44; *W.E.*,
II.i.33; *N.S.S.*, II.i.89; *L.T.*, 78. And *P.G.*, IV.iii.35.

200 *golden baites. 1 Hieronimo* (ed. A. Cairncross, Lincoln, Nebr.,
1967), I.118–119: 'Him with a golden bait will I allure / (For
courtiers will do anything for gold).' The image is a favorite
with Dekker. Cf. *S.H.R.*, F1v: 'The swallowing of the baytes
was (to those Soules) a pleasure, and their skipping to and fro,
when they were whipped, made all Hell fall into a laughing.
One of those baytes was *Promotion*, the second was *Gold*.'
Cf. *W.B.*, III.i.229: 'bait hookes with gold' (a phrase which
occurs again in *W.K.*, I.ii.72); and *O.F.*, I.ii.51: 'poysned
baits, hung vpon golden hookes'. *Sat.*, I.ii.111.

203 *Rosa solis,* literally, rose of the sun; a cordial originally made
from, or flavoured with, the juice of the plant sundew; then
spirits, especially brandy, entered into its composition
(*O.E.D.*). *N.G.*, pp. 78–79: 'drinke off this draught of *Rosa
solis*, to fetch life into them againe, after their so often
swounding'. *I.T.B.N.*, V.iv.104.

219 *I smell a rat.* Tilley, R31.

221 *serues seauen yeares,* the length of an apprenticeship. Cf.

1 H.W., V.ii.171–172: 'Has serud a prentiship to this mis-
fortune, / Bin here seuen yeares'.

IV.iii

22 *Iacke-mumble-crust.* Cf. *Sat.*, III.i.139–140, n.

35–36 *helter skelter...hangman.* With the present passage, Hérford
and Simpson (IX, 355) compare Jonson, *Every Man in his
Humour*, I.iv.91–92: '*Helter skelter*, hang sorrow, care 'll kill
a cat, vp-tailes all, and a louse for [Quarto reads 'poxe on']
the hangman.' And cf. *Look About You* (M.S.R.), lines
1258–1259: 'heere are two crackt groates / To helter skelter, at
some vawting house'.

35 *top and top gallant*, short for 'topsail and topgallant sail', with all
sail set, in full array. *M.G.*, p. 120: 'O my Gallant of Gallants,
my Top and Top Gallant, how many Horses hast thou kilde
in the Countrie with the hunting of Harlottries.' Tilley, T437.

35 *pell mell.* IV.ii.167.

36 *huftie tuftie.* The phrase means 'swaggering'. Nashe, in *Have
With You* (III, 73) speaks of Gabriel, who 'came ruffling it out,
huffty tuffty, in his suite of veluet', and in *Lenten Stuffe* (III,
174) of 'huftituftie youthfull ruffling comrades'. For its use,
as in the present passage, as a pledge in drinking, cf. Bacchus
in Nashe's *Summer's Last Will* (III, 267): 'Summer, wilt thou
haue a demy culuering, that shall cry husty tusty, and make
thy cup flye fine meale in the Element?' and McKerrow's note
(IV, 435) suggesting that 'husty tusty' 'looks like an error
for "hufty-tufty"'.

36 *hem. 2 H.W.*, I.ii.47, n.

38.2 *a set at Mawe*, a game at maw; it was played with a piquet pack
of thirty-six cards, and any number of persons from two to
six formed the party (*O.E.D.*). Cf. *V.D.*, H4v–I1, of the
confusion reigning in a prison:

But the time of munching being come, all the sport was to see, how the
prisoners...ranne vp and downe, to arme themselues against that
battaile of hunger. Some, whetting kniues that had meate, others
scraping Trenchers alowd, that had no meat: Some ambling down
staires for Bread and Beere...Euery chamber shewing like a Cookes

shop, where prouant was stirring. And those that had not prouander
in the manger, nor hay in the rack, walking vp and downe like staru'd
Iades, new ouer-ridden in Smithfield. This set at Maw being playd out,
all seem'd quiet.

An anonymous play (now lost) titled *The Set at Maw* was
being acted by the Admiral's Company during December
1594 and January 1595 (Henslowe's *Diary*, pp. 26–27).
M.M.L., II.i.243.

41–42. *tag and rag, cut and long taile.* Cf. Laneham's *Letter*
(*Progresses of Queen Elizabeth*, ed. Nichols, 1, 445): 'after
the brydegroom had made his coors, ran the rest of the band
a whyle, in sum order; but soon after, tag and rag, cut and
long tail'. Both terms are proverbial 'for a number of persons
of various sorts and conditions; all and sundry, esp. of the
lower classes' (*O.E.D.*). 'Cut' was a common phrase for a
horse; whether it signified 'cut-tail' or 'gelding' is uncertain.
It was also used of dogs. Nichols, in a note on the passage
already cited from Laneham, quotes Ulpian Fulwell, *Ars
Adulandi* (1576), G3: 'Yea, even their very dogs, Rug, Rig,
and Risbie, yea, cut and long-taile, they shall be welcome.'
For 'tag and rag', cf. *I.T.B.N.*, IV.ii.7. Tilley, C938, T9 and
T10.

42 *God bo'y. Sat.*, III.i.82.

44 *tri-lill.* For this exclamation, generally associated with the act of
drinking, cf. Greene, *James IV* (ed. Collins), lines 1134–
1135: 'Oh, sir, the wine runnes trillill down his throat', and
the editor's note (11, 359) defining the term as 'an onomatopoeic
word which as an adverb may be paraphrased "smoothly,
with a pleasant gurgle", "down joyfully with it!"' It is very
common. Lodge and Greene, *A Looking Glasse for London and
England* (ed. Collins), lines 1686–1688: 'Come, let vs to the
spring of the best liquor: whilest this lastes, tril-lill.' *Look
About You* (M.S.R.), lines 661–662: 'we'll drinke trylill I
faith'. Nashe, *Summer's Last Will* (III, 265): 'wine is a pure
thing, & is poyson to all corruption. Try-lill, the hunters
hoope to you.' *W.Y.*, p. 57: 'The Tinker being not to learne
what vertue the medicine had which he held at his lippes,

powred it downe his throate merily, and crying trillill, he
feared no plagues.' *R.A.*, B2v: 'Amongst Gentlemen that haue
full pursses, and those that crie trillill, let the world slide.'
S.H., V.ii.178.

61–62 *a man...hose on his head.* Tilley, M244.

64 *her Ladie in tawny coate.* Eccentric dress for a lady, since tawny
coats are ordinarily associated with strolling musicians (cf. e.g.
Chettle, *Kind-Hartes Dreame* (ed. Harrison, pp. 11–12); Jonson, *Poetaster*, III.iv.134–135), or summoners (*1 Henry VI*,
I.iii.28.2; and *R.G.*, IV.ii.219.1 and 257), or rejected lovers
(Field, *A Woman is a Weathercock*, II.i.25–26). In *Grim the
Collier of Croydon*, I.iii (1662), p. 10, the devil Belphegor
appears like a physician with 'Akercock *his man.in a Tawny
coat*'. See Linthicum, pp. 46–47.

82 *Cartho crogge,* i.e. *Gato (Gad hi) (Cerdd i) grogi,* Welsh for
'May she (Let her) (Go thou) hang.'

84 *O mon Iago,* i.e. *O myn Iago,* Welsh for 'O by [Saint]
James'.

90 *peppered,* trounced. *1 H.W.*, III.i.133.

111 *Man gras worthe whee,* i.e. *Mae 'ngras (Mae'n gras) wrthych
chwi,* Welsh for 'My grace (Our grace) is with you.'

120 *dresser,* the kitchen sideboard.

137–138 *Tawsone en Ennoh Twewle,* i.e. *Taw sôn, yn enw'r Diawl,*
Welsh for 'Hold thy tongue, in the name of the Devil.'

141–143 *Adologo whee bethogh en Thlonigh, en Moyen due,
Gwenthian. | Ne vetho en Thlonigh, Gna watha gethla Tee,* i.e.
Atolwg i chwi, byddwch yn llonydd er mwyn Duw, Gwenllïan,
Welsh for 'Prithee, be quiet, for God's sake, Gwenllïan', and
Ni fydda yn llonydd, gwna waetha gelli di, 'I shan't be quiet,
do the worst thou canst.'

146–148 *mon due Gwenthian, Me knockoth e pen, en vmbleth, pobe des,
and pobe nose. | Gwelogh olach vessagh whee, en herawgh, ee,* i.e.
Myn Duw, Gwenllïan, mi gnocia dy ben, [?], bob dydd a bob nos,
Welsh for 'By God, Gwenllïan, I'll knock thy head, [?], every
day and every night [*en vmbleth* = ? *yn unbleth* 'into one
plait'; ? *i vmaith* 'off'; ? *yn bellen* 'into a ball'; ? *yn blet* 'into
a pleat']', and *Gweld sich ola fuasech chwi (Gwell o'ch lladd*

fuasech chwi) '*y nharo i*, 'Seeing your last you'd be (Better killed you'd be) striking me.'

151–152 *En herawgh Ee? Me grauat the Legatee, athlan oth pendee, adroh ornymee on dictar, en hecar Ee*, i.e. '*Y nharo i? Mi grafa dy lygaid di allan o'th ben di o droi arna i (arni) mewn dicter*, [?], Welsh for 'Striking me? I'll scratch your eyes out of your head for turning on me (on her) in anger [*en hecar ee* = ? '*y nheigr i* 'my tiger'; ? '*yn egru i* 'provoking me'].'

168 *Stethe whee lawer*, i.e. *Steddwch chwi i lawr*, Welsh for 'Sit down.'

200 *culuerins*. Cf. *R.G.*, V.ii.46, n.

227–228 *shew you a faire paire of heeles*. *W.A.*, F4v–G1: 'they desired their gratious Empresse (*Money*) not to lye lasing thus in a chamber, but either that she would be more stirring...or else they vowed there were at least ten thousand...that shortly if this world lasted, would...shew her a faire paire of heeles, and from her fly into the hands of *Pouertie* their enemie'.

246 *kisse the poste*. II.i.32.

249 *boepeepe*. I.ii.3.

<h2 style="text-align:center">V.i</h2>

4 *a tale of Pignies*, i.e. 'pygmies'; see below, line 44. Chapter 64 of the edition of *The Voyages and Trauailes of Sir John Maundeuile Knight* published *c*. 1583 (entered S.R. 12 March 1582; STC 17251) treats 'Of the Land of Pigme, the people whereof are but three spans long' (sig. O4v). They are described by Pliny, *Natural History*, VII.2 (translated by Philemon Holland (1601), p. 156).

10 *ambrie*, 'a place for keeping victuals' (*O.E.D.*); a cupboard or storehouse. Chettle, *Piers Plainness*, p. 128: 'In his diet he was verie sparing, because he had small store of spare money to buy meate: and had not the scullerie at the Court been my best ambrie, I must either have left my master, or lost my life.' *V.M.*, II.iii.213.

13 *paltries*, rubbish, trash.

17–18 *wonders not of nine daies, but 1599*, when *P.G.* was written.

18 *Iohn Prester*. Prester John and his realms are described in the

final chapters (86–87, 97–99) of Mandeville, *Travels* (Sigs. R3–R3v, T1–T2v). *O.F.*, I.ii.197, n.

18 *Tamer Cams, Sat.*, V.ii.182, n.

18–19 *people with heds like Dogs.* Mandeville, *Travels*, chapter 61, tells 'Of the Iland named Macumeran [i.e. Nacumera], whereas the people haue heads like hounds' (sig. N4v). Pliny, vi.30 (p. 147) and vii.2 (pp. 155, 157).

25–26 *many without heads, hauing their eyes nose and mouths in their breasts.* Mandeville, *Travels*, chapter 62, tells 'Of a great Iland called Dodyn, where are many men of euill conditions' (O1v):

> the king of this Ile is a great Lord and mightie, and hee hath in euery Ile other kings vnder him, and in one of these Iles are men that haue but one eie, and that is in the middest of their front...And in another Ile dwell men that haue no heads, and their eyes are in their shoulders, and their mouth is on their breast (O2–O2v).

Pliny, v.8 (p. 96), and vii.2 (p. 156).

35 *Epimœi.* G. Hübsch in his edition of *Patient Grissil* explained the word as a combination of ἐπί and μοί meaning 'Egoisten'. This explanation was dismissed by W. Bang in a note on *Patient Grissil* printed in *Archiv für das Studium der neueren Sprachen und Litteraturen*, 107 (1901), 111–112. Bang suggested that '*Epimoei*' was a mistake for '*Ewaipanoma*', 'a nation of people whose heads appear not above their shoulders', mentioned in Raleigh's *Discovery of Guiana*, where 'they are reported to have their eyes in their shoulders, and the mouths in the middle of their breasts'. Could the word intended be '*Epigastrium*', defined in Thomas' *Dictionary* (1587) as 'all the bellie, from the bulke down to the priuy members' and where the plural is given as '*Epigastrii*'?

37 *them that haue but one leg, and yet will out run a horse.* Mandeville, *Travels*, chapter 51: 'In Ethiope are such men that haue but one foote, and they go so fast that it is a great meruaile' (sig. L3). Pliny, vii.2 (p. 156).

38 *banckrouts. W.H.*, III.ii.9, n.

44–45 *Pigmies...Cranes.* Neither of the sixteenth-century printed editions of Mandeville in English (1568 and *c.* 1583) makes any mention of the cranes. The manuscript of Mandeville's

Travels in the British Library (MS Cotton Titus c. XVI)
relates of the pygmies: 'And þei han often tymes werre with
the bryddes of the contree þat þei taken & eten' (ed. P.
Hamelius, Early English Text Society (London, 1919), I, 138,
lines 23–24): a passage which, as the editor notes (II, 112–113)
has been mistranslated from the French original, wherein the
birds are said to eat the pygmies. 'The Englisher reverses the
relation' (Hamelius, p. 113). Laureo's reference to the 'poore
and wretched... *Pigmies*' and 'the deuouring Cranes' in lines
46–47 makes it clear that the source for the present scene in
P.G. had the relation between cranes and pygmies right.
Pliny recounts it in VII.2 (p. 156):

And these pretie people ['the Pygmæi Spythamei'] *Homer* also hath
reported to be much troubled and annoied by cranes. The speech goeth,
that in the Spring time they set out all of them in battell array, mounted
upon the backe of rammes and goats, armed with bowes and arrowes,
and so downe to the sea side they march, where they make foule worke
among the egges and young cranelings newly hatched, which they
destroy without all pitie. Thus for three moneths this their journey and
expedition continueth, and then they make an end of their valiant
service: for otherwise if they should continue any longer, they were
never able to withstand the new flights of this foule, growne to some
strength and bignesse.'

Homer alludes to the death and destruction visited by cranes
on pygmies in *Iliad*, III.6.

44 *gig*, a whipping-top (*O.E.D.*).

59 *trudge*. O.F., V.ii.15, n.

82 *snaffled*. Cf. *The Mirror for Magistrates* (ed. L. B. Campbell
(Cambridge, 1938)), p. 246: 'lyke horses snaffled with the
byttes'.

100 *you haue fisht faire and catcht a frog*. Tilley, F767. *N.H.*,
V.i.483–484.

V.ii

8–10 *Sunne,... disperceth vapours with his beames*. Cf. *L.D.*,
III.iv.18, n.

16 *Tardaugh*, i.e. *Dydd da iwch*, Welsh for 'Good day to you.'

51.1 *carrying coales*, the task of the poorest drudges in great houses. Hence the phrase 'to carry coals' with its twofold meaning: (1) to do any dirty work; (2) to endure any insult. *W.H.*, III.iii.31.

52 *Cole-staffe*, i.e. cowl-staff, a pole used to run through the handles of a 'cowl' or tub so that it could be carried on the shoulders of two men.

56 *logger head.* *W.E.*, III.i.20, n.

87 *Tawsone.* III.ii.232.

88 *sol faes.* IV.ii.110.

109 *A wreath of willow*, the usual emblem of the forsaken lover. Massinger, *The Maid of Honour*, IV.v.27–29:

> if you forsake me,
> Send me word that I may provide a willow ghyrlond
> To weare when I drowne my selfe.

J.M.M., G3–G3v: 'His Armes were seuen-times folded together, like a withered garland of willow, worne carelessly by a forsaken Louer.' *W.K.*, V.ii.128–129.

135 *haue I done so?* i.e. 'put robes on Parasites' (line 133).

137 *Truth, sildome dwels in a still talking tongue.* Cf. the proverb 'That tongue does lie that speaks in haste' (Tilley, T400).

152 *aduersities colde I꒝ie hand.* Cf. *L.D.*, III.ii.65–66.

195 *nephewes*, i.e. grandchildren.

198 *looke not strange.* I.i.1; I.ii.235.

199–208 *These two are they...name.* At the end of the Ballad 'Of patient Grissel and a Noble Marquesse', the Marquess thus addresses Grissil's former detractors:

> And you that enuy her estate,
> Whom I haue made my louing mate,
>   now blush for shame, and honour vertuous life,
> The Chronicles of lasting fame,
> Shall euermore extoll the name
>   of patient *Grissel*, my most constant wife.

> (Lines 177–182)

201–202 *that multitude, | That many headed beastes.* *L.D.*, III.iv.21–22, n. And *P.G.*, III.i.147.

222 *cog a hoope.* Originally a drinking phrase, meaning 'turn on the tap and drink without stint' (*O.E.D.*). Tilley, C493.

236 *snip snap. O.F.*, I.i.49, n.
258 *brabble*, quarrel. *L.C.*, C4:

> Nothing could bee heard but noise, and nothing of that noise be
> vnderstood, but that it was a sound as of men in a kingdome, when on
> a suddaine it is in an vprore. Euery one brabled with him that he
> walked with, or if he did but tell his tale to his Councell, he was so
> eager in the verry deliuery of that tale, that you would haue sworne he
> did brabble.

268 *will tag her will.* III.ii.269.
278 *louertine*, 'addicted to love-making' (*O.E.D.*, which labels the
    term a nonce-word formed on the model of 'libertine', and
    cites the present passage as its only example).
282 *leade Apes in hell.* II.i.257.
299 *spride of buttrie. Sat.*, IV.i.142, n.
312 *Man gras wortha whee*, i.e. *Mae 'ngras (Mae'n gras) wrthych
    chwi*, Welsh for 'My grace (Our grace) is to you.'

SATIROMASTIX

INTRODUCTION

In the year following *Patient Grissil*, Dekker's play-writing activities for Henslowe continued unabated: an unaided play, *Truth's Supplication to Candelight* (January 1600);[1] *The Spanish Moor's Tragedy* (probably the play now known as *Lust's Dominion*), with Day and Haughton (February 1600);[2] *The Seven Wise Masters*, with Chettle, Day and Haughton (March 1600);[3] *The Golden Ass* or *Cupid and Psyche*, with Chettle and Day (April–May 1600);[4] *The Fair Constance of Rome*, Part One, with Drayton, Hathway, Munday and Wilson (June 1600, and perhaps Part Two, later in the month);[5] another unaided play, *Fortune's Tennis* (September 1600).[6] December found him altering his 1598 play, *Phaeton*, for performance at Court,[7] even as he had altered his *Fortunatus* the year before. But at this point, Dekker's work for Henslowe and the Admiral's Company has begun to taper off. The cessation of his activities for Henslowe in the fall of 1600 is conspicuous, and we hear nothing of him in Henslowe's records through the opening months of 1601. In April–May 1601, in collaboration with Chettle, he writes *King Sebastian of Portugal* for the Admiral's Men,[8] and then he disappears from Henslowe's Diary for over six months. It is during these periods that Dekker has begun to write for the chorister company of boy actors whose theatre near St Paul's Church[9] had been reopened early in 1600 after having been closed throughout the previous decade. Probably in the fall of 1601 (perhaps in collaboration with Middleton) he wrote *Blurt, Master-*

---

[1] *Henslowe's Diary*, p. 130. [2] *Ibid.*, p. 131.
[3] *Ibid.*, pp. 131, 132. [4] *Ibid.*, pp. 133, 134.
[5] *Ibid.*, pp. 135, 136. [6] *Ibid.*, p. 137.
[7] *Ibid.*, p. 137. [8] *Ibid.*, pp. 168, 169, 170.
[9] H. N. Hillebrand, *The Child Actors: A Chapter in Elizabethan Stage History* (Urbana, Illinois, 1926), p. 215.

Constable, or *The Spaniard's Night-walk* for the Children of Paul's; and sometime prior to 11 November 1601 (when it was entered in the Stationers' Register)[1] Dekker wrote *Satiromastix*, acted privately by the Paul's Company, and publicly at the Globe by the Chamberlain's Men. With this play he is suddenly found assuming a central role in the famous war of the theatres, which with Jonson and Marston as its principal opponents, had become increasingly heated over the past two years.

Why Dekker should have been involved in Marston's quarrel with Jonson is a mystery.[2] It is possible, indeed, that at the outset he was not directly involved in it, and that he wrote *Satiromastix* on a joint commission from the Chamberlain's Company (which had its own quarrel with Jonson, apparently stemming from the failure of their production of his *Every Man out of his Humour*) and the Paul's Company, which had been acting Marston's contributions to the quarrel (*Jack Drum's Entertainment* and *What You Will*) while its rival, the Children of her Majesty's Chapel, was staging Jonson's entries (*Cynthia's Revels* and *Poetaster*). If the notion of attacking Jonson in a play originated with Dekker, one would like to suppose that he would have devised a more adequate dramatic form for it than the one exhibited in *Satiromastix*. The commission (if that is what it was) seems to have reached him at a time when he was working on another play, a romantic tragedy or tragicomedy[3] set in the Norman court of King William Rufus, and he appears to have met the request for a satiric action directed against a contemporary literary personality by the simple expedient of inserting it, at whatever cost to dramatic congruity, into his pseudo-historical romance. The result is a dramatic medley that has been the despair of critics since Swinburne.[4] The need for haste

---

[1] Arber, III, 195.

[2] For a possible explanation, see the Introduction to *Lust's Dominion*.

[3] As originally conceived, the play may have been a tragedy, with the King's violation of Caelestine serving as Sir Walter Terill's motive for murdering him. Roscoe A. Small, *The Stage-Quarrel Between Ben Jonson and the So-Called Poetasters* (Breslau, 1899), pp. 121–122, gives an act-by-act summary of the presumptive tragedy, and suggests that 'With this major plot would have been combined the comic minor plot of the wooing of the Widow Minever by the two rivals Adam Prickshaft and the Welshman Sir Vaughan ap Rees' (p. 122).

[4] Swinburne writes of *Satiromastix*: 'It may be assumed, and it is much to be

in answering Jonson may have dictated the slapdash combination of satire and romance, though it is also possible to discern a fine insouciance in Dekker's casual response to the elaborately constructed *Cynthia's Revels* and *Poetaster*. As M. T. Jones-Davies has shrewdly remarked: 'Dekker bâtit sa parodie dans un esprit de pure dérision. Rien n'était trop absurde pour cette guerre absurde.'[1]

The blow that *Satiromastix* was to administer to Jonson was well advertized before it appeared. Rumors seem to have reached him not long after the production of *Cynthia's Revels* in the winter of 1600–1601[2] that the attack was being prepared, and he promptly set about anticipating it with *Poetaster*, urged on to what for him was unusual speed of composition. He wrote the play in fifteen weeks, as Envy announces in the induction (line 14), a point that is derided in *Satiromastix* (I.ii.363–364).[3] *Poetaster* seems to have reached the stage in the late spring or early summer of 1601.[4] *Satiromastix* followed in the fall.[5]

hoped, that there never existed another poet capable of imagining – much less of perpetrating – an incongruity so monstrous and so perverse' (*The Age of Shakespeare* (London, 1908), p. 67).   [1] I, 44.

[2] Chambers, III, 364. Small (*The Stage-Quarrel*, p. 24), who saw in V.xi.14–21 of *Cynthia's Revels* a reference to the execution of Essex on 25 February 1601, argued for a date of late February or March, but this is refuted by Chambers. Herford and Simpson (I, 394) suggest December 1600 as the date of the first performance.

[3] On the sequence that led from *Cynthia's Revels* to *Poetaster*, Herford and Simpson write (I, 415): 'No other play of Jonson's followed so swiftly on the heels of its predecessor, and the rapid execution points to circumstances of unusual urgency.'

[4] In *Poetaster*, III.iv.328–329, one of the players says: 'this winter ha's made vs all poorer, then so many staru'd snakes'. These, say Herford and Simpson (I, 415) are 'words which would hardly have been used later than May, and if the play had been performed later, would have been altered'. Small, *The Stage-Quarrel*, p. 25, dates the production of *Poetaster* in June 1601, but his calendar is out by at least a month as a result of his February/March date for *Cynthia's Revels* (see n. 2, above). G. B. Harrison, *Elizabethan Plays and Players* (Ann Arbor, 1956), p. 252, says that Jonson began to write *Poetaster* 'c. end of May' 1601 and gives 'c. 10th September' as the date of its first performance, but he gives no evidence for either date; both imply a chronological certainty unwarranted by the evidence that is available.

[5] The reference in *Satiromastix*, V.ii. 243, to 'the *Whipping a'th Satyre*' suggests that the play was not completed at least until after 14 August 1601 when the verse satire of that name was entered in the Stationers' Register (Arber, III, 190). Small, *The Stage-Quarrel*, p. 119, suggests a date of August or September 1601. Noting that Dekker could not 'have done much of his satire, until he had seen *Poetaster*, to many details of which it retorts', Chambers (III, 293) continues: 'It is perhaps rather fantastic to hold that, as [Dekker] chaffs Jonson for the boast that he wrote *Poetaster* in fifteen weeks..., he must himself have taken less.'

Sometime during the fall of 1601, at the height of the uproar which the stage quarrel occasioned, Jonson wrote an 'Apologetical Dialogue' intended as a kind of epilogue to *Poetaster*[1] wherein he declared, by way of justifying his attack on players and playwrights, that for

> three yeeres,
> They did prouoke me with their petulant stiles
> On euery stage

(lines 96–98)

In so far as one can judge from extant works, what seems, specifially, to have provoked him were representations of him in three plays, all the work of Marston: *Histriomastix*, *Jack Drum's Entertainment*, and *What You Will*. This impression accords with Jonson's remark to Drummond of Hawthornden years later that he 'wrote his Poetaster on' Marston, and that the beginning of his 'quarrels' with that dramatist 'were that Marston represented him in the stage'.[2]

Henslowe's *Diary* affords a tantalizing glimpse of Jonson and Dekker collaborating on the tragedy of *Page of Plymouth* between 10 August and 2 September 1599,[3] and of the two of them continuing at once to work on another tragedy, *Robert II, King of Scotts*, this time in association with Chettle and an 'other gentleman' whom Henslowe in an entry of 3 September does not name but who may have been Marston, to whom Henslowe refers on 28 September as 'the new poete'.[4] But during this very period the seeds of future strife were being planted, if they had not already been. Marston's *Histriomastix* has traditionally been dated August 1599, and was long held to be an old play which Marston partially

---

[1] The date for the 'Apologetical Dialogue' is Small's (*The Stage-Quarrel*, p 60). It was spoken but once on the stage; and while Jonson intended that it be printed in the quarto of 1602, it was suppressed 'by Authoritie', as Jonson himself noted in a statement to the reader at the end of the quarto (Herford and Simpson, IV, 317); it did not appear in print until the folio of 1616. *Poetaster* had angered lawyers and soldiers as well as players and playwrights (see Herford and Simpson, I, 29). In what follows, all quotations from Jonson's plays are from the Herford and Simpson edition.

[2] Herford and Simpson, I, 140. Jonson mentions Dekker only once in the conversations with Drummond, when he calls him a rogue (along with Sharpham, Day and Minsheu (Herford and Simpson, I, 133)).

[3] *Diary*, p. 123.

[4] *Ibid.*, p. 124.

revised at that time for performance by the Children of Paul's at their newly reopened theatre.[1] The play is now generally regarded as Marston's own,[2] and P. J. Finkelpearl has recently suggested that it was written, not for the Paul's Boys, but for the Christmas revels of 1598–1599 at the Middle Temple.[3] Whether Marston wrote the whole of *Histriomastix* or only revised portions of an earlier play, he is generally held to be responsible for its well-intentioned but somewhat embarrassing tribute to Jonson in the character of the learned moralist Chrisoganus whose efforts to instruct society are set over against the mindless entertainment provided for it by a vulgar company of players and their hack poet Post-hast (almost certainly based on Anthony Munday, whom Jonson himself had recently caricatured in *The Case is Altered*). To judge from what followed, Jonson was not pleased by Marston's efforts to follow in his tracks as a comic dramatist, nor was he pleased by Marston's portrait of him, perhaps because, as Finkelpearl has suggested, 'Marston put several speeches into Chrisoganus' mouth which sound like quotations from [Marston's own] *The Scourge [of Villanie]*, a poem Jonson thought ridiculous.'[4] When Jonson's *Every Man out of his Humour* was staged by the Chamberlain's Men, presumably at the end of 1599 or early in 1600, it contained a parody of some of Marston's fustian vocabulary, put in the mouth of one Clove who appears in the company of a witless companion named Orange during the scene in the middle aisle of St Paul's Cathedral, and who launches a battery of learned-sounding gibberish in order to attract the attention of the surrounding gallants.[5]

---

[1] Small, *The Stage-Quarrel*, pp. 82–85.

[2] See Alvin Kernan, 'John Marston's Play *Histriomastix*', *Modern Language Quarterly*, 19 (1958), 134–140.

[3] *John Marston of the Middle Temple* (Cambridge, Mass., 1969), p. 122.

[4] *Ibid.*, p. 122. For the view that the character of Chrisoganus was intended as a compliment to Jonson, see Small, *The Stage-Quarrel*, p. 89.

[5] G. B. Harrison, *Plays and Players*, pp. 254–255, has suggested that the parody of Marston's vocabulary did not occur in the stage version, but was added to the text when *Every Man out of his Humour* was printed in 1600. Three quarto editions were published in that year, the titlepages of all three proclaiming the text to contain 'more than hath been Publickely Spoken or Acted'. Clove and Orange are acknowledged during one of the intra-scenic exchanges between Mitis and Cordatus to be 'meere strangers to the whole scope of our play; only come to walke a turne or two, i' this

When he realizes that 'they marke vs not' he and Orange disappear from the play, but during their brief turn in it, Clove's verbal display has included in part the following:

Now, sir, whereas the *Ingenuitie* of the time, and the soules *Synderisis* are but *Embrions* in nature, added to the panch of *Esquiline*, and the *Inter-vallum* of the *Zodiack*, besides the *Eclipticke line* being *opticke*, and not *mentall*, but by the *contemplatiue* & *theoricke* part thereof, doth demonstrate to vs the *vegetable circumference*, and the *ventositie* of the *Tropicks*, and whereas our *intellectuall*, or *mincing capreall* (according to the *Metaphisicks*) as you may reade in Plato's *Histriomastix — — — (Every Man out of his Humour*, III.iv.21–29)

Marston's response to this put-down seems to have been the character of Brabant Senior in *Jack Drum's Entertainment* (acted by the Children of Paul's about August 1600; entered in the Stationers' Register on 8 September 1600).[1] It is a less respectful portrait of Jonson than the one that had been offered in *Histriomastix*. Brabant Senior is a character with a humour, which is to surround himself with gulls, that he may encourage them in their folly for the amusement of himself and a small circle of intimates. His nature is exploitative and abusive, and throughout the play it is condemned by another character, Planet, who looks on at Brabant Senior's complacent arrogance and deplores it. Planet thus describes him just before his first appearance:

> Oh the Prince of Fooles, unequald Ideot,
> He that makes costly suppers to trie wits:
> And will not stick to spend some 20. pound
> To grope a gull: that same perpetuall grin
> That leades his Corkie Jests to make them sinke
> Into the eares of his Deryders with his owne applause.[2]

Brabant Senior comes on, exulting in the 'feast of fooles' at which he has just entertained: 'tis the recreation of my Intellect, I think I speake as significant, ha, ha, these are my zanyes, I fill their paunches, they feed my pleasures, I use them as my fooles faith, ha, ha' (p. 193). In the course of the play he devises a plot whereby one

Scene of *Paules*, by chance' (III.i.17–19). *Every Man out of his Humour* was entered in the Stationers' Register on 8 April 1600 (Arber, III, 159).

[1] *Ibid.*, III, 172.

[2] Ed. Wood, III, 190. Quotations from *Jack Drum's Entertainment* in what follows are from this edition, to which reference is made by page-numbers in parentheses.

of his entourage, a lustful Frenchman in search of a woman, is
directed to Brabant Senior's own wife under the impression that
she is a courtesan. Brabant Senior assumes that she will indignantly
bid him be gone when his intentions are made known, and he
alerts his friends to the jest, that they may savor the frustrated
Frenchman's return. But the Frenchman returns full of thanks to
Brabant Senior, his ardor satisfied. Planet, who has earlier expressed
his hatred for such 'bumbaste wits'

> That are puft up with arrogant conceit
> Of their owne worth, as if *Omnipotence*
> Had hoysed them to such unequald height,
> That they survaide our spirits with an eye
> Only create to censure from above,
>
> (p. 229)

rejoices in the fact that he who has prided himself on his powers of
gulling others has gulled himself. As the comedy ends, Planet
crowns Brabant Senior with 'the Coronet of Cuckolds':

> Nay you shall weare it, or weare
> My Rapier in your gutts by heaven.
> Why doest thou not well deserve to be thus usde?
> Why should'st thou take felicitie to gull
> Good honest soules, and in thy arrogance
> And glorious ostentation of thy wit,
> Thinke God infused all perfection
> Into thy soule alone, and made the rest
> For thee to laugh at? Now you Censurer
> Be the ridiculous subject of our mirth.
> Why Foole, the power of Creation
> Is still Omnipotent, and there's no man that breathes
> So valiant, learned, wittie, or so wise,
> But it can equall him out of the same mould
> Wherein the first was form'd. Then leave proud scorne,
> And honest selfe made Cuckold, weare the horne.
>
> (p. 240)

The next entry in the quarrel is Jonson's *Cynthia's Revels*, staged
by the other newly reactivated chorister company, the Children
of her Majesty's Revels, at their newly opened theatre in the
Blackfriars in or about December 1600 (entered in the Stationers'
Register on 23 May 1601).[1] Here again we have an associated pair

---

[1] Arber, III, 185.

of satiric targets, but a much more elaborately developed pair than Clove and Orange in *Every Man out of his Humour*. *Cynthia's Revels* presents us with a pair of courtly affectations: Hedon, 'the *voluptuous*', and Anaides, 'the *impudent*' (induction, lines 57, 59). Mercury's characterization of Hedon stresses his foppery:

> Hee has a rich wrought wast-coat to entertaine his visitants in, with a cap almost sutable. His curtaines, and bedding are thought to bee his owne: his bathing-tub is not suspected. He loues to haue a fencer, a pedant, and a musician seene in his lodging a mornings.
> *Cupid.* And not a poet?
> *Mercury.* Fye no: himself is a rimer, and that's a thought better then a poet (*Cynthia's Revels*, II.i.42–49).

Mercury's characterization of Anaides reveals a coarser type: he is not in truth a courtier, but 'has two essentiall parts of the courtier, pride, and ignorance' (II.ii.77–78).

> He will censure or discourse of any thing, but as absurdly as you would wish. His fashion is not to take knowledge of him that is beneath him in clothes. Hee neuer drinkes below the salt. Hee do's naturally admire his wit, that weares gold-lace, or tissue. Stabs any man that speakes more contemptibly of the scholler then he. Hee is a great proficient in all the illiberall sciences, as cheating, drinking, swaggering, whoring, and such like: neuer kneeles but to pledge healths, nor prayes but for a pipe of pudding tabacco. He will blaspheme in his shirt. The othes which hee vomits at one supper, would maintaine a towne of garrison in good swearing a twelue-moneth (II.ii.85–97).

But the principal thing about Hedon and Anaides is their envy and their hatred of Crites. They scorn his scholarly labors: call him 'a whore-sonne booke-worme, a candle-waster' (III.ii.2–3), maintain that 'he smels all lamp-oyle, with studying by candle-light' (III.ii.11–12). Hedon observes in his frustration: 'How confidently he went by vs, and carelesly! neuer moou'd! nor stirr'd at any thing! did you obserue him?' (III.ii.13–15). Hedon goes on: 'this afflicts mee more then all the rest, that wee should so particularly direct our hate, and contempt against him, and hee to carrie it thus without wound, or passion! 'tis insufferable' (III.ii.19–22). He resolves to 'speake all the venome I can of him; and poyson his reputation in euery place, where I come' (III.ii.46–47). And he continues: 'if I chance to bee present where any question is made of his sufficiencies, or of any thing he hath done priuate, or publike, Ile censure it slightly, and ridiculously' (III.ii.49–51). Anaides has a better idea, since to censure Crites is to raise doubts about one's own judgment:

Approue any thing thou hearest of his, to the receiu'd opinion of it; but if it bee extraordinarie, giue it from him to some other, whom thou more particularly affect'st. That's the way to plague him, and he shall neuer come to defend himselfe. S'lud, Ile giue out, all he does is dictated from other men, and sweare it too (if thou'lt ha' mee) and that I know the time, and place where he stole it, though my soule bee guiltie of no such thing; and that I thinke, out of my heart, hee hates such barren shifts: yet to doe thee a pleasure, and him a disgrace, I'le dam' my selfe, or doe anything (III.ii.55–66).

Jonson sees to it that the detractors of Crites are made to bear witness to his virtues even as they plot their campaign of detraction. Crites, for his part, is superbly unconcerned at their efforts to slander his name:

> Doe, good detraction, doe, and I the while
> Shall shake thy spight off with a carelesse smile.
> Poore pittious gallants!
>
> (III.iii.1–3)

To be 'disprais'd' by such as them 'is the most perfect praise' (III.iii.16). If good men had spoken ill of him, he would have called his 'thoughts, and actions, to a strict accompt' (III.iii.21):

> But when I remember,
> 'Tis Hedon, and Anaides: alasse, then,
> I thinke but what they are, and am not stirr'd.
> The one, a light voluptuous reueller,
> The other a strange arrogating puffe,
> Both impudent, and ignorant inough
>
> (III.iii.22–27)

The last four lines made their impact. The Horace of *Satiromastix* is made to repeat them (at I.ii.153–156) with reference to Crispinus and Demetrius, thereby making perfectly clear the connection that existed for Dekker and Marston between the Hedon and Anaides of *Cynthia's Revels*, and the Crispinus and Demetrius of *Poetaster*.[1] Hedon had been termed a reveler in *Cynthia's Revels*,

---

[1] Small suggested that both these pairs are developed from satiric types that go back to *Every Man out of his Humour*, and that as Jonson originally conceived them, neither had anything to do with Marston or Dekker. The frivolous reveler Hedon in

187

and Crispinus is heard proudly using the term of himself in
Poetaster ('Why, I haue beene a reueller, and at my cloth of siluer
sute, and my long stocking, in my time, and will be againe –'
he babbles on to Horace in the scene in which he attaches himself
to the famous poet in the street and will not be shaken, determined
as he is to make an impression (III.i.175–177)). Later he is heard
assuring Minos, the apothecary to whom he owes fourscore
sesterces for sweetmeats and who has ordered his arrest: 'as I am
a gentleman, and a reueller, I'le make a peece of *poetrie*, and absolue
all, within these fiue daies' (III.iv.62–64). The impudence that
Crites has noted in *Cynthia's Revels* is equally evident to Horace
in *Poetaster* ('Man hath nothing giuen him, in this life, without
much labour', Crispinus assures Horace, and Horace adds: 'And
impudence' (III.i.277–279)). The Crispinus of *Poetaster* is an
utterly frivolous young man who plays at being a poet in odd
moments when he is not flirting or gossiping. But he has a great
deal of cheek, as he fully displays in the amusing scene when he
comes upon Horace and makes his impertinent bid for the famous
poet's attention. Horace manages to make his escape when
Crispinus is met by Minos and the lictors, out to arrest him. It is
then that Crispinus falls into the hands of the blustering Captain
Tucca who arranges for him to write for the players, and it is now
that Demetrius appears on the scene. According to the player
Histrio, he is 'a very simple honest fellow,...a dresser of plaies
about the towne, here; we haue hir'd him to abuse Horace, and
bring him in, in a play, with all his gallants' (III.iv.321–324).
'Why' asks Tucca, and the player's answer is direct enough:
'O, it will get vs a huge deale of money (Captaine) and wee haue

Cynthia's Revels who becomes Crispinus in *Poetaster* derives from Fastidious Briske
in *Every Man Out*. Anaides, the arrogant but empty railer of *Cynthia's Revels*
who becomes Demetrius in *Poetaster*, derives from Carlo Buffone in *Every Man
Out*. Hedon and Anaides represent the two types in a state of transition, as Jonson
began to adapt the general features of the types to the particular natures of his
enemies. Thus, says Small (*The Stage-Quarrel*, p. 35), Anaides 'is meant for Dekker
just in so far as the character coincides with the character of Demetrius. The remaining
phases of the character are merely a new version of the character of Carlo Buffone.'
Likewise, 'Hedon is Marston just in so far as his characteristics accord with those
of Crispinus; that is, in so far as he is represented as a poet and an enemy of Horace.
The remainder of his character is a repetition of that of Brisk' (*ibid.*, p. 42).

need on't; for this winter ha's made vs all poorer, then so many
staru'd snakes: No bodie comes at vs; not a gentleman, nor a –'
(III.iv.327–330). He alludes, of course, to the competition which
the adult companies were experiencing at just this time from the
companies of boy actors, and which is commemorated in *Hamlet*
(II.ii.325ff.). The player in *Poetaster* acknowledges that they do
not know much concerning Horace 'to make a play of', but is
undeterred: 'our Author will deuise, that, that shall serue in some
sort' (III.iv.333–334).

The envy and hatred that Hedon and Anaides have exhibited
for Crites in *Cynthia's Revels* is evident as well in *Poetaster*, especially in Demetrius' attitude toward Horace. In one of his rare out-
bursts (Jonson represents him as not particularly articulate) he
expresses his contempt for the poet and his ways: 'Horace! hee is
a meere spunge; nothing but humours, and obseruation; he goes
vp and downe sucking from euery societie, and when hee comes
home, squeazes himselfe drie againe. I know him, I' (IV.iii.104–
107). The matter of Horace's translating is a recurrent theme with
Demetrius, who views it as a form of plagiarism. In his doggerel
verses against Horace, he is made to say:

And (but that I would not be thought a prater)
I could tell you, he were a translater.
I know the authors from whence he ha's stole,
And could trace him too, but that I vnderstand hem not full and whole.
(V.iii.310–313)

Anaides, in *Cynthia's Revels* (III.ii.60) has threatened to 'giue out'
that all Crites 'does is dictated from other men', and later in
Cynthia's Revels he has sought to defame Crites' learning:

Death, what talke you of his learning? he vnderstands no more then a schoole-
boy; I haue put him downe my selfe a thousand times (by this aire) and yet I
neuer talkt with him but twice, in my life: you neuer saw his like. I could
neuer get him to argue with me, but once, and then, because I could not
construe an Author I quoted at first sight, hee went away, and laught at me
(*Cynthia's Revels*, IV.v.40–46).

Demetrius in *Poetaster* anticipates with relish the play that he will
write attacking Horace; he and his collaborator Crispinus will
'tickle him i' faith, for his arrogancie, and his impudence, in

commending his owne things; and for his translating: I can trace him i' faith. O, he is the most open fellow, liuing; I had as lieue as a new sute, I were at it' (IV.iii.120–123). Before the play can be written, however, Crispinus and Demetrius have become involved in the accusation of treason that Asinius Lupus levels against Horace, and when this is disproved, the two poetasters are charged with having 'most ignorantly, foolishly, and...maliciously, gone about to depraue, and calumniate the person and writings of Qvintvs Horacivs Flaccvs' (V.iii.224–227). The evidence that condemns them is from their own hands: in each case, a poem written against Horace. Crispinus' is a wicked parody of Marston's violent satiric style ('Rampe vp, my *genius*; be not retrograde: / But boldly nominate a spade, a spade' (V.iii.275–276)). Demetrius' lumbering verses betoken the lurching metres of the old morality plays:

> Our *Muse* is in mind for th'vntrussing a *poet*,
> I slip by his name; for most men doe know it:
> A *critick*, that all the world bescumbers
> With *satyricall* humours, and *lyricall* numbers
> (V.iii.302–305)

After the two have been found guilty, they are asked 'what cause they had to maligne Horace' (V.iii.447–448). Demetrius answers: 'In troth, no great cause, not I; I must confesse: but that hee kept better company (for the most part) then I: and that better men lou'd him, then lou'd me: and that his writings thriu'd better then mine, and were better lik't, and grac't: nothing else' (V.iii.449–453). Crispinus is unable to answer the question because the pills that Horace has given him a short time before now begin to work, and he is in the throes of vomiting up the more egregious particles of his vocabulary. He can say little as the play ends. Demetrius, whom Horace has forgiven, is forced to put on a fool's coat and cap, and both poetasters are made to take an oath never again 'to maligne, traduce, or detract the *person*, or writings of Qvintvs Horacivs Flaccvs' (V.iii.595–596). Nor must they ever again ambitiously affect 'the title of the *vntrussers*, or *whippers* of the age' (V.iii.605).

The threatened attack on Jonson when it came proclaimed its contempt for that last clause by calling itself *Satiromastix*, or *The untrussing of the Humorous Poet*. The plans for it as anticipated in

Poetaster call for two authors, and Dekker's plural 'Poetasters' in his prefatory address 'To the World' (line 9; see Commentary) has led to a general assumption that Marston aided him in the play. This is possible so far as a contribution to the dramatic portraiture and the satiric strategies are concerned, but Marston had nothing at all to do with the actual writing of the play. His contribution may best be assessed by the features which *Satiromastix* shares with his own *What You Will*. This seems to have been his last unaided contribution to the quarrel, and the date of it is uncertain, but it probably came sometime between *Cynthia's Revels* and *Poetaster*, in the spring of 1601.[1] The barbs at Jonson which Marston included in the character of Lampatho Doria are in a sense a continuation of those he had developed in the character of Brabant Senior in *Jack Drum's Entertainment*. Lampatho is found in one of his early scenes encouraging a foppish French lord in his folly, addressing him with elaborate politeness to his face and mocking him behind his back to Quadratus, who is to *What You Will* what Planet was to *Jack Drum's Entertainment*. Quadratus is both fascinated and repelled by Lampatho's hypocrisy: 'thou Janus! thou poltroon! thou protest! thou earwig that wrigglest into men's brains! thou dirty cur, that bemirest with thy fawning!' (*What You Will*, II.i.111–114).[2] When crossed, Lampatho can turn vicious:

> So Phoebus warm my brain, I'll rhyme thee dead.
> Look for the satire: if all the sour juice
> Of a tart brain can souse thy estimate,
> I'll pickle thee.
> (II.i.121–124)

The envy which Hedon and Anaides displayed in *Cynthia's Revels* is attributed to Lampatho in *What You Will*. Thus Quadratus:

> Unwind youth's colours, display ourselves,
> So that yon envy-starved cur may yelp
> And spend his chaps at our fantasticness.
> (II.i.130–132)

The scholar's lack of social graces which made Crites a mark of reproach to would-be courtiers such as Hedon and Anaides is

[1] *Ibid.*, pp. 101–107.
[2] Quotations from *What You Will* are from the text in Bullen's edition of Marston's *Works*.

developed as a theme in *What You Will*, though of course with
a difference. In *Cynthia's Revels*, Crites' scholarly sobriety caused
him to stand out as the one serious, responsible human being in
a society of affected fops and their ladies. In *What You Will*,
Lampatho's scholarly endeavors are but a single phase of his career
and his personality; they are for the most part in the past; he has
come to recognize their futility, and is nothing loath to put them
behind him (rather in the manner of a humor) and become himself
a gallant, which by the end of the play he is bidding fair to do,
having won the hand of one of the wittiest and wealthiest women in
it. What emerges is the portrait of a calculating time-server with
a very shrewd eye for the effects that will work to his advantage.
The mood of the railing satirist descends upon him:

> Dirt upon dirt, fear is beneath my shoe.
> Dreadless of racks, strappadoes, or the sword –
> Maugre informer and sly intelligence, –
> I'll stand as confident as Hercules,
> And, with a frightless resolution,
> Rip up and lance our time's impieties.
> Open a bounteous ear, for I'll be free:
> Ample as Heaven, give my speech more room;
> Let me unbrace my breasts, strip up my sleeves,
> Stand like an executioner to vice,
> To strike his head off with the keener edge
> Of my sharp spirit.   (III.ii.144–156)

But as his audience (Quadratus, the French fop Laverdure, the
fawning Simplicius) urge him on, he rounds upon them in a fierce
change of mood:

> *Laverdure.* 'Tis most gracious; we'll observe thee calmly.
> *Quadratus.* Hang on thy tongue's end. Come on! prithee do.
> *Lampatho.* I'll see you hanged first. I thank you, sir, I'll none.
> This is the strain that chokes the theatres;
> That makes them crack with full-stuff'd audience;
> This is your humour only in request,
> Forsooth to rail; this brings your ears to bed;
> This people gape for; for this some do stare.
> This some would hear, to crack the author's neck;
> This admiration and applause pursues;
> Who cannot rail? my humour's changed, 'tis clear:
> Pardon, I'll none; I prize my joints more dear.
>   (III.ii.162–173)

The play contains a number of jocular references to Lampatho's nocturnal scholarly labors by candle-light. Quadratus is given to calling him 'Lamp' in allusion to these: 'Come, then, Lamp, I'll pour fresh oil into thee' (IV.i.185); the gibe goes back to *Cynthia's Revels*, and is carried on into the opening of I.ii of *Satiromastix*, with Horace and his candle at his labors of poetry (and see the Commentary on *Satiromastix*, I.ii.283 regarding Horace's rug-gown). Lampatho lashes out throughout the play when crossed: 'I'll be revenged', he cries, and Quadratus asks 'How, prithee? in a play?' (IV.i.172–173). He accuses Quadratus of scorning reproof, and Quadratus replies with an imitation of Crites' speech from *Cynthia's Revels*, III.iii.18ff. ('If good Chrestvs, / Evthvs, or Phronimvs, had spoke the words, / They would haue moou'd me, and I should haue call'd / My thoughts, and actions, to a strict accompt / Vpon the hearing: But when I remember, / 'Tis Hedon, and Anaides: alasse, then, / I thinke but what they are, and am not stirr'd'). Here is Quadratus:

> should discreet Mastigophoros,
> Or the dear spirit acute Canaidus
> (That Aretine, that most of me beloved,
> Who in the rich esteem I prize his soul,
> I term myself); should these once menace me,
> Or curb my humours with well-govern'd check,
> I should with most industrious regard,
> Observe, abstain, and curb my skipping lightness;
> But when an arrogant, odd, impudent,
> A blushless forehead, only out of sense
> Of his own wants, bawls in malignant questing
> At others' means of waving gallantry, –
> Pight foutra!
>
> (*What You Will*, II.i.169–181)

All these details from Marston's play have contributed to the craven, time-serving, sycophantic portrait of Horace in *Satiromastix*. Further, the character of Asinius Bubo, Horace's fawning admirer in *Satiromastix*, has a great deal in common with Lampatho's dim-witted admirer, Simplicius Faber in *What You Will*.

In writing *Satiromastix*, Dekker calmly appropriated the four principal satiric figures of *Poetaster* to his own purpose: Jonson's Horace, the high-principled and serenely noble poet who has the

confidence and respect of all right-thinking men in Rome, including his venerable fellow-poet Virgil, and who is welcomed into
the presence of Augustus Caesar, becomes in *Satiromastix* an
ambitious toady seeking to get ahead by his poetic powers of
flattery which can also be turned on occasion to powers of railing
and denunciation; he is by turns arrogant and sniveling, an incor-
rigible hypocrite, a braggart who is in fact a coward, one who
alternately threatens and cajoles. Jonson's poetasters, Crispinus
and Demetrius, become in *Satiromastix* two responsible young
courtiers who look on in dismay at Horace's continual abuse of
the privileges of friendship as he violates confidences to make
sensational matter for satire, and all in the name of exposing vice
in the cause of virtue. They acknowledge his native poetic talent
and are distressed at his vulgar and unseemly use of it to make his
way in society. Tucca, who in *Poetaster* was the loud-mouthed
captain who brought Crispinus together with Demetrius and the
players, is still loud-mouthed in *Satiromastix*, where he has assumed
something of the role of principal satirist; he functions as the chief
decrier of Horace's blatant hypocrisy. Yet for all the unkind
allusions to Jonson's character, to say nothing of the unflattering
allusions to his physique – 'his red, pockmarked face, thin beard,
staring eyes, hollow cheeks, shapeless nose, loud voice', – and the
gleefully taunting references to his piquant personal history 'as
bricklayer, homicide, jailbird, converted Papist, and itinerant
actor dismissed from his company for lack of talent',[1] *Satiromastix*
somehow avoids being a mean-spirited play. Its tone is firm and
clear: it combines a decent (not extravagant) respect for Jonson's
poetic skills, a willingness up to a point to indulge certain personal
peculiarities of his in respect of these, and the decisive announcement that enough is enough, and that Dekker the dramatist and
that segment of public opinion which he represents will no longer
tolerate Jonson's egregious behavior.

What at bottom the war of the theatres was about was the moral
responsibility of the satirist. How disinterested in fact was his
exposure of folly and vice? How much secret pleasure did he take
in railing against what he insisted were general types of offenders

---

[1] Both lists of descriptives are from Price, p. 58.

but which often seemed to bear a striking resemblance to particular persons? Could he who so arrogantly judged others bear the light of judgment on his own behavior? These are the questions which, in one way or another, all the plays connected with the stage quarrel – Marston's, Jonson's, Dekker's *Satiromastix* – ask, and they obviously were of importance to a wider dramatic circle; Shakespeare discusses the issue in a famous exchange between Duke Senior and Jacques in *As You Like It* (II.vii.62ff.). What finally was most devastating about *Satiromastix* was the manner in which it measured Jonson against the standard of moral responsibility he had been at pains to define for society in three massive comical satires, and found him lacking. In the 'Apologetical Dialogue' to *Poetaster*, he announced his intention to abandon comedy, the muse of which had proved 'so ominous' to him, and to try 'If *Tragoedie* haue a more kind aspect' (line 224). Meanwhile, September 1601 found him back with Henslowe, writing additions to the despised *Spanish Tragedy*.[1]

Satiromastix was entered in the Stationers' Register on 11 November 1601, and *Poetaster* a month later, on 21 December; in the event, neither play was printed until the following year, but by the end of 1601, the stage quarrel may be assumed to have spent itself.

Its story has an epilogue. In Cambridge during the Christmas holidays of 1601–1602, the students of St John's College performed a new play that constituted the third part of a trilogy that had been begun three years before. In the Christmas season 1598–1599, the students had performed a play titled *The Pilgrimage to Parnassus*. So successful was it that a sequel (now known as *The Return from Parnassus*, Part One) was acted in the following Christmas season. No performance of either play was given in the season 1600–1601, but now for the Christmas festivities of 1601–1602 a final installment (known as *The Return from Parnassus*, Part Two) was presented. The author or authors of all three plays

---

[1] Henslowe records a payment of £2 to Jonson for this purpose on 25 September 1601 (*Diary*, p. 182). On 22 June 1602, Jonson received £10 for further new additions to *The Spanish Tragedy* (called 'Jeronimo' in both entries), plus 'A Boocke called Richard crockbacke' (*Diary*, p. 203).

are unknown, but he or they were obviously members of the Cambridge academic community with a marked interest in contemporary literary matters. Both parts of *The Return from Parnassus* especially display considerable familiarity with recent developments in the literary world, specifically in relation to such personalities as Marston, Hall, Nashe, Gabriel Harvey and Shakespeare; and near the end of the second *Return* the author, in what has become a *locus classicus* for the subject, makes reference to the recent stage quarrel.

The two Cambridge graduates whose unavailing efforts to make a living after they leave the university are the subject of both parts of the *Return* are at a particularly low ebb in their fortunes, and apply to the Chamberlain's Men for jobs as actors. They are interviewed by Burbage and Kempe, who have a brief scene together (IV.iii) before the applicants appear. Kempe, who is not optimistic about the dramatic talents of scholars, speaks:

Few of the vniuersity men pen plaies well, they smell too much of that writer *Ouid*, and that writer *Metamorphoses*, and talke too much of *Proserpina* & *Iuppiter*. Why heres our fellow *Shakespeare* puts them all downe, I and *Ben Ionson* too. O that *Ben Ionson* is a pestilent fellow, he brought vp *Horace* giuing the Poets a pill, but our fellow *Shakespeare* hath giuen him a purge that made him beray his credit.[1]

The nature of the purge which Shakespeare administered to Jonson has been the subject of immense speculation. That Shakespeare followed the quarrel with interest is obvious from the famous reference to it in *Hamlet* (II.ii.325–362), but none of the efforts to discover in a Shakespearean play something that might be identified as a purge to Jonson have ever won much acceptance.[2] 'The purge ought to be *Satiromastix*', Chambers wrote in *The Elizabethan Stage* (IV, 40): 'though there is nothing to indicate that Shakespeare had any responsibility for *Satiromastix*, it is just conceivable that a Cambridge man, writing before the play was

---

[1] *The Three Parnassus Plays*, p. 337.

[2] *Troilus and Cressida* is the play that has been most often investigated for this purpose. See, e.g., Small, *The Stage-Quarrel*, p. 170, where after a lengthy examination of the play it is concluded 'that the character of Ajax is a hit at Jonson,...and that very likely this play is the "purge" mentioned by Kempe in ii Return from Parnassus'.

assigned to Dekker in print, may have thought that he had'. And
J. B. Leishman, in a note on the passage (line 1772) in his edition
of *The Three Parnassus Plays*, views the purge as 'almost certainly
Satiromastix'. He concludes in an Appendix on the subject:

It may well be that, for the majority of Elizabethan playgoers and playreaders, the Globe and the Chamberlain's Men were as much 'Shakespeare's
theatre' and 'Shakespeare's Company' as for us of to-day, and that, in their
eyes, Shakespeare was as much responsible for what was done at the Globe as,
in the eyes of the law, a husband is responsible for the torts of his wife.[1]

The Commonplace Book of Edward Pudsey, preserved in the
Bodleian Library (MS Eng. poet. d. 3), contains quotations from
a number of plays that were being acted in the years just before
and after 1600, including Chapman's *Blind Beggar of Alexandria*;
Jonson's *The Case is Altered*, *Every Man out of his Humour*,
Cynthia's Revels, *Poetaster*, Marston's *Jack Drum's Entertainment*
and both parts of *Antonio and Mellida*; Shakespeare's *Merchant
of Venice*; and Dekker's *Satiromastix*. Pudsey devotes a full page
of his table-book (fol. 42v) to quotations from what he calls 'The
Untrussing of the Poet': a page that follows appropriately on a
page-and-a-half of quotations from *Poetaster*. The passages from
Dekker's play that he found noteworthy are given in an appendix
at the end of the Commentary. Pudsey's headings for certain of the
extracts are printed in the left-hand margin. Twice at the end of
lines he has inserted (apparently at another date) quotations from
Blurt, Master-Constable, a fact that contributes to the evidence for
Dekker's authorship of that play. The passages in *Satiromastix* to
which Pudsey's quotations refer are identified by act-, scene- and
line-numbers in square brackets. Quotations from *Blurt* are referred
to act-, scene- and line-numbers in Bullen's text of that play in
vol. 1 of his edition of Middleton. To all of these, Pudsey's quotations
often bear only an approximate resemblance. As Halliwell-Phillips
has noted inside the manuscript, 'from the inaccurate state of many
of [the quotations], it may be reasonably concluded that they have
not been taken from the printed editions & that they are, in
all probability, copies of brief short-hand or other notes taken by
Pudseye at the theatres'.

---

[1] *The Three Parnassus Plays*, p. 370.

Reference is made in the Commentary to the work of the following editors of *Satiromastix*: J. H. Penniman (Boston, 1913); H. Scherer (Louvain, 1907).

COMMENTARY

Titlepage

3 *vntrussing*. The play's subtitle had been anticipated in Jonson's *Poetaster*, IV.vii.26–27 (Tucca concerning the play that Demetrius Fannius has been engaged to write against Horace): 'Come, wee'll goe see how forward our iourney-man is toward the vntrussing of him.' The verses of Demetrius that are read during his and Crispinus' arraignment begin: 'Our *Muse* is in mind for th'vntrussing a *poet*' (V.iii.302). And the oath of good behavior administered to Demetrius and Crispinus at the end of the arraignment stipulates among other things that neither shall 'at any time (ambitiously, affecting the title of the *vntrussers*, or *whippers* of the age) suffer the itch of writing to ouer-run your performance in *libell*' (V.iii.604–607). W.I. in *The Whipping of the Satyre* (1601) thus addresses himself to the 'Humourist' (Jonson):

> Come on your wayes, I'le ye no more reproue,
> But what your friends bad, that perfourme I must,
> Correct ye sharpely, not for hate, but loue;
> Stand not on points, then they must be vntrust (sig. G2)

See *Sat.*, V.ii.243, n.

10 *Non recito cuiquam nisi* Amicis *idq; coactus*. Horace, *Satires*, I.4.73. 'This must, it seems, be an ironical thrust at Jonson's self-parade as Horace in *The Poetaster*' (R. B. Sharpe, 'Title-Page Mottoes in the Poetomachia', *Studies in Philology*, 32 (1935), 215).

Ad Lectorem (1, 306)

1 *the Trumpets sounding thrice*. O.F., II.ii.308, n.
2 *this short Comedy of Errors*. *1 H.W.*, IV.iii.24; *M.G.*, p. 131. *N.F.H.*, F3v: 'his ignorance (arising from his blindnesse) is the only cause of this Comedie of errors'.

Dramatis Personæ

1 *William Rufus*, born *c.* 1056, the son of William I the Conqueror, he reigned as William II of England from 1087 to 1100. His death came on 2 August 1100: while hunting in the New Forest, 'he was slaine with an arrow; which being shot unto a Deere, unfortunately glanced upon him' (William Martyn, *The Historie and Lives of the Kings of England* (1638), p. 14). Dekker took over nothing but the name and the lecherous reputation of the King. Martyn continues:

And thus ended the troublesome, yet victorious, reigne of King *William*, third sonne to the Conquerour: who being of a wanton disposition, neglecting marriage, and daily solacing himselfe among his Whores and Concubines, died without any lawfull issue of his bodie. Hee was of a comely stature, firmly compacted in his limbes, very strong, active, and healthy, exceeding lecherous and covetous, of an high courage, and nobly valorous, constant in his resolutions, scorning Fortune, and all troubles (p. 15).

2 *Sir Walter Terill*. William Rufus' death in the hunting accident in the New Forest was probably an assassination, and his alleged slayer was Walter Tirel, lord of Poix in Ponthieu. Tirel may have been acting under orders from William Rufus' younger brother, Henry, who promptly seized the English throne as King Henry I.

7 *Crispinus*. The character is taken over from Jonson's *Poetaster*, where his full name is Rufus Laberius Crispinus, and he functions as a satire on Marston. Jonson chose the name 'Rufus' because of Marston's red hair. It is dropped in *Satiromastix*, perhaps because of possible confusion with William Rufus. Herford and Simpson (IX, 535) – following Small, *The Stage-Quarrel*, p. 26 – cite one of the Horatian sources (*Satires*, 1.4.14–16) for the name 'Crispinus': 'a bad and voluminous poet [who] challenged Horace to see which of them could write faster'. Small notes that the name is also mentioned by Horace in *Satires*, 1.1.120; 1.3.139; 11.7.45.

8 *Demetrius Fannius*. From *Poetaster*; Jonson's satire on Dekker. Herford and Simpson (IX, 536) – following Small, *The Stage-*

Quarrel, p. 27 – note the Horatian sources of the names: Demetrius was a musician whom Horace calls a monkey (*Satires*, 1.10.18 with the Scholiast's note, and 90) and a backbiter (1.10.78–79). Fannius was a feeble poet whom Horace mentions in *Satires*, 1.4.21–22 and 1.10.78–80.

9 [*Pantilius*] *Tucca.* From *Poetaster*; the backbiter ('cimex Pantilius') in Horace (*Satires*, 1.10.78), as Small (*The Stage-Quarrel*, p. 26) and Herford and Simpson (IX, 535) have noted. The name 'Tucca' appears in Everard Guilpin's *Skialetheia* (1598), B8v, 'Satyre Preludium', in an account of the varieties of poetical persuasions to love:

> A third that falls more roundly to his worke,
> Meaning to moue her were she Iew or Turke:
> Writes perfect *Cat and fidle*, wantonly,
> Tickling her thoughts with masking bawdry:
> Which read to Captaine *Tucca*, he doth sweare,
> And scratch, and sweare, and scratch to heare
> His owne discourse discours'd: and *by the Lord*
> *It's passing good: oh good!* at euery word:
> When his Cock-sparrow thoughts to itch begin,
> He with a shrug sweares't *a most sweet sinne.*

The Captain Tucca of *Skialetheia*, *Poetaster*, and *Satiromastix* is generally held to be the same person, and was based in some degree on a contemporary London personality, Captain Jack Hannam (see Dekker's prefatory address 'To the World', lines 29–34, and the note on line 33). Marston seems to have treated the same character under the name 'Tubrio' in *Certaine Satyres*, I, 89–124 and II, 118; *The Scourge of Villanie*, 'In Lectores', 76; *Satyre* VII, 100–138; and as Capro in *The Scourge of Villanie*, VI, 73ff. Davenport, pp. 223–226, suggests that something of the contemporary reputation of Barnabe Barnes also enters into the satirists' treatment of the swaggering captain.

10 *Horace.* The great Roman poet (65–8 B.C.). He is the protagonist of *Poetaster*, maintaining the integrity of poetry in spite of the attacks of mean-spirited and ignorant hacks. His characterization in the play was widely assumed to be a Jonsonian self-portrait.

11 *Asinius Bubo.* Dekker's parody of the name 'Asinius Lupus', a character in *Poetaster.* The two characters have nothing in common.

Ad Detractorem

1–3 *Non potes... esse nihil.* Martial, XIII.2.4–8. Dekker's rejoinder to Jonson's *Ad Lectorem,* with its adaptation of the last four lines of Martial's epigram, VII.12, printed after the list of 'Persons of the Play' in the 1602 quarto of *Poetaster*:

> Ludimus innocuis verbis, hoc iuro [*Ludimus innocui: Scis hoc bene: iuro* in the original] potentis
> Per Genium Famæ, Castalidumque gregem:
> Perque tuas aures, magni mihi numinis instar,
> Lector, inhumana liber ab Inuidia.

For Webster's later use of Martial, XIII.2.4–8, cf. the address 'To the Reader' that prefaces the 1612 quarto of *The White Devil* (lines 3 and 14–15).

To the World

4–5 *Monstrum... ademptum.* Virgil, *Aeneid,* III.658.

9 *Poetasters.* The plural has been taken by Herford and Simpson as evidence that Marston aided Dekker in writing *Satiromastix.* They cite the present passage in a note on *Poetaster,* III.iv.335, where Demetrius has been introduced as 'a dresser of plaies' hired to abuse Horace, and Tucca says 'my Parnassus [i.e. Crispinus], here, shall helpe him'. And they note that Jonson in the 'Apologetical Dialogue', line 154, at the end of *Poetaster* speaks of 'the vntrussers'.

10 *Chopins,* high raised shoes with cork soles. Cf. Barry, *Ram-Alley,* Act V (ed. Hazlitt, *Old Plays,* X, 366–367), quoted in the note on I.i.0.1; and *Hamlet,* II.ii.427. *M.M.L.,* IV.iv.38.

15–16 *Burgonian... against him.* The reference is to John Barrose, the Burgonian fencer whose execution in July 1598 is recorded by Stow (*Annales* (1605), p. 1308):

> Also *Iohn Barrose,* a *Burgonian* by nation, and a Fencer by profession, that lately was come ouer and had chalenged all the Fencers of England, was hanged without Ludgate, for killing of an officer of the Citie which

had arrested him for debt, such was his desperatnesse, and brought such reward as might be an example to other the like.

His reputation as a fencer is affirmed by Martius ('Who nere discourseth but of fencing feates') in Marston's *The Scourge of Villanie*, XI, 60–63:

> Then fals he in againe,
> Iading our eares, and some-what must be saine
> Of blades, and Rapier-hilts, of surest garde,
> Of *Vincentio*, and the *Burgonians* ward.

Guilpin, in *Skialetheia*, Satire V (1598), D5v, refers to 'the *Burgonians* tragedy'.

20 *Bun-hill. R.G.*, IV.ii.9–10, n.

21 *Se defendendo*, in self-defense. Cf. the Gravedigger's blunder in *Hamlet*, V.i.6–9:

> *1. Clown.* How can that be, unless she drown'd herself in her own defense?
> *2. Clown.* Why, 'tis found so.
> *1. Clown.* It must be *se offendendo*, it cannot be else.

29 *his Arraignement*, Jonson's *Poetaster or The Arraignment*, acted in 1601, printed in quarto in 1602. Cf. *Sat.*, IV.iii.197.

29–30 *Cat-a-mountaine*. Topsell, *The Historie of Foure-Footed Beastes* (1607), p. 577, explains the term as an English name for the leopard, and *O.E.D.* defines it as 'the leopard or panther'. But Dekker, in *B.H.*, 419–420, regards 'Leopard' and 'Cat-A-Mountaine' as two distinct beasts. As a term of ferocity, cf. Falstaff's reference to Pistol's 'cat-a-mountain looks' in *The Merry Wives of Windsor*, II.ii.26–27. Cf. *Sat.*, III.i.186.

30 *mewes*. Representing the cry of a cat, and used as a derisive exclamation; a favorite expression of Dekker's, especially in dedicatory epistles. *S.H.R.*, 'Not to the Readers: but to the Vnderstanders' (A3): 'A thousand palats must bee pleased with a thousand sawces: and one hundred lines must content fiue hundred dispositions. A hard taske: one sayes, it is too harsh another, too supple: another too triuiall: another too serious. The first reades, and mewes: the second reades, and

railes: the third reades, and rackes me: the fourth reades, and rends me.' *K.C.*, 'To the Reader' (A4): 'In the self-same scuruey manner doe the world handle poore bookes: when a Reader is intreated to bee curteous, hee growes vnciuil: if you sue to his worship, and giue him the stile of *Candido Lectori*; then hee's proud, and cries mew.' Cf. *1 H.W.*, III. iii.22, n.; *R. G.*, prologue, 6; *W.K.*, II.iii.105. And *Sat.*, I.ii.94.

31 *Stigmaticke*, one stigmatized by nature, deformed, ugly. Greene, *Orpharion* (XII, 66–67): 'for such as nature hath either slipt ouer with negligence, or made in her melancholy, so that they are ill fauored and deformed eyther in face or body: such I holde as a principle to be counted stigmaticall, as noted by nature to be of a bad constitution'. The Devil in *S.H.R.* (D3) speaks of 'that *Stigmaticall Virago Vertue*'. Cf. *W.K.*, III.i.169.

33 *Capten Hannam*. Jack Hannam; he was the captain of a company in Drake's expedition against Spain which sailed in September 1585 (F. P. Wilson, 'An Ironicall Letter', *Modern Language Review*, 15 (1920), 80).

36 *Test*. A continuation of the image of minting, a 'test' being originally 'the cupel used in treating gold or silver alloys or ore' (*O.E.D.*).

50–51 *Detraction...Enuy.* They are personified as hags, dwelling near neighbor one to another, in Spenser, *The Faerie Queene*, V.xii.28. Marston (in 1598) had addressed a preface 'To *Detraction*' ('Enuies abhorred childe') at the beginning of *The Scourge of Villanie*. Cf. the 'Defiance to Enuie' at the beginning of Hall's *Virgidemiarum* (1597), and of Middleton's *Micro-Cynicon* (1599). Envy speaks the induction to *Poetaster*, and cf. the prologue to that play, especially lines 6–10. For Envy and her snakes, cf. *M.E.*, 1368–1369; *I.T.B.N.*, 'To my Loving, and Loved Friends', 30; *T.T.*, 280.

53 *Nauci*, a nutshell, trifle (*naucum*).

54 *Venusian*. Referring to the birthplace of the real Horace, the town of Venusia (now Venosa) in Apulia. Horace, in *Poetaster* (III.v.58) speaks of 'the *Venusian* Colonie' (a scene omitted from the quarto text of the play).

55 *Populus me sibylat at mihi plaudo.* Horace, *Satires*, 1.1.66.
56 *Malim Conuiuis quam placuisse Cocis.* Martial, IX.81.4.

I.i

0.1 *strewing.* With the opening scene, cf. Barry, *Ram-Alley*, Act V
(ed. Hazlitt, *Old Plays*, x, 366–367):

> *Enter* Adriana *and another, strawing herbs.*
> *Adr.* Come, straw apace; Lord, shall I never live
> To walk to church on flowers? O, 'tis fine,
> To see a bride trip it to church so lightly,
> As if her new chopines would scorn to bruise
> A silly flower

On the custom of strewing herbs and flowers from the house
where persons betrothed resided to the church where they
were married, see Hazlitt, *Popular Antiquities*, II, 69–71.

14 *ietting*, strutting. *The Fair Maid of Bristow* (ed. A. H. Quinn,
(Philadelphia, 1902)), line 904: 'See how that bold face ieats
it like a bride.'

32 *gloues*, given to the guests at a wedding. Greene, *Greenes Vision*
(XII, 227): 'Well, on a Sunday it was, and the maids flockt to
Kates fathers house, striuing to make the Bride handsome,
who had a fresh Gowne of home-spun Cloath, and was very
finelie dizond in a little Cappe, and a faire paste: the Glouer
sould two doozen of two peny Gloues, which she gaue to her
friends.' And Field, *Amends for Ladies*, I.i.403–407: 'I am
come from master *Ingen* this morning who is married or to be
married, and though your Ladyships did not honor his
Nuptials with your presence, he hath by me sent each of you
a paire of gloues.' See Hazlitt, *Popular Antiquities*, II, 75–
77.

34 *Rosemary*, used at both weddings and funerals. *W.Y.*, p. 46:
'for the Rosemary that was washt in sweet water to set out the
Bridall, is now wet in teares to furnish her buriall'. See Hazlitt,
Popular Antiquities, II, 71–74. *N.S.S.*, V.ii.0.2, n; 2 *H.W.*,
V.ii.269–271.

39 *leade Apes in hell. P.G.*, II.i.257; *Sat.*, II.i.140.

48 *Rebatoes*, linen-covered wire frames to which the ruff was

pinned, worn by both sexes from about 1590 to 1630. Nashe, *Christs Teares* (II, 151): 'I see Gentleweomen baking in their painting on their faces by the fire, and burning out many pounds of Candle in pinning their treble rebaters, when they wil not bestow the snuffe of a light on looking on anie good Booke.' Stubbes, in *The Anatomie of Abuses* (p. 52) speaks of 'two great stayes' with which the devil ('king and prince ouer all the children of pride') bears up and maintains 'his kingdome of great ruffes':

the one arch or piller wherby his kingdome of great ruffes is vnder-propped, is a certaine kind of liquide matter which they call Starch, wherein the deuill hath willed them to wash and diue his ruffes wel, which, when they be dry, wil then stand stiffe and inflexible about their necks. The other piller is a certain deuice made of wyers, crested for the purpose, whipped ouer either with gold, thred, siluer or silk, & this hee calleth a supportasse, or vnderpropper. This is to be applyed round about their necks vnder the ruffe, vpon the out side of the band, to beare vp the whole frame & body of the ruffe from falling and hanging down.

G.H., B4: 'your trebble-quadruple *Dædalian* ruffes, nor your stiffe necked *Rebatoes* (that haue more arches for pride to row vnder, then can stand vnder fiue London Bridges)'. *P.G.*, III.ii.243. And *Sat.*, II.i.59–63.

48 *poaking.* Cf. II.i.63, and *1 H.W.*, II.i.13, n.

56 *Virginall Iackes.* The jack was 'an upright piece of wood fixed to the back of the key-lever, and fitted with a quill which plucked the string as the jack rose on the key's being pressed down' (*O.E.D.*). *G.H.*, C3: 'thy teeth (as if thou wert singing prick-song) stand coldly quauering in thy head, and leap vp and downe like the nimble Iackes of a paire of Virginals'. For the bawdy *double-entendre* of the present passage, cf. *1 H.W.*, V.ii.266–267; *2 H.W.*, IV.iii.10–11; *N.H.*, I.iii.42–43; *N.S.S.*, IV.ii.26–27.

66 *pew-fellow,* associate. *B.L.*, H3: 'The *Foyst* and the *Nip* (that is to say the Pocket diuer and the cut pursse) are pewfellowes together and of one religion.' *N.F.H.*, C3v. *W.H.*, II.i.208–209; V.i.172; *N.H.*, II.i.6; *I.T.B.N.*, III.iii.48; *L.D.*, V.iii.49.

69–70 *pul'd...eares?* Cf. *W.H.*, V.iv.295–297: 'all the Noise

that went with him poore fellowes haue their Fidle-cases
puld ouer their eares'.

71 *noyse*, band of musicians. *B.L.*, CI–CIV: 'neither are they any
of these terrible noises (with thridbare cloakes) that liue by
red lattises and Iuy-bushes, hauing authoritie to thrust into
any mans roome, onely speaking but this, *Will you haue any
musique?*' And cf. *W.H.*, V.iv.295–297, quoted in the preceding note. In the present passage, 'went' (line 71) = 'began
to play'.

72 *villiacoes*, from the Italian *vigliacco*, defined by Florio as 'a
raskal, a villain, a base, vile, abiect skuruie fellow, a scoundrell'.
B.L., C2: 'my poore *Villiaco*'. The word is very common;
e.g. Jonson, *Every Man out of his Humour*, V.iii.68; Chapman,
Sir Giles Goosecap, III.i.154. And cf. *S.T.W.*, IV.ii.54, n.

74–75 *burnt wine and sugar*. *J.M.M.*, H3–H3v: 'to shew how
much they deserued to comfort him, they askt him what he
would drinke next his heart, but he that not an houre before
had nothing but daggers in his mouth, leaps about their necks,
cals them mad *Greekes*, true *Troians*, commands a gallon of
sacke & suger to be burnt for the *Sergiants*'. *K.C.*, LI, of the
spirit of the dead Nashe,who

inueyed bitterly (as he had wont to do) against dry-fisted Patrons,
accusing them of his vntimely death, because if they had giuen his *Muse*
that cherishment which shee most worthily deserued, hee had fed to his
dying day on fat Capons, burnt sack and Suger, and not so desperately
haue ventur'de his life, and shortend his dayes by keeping company
with pickle herrings.

W.H. V.i.113.

75–76 *curry theyr strings*. Cf. *W.H.*, V.iii.85: 'curry your instru-
ments: play and away'.

99 *Crop*. 'A pouch-like enlargement of the oesophagus or gullet in
many birds, in which the food is partially prepared for
digestion' (*O.E.D.*). Here used presumably for the sake of the
quibble in the following lines. Cf. Webster, *Appius and
Virginia*, II.ii.83–85:

> Come you birds of death,
> And fill your greedy croppes with humane flesh;
> Then to the City flie, disgorge it there.

111–112 *when we are at Church bring wine and cakes.* For the custom
of serving wine with pieces of cake or wafers (called 'sops')
immersed in it during a marriage ceremony, see Hazlitt,
Popular Antiquities, II, 84–86 (where the present passage is
cited).

130 *by my truely.* A mild asseveration. Dryden, *Sir Martin Mar-all*,
Act IV (ed. Summers, II, 121): 'My old Lady may do what she
will, forsooth, but by my truly, I hope she will have more care
of me, then to marry me yet; Lord bless me, what should I do
with a Husband?' *W.H.*, II.i.122.

135 *Drinke that shilling*, i.e. accept that shilling as a tip. Cf. *2 H.W.*,
I.i.176: 'Drinke vp this gold.'

I.ii

0.1 *a candle.* With the present stage direction, Herford and Simpson
(IX, 584) compare the 'Apologetical Dialogue' at the end of
Poetaster, lines 212–213, where the Author speaks of the
agony of bringing forth his 'long-watch'd labours': 'Things,
that were borne, when none but the still night, / And his
dumbe candle saw his pinching throes.' And *Cynthia's Revels*,
III.ii.2–3, where Crites is called 'a whore-sonne booke-
worme, a candle-waster' and (lines 11–12) said to smell 'all
lamp-oyle, with studying by candle-light'. Tucca's words to
Horace at *Sat.*, IV.i.138: 'Goe not out Farding Candle', may
be a similar fling at Jonson's labors. See introduction, p. 193.

7 *Eoan*, from Latin *Eous*, of dawn, of the morning. Drayton, *Ode
to the New Year*, 19, speaks of '*Eoan* brightnesse'.

8–20 *O me thy Priest inspire...spright and flame.* Cf. Jonson,
Underwood, XXV ('An Ode to Iames Earle of Desmond, writ
in Queene Elizabeths time, since lost, and recovered'), lines
8–13:

> *Cynthius*, I applie
> My bolder numbers to thy golden *Lyre*:

O, then inspire
Thy Priest in this strange rapture; heat my braine
    With *Delphick* fire:
That I may sing my thoughts, in some unvulgar straine.

Herford and Simpson (XI, 62) date the poem *c.* 1600. Jonson's autograph manuscript of the *Ode* is preserved in the library of Christ Church, Oxford (lines 1–23 reproduced in Herford and Simpson, VIII, 178). In line 9, for 'bolder numbers' Jonson originally wrote 'flowing numbers'; cf. *Sat.*, I.ii.19. Though not printed until 1640, Jonson's *Ode* to the Earl of Desmond must have been known to Marston and Dekker; cf. *Sat.*, I.ii.92. '*Delphick*' in line 12 (quoted above) is one of the 'new-minted Epithets' which Marston – in 'To those that seeme iudiciall perusers', prefixed to *The Scourge of Villanie* (ed. Davenport, p. 100) – attributed to Torquatus, who has been identified with Jonson.

19 *In flowing numbers fild with spright and flame.* A parody of Jonson's *Ode* to the Earl of Desmond, line 9 (see preceding note), and of *Poetaster*, III.i.12: 'In flowing measure, fill'd with flame, and spright.' The line occurs in the ode Horace is composing when he is interrupted by Crispinus (Marston).

21 *ningle*, mine ingle (intimate, favorite). The word, in its meaning 'catamite', often has dubious connotations, as in the reference to Jove and 'his Ningle *Ganimed*' in *2 H.W.*, I.i.7, and *R.G.*, III.iii.62–63: 'fencers and ningles, / (Beasts *Adam* nere gaue name to)'. The Clown uses it of the diabolic dog in *W. of E.*, III.i.126, 130, 141, and *passim*. And cf. *G.H.*, F3v: 'had none in your company, but your *Perinado* or your *Inghle*'. The word is often associated with players, as in the reference to '*Enghles & Plaiers-Boyes*' in *N.G.*, p. 65. In *I.T.B.N.*, II.i.95, the word is used of a soldier, scholar, and mariner who are about to present a show. In *Poetaster*, Ovid senior, having heard a rumor that his son plans to write for the stage, says indignantly: 'What? shall I haue my sonne a stager now? an enghle for players? a gull? a rooke? a shot-clogge? to make suppers, and bee laught at?' (I.ii.15–17). Cf. Marston, *Histriomastix*, Act II (ed. Wood, III, 260):

Gulsh. I but how if they doe not clap their hands.

Post. No matter so they thump us not, Come, come, we poets have the kindest wretches to our Ingles.

Belsh. Why whats an Ingle man?

Post. One whose hands are hard as battle-dores with clapping at bald-nesse.

Later (Act IV; p. 282), an Ingle appears in conversation with the players:

> *Gul.* You weare the hansom'st compast hilt I have seene;
> *Ingle.* Doth this fashion like my friend so well.
> *Bel.* So well I meane to weare it for your sake.
> *Ingle.* O can deny thee nothing if I would.

Later still (Act V; p. 286) one of the players says: 'Well, I have a Brewer to my Ingle, / Heele furnish me with a horse great inough.' And cf. *Merrie Conceited Jests of George Peele* (1607), p. 22:

There was a Gentleman, who God had indued with good liuing to maintaine his small wit: he was not a foole absolute: although in this world he had good fortune and he was in a manner an Ingell to *George*, one that tooke great delight to haue the first hearing of any worke that *George* had done, himselfe being a writer, and had a Poeticall inuention of his owne.

Thus used, in the sense of a patron of players (or of a poet-dramatist), Asinius Bubo is something of an ingle himself, but he is always heard using the term; it is never used of him. His use of it throughout the present play seems to mean nothing more than 'familiar friend', as in Jonson's *The Case is Altered*, I.ii.2–3: 'What *Signior Antonio Balladino*, welcome sweet Ingle' (and so throughout that play, e.g., II.vii.86; IV.v.33). Cf. *V.M.*, II.i.34, and *1 H.W.*, III.i.141–142: 'its a common thing to call Coz, and Ningle now adayes all the world ouer'. And cf. *1 H.W.*, I.ii.117 ('yngle'), n.

22 *the nine Muses be his midwiues.* Cf. *Poetaster*, III.i.13–14, Crispinus' greeting to Horace: 'Sweet *Horace*, *Minerva*, and the *Muses* stand auspicious to thy desseignes.'

30 *a sacke-full of newes.* Though the earliest extant edition of the jest-book titled *The Sackful of News* is dated 1673, it had been

entered in the Stationers' Register more than a century before, in 1557–1558, and often thereafter, and seems to have had a number of sixteenth-century editions. There was a copy in Captain Cox's library, as described in Laneham's *Letter* concerning the Queen's entertainment at Kenilworth in the summer of 1575 (Nichols, *Progresses of Queen Elizabeth*, I, 454). See F. P. Wilson, *Shakespearian and Other Studies*, ed. Helen Gardner (Oxford, 1969), p. 285. *W.H.*, V.iv.188.

36 *Dam me ift be not the best that euer came from me.* A hit at Jonsonian confidence. Cf. *Cynthia's Revels*, epilogue, 20: 'By God 'tis good, and if you lik't, you may'; and the prologue (armed in 'a well erected confidence') to *Poetaster*, lines 15–20:

> put case our Authour should, once more,
> Sweare that his play were good; he doth implore,
> You would not argue him of arrogance:
> How ere that common spawne of ignorance,
> Our frie of writers, may beslime his fame,
> And giue his action that adulterate name.

In *The Return from Parnassus*, Part Two, lines 297–299, Jonson is said to be 'a bould whorson, as confident now in making of a booke, as he was in times past in laying of a brick'. Demetrius (Dekker) in *Poetaster* (IV.iii.120–121) attacks Horace (Jonson) 'for his arrogancie, and his impudence, in commending his owne things'. And cf. *Every Man out of his Humour*, induction, 220–222.

43 *leafe*, i.e. of tobacco. Concerning the contemporary enthusiasm for tobacco and the art of smoking it, cf. *G.H.*, B2v–B3:

> If there be any strength in thee, thou beggerly monarke of *Indians*, and setter-vp of rotten-lungd chimney-sweepers (*Tobacco*) I beg it at thy smoaky hands: make me thine adopted heire, that inheriting the vertues of thy whiffes, I may distribute them amongst all nations, and make the phantastick *Englishmen* (aboue the rest) more cunning in the distinction of thy *Rowle Trinidado*, *Leafe* and *Pudding*, then the whitest toothd Blackamoore in all *Asia*. After thy pipe, shal ten thousands be taught to daunce, if thou wilt but discouer to me the sweetnesse of thy snuffes.

And F3v: 'From thence you should blow your selfe into the Tobacco-Ordinary, where you are likewise to spend your iudgement (like a *Quacksaluer*) vpon that mysticall wonder, to bee able to discourse whether your *Cane* or your *Pudding* be sweetest, and which pipe has the best boare, and which burnes black, which breakes in the burning, &c.'

47 *fore-head and swelling.* Cf. *R.G.*, II.i.12–14: 'And indeed the raysing of the woman is the lifting vp of the mans head at all times, if one florish, tother will bud as fast I warrant ye.'

57 *O pure, rich,...on, on.* With Asinius' praise of Horace, cf. the raptures of Simplicius Faber at the verbal powers of Lampatho Doria as described in Marston's *What You Will*, II.i.49–55:

> Doth he but speak, 'O tones of heaven itself!'
> Doth he once write, 'O Jesu admirable!'
> Cries out Simplicius. Then Lampatho spits,
> And says, 'faith 'tis good.'

66 *by this Candle (which is none of Gods Angels).* Apparently, as Bang (quoted by Scherer) and Parrott (in his edition of Chapman) have suggested, a parody of *The Blind Beggar of Alexandria*, VI.35–36: 'Now, by this pistol, which is God's angel' (where the phrase 'God's angel' = 'God's messenger of death' (Parrott, II, 679)). Dekker parodies the passage again in *N.H.*, II.i.183–184: 'by this Iron (which is none a gods Angell)'. Cf. *1 Henry IV*, III.iii.33–35, Falstaff to Bardolph: 'If thou wert any way given to virtue, I would swear by thy face; my oath should be "By this fire, that's God's angel."' The basis of the oath is Psalm 104: 4, where it is said that the Lord 'maketh his angels spirits; his ministers a flaming fire'.

94 *Musco*, i.e. musk-cod (or musk-cat), a perfumed fop (cf. II.ii.24, n.). With the present passage, cf. *G.H.*, BIV:

> A fig therefore for the new found Colledge of *Criticks*. You Courtiers that. . .at the rusticall behauiour of our Countrie Muse, will skrew forth worse faces then those which God and the Painter has bestowed vpon you, I defie your perfumd scorne: and vow to poyson your Muske cats, if their ciuet excrement doe but once play with my nose. You *ordinary Gulles,* that through a poore and silly ambition to be thought you inherit the reuenues of extraordinary wit, will spend your shallow censure vpon the most elaborate Poeme, so lauishly, that all the painted table-men about you, take you to be heires apparant to rich *Midasse*.

94 *cryed Mew.* Cf. 'To the World', 30, n.

95 *Rooke*, simpleton, gull. Jonson, *Every Man in his Humour*,
I.v.88–89: 'Hang him, rooke, he! why, he has no more
iudgement then a malt-horse'; and *The Case is Altered*,
II.vii.54–55: 'Why but me thinkes such rookes as these
should be asham'd to iudge.' *W.Y.*, (p. 14):

> Not for applauses, shallow fooles aduenture,
> I plunge my verse into a sea of censure,
> But with a liuer drest in gall, to see
> So many Rookes, catch-polls of poesy,
> That feede vpon the fallings of hye wit,
> And put on cast inuentions, most vnfit,
> For such am I prest forth in shops and stalls,
> Pasted in Powles, and on the Lawyers walls
> For euery Basilisk-eyde Criticks bait,
> To kill my verse, or poison my conceit.

Cf. *Sat.*, I.ii.163, and II.ii.28. *N.H.*, I.ii.50.

100–101 *the Palinode, which I meane to stitch to my Reuels.* The
reference is to the Palinode which closes Jonson's *Cynthia's
Revels*, acted in 1600, printed in quarto in 1601. *N.G.*, p. 71:
'sung extemporall *Odes* in thine honor, & *Palynodes* in
recantation of all former good opinions held of niggardly
patrons'. *J.M.M.*, H3v:

> And whereas before their coming into his roome, he had a foolish
> humor to pistoll them with paper-bullets shot out of pen & inke-
> hornes, he protesteth (with his eyes lifted vp to heauen, higher then his
> heade) that now he will w[r]ite *Palinodes Recantations*, and *Retractions*,
> yea he will presently eate his owne words, though he were sure like
> *Earle Goodwines* drinke they should choake him.

109 *Angels. O.F.*, I.ii.35, n. Cf. *Sat.*, I.ii.369, and III.i.94, 114.

111 *golden baites. P.G.*, IV.ii.200.

117 *neck-verse.* A Latin verse printed in black letter, usually the
beginning of Psalm 51 (*Miserere mei Deus, secundum magnam
misericordiam tuam*), formerly set before one who
claimed benefit of clergy (freedom from penalty imposed by
a secular court); the ability to read established one's right to
the benefit. For the fling at Jonson, see IV.i.136, n.

120–121 *of what fashion is this knights wit, of what blocke? O.F.*,

II.ii.302, n. Cf. *Poetaster*, IV.v.150–152: 'Why, you whore-son block-head, 'tis your only blocke of wit in fashion (now adaies) to applaud other folkes iests.'

125 *lantskip.* Cf. *V.M.*, V.i.10, n.; *W.B.*, prologue, 9–10; *B.H.*, 52; *L.T.*, 106.

126 *sumpter horses, carry good cloaths. 1 H.W.*, IV.i.67–68, n.

128 *the horses walking a'th top of Paules.* The much-noted event that Chamberlain reported to Carleton in a letter of 3 February 1601: 'We have dayly here many new experiments made, as the last weeke one came hopping from Charing Crosse into Powles bounde in a sacke, and this morning another carried up a horse and rode upon him on the top of Powles steeple' (*Letters of John Chamberlain*, ed. N. E. McClure (Philadelphia, 1939), I, 118). In *G.H.*, the gallant visiting St Paul's for the first time is advised to go first to the top of the steeple:

From hence you may descend to talke about the horse that went vp, and striue if you can to know his keeper, take the day of the Moneth and the number of the steppes, and suffer your selfe to beleeue verily that it was not a horse, but something else in the likenesse of one. Which wonders you may publish when you returne into the country, to the great amazement of all Farmers daughters that will almost swound at the report (sig. D3).

Among the complaints voiced by Paul's Steeple in *D.T.* is a reference to the occasion: 'Some (seeing me so patient to endure Crowes and Dawes) pecking at my ribs, haue driuen tame Partridges ouer my bosome, others euen riding ouer me, and Capring vpon my backe, as if they had bin curvetting on the horse, which in despight they brought to Trample vpon me' (sig. D4). The horse was the one owned by Banks (see below, I.ii.306, n.). *J.M.M.*, C2v; *M.G.*, p. 126; *N.H.*, IV.i.77.

130 *prepcsterously behinde your backe.* The phrase quibbles on the sense of 'preposterous' meaning 'inverted in order'. Cf. Henry King, *The Exequy*, 21–22: 'Nor wonder if my time go thus / Backward and most preposterous'.

133 *lymping tongu'd captaine.* For Tucca's stammering, see V.ii.179, 185, and *Poetaster*, I.ii.179–180; IV.v.76–77.

133–134 *poor greasie buffe Ierkin.* Greene, *A Quippe for an Upstart Courtier* (XI, 249): 'one of them had a buffe leather ierkin all greasie before with the droppings of beere that fell from his beard'. And Jonson, *Epicoene*, III.i.52–55, Mistress Otter to her Captain: 'And did not I take you vp from thence, in an old greasie buffe-doublet, with points; and greene vellet sleeues, out at the elbowes? you forget this.'

134 *out of his Element.* An affected phrase: cf. *Twelfth Night*, III.i.57–59: 'who you are, and what you would, are out of my welkin – I might say "element", but the word is overworn'. For the ridicule that may be implicit in Jonson's use of the phrase in *Cynthia's Revels*, I.iv.85 and *Poetaster*, I.ii.33, and Dekker's use of the phrase here and at I.ii.187–188 and V.ii.326, see A. H. Marckwardt, 'A Fashionable Expression; its Status in *Poetaster* and *Satiromastix*', *Modern Language Notes*, 44 (1929), 93–96.

135 *dudgion wit.* With the present passage, Herford and Simpson cf. *Poetaster*, I.ii.248: 'And desp'rate [quarto: 'dudgeon'] censures stab at *poesie*.' 'Dudgeon' was 'A kind of wood... used by turners, esp. for handles of knives, daggers, etc.' (*O.E.D.*).

141 *copper-lace*, imitation gold or silver lace, used for the actors' gowns. Tucca, in *Poetaster* (III.iv.197–199), says to one of the players: 'I heare, you'll bring me o' the stage there; you'll play me, they say: I shall be presented by a sort of copper-lac't scoundrels of you.' Henslowe's *Diary*, p. 49, under date of 28 November 1596, records the loan of 40s. 'vnto marten slater to by coper lace & frenge for the playe of valteger'. *G.H.*, E3: 'By sitting on the stage, you may...examine the play-suits lace, and perhaps win wagers vpon laying tis copper.' Cf. *Sat.*, IV.iii.203–204.

143 *a prepar'd troope of gallants.* Cf. *Poetaster*, III.iv.322–324, where the player says of Demetrius (Dekker), 'a dresser of plaies about the towne': 'we haue hir'd him to abuse Horace, and bring him in, in a play, with all his gallants'.

144 *vnsalted.* Cf. *Poetaster*, IV.iii.87–88, Tucca concerning Crispinus' verses (stolen from Horace): 'shew 'hem; they

haue salt in 'hem, and will brooke the aire'. Concerning
salsus (the salted, sharp) as an ingredient of wit, see Quintilian,
Institutes, VI.3.18–19.

147 *Dor*, buffoon.

148 *cob-web-lawne*, a transparent lawn. Perhaps suggested by
Every Man out of his Humour, II.iii.209–219 (Carlo of
Saviolina's wit): 'shee speakes as shee goes tir'd, in cob-web
lawne, light, thin: good enough to catch flies withall'. Or
Cynthia's Revels, III.iv.80–86 (Crites' derisive account of the
follies to be witnessed at court):

> Then fall they in discourse
> Of tires, and fashions, how they must take place,
> Where they may kisse, and whom, when to sit downe,
> And with what grace to rise; if they salute,
> What curt'sie they must vse: such cob-web stuffe,
> As would enforce the common'st sense abhorre
> Th'*Arachnean* workers.

S.D.S., E4v–F1, of Apishness: 'when his Court remoues, hee
is folowed by *Tobacconists*, *Shittlecock-makers*, *Feather-
makers*, *Cob-web-lawne-weauers*, *Perfumers*, young Countrie
Gentlemen, and *Fooles*'.

149–151 *Why should I care...report me wrong'd*. The lines are
lifted *verbatim* from the quarto text of *Cynthia's Revels*,
III.iii.8–10, where they are part of Crites' scornful soliloquy
denouncing Hedon and Anaides. In the 1616 folio text,
Jonson changed 'Why' (line 149) to 'What'.

153–156 *I thinke...enough*. From *Cynthia's Revels*, III.iii.24–27.
For 'moou'd' (line 153) Jonson's text reads 'stirr'd', for
'arrogant' (line 156) Jonson's text reads 'ignorant'. See
introduction, p. 187.

157 *Criticus*. The name of the principal character in the quarto
version of *Cynthia's Revels*; altered to 'Crites' in the text of
the 1616 folio. For Dekker's identification of the character
with Jonson, cf. *Sat.*, I.ii.311–314.

173 *whiffe*, a form of inhaling; a technical term in the art of tobacco-
smoking. Cf. Marston, *Jack Drum's Entertainment*, Act 1 (ed.
Wood, III, 189): 'Just like a whiffe of Tabacco, no sooner in

at the mouth, but out at the nose'. Instruction in the art is
advertised in *Every Man out of his Humour*, III.iii.47–64,
and III.vi.137–149. *G.H.*, E1 (of the young gallant in an
ordinary):

And heere you must obserue to know in what state Tobacco is in
towne, better then the Merchants, and to discourse of the Potecaries
where it is to be sold, . . . : then let him shew his seuerall tricks in taking
it. As the *Whiffe*, the *Ring*, &c. For these are complements that gaine
Gentlemen no mean respect, and for which indeede they are more
worthily noted, I ensure you, then for any skill that they haue in learning.

W.K., I.ii.92.

174 *tickling geare. 1 H.W.*, II.i.67, n.

180 *pudding*, tobacco rolled into a tight stick or cane in the shape
of a sausage ('pudding'); it had to be shredded by the knife
before smoking. *Cynthia's Revels*, II.ii.93–94: 'neuer kneeles
but to pledge healths, nor prayes but for a pipe of pudding
tabacco'. And Marston, *What You Will*, II.i.26–27: 'Ha, ye
dear rogue, hast any pudding tobacco?' Cf. the passages
quoted in the note on line 43, above. *R.G.*, III.ii.198.

180 *a Lady...tooke a pype full or two.* Howes in his continuation
of Stow's *Annales*, under the year 1614 writes: 'Tobacco, was
first brought, and made knowne in England by sir *Iohn
Hawkins*, about the yeere one thousand fiue hundred sixty-
fiue, but not vsed by englishmen in many yeers after, though
at this day, commonly vsed by most men, & many women'
(*Annales* (1615), p. 948).

184 *take him in snuffe*, take offense at him. The phrase is here used
with a quibble on 'snuff' meaning 'inhale'; where there is so
much fool as Asinius to fill the nostrils, Demetrius has no
need to take tobacco. The phrase originally had reference to
the unpleasant smell from the smoking snuff of a candle.
S.D.S., D4: 'O *Candle-light*, howe hast thou stuncke then,
when they haue popt thee out of their companye: howe hast
thou taken it in snuffe, when thou hast been smelt out.' The
phrase is very common. Cf. *Every Man in his Humour*
(Q 1601), III.iv.123–124; *Poetaster*, II.i.61; *Blurt, Master-
Constable*, IV.iii.24; *The Pilgrimage to Parnassus*, 173;

I Henry IV, I.iii.41; Marston, *Certaine Satires*, II.18; *Every Man out of his Humour*, induction, 180–181.

188 *hit me ith teeth*, reproach me. Tilley, T429. *P.G.*, III.i.108; *W.H.*, III.iii.75–76; *R.G.*, IV.ii.35; V.i.25; *V.M.*, II.i.78.

188–189 *the greatest Clarkes are not the wisest men.* Tilley, C409.

190 *As in presenti.* Cf. Middleton, *A Chaste Maid in Cheapside*, IV.i.53–54: 'He was eight years in his grammar, and stuck horribly / At a foolish place there call'd *as in presenti*.' The pun on 'as' is very common, and is derived from William Lily's *Shorte Introduction of Grammar generally to be vsed... of all those that intende to attaine the knowledge of the Latine tongue*, where in the Latin part some hexameters headed 'G. L. de simplicium verborum primae coniugationis, communi praeterito' begin 'As in presenti, perfectum format in aui, / Vt no nas naui, vocito vocitas vocitaui' (edn. 1567, sig. C6). One of the schoolboys is found struggling with the passage in the scene of the Latin lesson in Marston's *What You Will*, II.ii.56–58:

Hol. Pree, master, what word's this?
Pedant. Ass! Ass!
Hol. As in presenti perfectum format in, in, in –

Nashe, in *Strange Newes* (I, 282), calls Gabriel Harvey 'this Asse *in presenti*, this grosse painted image of pride'.

191 *turne ouer a new leafe.* Tilley, L146. For the pun on 'leaf' (of book and of tobacco), cf. Marston, *The Scourge of Villanie*, 'In Lectores prorsus indignos', 7–13 (ed. Davenport, p. 96):

> Shall each odd puisne of the Lawyers Inne,
> Each barmy-froth, that last day did beginne
> To reade his little, or his *nere a whit*,
> Or shall some greater auncient, of lesse wit,
> (That neuer turnd but browne Tobacco leaues
> Whose sences some damn'd *Occupant* bereaues)
> Lye gnawing on thy vacant times expence?

2 H.W., II.i.44; *M.M.L.*, II.ii.105; *W.H.*, I.i.83.

194 *Inke all gall.* Cf. II.i.120.

198 *Anotomy*, a cadaver; a body for dissection. *N.F.H.*, F4v: 'the Barbar-Surgions had begde the body of a man at a Sessions

217

to make an Anatomie'. *Canaans Calamitie* (1618), G4v: 'like Anotamy of all flesh beryuen'. *2 H.W.*, V.ii.73.

206–207 *write on paper,* | *Made of these turning leaues of heauen, the cloudes.* Cf. *B.L.*, B2v: 'yea, in the verie clowds are written lessons of Diuinitie for thee, to instruct thee in wisdome: the turning ouer their leaues, teach thee the variations of seasons'.

237 *winch.* 'Of a horse: To kick restlessly or impatiently' (*O.E.D.*, *v.*¹2).

238–244 *If you sweare...same man?* A difficult passage. The meaning seems to be: 'If you (Horace) swear to this effect: "Damn me, Fannius or Crispinus, either to the law, to poets, or to players, if I should brand either of you, tax you, scourge you" – can I (Demetrius) wonder then that of five hundred, four (hundred?) should all point their fingers in one instant at one and the same man for being thus forsworn?'

239 *law* (*Our kingdomes golden chaine*). Percy Simpson, in W. H. Williams' *Specimens of Elizabethan Drama* (Oxford, 1905), p. 509, quotes Day, *Law Tricks*, I.i (ed. Bullen, p. 127):

> *Lu.* Wrong not the Law.
> *Poly.*   I cannot, 'tis diuine;
> And ile compare it to a golden chaine
> That linkes the body of a Common-Wealth
> Into a firme and formal Vnion.

247–248 *purge* | *Your sicke and daungerous minde of her disease.* An echo of the purging of Crispinus in *Poetaster*, V.iii.391ff. Cf. *Sat.*, I.ii.368–369.

270 *stile.* The pun on 'stile'/'style' is common. See Chaucer, *The Squire's Tale, Canterbury Tales*, F 105–106: 'Al be it that I kan nat sowne his stile, / Ne kan nat clymben over so heigh a style.' Jonson has it in the quarto (but not the folio) version of *Every Man in his Humour*, I.ii.55–57: 'Here is a *style* indeed, for a mans sences to leape ouer, e're they come at it: why, it is able to breake the shinnes of any old mans patience in the world.' Marston, *The Insatiate Countesse*, Act II (ed. Wood, III, 27): 'I marry, here's a stile so high, as a man cannot helpe a Dog o'er it.' Shakespeare, *Much Ado About Nothing*, V.ii.6–7. Dekker employs the quibble again in *W.E.*, IV.ii.41.

279 *bastards... Muses.* Scherer (p. 90) cites *W.Y.*, p. 6: 'Alas, poore wenches (the nine Muses!) how much are you wrongd, to haue such a number of Bastards lying vpon your hands?' Cf. *Sat.*, IV.ii.149–150.

280 *gorgeous gallery of gallant inuentions.* The title of a poetical miscellany, compiled by Thomas Proctor and published in 1578.

281 *lyme and hayre-rascall.* In reference to Jonson's early career as a bricklayer, '"lyme and hayre" being constituents of mortar' (Penniman, p. 407).

283 *Rug,* a rug-gown, made of hairy frieze and worn by scholars. Cf. *Every Man out of his Humour,* III.vii.18–21: 'You skie-staring cocks-combs you, you fat braines, out vpon you; you are good for nothing but to sweat night-caps, and make rug-gownes deare!' And Marston, *What You Will,* IV.i.179–180, where the scholarly Lampatho Doria says: 'Lamp-oil, watch-candles, rug-gowns, and small juice, / Thin commons, four o'clock rising, – I renounce you all.'

284 *Knights ath Poste.* O.F., I.ii.1, n.

285 *copper-fact.* Cf. below, 367–368, n.

287 *not done yet.* The first of several references to Jonson's slowness of composition. Cf. below, 363, n.

289 *thin-bearded.* Scherer (p. 91) cites one of the epitaphs written by 'a companion' of Jonson's and quoted in the *Conversations with Drummond,* XVII: 'here lyes honest Ben / that had not a beard on his chen' (Herford and Simpson, I, 149). Cf. *Sat.*, V.ii.251.

290 *is this thy Tub Diogines?* In allusion both to the Cynic philosopher of the fourth century B.C., Diogenes of Sinope on the Euxine (said to have lived in a large earthenware tub as part of his program of repudiating civilized customs), and to Jonson's early comedy, *A Tale of a Tub,* written *c.* 1597–1598.

293 *goates pizzel.* 2 *H.W.*, IV.iii.90, n.

293 *Caine.* Like the epithet in the preceding note, an allusion to Asinius' small stature, coupled with a reference to his addiction to smoking, 'cane' being a kind of tobacco. See the quotation from *G.H.*, F3v, quoted in the note on line 43, above.

301 *Sarsens-head at Newgate.* According to Stow, 'a fayre and large Inne for receipt of trauellers, and hath to signe the sarasens head' (*Survey*, II, 34). It was near St Sepulchre's Church, Holborn. Deloney, *The Gentle Craft*, Part Two (p. 178): 'Thereupon *Harry* tooke his knife, and, cutting his finger, all to smeared *Tom-Drums* face with his bloud, that hee made him looke like the Image of *Bred-streete* corner, or rather like the *Sarazines-head* without *New-gate*.' *S.T.M.*, 8; *S.H.*, V.i.14.

302 *dunkirkes guts*, 'narrow passage' (Scherer, p. 92), so called from the channel port.

304 *bench-whistler*, a tavern loafer. *B.L.*, C4: 'all the Bench-whistlers from one end to the other, gaue a ringing *Plaudite* to the *Epilogue* of his speech'. Chapman, *All Fools*, II.i.177–178: 'Y'are but bench-whistlers nowadays to them [poets] / That were in our times.' Tilley, B307.

304–305 *a dagger Pye.* The Dagger in Holborn and the Dagger in Cheapside were both famous for pies. Cf. *Churchyardes Chippes*, Part One (1575), 20*b*:

> like maistres Grace:
> That at the daggar dwelled oens,
> Who made good pies of Mari boens

R. Johnson, *The Pleasant Conceites of Old Hobson* (1607), B2v: 'Euermore when Maister *Hobson* had any buisines abroad, his prentises wold ether bee at the tauerne, filling there heads with wine, or at the dagger in cheapside cramming their bellies with minced pyes.' And cf. Heywood, *If You Know Not Me, You Know Nobody*, Part Two (ed. Shepherd, I, 257):

> *Hob*...And where haue you been?
> *3. Pren.* At breakfast with a Dagger-pie, sir.

O.F., II.ii.98–99.

305 *browne-bread-mouth stinker.* Brown bread was made of wheat mixed with bran. Harrison, *Description of England* (ed. Furnivall, I, 153–155):

> Of bread made of wheat, we haue sundrie sorts, dailie brought to the table, whereof the first and most excellent is the mainchet, which we

commonlie call white bread... The next sort is named browne bread, of the colour, of which we haue two sorts, one baked vp as it cometh from the mill, so that neither the bran nor the floure are any whit diminished... The other hath little or no floure left therein at all... and it is not onelie the woorst and weakest of all the other sorts, but also appointed in old time for seruants, slaues and the inferiour kind of people to feed vpon.

W.A., C4, of Low Country soldiers: 'fed vpon cabbage, vpon rootes, & vpon Christmas day (in stead of minched pyes) had no better cheere than prouant (mouldy Holland cheese, and course browne bread)'. For its use as a term of opprobrium, cf. Nashe, *Christs Teares*, II, 124: 'It is the superaboundance of witte that makes Atheists: wil you then hope to beate them down with fusty brown-bread dorbellisme?' And *S.H.*, II.iii.59: 'auaunt kitchinstuffe, rip you brown bread tannikin'.

306 *Bankes his horse.* This was the famous Morocco, a bay gelding owned by the horse-trainer Banks. Among the many tricks in its performing repertoire, it could dance, add up a throw of dice, tell the number of pence in a silver coin, bow when the King of Scots and Queen Elizabeth were named, and 'bite and strike at you' at mention of the King of Spain. The horse was exhibited at the 'Crosse Keyes in Gracious-streete' before Tarlton's death in 1588, according to *Tarlton's Jests* (1638), C2–C2v, and at 'Belsavage, without Ludgate' in 1595, according to the preface to the tract *Maroccus Extaticus, or Bankes Bay Horse in a Trance*, 1595 (Percy Society (1843), IX, iii). A ballad 'shewing the strange qualities of a yonge nagge called Morocco' was entered in the Stationers' Register on 14 November 1595 (Rollins, no. 2430). Dekker mentions Banks' horse in the following pamphlets: *W.Y.*, p. 6: 'These are those ranck-riders of Art, that haue so spur-gald your lustie wingd *Pegasus*, that now he begins to be out of flesh, and (euen only for prouander-sake) is glad to shew tricks like *Bancks* his Curtall.' *S.D.S.*, F2: 'they doe it (as *Bankes* his horse did his *tricks*) onely by the eye, and the eare'. *L.C.*, K2: 'more strange Horse-trickes plaide by such Riders, then *Bankes* his curtall did euer practise (whose Gamballs of the two, were the honester)'. Cf. *Sat.*, I.ii.128, n.

311 *Pediculous*, infested with lice, lousy.

312 *Asper...Criticus...Horace.* The names under which Jonson
    was assumed to have presented himself in, respectively, *Every
    Man out of his Humour* (1599), *Cynthia's Revels* (1600; cf.
    Sat., I.ii.157, n.), and *Poetaster* (1601).

312–313 *thy tytle's longer a reading then the Stile a the big Turkes.*
    Scherer (p. 92), after Koeppel, compares *I Henry VI*, IV.vii.72–
    74:

> Here's a silly stately style indeed!
> The Turk, that two and fifty kingdoms hath,
> Writes not so tedious a style as this.

313 *the big Turkes*, i.e. the Turkish Sultan's, the Grand Turk's.

319 *Hunkes*, the blind bear, the baiting of which was one of the
    attractions of Paris Garden. Sir John Davies mentions him in
    his *Epigrams* of c. 1594, no. 43 (ed. R. Krueger (Oxford,
    1975), pp. 148–149):

> Publius student of the common law,
> Oft leaves his bookes, and for his recreation:
> To Paris Garden doth himselfe Withdrawe,
>
> To see olde Harry Hunkes and Sacarson.

W.A., B2: 'At length a blinde *Beare* was tyed to the stake, and
in stead of baiting him with dogges, a company of creatures...
took the office of Beadles vpon them, and whipt monsieur
Hunkes, till the blood ran downe his old shoulders.' And cf.
S. Rowlands, *The Knave of Harts* (1612), F4:

> an vnfortunate two-legged *Beare*,
> Who though indeede he did deserue no ill,
> Some Butchers (playing Dogs) did well-nye kill:
> Belike they did reuenge vpon him take,
> For *Hunckes* and *Stone*, and *Paris-gardens* sake
> With all the kindred of their friend old Harry

M. P. McDiarmid ('The Stage Quarrel in *Wily Beguiled*',
Notes and Queries, 201 (1956), 380–383) suggests a reference
to Jonson under the same name in *Wily Beguiled* (M.S.R.
(1912), prepared by W. W. Greg), lines 1613–1617: 'I am

none of these sneaking fellowes that wil stand thrumming of
Caps, and studying vppon a matter, as long as *Hunkes* with
the great head has beene about to show his little wit in the
second part of his paultrie poetrie.' Cf. *Sat.*, V.ii.244.

320 *gull-groper.* Halliwell, noting the occurrence of the term in the
present play, defined 'gull-gropers' as 'Usurers who lend
money to the gamesters'. Penniman (p. 409) declared 'to
"grope a gull" was to swindle'. Neither seems right. 'Grope'
has the meaning 'examine, sound, probe' (*O.E.D.*, *v.*4.c).
Thus 'gull-groper' means one given to investigating or exposing fools. Cf. Marston, *Jack Drum's Entertainment*, Act I
(ed. Wood, III, 190):

> He that makes costly suppers to trie wits:
> And will not stick to spend some 20. pound
> To grope a gull.

And Jonson, *Cynthia's Revels*, IV.iii.382, Phantaste of the
foolish Asotus: 'Call him hither, 'tis good groping such a
gull.'

324 *thou sayst Crispinus Sattin dublet is Reauel'd out heere.* Jonson
had so done in *Poetaster*, III.i.66–70:

Cris. Pray thee, Horace, obserue.
Hora. Yes, sir: your sattin sleeue begins to fret at the rug that is vnderneath it,
I doe observe: And your ample veluet bases are not without euident staines
of a hot disposition, naturally.

325 *and that this penurious sneaker is out at elboes.* The sneer at
Demetrius occurs in *Poetaster*, III.iv.318–324:

Tvcc. . . . what's he, with the halfe-armes there, that salutes vs out of his
cloke, like a *motion?* ha?
Hist. O, sir, his dubblet's a little decaied; hee is otherwise a very simple
honest fellow, sir, one Demetrivs, a dresser of plaies about the towne,
here; we haue hir'd him to abuse Horace, and bring him in, in a play,
with all his gallants.

326 *ban-dog*, a dog so ferocious that it had to be kept fastened up
(where 'ban' = 'band', *O.E.D.*, *sb.*[1] 5: 'A leading-string,
strap, or chain'). *D.D.*, E3v: 'Base *Heapes* tumbled together,
who all yell'd / Like bandogs tyed in kennels'. *S.D.S.*, F1v:

'filthy wide-mouthed bandogs'. *S.H.*, I.iv.9; *V.M.*, II.iii.112; *W. of E.*, IV.i.235; *L.D.*, IV.iv.30. And *Sat.*, IV.i.133.

330 *olde Coale*. Tucca's response to Horace's 'Ile laye my handes vnder your feete' (lines 327–328). The term is sometimes used for a pander, as explained in Marston's *The Malcontent*, II.ii.1–9:

> *Malevole.* Bless ye, cast o' ladies! – Ha, Dipsas! how dost thou, old coal?
> *Maquerelle.* Old coal!
> *Malevole.* Ay, old coal; methinks thou liest like a brand under billets of green wood. He that will inflame a young wench's heart, let him lay close to her an old coal that hath first been fired, a pand'ress, my half-burnt lint, who, though thou canst not flame thyself, yet art able to set a thousand virgins' tapers afire.

Cf. *2 H.W.*, IV.i.224; *W.H.*, II.i.126.

331–332 *rowly powlies*, compeers, corrivals, equals. Cf. Jonson, *A Tale of a Tub*, II.ii.15: 'What? Rowle-powle?...All fellowes?' And *Poetaster*, I.ii.24–29: 'How now, good man slaue? what, *rowle powle*? all riualls, rascall? why my master of worship, do'st heare? Are these thy best proiects? is this thy desseignes and thy discipline, to suffer knaues to bee competitors with commanders and gent'men? are wee *paralells*, rascall? are wee *paralells*?' Herford and Simpson have noted (IX, 285) that while *O.E.D.* explains 'rowle powle' as 'A worthless fellow; a rascal', 'both the Jonson passages and their context suggest a levelling of social distinction'. In support of this meaning, they cite S. Rowlands, *Hell's Broke Loose* (1605), B3: 'Wee'le ayme our thoughts on high, at Honors marke: / All rowly powly; Tayler, Smyth, and Clarke'; and they note that here *O.E.D.* queries the word as an adverb, meaning 'Pell-mell, without distinction'. The present passage is further evidence that Herford and Simpson are right in their suggestion that 'rowle powle' implies a levelling of social distinction. Cf. also *Blurt, Master-Constable*, I.ii.95–98:

> *Laz.* I have the general's hand to pass through the world at my pleasure.
> *Blurt.* At your pleasure! that's rare. Then, rowly, powly, our wives shall lie at your command.

332 *Damons . . . Pithyasse*. Richard Edwards' *Damon and Pithias*
(earliest extant edition, 1571, but acted *c.* 1564–1565) had
dramatized the classical story. The more recent *Damon and
Pithias* of Chettle, for which Henslowe paid advances to the
author between 16 February and 27 April 1600 (it was licensed
on 16 May 1600) is lost. See Henslowe, *Diary*, pp. 63, 131,
133, 134. The point of the present reference seems to be solely
to give Tucca an occasion to call Horace 'their Pithy-asse',
perhaps in retaliation for the manner in which Jonson had
played with the name 'Crispinus, alias Crispinas' in *Poetaster*,
V.iii.218. Cf. *Sat.* II.ii.38: 'as for *Crispinus*, that Crispin-asse'.

337 *fels't into the hands of sattin*. For the pun on Satan, cf. *I.T.B.N.*,
IV.ii.112, n.

339 *Gorboduck*. Cf. *Poetaster*, V.iii.439–440 (Tucca to the Lictors
as they put the case of vizards on his head): 'Hold your hook't
talons out of my flesh, you inhumane *Gorboduckes*.' Jonson
changed the word to '*Harpies*' in the 1616 folio. The allusion
is to Gorboduc, the legendary British king whose division of
his kingdom between his two sons, Ferrex and Porrex, led
to civil war and the murder of the elder by the younger. Sackville and Norton's tragedy on the subject was acted before the
Queen on 18 January 1562; there were printed editions in
1565, *c.* 1571, and 1590. Day's edition of *c.* 1571 carries the
title *The Tragidie of Ferrex and Porrex*. Henslowe, between
18 March and 13 April 1600, made four payments (the last
one 'in full') to William Haughton for 'A Boocke called
ferex & porex' (*Diary*, pp. 132, 133). The play, which is lost,
was licensed sometime between 7 and 10 May 1600 (*Ibid*,
p. 134). Cf. *Sat.*, I.ii.392.

342 *heyre apparant of Helicon*. Cf. *W.Y.*, p. 5: 'they giue out, that
they are heires-apparent to *Helicon*, but an easy *Herald* may
make them meere yonger brothers'.

347 *Mary muffe. 1 H.W.*, II.i.41, n.

347 *man a ginger-bread*. Cf. *Blurt, Master-Constable*, II.ii.312–314:
'I am so choked still with this man of gingerbread, and yet I
can never be rid of him!' There is perhaps an echo of *Poetaster*,
IV.iii.160–163:

Deme. I'le goe write, sir.

Tvcc. Doe, doe, stay: there's a drachme, to purchase ginger-bread, for thy *muse.*

'Figures made of gingerbread frosted and ornamented gave rise to the expression, meaning showy, unsubstantial' (Penniman, p. 410). Cf. *S.D.,* III.i.36.

347–348 *small coale. W.H.,* III.iii.1.

355–356 *when thou ranst mad for the death of Horatio.* The reference is to Jonson's performance as Hieronimo in Kyd's *The Spanish Tragedy,* presumably both as a strolling player and at Paris Garden, in his acting days. The play, originally produced between 1584 and 1589, was revived in 1597. Cf. *Sat.,* IV.i.131–132.

356 *thou borrowedst a gowne.* For the suggestion that 'Jonson perhaps reverted to this reminiscence' in *The Alchemist,* IV. vii.67–71, see Herford and Simpson, I, 14 (n. 2).

356 *Roscius,* the famous Roman actor (d. 62 B.C.). Cf. *B.R.W.R.,* p. 201: 'the onely Roscius of the time, and one of the best Actors that euer stept on stage'. For the identification, in the present passage, of Roscius with Burbage, see Penniman, p. 411.

362 *wut,* wilt. Cf. Tucca's similar use of 'shat' (shalt) at III.i.206.

363 *fifteene weekes.* A hit at Jonson's slowness of composition. Cf. Envy's prologue to *Poetaster,* 14–17:

> these fifteene weekes
> (So long as since the plot was but an *embrion*)
> Haue I, with burning lights, mixt vigilant thoughts,
> In expectation of this hated play.

And the 'Apologetical Dialogue' at the close of *Poetaster,* 193–195:

> *Pol.* . . . they say you are slow,
> And scarse bring forth a play a yeere.
> *Avt.*   'Tis true.
> I would they could not say that I did that.

In *The Return from Parnassus,* Part Two, lines 296–297, Jonson is said to be 'so slow an Inuentor, that he were better betake himselfe to his old trade of Bricklaying'. In fact, that

Jonson should write a play within the space of fifteen weeks
was for him something of a record. See Introduction, p. 181.

363–364 *Cockatrices egge*. Cf. Isaiah 59: 5: 'They hatch cockatrice'
eggs, and weave the spider's web: he that eateth of their eggs
dieth, and that which is crushed breaketh out into a viper.'
L.C., H4: 'Shee is the Cockatrice that hatcheth all these egges
of euills.' The cockatrice, or basilisk, was a fabled reptile
hatched by a serpent from a cock's egg, and reputed to kill
by its mere glance. The present passage is probably an echo
of Envy's prologue to *Poetaster*, 35–37:

> Are there no players here? no poet-apes,
> That come with basiliskes eyes, whose forked tongues
> Are steept in venome, as their hearts in gall?

367–368 *saffron-cheeke*. Cf. line 285: 'copper-fact rascal'; both this
and the present passage are allusions to Jonson's dark complexion.

368 *Sun-burnt Gipsie*. Cf. Drayton, *Englands Heroicall Epistles*,
'Mistress Shore', 114: 'a Sunne-burnt base Egyptian'. And
Nashe, *Christs Teares*, 'To the Reader', II, 180: 'Sixe and
thirtie sheets of mustard-pot paper since that hath he [Harvey]
published against me, wherein like a drunken beggar he hath
rayled most grossely, and imitated the rascally phrase of
sunne-burnt rogues in the field.' *L.D.*, III.ii.206.

368–369 *giue... Pilles*. An echo of the purgation administered by
Horace to Crispinus in *Poetaster*, V.iii.391ff. Cf. *Sat.*, I.ii.247–
248.

369 *ten shillings... Angelica*. With a pun on 'angel', a gold coin
the value of which was 10s. (*Shakespeare's England*, I, 341).
But see as well the following note.

369–370 *Angelica... tumbler*. This would appear to be another
allusion to 'the nimble tumbling Angelica' whom Marston
mentions in *The Scourge of Villanie*, XI, 101, and the present
passage may give further support to the identification, suggested by Chambers, II, 263, n. 4, of Marston's Angelica with
Angelica Alberghini, who by 1580 was the wife of Drusiano
Martinelli, an Italian actor known to have been in London in

January 1579; the present reference, together with Marston's, may, as Chambers suggested, indicate a later visit. Whether or not Angelica was an acrobat is not certain, but it seems likely that she was. Acts of tumbling were prominent features of performances by the Italian companies. In November 1573 Thomas Norton complained of 'the unchaste, shamelesse and unnaturall tomblinge of the Italian weomen'; and among the Chamber Accounts for 1577–1578 is an item 'for a matres hoopes and boardes with tressells for the Italian Tumblers' (Chambers, II, 262).

372 *Goe by Ieronimo.* The much-parodied tag from *The Spanish Tragedy*, III.xii.31; in Kyd's play, it is spoken by Hieronimo himself. Horace (Jonson) is here being taunted for his association with the role (cf. lines 355–356). Dekker quotes the line elsewhere in *S.H.*, I.ii.41–42; *W.H.*, II.ii.185.

373 *when.* An exclamation of impatience. Cf. *Respublica* (ed. J. S. Farmer, *'Lost' Tudor Plays* (London, 1907), p. 264): 'Come, off at once! when? come off!' Shakespeare, *Julius Caesar*, II.i.5: 'When, Lucius, when? Awake, I say!' *Richard II*, I.i.162–163: 'When, Harry? when? / Obedience bids I should not bid again.' *S.H.*, III.ii.8; *P.G.*, III.i.50; *I.T.B.N.*, II.iii.70, 73; *M.M.L.*, III.ii.71; *W.E.*, IV.ii.100; *L.D.*, V.ii.76; *2 H.W.*, II.ii.43. And *Sat.*, IV.iii.169.

374 *Mœcenas.* Born between 74 and 64 B.C., he was the patron of a literary circle that included Virgil and Horace. He died in 8 B.C. Jonson includes him among the *Dramatis Personae* of *Poetaster*. With the whole of the present passage, wherein Tucca proposes a gift of money for a compliant Horace and pronounces himself his Maecenas, cf. the exchange between Quadratus and Lampatho Doria in Marston's *What You Will*, II.i.228–233:

Lam. I protest –
Qua. Nay, leave protests; pluck out your snarling fangs. When thou hast means, be fantastical and sociable. Go to: here's my hand; and you want forty shillings, I am your Mecaenas, though not *atavis edite regibus*.

Cf. *Poetaster*, I.ii.163.

374 *dam vp's Ouen-mouth*. Penniman (p. 412) compares Nashe, *Christs Teares* (II, 124): 'damme vp the Ouen of your vttrance'.

375 *vauward*, vanguard.

375–376 *yonder foure Stinkers*, i.e. Crispinus, Demetrius, Horace, and Asinius.

376 *the Knight*, i.e. Sir Quintilian.

377 *Summa totalis*. *N.F.H.*, H2: 'but what is your *Summa totalis*, (quoth *Charon*), *Summa totalis*, answers the other commes to three shillings and a pennie.' *G.H.*, D2v: 'bee an absolute confirmed Foole, in *Summa Totali*'. And Middleton, *The Family of Love*, V.iii.400: '*Summa totalis*, a good audit ha' you made.'

385 *Tilt-yard*. Stow writes of the City of Westminster: 'South from Charing crosse on the right hand, are diuers fayre houses lately builded before the Parke [St James Park], then a large Tilt yard for Noblemen and other to exercise themselues in Iusting, Turn[ey]ing, and fighting at Barryers' (*Survey*, II, 101).

388 *golles*. A cant term for 'hands'. *Poetaster*, V.iii.187–188: 'Make 'hem hold vp their spread golls.' *W.Y.*, p. 54: 'held vp his gowty golles and blest himself'. *1 H.W.*, I.iv.49; V.ii.453; *N.S.S.*, II.ii.65; *R.G.*, I.ii.240.

388 *a Souldiers Spur-royall*. A spur-royal was a gold coin (a rial) with a value, during the reigns of Elizabeth and James I and VI, of 15s. It bore on the reverse a blazing sun with rays which resembled the rowel of a spur. The 'Souldiers' spur-royal was evidently a shilling, though I have not encountered the phrase elsewhere.

391–392 *deuide my Crowne*, i.e. give a half-crown, which is the total sum of Tucca's gift; he has offered 'a Souldiers Spur-royal' (= 1s.), has doubled it ('double presse-money'), making 2s., and now adds a teston (a silver coin valued at 6d.).

392 *Porrex*. Cf. line 339, n.

393 *Mandrake*. As a term of abuse, cf. Shakespeare, *2 Henry IV*, I.ii.14–15: 'Thou whoreson mandrake'. Jonson, *Epicoene*, IV.ii.90: 'O viper, mandrake!'

393 *Skeldring*, begging (used especially of the disbanded or wounded soldier); but the word also carries the sense of 'cheating'. It occurs frequently in *Poetaster*, where it is always used by or about Tucca. He is called 'the madde skeldring captaine' (I.i.24–25); he says of players: 'An honest decayed commander, cannot skelder, cheat, nor be seene in a bawdie house, but he shall be straight in one of their wormewood *comoedies*' (I.ii.49–51); he says to one of their numbers: 'There are some of you plaiers honest gentl'-man-like scoundrels,...and are companions for gallants. A man may skelder yee, now and then, of halfe a dozen shillings, or so' (III.iv.152–156); at the arraignment of Crispinus and Demetrius he says in an aside: 'Would I were abroad skeldring for a drachme, so I were out of this labyrinth againe' (V.iii.183–184). Dekker, in the dedicatory Epistle to *S.D.S.*, A3v, says of the practice of dedicating the same book to sundry patrons: 'That art of *Skeldring* I studie not'; later in the same tract he speaks of 'skeldring soldiers, and begging schollers' (F2v). And cf. *G.H.*, E2: 'And no question if he be poore, he shall now and then light vpon some *Gull* or other, whom he may skelder (after the gentile fashion) of money.' *R.G.*, V.i.104.

394 *farewell my sweet.* A form of address that seems to have been associated with swaggering gallants. Cf. Guilpin, *Skialetheia*, Epigram 53, 'Of Cornelius' (1598), B4v:

> He wallows in his walk his slop to grace,
> Sweares *by the Lord*, daines no salutation
> But to some iade that's sicke of his owne fashion,
> As *farewell sweet Captaine*

And Marston's Tubrio in *The Scourge of Villanie*, VII, 105–106:'He that salutes each gallant he doth meete, / With *farewell sweet Captaine, kind hart, adew*.' For a discussion of the features that Tubrio shares with the Tucca of both *Poetaster* and *Satiromastix*, see Davenport (ed.), *The Poems of John Marston*, pp. 223–226.

394–395 *Amadis de Gaule.* Anthony Munday's translation (from the French of Nicholas de Herberay) of the first book of this Spanish romance was published *c.* 1590 (the titlepage is missing

from the only extant copy); the second book (translated by
'Lazarus Pyott') appeared in English in 1595. Translations of
Parts Three and Four were printed in 1618. See G. R. Hayes,
'Anthony Munday's Romances of Chivalry', *Library*, 4th
Series, 6 (1926), 61–63, 68, and J. J. O'Connor, *Amadis de
Gaul and its influence on Elizabethan literature* (New Brunswick,
N.J., 1970).

399 *March faire.* Jonson, *The Case is Altered*, V.xiii.66–67:
'March faire al, for a faire March, is worth a kings ransome.'
And Fletcher, *Wit Without Money*, IV.v.12:

> *Isab.* Forward with the meat now!
> *Rog.* Come, gentlemen, march fairly.

S.H., V.ii.210; *2 H.W.*, IV.iii.45.

II.i

1 *Lungis*, 'a long, slim, awkward fellow; a lout' (*O.E.D.*). Cf.
Beaumont, *The Knight of the Burning Pestle*, II.320–321:
'the foule great Lungeis laid unmercifully on thee'.

8 *stronge backe, and a soft bellie.* Cf. *G.H.*, B3v: 'Good Cloathes
are the embrodred trappings of pride, and good cheere the
very *Eringo-roote* of gluttony: so that fine backes, and fat
bellies are Coach-horses to two of the seuen deadly sins.'

12–16 *implements...of a Lady...Coach, and my fan.* Marston,
What You Will, I.i.190–191 (of a widow who is determined to
marry a knight):

> *Ran.* Then must my pretty peat be fann'd and coach'd?
> *Jaco.* Muff'd, mask'd, and ladied.

22–24 *fetcht...farre...good for Ladies.* An allusion to the
proverb 'Dear bought and far fetched are Dainties for ladies'
(Tilley, D12). Allusions to the proverb are numerous: e.g.
Marston, *The Malcontent*, V.iv.66; Jonson, *Cynthia's Revels*,
IV.i.18; Day, *Law Tricks*, Act IV (ed. Bullen, p. 168); Lyly,
Euphues (ed. Bond, I, 236). The Stationers' Register, for the
period 22 July 1566–22 July 1567, records an entry for 'a play

intituled *farre fetched and Deare bought ys good for lad[i]es'*
(Arber, I, 331).

23 *Low Countries.* Penniman (p. 414) quotes Gosson, *Quippes for
Vpstart Newfangled Gentlewomen* (1595), A4: 'These Holland
smockes so white as snowe, / and gorgets braue with drawn
work wrought'.

39–42 *crow ouer...cocke...combe.* Cf. *2 H.W.*, V.ii.61–62: 'This
is the Hen, my Lord, that the Cocke (with the Lordly combe)
your Sonne-in-law would crow ouer, and tread.' *R.G.*,
III.ii.192–194: ' 'tis one of *Hercules* labours, to tread one of
these Cittie hennes, because their cockes are stil crowing ouer
them'.

44 *browne study.* *N.G.*, p. 69: 'As for the Citie, thats so full of
Crafts-men, there is no dealing with their misteries: the nine
Muses stand in a brown study, when they come within their
liberties.' *N.F.H.*, GIV: 'being told that hell is iust so many
miles from earth, as earth is from heauen, he stands in a
browne study, wondring...how it should happen, that he
tooke rather the one path then the other'. Tilley, S945.

59–63 *Rebato...pinning...poaked.* I.i.47–48.

66 *the cloute* (French *clou*), the wooden pin, usually painted white,
by which the target was fastened to the butt. Cf. *Love's
Labour's Lost*, IV.i.134: 'Indeed 'a must shoot nearer, or
he'll ne'er hit the clout.'

71 *siluer voice.* Cf. *O.F.*, I.i.330, n.

75 *a Hall.* An exclamation used to make room in a crowded
apartment when an open space was required for a dance or
a masque. Cf. Chapman, *May-Day*, V.i.109–110: 'Welcome,
gallants! Oh, the room's too scant; a hall, gentlemen!' And
Chapman, *The Widow's Tears*, III.ii.1–6: 'A hall, a hall!
Who's without there? *Enter two or three with cushions.* Come
on, y'are proper grooms, are ye not?...Their honours are
upon coming, and the room not ready. Rushes and seats
instantly!' *Romeo and Juliet*, I.v.26: 'A hall, a hall! give
room! and foot it, girls.'

81–82 *key-colde*, 'as cold as a key; very cold; esp. cold in death'
(*O.E.D.*). *S.D.S.*, C2v: 'To knocke, hee thought it no

policy, because such fellowes are commonly most churlish, when they are most intreated, and are key-cold in their comming downe to Strangers, except they be brybed.' Tilley, K23.

106 *puʒd*, buzzed (Scherer, p. 97).

106 *a hundred merie tales.* The popular jest-book was printed by Rastell in 1526; there are entries in the Stationers' Register for the period 1557–1558 (Arber, I, 75) and 15 January 1582 (*ibid.*, II, 405). There was a copy in Captain Cox's library according to the Laneham *Letter* (Nichols, *Progresses of Queen Elizabeth*, I, 454). Benedick accused Beatrice of getting her wit out of it in *Much Ado About Nothing*, II.i.129–131.

108 *Sapline*, chaplain (Scherer, p. 97).

109 *prease*, press (Skeat and Mayhew).

110 *celler.* A quarto misprint for 'coller' (i.e. choler)? Cf. line 121.

113 *take shalke for shees.* Tilley, C218 ('No more like than Chalk and cheese' or 'To give chalk for cheese'). *W.A.*, G1: 'Whereas through the extreame deadnesse of time and terme, we all run backward in our condition, hauing great rents to pay, and greater scores, which will neuer bee paid, guests now being glad if they can make vs take chalke for cheese'.

122 *I neither know that Horace.* So much for the imperial intimacy of Jonson's Horace with Augustus Caesar in *Poetaster*.

129 *Miniuer cappe. S.H.*, V.iv.49.

131 *daunce...the saking of the seetes. S.H.*, IV.iv.82, n.

140 *Leades Apes in hell.* I.i.39.

154 *your hot beautie's melt.* Cf. Capulet to his servants in *Romeo and Juliet*, I.v.28: 'And quench the fire, the room is grown too hot.'

161 *fadom.* 'A fathom was the extent of the out-stretched arms. Here it means what they embrace, the bride' (Penniman, p. 415).

167 *back-bite. W.H.*, V.i.94.

188 *yellow*, the color of jealousy. *2 H.W.*, I.i.111–112, n.

209 *Endimions. G.H.*, C1v: 'looke vppon *Endymion*, the Moones Minion, who slept threescore & fifteene years and was not a haire the worse for it'. *M.M.L.*, V.ii.78; *V.M.*, II.ii.46.

210 *dyet drinkes.* V.i.141.

II.ii

4–5 *Pee and Kue.* 'Pee' = 'a coat of coarse cloth worn by men, esp. in the 16th century' (*O.E.D., sb.*¹). 'Cue' = 'humour, disposition, mood, frame of mind (proper to any action)' (*O.E.D., sb.*² 4). Tilley, P1.

8 *Critist,* critic. See *M.E.,* 54, n.

13 *grace,* 'the permission which a candidate for a degree is required to obtain from his College or Hall' (*O.E.D.*).

15 *Beagle. W.H.,* III.iv.3, n.

16 *it passes.* Cf. Shakespeare, *Troilus and Cressida,* I.ii.166–167: 'all the rest so laugh'd, that it pass'd'. And *Wily Beguiled,* (M.S.R.), lines 1433–1434: 'her father oth tother side, he yoles at her, and ioles at her; and shee leades such a life for you it passes'.

18 *Conniue.* The affected Madam Moria uses the word in *Cynthia's Revels,* IV.ii.41–42: 'and therefore there is more respect requirable, howsoere you seeme to conniue'.

24 *Muske-cod,* literally a small bag or purse used for perfumes; used figuratively for a fop. Cf. *Every Man out of his Humour,* V.vi.11; Marston, *Antonio and Mellida,* III.ii.108. *M.M.L.,* I.i.55; *N.S.S.,* II.i.33. Cf. *Sat.,* I.ii.94, n.

28 *Rooke.* I.ii.95, 163.

34 *spangle babies.* Cf. *P.G.,* II.i.19–23: 'for my briske spangled babie wil come into a Stationers shop, call for a stoole and a cushion, and then asking for some greeke Poet, to him he falles, and there he grumbles God knowes what, but Ile be sworne he knowes not so much as one Character of the tongue'.

35 *true heires of Master Iustice Shallow.* The two Shakespearean plays in which he figures were of recent date. *2 Henry IV* was presumably acted in 1598 and printed in 1600; *The Merry Wives of Windsor* was written *c.* 1597 and printed (in a corrupt version) in 1602. Cf. Jonson, *Every Man out of his Humour,* V.ii.22: 'this is a kinsman to iustice Silence', and Nicholson's suggestion (cited in Herford and Simpson's note, IX, 473) that such a kinsman may mean 'a Shallow'.

38 *Crispinus, that Crispin-asse.* I.ii.332, n.

39 *Fannius his Play-dresser. Poetaster,* III.iv.321–324: 'one Demetrivs, a dresser of plaies about the towne, here; we haue hir'd him to abuse Horace, and bring him in, in a play, with all his gallants'.

41–42 *cut an Innocent Moore i'th middle, to serue him in twice; and when he had done, made Poules-worke of it.* This bit of theatrical gossip has occasioned much speculation. Horace charges Fannius (Dekker) with having made two plays out of a previously existing one (dealing presumably with a 'Moore') and purveying them either (1) to two separate acting companies, one of which was the Children of Paul's, or (2) selling both plays to Paul's (either meaning could be implied in 'serue him in twice' and 'made Poules-worke of it'). Dekker, the author of *Satiromastix,* does not deny the charge. The 'Moore' has sometimes been identified with Muly Mahamet in Peele's *The Battle of Alca≥ar.* Originally written in 1588 or 1589 and printed in 1594, Peele's play had recently (sometime between 1598 and 1600) been revived by the Admiral's Company. Jonson had parodied it in *Poetaster* when one of Tucca's pyrgi announces (III.iv.266): 'you shall see mee doe the Moore'; he returns at line 345 and recites seven lines from II.iii of *The Battle* (lines 468, 472–477; *Poetaster,* III.iv.345– 352). Another contemporary play in which the Moor Muly Mahamet appears is *The Famous Historye of the life and death of Captaine Thomas Stukeley;* this is usually identified with the *Stewtley* which Henslowe recorded as a 'new' play acted by the Admiral's men on 11 December 1596 (*Diary,* p. 55). It too seems to have been revived (and altered) shortly before the production of *Satiromastix. Stukeley* was entered in the Stationers' Register on 11 August 1600, and printed in 1605 in a text the incoherence of which caused R. Simpson (in his *The School of Shakespeare* (London, 1878), I, 140) to suggest that part of a play on Don Antonio had been inserted into one dealing with Stukeley's exploits in England, Ireland, Spain, Rome, and Africa. Fleay (I, 127), speculating from the present passage in *Satiromastix,* thought that the 1605

Stukeley text represented a play that Dekker had made up for the Paul's company *c.* 1600 out of the earlier *Stewtley* and a *Mahomet* by Peele. 'But surely', as Chambers (IV, 47) remarked concerning this conjecture, 'there is a difference between making two plays out of one and making one play out of two'. Perhaps as a consequence of the rumor which reached England in the late 1590s, to the effect that Sebastian, King of Portugal, believed killed at the battle of Alcazar (August 1578), was still alive, there was around the turn of the century renewed interest in the disastrous battle, the personalities who participated in it (Muly Mahomet, Stukeley, Sebastian), and the crisis over the succession to the Portuguese throne which it triggered. The claimant to the throne (after Philip II of Spain had seized it) was Don Antonio, Prior of Crato, who came to England in 1580, and whose claim was backed by Queen Elizabeth through the decade that followed; he makes a shadowy appearance in Dekker's *Whore of Babylon*, II.i.264 (see the note on that passage), and appears in some of the later scenes of the extant text of *Stukeley*. In the period just before *Satiromastix*, Dekker and Chettle had written a play (now lost) about King Sebastian of Portugal; Henslowe paid them for it 'in full' on 22 May 1601 (*Diary*, p. 170). Can this be the explanation of the present passage? In such a view, the Innocent Moore that was cut in the middle would be the old play dealing with Sebastian, Antonio, and the Battle of Alcazar from which Dekker in his capacity as play-dresser borrowed scenes and introduced them into the revised *Stukeley*, and from which he may also have drawn for his and Chettle's *King Sebastian*. This was an Admiral's play, as *Stewtley* had been. But the titlepage of the 1605 quarto of *Stukeley* advertises the play simply 'As it hath been Acted', without naming a company. Might it have been Paul's? If so, it would qualify as one of the 'mustie fopperies of antiquitie' with which Marston in *Jack Drum's Entertainment* (ed. Wood, iii, 234) charged the company with filling out its repertoire in the first months after the theatre had reopened early in 1600. Any play dealing with Stukeley,

Sebastian, or the battle of Alcazar would inevitably share a fund of common subject material, and a Moor, directing the battle where they all met their fate, would be a principal figure in each. It is possible, however, that the passage alludes instead to *The Spanish Moor's Tragedy*, in which Dekker certainly and Marston very probably had a hand. See the Introduction to *Lust's Dominion*.

43 *Poet-apes*. Herford and Simpson (IX, 537), in their note on the induction (Envy's prologue) to *Poetaster*, 35, where the phrase occurs ('Are there no players here? no poet-apes'), quote Sidney, *An Apology for Poetry* (ed. G. Gregory Smith, *Elizabethan Critical Essays* (2 vols., Oxford, 1904), I, 205): 'the cause why it [poetry] is not esteemed in Englande is the fault of Poet-apes, not Poets'. Cf. Jonson, Epigram LVI ('On Poet-Ape'). And *Sat.*, V.ii.339.

46 *trudge*. *O.F.*, V.ii.15, n.

49 *Rosamond*, Rosamond Clifford (born *c.* 1140, died *c.* 1176), the mistress of Henry II who concealed her at Woodstock in what came popularly to be known as a 'maze', where she was sought out by Queen Eleanor and murdered. In the years just prior to 1601 her story had been dealt with poetically by Warner in the third edition of *Albions England* (1592), Book VIII, Chapter 41, by Daniel in *The Complaint of Rosamond* (1592), and by Drayton in *Englands Heroicall Epistles* (1597). A ballad *On the Death of Faire Rosamond* first appears in the 1607 edition of Thomas Deloney's *Strange Histories*; if Deloney is really the author it had to have been written before his death in 1600, and before 1593 if it was in the lost first edition of *The Garland of Good Will*. See Deloney's *Works*, pp. 297–302, 562–564; and *Roxburghe Ballads*, VI, 667–675. *W.H.*, IV.ii.82.

57–59 *That we...straine*. Adapted from the opening lines of the prologue to *Cynthia's Revels*:

> If gracious silence, sweet attention,
> Quicke sight, and quicker apprehension,
> (The lights of iudgements throne) shine any where;
> Our doubtfull authour hopes this is their sphere.

> And therefore opens he himselfe to those;
> To other weaker beames, his labours close:
> As loth to prostitute their virgin straine,
> To eu'rie vulgar, and adult'rate braine.

60–62 *No, our...feare*. Cf. the end of the prologue to *Cynthia's Revels*:

> Pied ignorance she [the author's muse] neither loues, nor feares.
> Nor hunts she after popular applause,
> Or fomie praise, that drops from common iawes:
> The garland that she weares, their hands must twine,
> Who can both censure, vnderstand, define
> What merit is: Then cast those piercing raies,
> Round as a crowne, in stead of honour'd bayes,
> About his *poesie*; which (he knowes) affoords
> Words, aboue action: matter, aboue words.

III.i

1 *a the bow hand wide*, literally, too far left (the bow hand being the left, in which the bow was held); wide of the mark. Tilley, B567. Beaumont and Fletcher, *The Coxcomb*, I.iii.1–2:

> *Uberto*. Well, you must have this wench then.
> *Richardo*. I hope so, I am much o'th bow hand else.

1 H.W., I.ii.86.

27 *in hugger mugger*, in secret, privately. *N.F.H.*, C4v: 'discharg'd their great bellies there, like whores in hugger mugger'. *S.H.R.*, E1v: 'what I giue to them shall be in Hugger-Mugger'. Chettle and Day, *The Blind Beggar of Bednal Green*, IV.iii (ed. Bullen, *Works of Day*, p. 89): 'I do but stay here to talk 3 or 4 cold words in hugger-mugger with the Blind-beggars Daughter.' *Hamlet*, IV.v.84. *N.H.*, IV.i.120.

28–29 *haue his blew coate pul'd ouer his eares*, i.e. be dismissed. Cf. V.ii.228, and *2 H.W.*, I.ii.188, n. A blue coat was the identifying dress of a serving-man. Cf. *2 H.W.*, I.ii.196, n.

39 *markes*.

A denomination of weight formerly employed (chiefly for gold and silver) throughout western Europe; its actual weight varied considerably, but it was usually regarded as equivalent to 8 ounces (= either $\frac{2}{3}$ or $\frac{1}{2}$ of a pound, according to the meaning given to the latter term)... In England, after the Conquest, the ratio of 20 sterling pennies to an ounce was the basis of computation; hence the value of the mark became fixed at 160 pence = 13*s*. 4*d*. or ⅔ of the pound sterling (*O.E.D., sb.²*).

R.G., I.i.83.

45 *Salamander*, a lizard reputed to live in fire; here used with reference to Peter's red face. Cf. *J.M.M.*, E1: 'make gloues for friends, (like Salamanders skins) able to resist the heate of the low country: for though they are farre from the Sunne, they alwaies liue in the fire'. *D.D.*, E1v: 'Ten thousand *Salamanders* (whose chill thawing / Puts *Bonfires* out).' *N.H.*, IV.i.180; *M.M.L.*, I.ii.52, n.

53 *incontinent. R.G.*, IV.ii.30–31.

54 *Mandilian*, 'a kinde of military garment, a loose Cassock' (*The New World of English Words*, Ed. Phillips (1658)). *G.H.*, C2v: 'But you *Babiownes*, and you Iack-an-apes (being the scum, and rascality of all the hedge-creepers) they go in ierkins and mandilions.' *O.P.*, M3v: 'nothing makes them Souldiers but old Mandilions, which they buy at the Broakers'. Scherer (p. 101), sees an allusion to Jonson's service as a soldier in the Low Countries in 1591–1592. *W.B.*, V.vi.39. *Sat.*, V.ii.177.

58 *on vrd*, i.e. one word (Penniman, p. 418).

64 *breake my armes*, with which the letter was sealed.

67 *tis no libell, for heere is my hand to it.* Cf. *Poetaster*, V.iii.54–56, concerning the supposedly libellous picture Lupus has found in Horace's study:

> *Caes.* Shew it to *Horace*: Aske him, if he know it.
> *Lvpv.* Know it? His hand is at it, *Caesar.*
> *Caes.* Then 'tis no libell.

82 *God bo'y*. Cf. IV.iii.157. *N.H.*, I.iii.178; *P.G.*, IV.iii.42.

86–87 *put my nose from his ioynt.* Tilley, N219.

94 *a good Ansell*, i.e. angel, with a quibble on the gold coin. Cf. *O.F.*, I.ii.35, and *Sat.*, I.ii.109.

103 *Diues...crummes.* Luke 16: 21. As Penniman notes (p. 419), the name 'Dives' is from the Vulgate. Cf. *W.Y.*, p. 33: '*Laʒarus* laie groning at euery mans doore, mary no *Diues* was within to send him a crum, (for all your Gold-finches were fled to the woods).' (For 'Gold-finches', cf. *Sat.* III.i.129.) There seem to have been a number of dramatic treatments of the story (all of which are now lost) throughout the sixteenth

century. Among the plays acted by the boys of Ralph Radcliff's school at Hitchin, *c.* 1546, was a *De Laẓaro a Diuitis aedibus Abacto* (A. Harbage and S. Schoenbaum, *Annals of English Drama, 975–1700* (London, 1964), p. 28). A play titled 'the Dialogue of Diues' is mentioned in Greene's *Groats-worth of Wit*, XII, 132; one titled *Dives and Laẓarus* is mentioned in *Sir Thomas More* (M.S.R., line 921); and '*The Divell and Dives*; (a Comedie.)' is mentioned in *Histriomastix*, Act II (ed. Wood, III, 263). A *Dives and Laẓarus* was performed by English actors in Gräz in February 1608 (*Annals*, p. 206). A puppet play titled *The Story of Dives and Laẓarus* was licensed on 16 July 1619 (*ibid.*, p. 206). For ballads on the subject printed in the last half of the sixteenth century, see Rollins, nos. 614, 1757, 2293, 2589. Cf. *W.A.*, sig. B2.

104 *Frier Tucke*, Robin Hood's chaplain. He was a figure in the two Robin Hood plays (*The Downfall of Robert, Earl of Huntington* and *The Death of Robert, Earl of Huntington*) for which Henslowe records payment to Munday for Part One on 15 February 1598 (*Diary*, p. 86), and to Munday and Chettle and a representative for the Admiral's men for Part Two between 20 February and 8 March 1598 (*ibid.*, p. 87). Both parts were licensed on 28 March 1598 (*ibid.*, p. 88); they were printed in 1601. Tucca is referring to Sir Adam. *1 H.W.*, V.ii.338.

105 *Oyster-pye*, i.e. Miniver; but oyster pies are regularly included in lists of aphrodisiacs. Cf. *Cynthia's Revels*, II.ii.55: 'potato's, or oyster-pyes' (Herford and Simpson, IX, 500, say there is no suggestion of aphrodisiacs in this passage, but they are wrong). Marston, *The Scourge of Villanie*, II, 34–36:

> Pert *Gallus*, slilie slippes along, to wage
> Tilting incounters, with some spurious seede
> Of marrow pies, and yawning Oystars breede.

And cf. *I.T.B.N.*, I.iii.29–31, a list of provocatives that includes

> lam-stones,
> Fat sweete-breads, luscious maribones,
> Artichoke, and oyster-pyes.

108–109 *first part of the Mirrour of Knighthood.* Cf. Tucca to Ovid senior in *Poetaster* (quarto 1602), I.ii.156–157: 'Why, what should I say? or what can I say, my most *Magnanimous Mirror of Knighthood?*' (altered to 'my flowre o' the order' in folio 1616). The reference is to the Spanish romance by Diego Ortúñez de Calahorra, translated into English by Margaret Tyler under the title *The Mirrour of Princely Deedes and Knighthood* and published *c.* 1578 (subsequent editions *c.* 1580 and *c.* 1599). Succeeding parts of the romance (to the total of nine) appeared in English between 1585 and 1601. *2 H.W.*, III.ii.81–82.

111 *Tiborne.* The Tyburn gallows 'stood, there is reason to believe, on the site of Connaught Place, and near its south-west corner, though No. 49 Connaught Square is said to be the spot' (Wheatley and Cunningham, III, 413).

113 *a viȝard in a bagge.* The expression is apparently equivalent to money in her purse, 'vizard' being used for 'face' in respect to the faces on coins (such as the 'Angell', line 114). Cf. *2 H.W.*, III.ii.31: 'cash and pictures', where 'pictures' mean 'coins'.

115 *this chaine.* 'Chains were worn by most citizens, and were provided by the wealthy for their retainers; every well-dressed gentleman wore a gold chain' (*Shakespeare's England*, II, 115). Beaumont and Fletcher, *The Coxcomb*, V.i.43–44: 'goe thy wayes, thou wilt sticke a bench, spit as formally, and shew thy agot, and hatch'd chaine as well as the best of them'. *S.H.*, III.ii.127.1; *N.H.*, I.ii.93; *R.G.*, IV.i.12; *I.T.B.N.*, V.iv.32, 253–254.

116 *Friskin,* a gay, frisky person, applied to either sex. Cf. Nashe, *Have With You*, III, 122: 'hys Wench or Friskin was footing it aloft on the Greene'. A character (a tailor) is named Friskin in Davenant's *The Unfortunate Lovers* (1638). Cf. *Sat.*, *Epilogus*, 13–14.

116 *haue her ath hip,* have an advantage over her; have her at my mercy. The term is from wrestling. Tilley, H474.

119 *Lady ath Lake.* Nyneve (Viviane), the mistress of Merlin in the Arthurian romances. But the phrase is used jocularly of

any old woman. Cf. Day, *The Isle of Gulls*, Act V (ed. Bullen, p. 310): 'This gallant *Iuventus* of fourscore that, like my Lady of the Lake, displaies against al comers'. *B.L.*, D3: 'this olde Lady of the Lake'.

119 *Sir Tristram*. Tristram de Lyones, one of the Arthurian heroes, named here by Tucca because of his reputation as a master of the chase, and so of venery. Malory (*Works*, ed. E. Vinaver, 2nd ed. (Oxford, 1967), 1, 375) tells of his early education:

> And so in harpynge and on instrumentys of musyke in his youthe he applyed hym for to lerne. And aftir, as he growed in myght and strength, he laboured in huntynge and in hawkynge – never jantylman more that ever we herde rede of. And as the booke seyth, he began good mesures of blowynge of beestes of venery and beestes of chaace and all maner of vermaynes, and all the tearmys we have yet of hawkynge and huntynge. And therefore the booke of [venery, of hawkynge and huntynge is called the booke of] sir Trystrams.

Later, Arthur says to him: 'For [of] all maner of huntynge thou beryste the pryce, and of all mesures of blowynge thou arte the begynnynge, of all the termys of huntynge and hawkynge ye are the begynner, of all instirmentes of musyk ye ar the beste' (*ibid.*, 11, 571). The 'book' alluded to is *The Booke of Hawking, Hunting and Blasing of Arms* (St Albans, 1486); S.T.C. 3308. Sir Tristram's fame as the patron of hunting persists into the Renaissance, e.g. in *The Faerie Queene*, VI.ii.28–32. But since, as a character says in *Westward Ho*, III.iv.56, 'hunting, and venery are words of one signification', the name of Sir Tristram is often found in the later Elizabethan and Jacobean drama to signify a fornicator. Thus in Beaumont and Fletcher's *Philaster*, IV.ii.14–16, one of the Woodmen says of the lecherous Pharamond: 'I thinke he should love venery, he is an old sir *Tristram*: for if you be remembred, he forsooke the Stagge once, to strike a raskall milking in a medow, and her he kild in the eye.' And Middleton, *A Trick to Catch the Old One*, IV.v.18–19, where Dampit addresses Lamprey (whose aphrodisiac name points to his libertine nature): 'What, Sir Tristram? You come and see a weak man here, a very weak man.' On 13 October 1599 Henslowe records a payment of £3 to Thomas Downton 'for the Booke of Trystram de lyons' (*Diary*, p. 124); of this play, which may have been a revision of an older one (*Annals*, p. 70), nothing else is known. *N.H.*, V.i.359.

121–122 *weare her gloue in thy Worshipfull hatte.* See the opening of *Blurt, Master-Constable* (1602) A2: '*Enter* Camillo *with* Violetta, Hipolito, Baptista, Bentiuolio, & Virgilio, *as returning from warre, euery one with a Gloue in his hat, Ladies with them.*'

122 *brooch.* Men wore brooches in their hats, both as an ornament and also to clasp the feather. Cf. Ganymede in Marlowe's *Dido*, I.i.46–47: 'I would have a jewell for mine eare / And a fine brouch to put in my hat.' And the old courtier Curvetto's account of his dress in *Blurt, Master-Constable*, II.ii.209–212:

> A little simpering ruff, a dapper cloak
> With Spanish-button'd cape, my rapier here,
> Gloves like a burgomaster here, hat here
> (Stuck with some ten groat brooch).

Poetaster, I.ii.161–162: 'Honour's a good brooch to weare in a mans hat, at all times.' *I.T.B.N.*, II.i.49; *W.K.*, I.ii.30–31.

128 *yonder Cucko*, i.e. Sir Adam; the allusion is to his baldness (referred to in lines 86 and 132). Cf. *O.F.*, II.ii.17–18: 'mens wits in these daies, a're like the Cuckoo, bald once a yeere'. Dekker alludes elsewhere to the bird's traditional moulting period. Cf. *G.H.*, C2v:

> and as those excellent birds...called woodcocks...hauing all their feathers pluckt from their backes, ...or as the Cuckooe in Christmas, are more fit to come to any Knights board, and are indeed more seruice-able then when they are lapt in their warme liueries: euen so stands the case with man. Truth (because the bald-pate her father *Time*, has no haire to couer his head) goes (when she goes best) starke naked.

> *S.D.S.*, B3: 'Then flyes he out like an Irish rebell, and keepes aloofe, hiding his head, when he cannot hide his shame: and though he haue fethers on his back puld from sundry birds, yet to himselfe is he more wretched, then yᵉ Cuckoo in winter, that dares not be seene.'

129 *Gold-finch*, rich man. Dekker employs the metaphor elsewhere. Cf. *W.Y.*, p. 33 (quoted in the note on line 103, above). *P.W.*, C3v: 'his faire Mistresse,... being loath to loose such a Gold-Finch, that sung so sweetly in her eare'. *W.A.*, F3v: 'It was excellent musicke... to heare how euery particular regiment in *Pouerties* Camp, threatned to plague the Gold-finches of the Cittie, and to pluck their feathers.' The term is used of gold coins in *V.D.*, H2 ('his nest being halfe fild with such Gold-finches, he neuer stayes till the rest be fledge'), and of a purse in *Blurt, Master-Constable*, IV.i.9–11:

> if this goldfinch, that with sweet notes flies,
> And wakes the dull eye even of a puritan,
> Can work, then, wenches, Curvetto is the man.

Cf. Jonson, *Cynthia's Revels*, IV.iii.417–419: 'Sir, we will acknowledge your seruice, doubt not: henceforth, you shall bee no more Asotvs to vs, but our *gold-finch*, and wee your cages.' *W.K.*, I.ii.89.

131 *smug*. *P.G.*, III.ii.132, n.

131 *Belimperia*. The heroine of Kyd's *The Spanish Tragedy*.

132 *Derricke*, the name of a contemporary hangman at Tyburn. Cf. Middleton, *The Blacke Booke* (1604), E4: 'execute these Places and Offices as truely, as *Dericke* will execute his place and Office at Tyburne'. Dekker alludes to him often. *W.Y.*, p. 61: 'imagining that many a thousand haue bin turned wrong-fully off the ladder of life, and praying that *Derick* or his executors may liue to do those a good turne, that haue done so to others'. *S.D.S.*, C1: 'The theefe that dyes at *Tyburne* for a robbery, is not halfe so dangerous a weede in a Common-wealth, as the *Politick Bankrupt*. I would there were a *Derick* to hang vp him too.' *J.M.M.*, F1: 'might I haue beene her Iudge, shee should haue had her due, and danst *Derriks* dance in a hempen halter'. *B.L.*, G2v: 'for he rides circuite with the Deuill, and *Dericke* must bee his host, and *Tyborne* the Inne at which he will light'; and 13: 'Where I leaue them, as to the hauen in which they must all cast Anchor, if *Dericks* Cables do but hold, and vnlesse they amend.' *G.H.*, C1: 'who

knowes not that the Neapolitan, will (like *Derick* the hang-man)
embrace you with one arme, and rip your guts with the other?'
M.G., p. 124: '*Harlots*, which make men more miserable then
Dericke.'

132–133 *Susanna... Elders.* The story is in the Apocryphal book
of Daniel. It seems to have had a number of English stage
versions in the latter half of the sixteenth century, only one of
which is clearly extant. Among the plays acted by the boys of
Ralph Radcliff's school at Hitchin, *c.* 1546, was a *De Susanne
per Iudices Iniquos ob Lese Pudicitie Notam Diuini Liberatione.*
A 'playe of Susanna' was entered in the Stationers' Register
in 1568–1569 (Arber, I, 383); this may be identical with *The
Commody of the moste vertuous and Godlye Susanna* by Thomas
Garter, published in 1578. (Chambers' statement, III, 319, that
no copy of Garter's play is known is no longer true, a copy –
now in the Folger Shakespeare Library – having come to
light in the mid-1930s; see B. I. Evans, *TLS* (2 May 1936),
372.) An interlude titled *Susanna's Tears*, dated *c.* 1570 by
Harbage and Schoenbaum (*Annals*, p. 40), is in the publishers'
advertisement lists of Archer (1656) and Kirkman (1661).
A *Susanna* is given in the list of Rogers and Ley (1656), from
which Archer's list is derived. The *Susanna* that was performed by English actors at Stuttgart in September 1603 was
probably a Continental play (see *Annals*, p. 206, and *Chambers*,
II, 283). See M. T. Herrick, 'Susanna and the Elders in
Sixteenth-Century Drama', *Studies in Honour of T. W.
Baldwin* (Urbana, Ill., 1958), pp. 125–135. A ballad titled
godly and constante wyse Susanna was entered in the Stationers'
Register during the period 1562–1563 (Rollins, no. 991). It
was licensed anew as 'The storye of *Svsanna* being the xiijth
Chapter of Danyell' on 8 September 1592 (Rollins, no. 2528).
It is printed in *Roxburghe Ballads*, I, 190.

137 *father time*, addressed to Sir Adam, and another allusion to his
baldness. Cf. the referen̄ce to 'the bald-pate... father *Time*'
in *G.H.*, quoted in the note on line 128, above.

137–138 *mother-Winter*, i.e. Miniver. See lines 110–112.

139 *Birde-bolt*, a blunt-headed arrow used for shooting birds with-

out piercing them. *Love's Labour's Lost*, IV.iii.22–24:
'Proceed, sweet Cupid; thou hast thump'd him with thy
bird-bolt under the left pap.' *Much Ado About Nothing*,
I.i.41–42: 'my uncle's fool, reading the challenge, subscrib'd
for Cupid, and challeng'd him at the burbolt'. *Pilgrimage to
Parnassus*, 682–685: 'that litell gallowes Cupid hath latelie
prickt mee in the breech with his great pin, and almoste
kilde mee thy woodcocke with his birdbolte'. *W. of E.*,
II.i.214.

139–140 *mother Mumble-crust*, the old nurse in Udall's *Royster
Doyster*, written *c.* 1545–1553; it was entered in the Stationers'
Register *c.* October 1566 and published in an undated edition,
possibly in the same year. In the anonymous play of *Misogonus*,
probably acted by the students of Trinity College, Cambridge
c. 1568–1574, and preserved in a manuscript (now in the
Huntington Library) dated 1577, Madge is called 'mage
mvmblecrust' in III.i.44 (ed. Bond, *Early Plays from the
Italian*). The word implies a toothless person. Cf. Middleton
and Rowley, *The Spanish Gipsy*, II.i.225–226: 'Farewell, old
greybeard; – adieu, mother mumble-crust.' *S.H.*, I.iv.5;
P.G., IV.iii.22; *W.E.*, IV.ii.4–5.

140 *whim-wham*, 'A fanciful or fantastic object; *fig.* a trifle; in early
use chiefly, a trifling ornament of dress, a trinket' (*O.E.D.*,
citing this example). The phrase occurs in Marston's *The
Malcontent*, I.iii.56. *M.M.L.*, IV.i.6.

142 *learned Dunce*, Duns Scotus, the Scholastic philosopher
(1265–1308).

144 *bumble-broth*. *O.E.D.* (*s.v.* 'Bumble' *sb.*², 4, *attrib.* and *comb.*)
wonders if such combinations as 'bumble-bath' and 'bumble-
broth' mean something in the order of 'a mess, "pickle,
soapsuds"' and cites the present example together with John
Taylor, the Water Poet, *Praise Clean Linn.*: 'Laundresses are
testy...when they are lathering in their bumble broth.' But
none of this explains the present passage. Cf. Dryden, *The
Kind Keeper*, Act I (ed. Summers, IV, 279): 'Before *George*,
a proper fellow! and a Swinger he shou'd be, by his make!
the Rogue wou'd bumble a Whore, I warrant him!' And

Summers' note (IV, 538): 'bumble' is 'A rare slang term for to copulate with; to vault'.

148 *point*, 'A tagged lace or cord, for attaching the hose to the doublet, lacing a bodice, etc.; often used as a type of something of small value' (*O.E.D.*).

155 *Gutter-Lane*. Stow (*Survey*, I, 349), commenting on the changes in place names 'of late time by corruption', cites among other examples 'gutter lane, for guthuruns lane'. Of this, he writes elsewhere that it is 'so called of *Guthurun* sometime owner thereof: the inhabitants of this lane of old time were Goldbeaters' (*ibid.*, I, 314).

162 *mother Bunch*. S.H., IV.iv.110–111, n.

163 *Gwyniuer*. Another of Tucca's Arthurian references. For the use of the name of Arthur's queen as a term of abuse for an old woman, cf. Beaumont and Fletcher, *The Scornful Lady*, V.i.80, where the Elder Loveless says to Abigail the serving-woman, 'Now Lady Guiniver, what newes with you?' And cf. Aphra Behn, *The Younger Brother, or the Amorous Jilt*, IV.iii (*The Works of Aphra Behn*, ed. Montague Summers (6 vols., London, 1915), IV, 380): 'Ha – Old Queen *Gwiniver*, without her Ruff on?' with Summers' note (IV, 422) wherein the present passage is cited. The name is used disparagingly in Jonson, *Every Man out of his Humour*, II.iii.68; Marston, *The Malcontent*, I.iii.53; and William Rowley, *A Shoemaker a Gentleman*, IV.i.168.

164 *Shittle-cockes*. Small pieces of cork fitted with feathers, used as the object to be bandied back and forth in the game of battledore and shuttlecock. *W.E.*, III.i.40.

165–166 *West Indyes...discouer*. For the erotic image, cf. Donne, 'To his Mistress Going to Bed', lines 27–30.

171 *my moldie decay'd Charing-crosse*. Cf. Deloney, *The Gentle Craft*, Part Two, p. 188: 'why man she is not so old as charing Crosse for her gate is not crooked nor her face withered'. Stow reports of it:

Neare vnto this Hospitall [S. Marie Rounciuall] was an Hermitage, with a chappell of S. *Katherine*, ouer against Charing crosse, which crosse, builded of stone, was of old time a fayre peece of worke there made by commandement of *Edward* the first, in the 21. yeare of his raigne, in memorie of Helianor his deceased Queene (Stow, *Survey*, II, 100–101).

Dekker writes 'An Encomion of Charing Crosse' and its ruinous condition in *D.T.*, A3v–A4. Westminster addresses London concerning

that Auncient and eldest* [marginal note: '*Charing Crosse.'] Sonne of mine, with his Limbes broken to peeces, (as if hee were a Male-factor, and hadde beene tortured on the *Germaine* Wheele:) his *Reuerend Head* cut off by the cruelty of *Time*; the Ribbes of his body bruized; His Armes lop't away; His backe (that euen grew crooked with age) almonst [*sic*] cleft in sunder: yea, and the ground (on which hee hath dwelt so many* [marginal note: '*316. yeeres since Charing Crosse was builded by Ed: I, Anno. Chri. 1291.'] hundreds of yeeres) ready to bee pulled from vnder his feete, so that with greefe his very heart seemes to be broken.

Its antiquity is regularly stressed in contemporary references, as in the list of London sights enumerated in S. Rowlands, *Good Newes and Bad Newes* (1622), F2v: 'The old *Exchange*, the new *Exchange* and all. | The water-workes, huge *Pauls*, old *Charingcrosse*'. *W.H.*, II.i.35–42.

172 *patch-pannell*, 'one who is shabby or wears worn-out clothes' (A. B. Grosart, Glossarial-Index to *The Works of Gabriel Harvey* (3 vols., London, 1884–1885), III, 175). Cf. Harvey, *Pierces Supererogation* (ed. Grosart, II, 280): 'emprooue himselfe as ranke a bungler in his mightiest worke of Supererogation, as the starkest Patch-pannell of them all'.

174 *Long Meg a Westminster.* Her exploits were celebrated in *The Life of Long Meg of Westminster: containing the mad merry prankes she played in her life time, not onely in performing sundry quarrels with diuers ruffians about London; but also how valiantly she behaued herselfe in the warres of Bolloigne*, of which the earliest extant edition is dated 1620, though it was entered in the Stationers' Register on 18 August 1590. (The S.T.C. wrongly records an edition of 1582. The British Library copy of a 1582 edition, reported by F. O. Mann (Deloney's *Works*, p. 531), has a faked titlepage; see Wilson, *Studies*, p. 321.) A native of Lancashire in the reign of Henry VIII, she took

service in a London tavern, and served in the Boulogne war
of 1544. Her name was a byword for a virago. Lyly, in *Pappe
with an Hatchet* (c. 1589), asks: 'O doost remember, howe
that Bastard *Iunior* complaines of brothells, and talkes of long
Megg of *Westminster*' (*Works*, III, 403). Ballads dealing with
her were entered in the Stationers' Register on 27 August
1590 and 14 March 1595 (Rollins, nos. 1524, 1614). Harvey
mentions her in *Pierce's Supererogation* (1593): 'Phy, long
Megg of Westminster would haue bene ashamed to disgrace
her Sonday bonet with her Satterday witt. She knew some
rules of Decorum: and although she were a lustie bounsing
rampe, some what like Gallemella, or maide Marian, yet was
she not such a roinish rannell, or such a dissolute gillian-
flurtes, as this wainscot-faced Tomboy' (*Workes*, ed. Grosart,
II, 229). Deloney softened her character when he adapted it to
the story of Richard Casteler in the second part of *The Gentle
Craft* (presumably printed in 1598). Between 14 February
1595 and 28 January 1597, Henslowe records sixteen performances by the Admiral's men of a play titled *Long Meg of
Westminster* (*Diary*, pp. 27–28, 30–31, 54–56). The play is
lost, but it was evidently still being acted c. 1611 to judge from
the reference in Field's *Amends for Ladies*, II.i.152–153:
'Faith I haue a great mind to see long-megg and the ship at
the Fortune.' *W.H.*, V.iii.1; *R.G.*, V.i.2. Tilley, M865.

177 *deuill a Dow-gate*. A ballad entitled 'the Devell of Dowgate
and his sonne' was entered in the Stationers' Register on
5 August 1596 (Rollins, no. 569). Years later, on 17 October
1623, a play called *The Devill of Dowgate, or Usury put to Use*
was licensed by Sir Henry Herbert. It was said to be 'Acted
by the king's servants' and to be the work of Fletcher (see
Bentley, III, 328–329). Both the ballad and the play are lost.
Concerning Dowgate, Stow writes: 'Downegate warde
beginneth at the south end of Walbrooke warde, ouer against
the East corner of Saint *Johns* church vpon Walbrooke, and
descendeth on both the sides to Downegate, on the Thames,
and is so called of that downe going or descending thereunto:
and of this Downgate the ward taketh name' (*Survey*, I, 229;

but cf. Kingsford's note, II, 277: ' "Downe", and its explanation, seem to be guesses of Stow's.'). What the 'devil' was
seems to be unknown. Cf. Nashe, *Have With You*, III, 121:
'*Fasilia*, the daughter of *Pelagius*, King of *Spain*, was torne
in peices by a Beare: & so I hope thou wilt tear her and tug
with her, if she begin once to playe the *Deuill of Dowgate*.'
Wily Beguiled (M.S.R.), lines 1454–1456: 'strut before her...
as if hee were gentleman Vsher to the great *Turke*, or the
Diuell of *Dowgate*'.

178 *my wide mouth at Bishops-gate*. The reference is to the sign of
the Mouth tavern outside Bishopsgate. Cf. Haughton, *Englishmen for my Money* (M.S.R.), lines 2108–2110: 'He lookes like
the signe of the Mouth without Bishops gate, gaping, and a
great Face, and a great Head, and no Body.' *L.C.*, D2: 'a
paire of eies that stared as wide as the mouth gapes at Bishops-
gate'. It is named among the list of taverns enumerated by
their signs in the ballad *London's Ordinarie*; or, *Every Man
in his Humour*, lines 71–72 (*Roxburghe Ballads*, II, 24–28):
'But he that hath no money in his purse / May dine at the
signe of the Mouth.'

180 *dame Annis a cleere*. Stow writes of the wells to the north of
London

in the Suburbes sweete, wholesome, and cleare, amongst which *Holywel*,
Clarkes wel, & *Clementes wel*, are most famous and frequented by Schollers, and youths of the City in sommer euenings, when they would
walke foorth to take the aire...Somewhat North from *Holywell*, is
one other well curbed square with stone, and is called *Dame Annis the
cleare*, and not farre from it but somewhat west, is also one other cleare
water called *Perillous pond*, because diuerse youthes swimming therein
haue been drowned (*Survey*, I, 16).

Richard Johnson, *The Pleasant Walkes of Moorefields: a
dialogue between a Country Gentleman and a Citizen* (1607),
B2v:

Gent. But, sir, here is stones set vpright, what is the meaning of them?
Citiᶎ. Marry where they stand, runnes...from a spring called dame
Annis de Cleare called by the name of a rich London widow, called
Annis Clare, who matching herself with a riotous Courtier in the time of
Edward the first, who vainely consumed all her wealth, and leauing her

in much pouertie, there drowned she herself, being then but a shallow ditch or running water.

For the bawdy connotations of the name as an epithet for Miniver in the present passage, cf. Greene, *A Disputation Between a Hee Conny-catcher, and a Shee Conny-catcher*, X, 234, where Nan explains how the world's economy would suffer without whores: 'What should I say more *Lawrence*, the Suberbes should haue a great misse of vs, and *Shordish* wold complaine to dame Anne a Cleare, if we of the sisterhood should not vphold her iollitie.'

184 *Madge-owlet*. 'Madge' was a popular name for the owl. Herford and Simpson (IX, 362), in a note on *Every Man in his Humour*, II.ii.23, quote Swan, *Speculum Mundi* (1643), p. 397: 'Also there is Vlula; and this is that which we call the Howlet, or the Madge.' As a derisive term for a woman, cf. Day, *The Isle of Gulls*, II.iv (ed. Bullen, p. 261): 'the rare and neuer enough wondred at *Mopsa*, the black swan of beauty & madg-howlet of admiration'. Brome, *Covent Garden Weeded*, I.i (ed. Shepherd, ii, 14): 'Here old *Madge*, and to all the birds that shall wonder at thy howletship, when thou rid'st in an Ivy-bush call'd a Cart.' *W.H.*, V.iii.53.

186 *Cat-a-mountaine*, whore. *P.W.*, D4v: 'You talke of the poore Cat-a-mountaines in *Turnebull*, who venture vpon the pikes of damnation for single money.' And *Bartholomew Fair*, IV.v.77, where Knockhum calls the quarrel of Alice and Ursula 'Cat-a-mountaine-vapours'. Cf. *Sat.*, 'To the World', 29–30.

186–187 *Sislie Bum-trincket*. *S.H.*, I.i.158.

188 *Tripe-wife*. Cf. *S.H.*, II.iii.60–61, Simon Eyre to his wife: 'haue not I tane you from selling tripes in Eastcheape'. Marston, *The Malcontent*, I.v.6.

190 *Mother Red-cap*. Between 22 December 1597 and 5 January 1598, Henslowe records three payments to Drayton and Munday 'for a boocke called mother Read cape' (*Diary*, pp. 74, 85–86). There is evidence that the play was actually performed. Properties for it are listed in the inventory for the Admiral's men of 10 March 1598 (*ibid.*, p. 320), and it is

included among their stock of play-books for the same period
(*ibid.*, p. 324). The play is lost, as is the jest-book titled
*Mother Redcap Her Last Will and Testament, Containing
Sundry Conceited and Pleasant Tales Furnished with Much
Variety to Move Delight* (Stationers' Register, 10 March
1595; Arber, II, 293). Was the title-character an ale-wife?
Cf. Heywood, *The Wise-woman of Hogsdon*, Act II (ed.
Shepherd, V, 295): 'Come *Haringfield*, now wee have beene
drinking of Mother Red-caps Ale, let us now goe make some
sport with the Wise-woman.' The character is referred to
later in Act IV of the same play (V, 332): 'this over against
mother Red-caps is her house'. Cf. *Sat.*, V.ii.281.

191 *Grimalkin*, a name given to a cat, and derisively applied to an
old woman.

191 *Maggot-a-pye*, a magpie (i.e. an idle chatterer).

194 *a Gentle*, 'A maggot, the larva of the flesh-fly or blue-bottle,
used as bait by anglers' (*O.E.D.*). Tucca's pun contains a play
on both 'Maggot' and 'Gentlewoman' in the two preceding
lines.

195 *Cap-a-maintenance...naked sword.* Symbols of official dignity
borne before a king at his coronation or before the Lord
Mayor of London. Massinger, *The City Madam*, IV.i.70–72.

> I see Lord Major written on his forehead;
> The Cap of Maintenance, and Citie Sword
> Born up in state before him.

Both are used with obvious *double entendre.* Cf. *The Return
from Parnassus*, Part One, lines 377–378: 'we muste prouide
vs a poore capp of mantenance'. For the 'naked sword', cf.
Tourneur, *The Atheist's Tragedy*, II.v. (ed. Nicoll, p. 209):
'he was ready euen to haue drawne his naked weapon vpon
mee'. *N.H.*, I.ii.6.

196 *Lettice-cap.* It was 'of grey fur, resembling ermine, the ladies'
style having three corners "like the forked cappes of Popishe
Priestes"' (Linthicum, p. 225, quoting Stubbes). It was worn
as a means of inducing sleep. Cf. Beaumont and Fletcher,
Thierry and Theodoret, V.ii.8; and Fletcher, *Monsieur Thomas*,
III.i.10.

199 *hot-cockles*, 'from the French hautes-coquilles, is a play in which one kneels, and covering his eyes lays his head in another's lap and guesses who struck him'. (Strutt, *Sports and Pastimes*, ed. Cox, p. 308). *S.T.W.*, IV.ii.48; *W.E.*, III.i.124.

200 *Gammer Gurton...needle*. The 'Ryght Pithy, Pleasaunt and merie Comedie: Intytuled *Gammer Gurtons Nedle*' was presumably written by William Stevenson and first performed by the students of Christ's College, Cambridge, *c.* 1553. It was entered in the Stationers' Register under the title 'Dyccon of Bedlam' in 1563, but the earliest extant edition bears the date 1575. The play was still being acted in the 1590s, on the Continental if not on the English stage; there is a record of a performance by English actors in Frankfurt on 30 August 1592 (Chambers, II, 274). *W. of E.*, IV.i.251–252.

201 *thy teeth stand like the Arches vnder London Bridge*. Miniver's teeth are mainly gaps; cf. above, lines 139–140, n. *G.H.*, B4: 'stiffe necked *Rebatoes* (that haue more arches for pride to row vnder, then can stand vnder fiue London Bridges)'.

203 *in Stag, in Buffe*. 'Stag' refers to the color of the buff leather jerkin that Tucca wears. 'Buffe' was 'a very stout kind of leather made of oxhide, dressed with oil, having a fuzzy surface, and a dull whitish-yellow colour' (*O.E.D.*). It was common military attire. Cf. above, I.ii.133–134, n., and *2 H.W.*, I.iii.30–31. *W.B.*, V.iii.37; *I.T.B.N.*, II.i.107.

206 *shat*, shalt. Cf. I.ii.362: 'What wut end? wut hang thy selfe now?'

206–207 *march with two or three hundred linkes before me*. Tucca produces Sir Quintilian's chain, on the links of which he here puns along with the meaning of 'links' as torches.

209–210 *Ladie ath Hospitall*. The hospital of the Priory of St Mary of Bethlehem; since 1546 it had been administered by the city of London as a hospital for the insane. Tucca's string of puns brings him to it through association with 'chain'd' (line 209), which glances both at the notion of going attired in a chain of gold and of being bound like a madman. Cf. line 216: 'Ioane-a-bedlam', and *W.B.*, II.ii.179, n.

212 *three or foure payre of Knights.* 'A pack of cards was called a "pair", and Knight was an old name for the knave at cards' (Penniman, p. 422, citing Nares). The preference of rich citizens' widows for knights is a common subject for the satirists. Cf. Marston, *What You Will*, I.i.184–189:

> Therefore my widow she cashiers the blacks,
> Forswears, turns off the furr'd-gowns, and surveys
> The beadroll of her suitors, thinks and thinks,
> And straight her questing thoughts springs up a knight;
> Have after then amain, the game's a-foot,
> The match clapp'd up; tut, 'tis the knight must do't.

213 *flye out. L.D.*, II.ii.55.

216 *dub'd. W.H.*, V.i.54–55.

218 *Ladified.* S. Rowlands, *Good Newes and Bad Newes* (1622), B1:

> she vnto a Gallant Knight inclines,
> And would be Madam'd, Worship'd, Ladified,
> And in the Leather-carted fashion ride.

See *Sat.*, III.i.221.

221 *foote-cloth. O.F.*, I.ii.153–154, n.

221 *carted.* A quibble on the usual punishment of bawds; they were drawn through the streets in carts and so exposed to public shame. *I.T.B.N.*, I.i.51, n.

221 *drawne.* A further quibble on the usual punishment of criminals, who were drawn and quartered.

222 *Coacht.* Stow writes of the widespread use of coaches at this date: 'but now of late yeares the vse of coatches brought out of Germanie is taken vp, and made so common, as there is neither distinction of time, nor difference of persons obserued: for the world runs on wheeles with many, whose parents were glad to goe on foote' (*Survey*, I, 84). The taste for them among the wives and daughters of citizens is often noted; Gertrude in *Eastward Ho*, III.ii is a famous example, and cf. *Poetaster*, IV.ii.17. *Bartholomew Fair*, IV.v.94–102:

> *Kno.*. . .I'le prouide you a Coach, to take the ayre in.
> *Win.* But doe you thinke you can get one?
> *Kno.* O, they are as common as wheelebarrowes, where there are great

dunghills. Euery Pettifoggers wife has 'hem, for first he buyes a Coach, that he may marry, and then hee marries that hee may be made Cuckold in't: For if their wiues ride not to their Cuckolding, they doe 'hem no credit.

S. Rowlands, *Humours Looking Glasse* (1608), B3v:

> And she is neuer merry at the heart,
> Till she be got into her leatherne Cart.
> Some halfe a mile the Coach-man guides the raynes,
> Then home againe.

N.F.H., H2: 'he doubts there is some secrete Bridge made ouer to Hell, and that they steale thither in coaches, for euery Iustices wife, and the wife of euerie Cittizen must be iolted now'. According to a notice added by Howes to the 1631 edition of Stow's *Annales* (p. 867), the origin of coaches in England was thus:

> In the yeare 1564 Guilliam Boonen, a Dutchman, became the Queene's Coachman, and was the first that brought the use of coaches into England. . . Then little by little they grew usuall among the Nobilities, and others of Sort, and within twentie yeeres became a great trade of Coachmaking. . .Lastly, even at this time, 1605, began the ordinary use of Caroaches.

222 *Iigga-Iogge.* For the ballad tune titled (apparently) 'Jigg a Jog goo', see Simpson, pp. 385–386. *S.H.*, I.ii.61.

222 *a Hood. . .flap.* Cf. *S.H.*, III.ii.132–134: 'I shal make thee a Lady, heer's a French hood for thee, on with it, on with it, dresse thy browes with this flap of a shoulder of mutton, to make thee looke louely'; and V.i.14–15: 'this french flappe'. 'The French hood (1520's–1590 and unfashionably to *c.* 1630) was small and rounded, made on a stiff frame and worn far back on the head exposing the hair' (Phillis Cunnington, *Costume in Pictures* (London, 1964), p. 36). Jonson, *A Tale of a Tub*, IV.v.92–96:

> *Awd.*. . . Can you make me
>   A Lady, would I ha' you?
> *Pol.*   I can gi' you
>   A silken Gowne, and a rich Petticoat:
> And a french Hood. (All fooles love to be brave:
> I find her humour, and I will pursue it.)

In their note on this passage, Herford and Simpson (IX, 301) comment on the fact that the French Hood was 'regarded by city dames as a genteel fashion long after it was out of date elsewhere'.

226 *Maide-marian*, the companion of Robin Hood, and a performer in the May-day pageants. Her name was a synonym for a prostitute, 'a lustie bounsing rampe' as Harvey puts it (see the passage from *Pierce's Supererogation* quoted in the note to line 174 above). And cf. *I Henry IV*, III.iii.114–115, Falstaff to the Hostess: 'and for womanhood, Maid Marian may be the deputy's wife of the ward to thee'. She made a more virtuous figure in Munday's Robin Hood plays, *The Downfall and Death of Robert, Earl of Huntington*, where she was identified with the 'chaste Matilda,...poysoned at Dunmowe by King Iohn' (see the note to line 104 above).

227 *Alexis secrets.* Scherer was persuaded that this must be taken together with the earlier references to 'Anthony' and 'Cleopatria', and found in it an allusion to Shakespeare's *Antony and Cleopatra*, I.ii, wherein Alexas brings forth the Soothsayer who can read a little 'in nature's infinite book of secrecy'. He therefore supposed that Dekker must have known an *Ur-Antonius* (to be distinguished from both the Garnier–Pembroke *Antonius* and from Daniel's *Cleopatra*) that was either the work of an unidentified dramatist, or an early version by Shakespeare of his own later play. Neither Scherer nor Penniman recognized that 'Alexis secrets' refers to the voluminous and highly popular series of treatises known as the *Secrets of Alexis of Piemont*. The first of these was published in English translation in 1558 (S.T.C. 293). The *Second Part of the Secrets* followed in 1560 (S.T.C. 300); a *Third and Last Part of the Secrets* appeared in 1562 (S.T.C. 305), and a *Fourth and Final Book of Secrets* in 1569 (S.T.C. 309). An edition of *Secrets* in four parts appeared in 1595 (S.T.C. 312). Part Two was still appearing, 'newly corrected and augmented', in 1614 (S.T.C. 304).

228 *Rose...the Beare-garden.* The Rose Theatre was built by Henslowe, in partnership with John Cholmley, in 1587. It

was occupied by the Admiral's men from 1594 to 1600. It seems not to have been used for plays after 1603, and is referred to as 'the late playhouse' in 1606 (Chambers, II, 406–410). The Bear Garden, also called Paris (or Parish) Garden, was an amphitheatre where bear-baitings were held. Both the Rose and the Bear Garden were located near to each other on the Bankside. Norden's map of London (1593) 'shows "The Beare howse", a little west and north of "The play howse", which is the Rose' (Chambers, II, 461–462).

232 *Mary Ambree*, the unhistorical heroine of a ballad in *Bishop Percy's Folio Manuscript* (ed. J. W. Hales and F. J. Furnivall (3 vols., London, 1868), I, 515): *The valorous acts performed at Gaunt by the brave bonnie lass Marye Aumbree, who in revenge of her lovers death did play her part most gallantly.* See Rollins, nos. 2803, 2804. This celebrates her share in the effort made in 1584 to recapture Ghent with the aid of English volunteers after Parma's successes in the Netherlands. Her name comes to mean 'Amazon', 'virago'. She is often mentioned in drama: e.g. Jonson, *A Tale of a Tub*, I.iv.22 and *Epicoene*, IV.ii.123; Marston, *Antonio and Mellida*, I.i.104; Field, *Amends for Ladies*, II.i.47; Beaumont and Fletcher, *The Scornful Lady*, V.iv.98. *W.H.*, V.iii.5.

235–236 *walke arme in arme . . . Newgate*, i.e. as if they were chained together, like inmates of the prison. Cf. *1 Henry IV*, III.iii.88–90:

Falstaff.. . . . .How now, lad?. . . .must we all march?
Bardolph. Yea, two and two, Newgate fashion.

257 *yerke*, 'to lash with satire or ridicule' (*O.E.D.*, *s.v.* jerk, *v.*I). Cf. Marston, *Scourge of Villanie*, *Proemium in librum primum*, 19–20: 'Quake guzzell dogs, that liue on putred slime, / Skud from the lashes of my yerking rime.' And Virgil's scornful reference to the 'ierking *pedants*, / Players, or such like *buffon*, barking wits' who would attack Horace, in *Poetaster*, V.iii.371–372. *W.B.*, II.i.118.

264 *stinckers. M.M.L.*, IV.iii.14.

264 *Screech-owle. W.H.*, IV.ii.127.

266 *mother Mum-pudding.* Stow writes of the buildings in petty
   Wales, Tower Street ward: they have for many years 'fallen
   to ruine, and beene letten out for stabling of horses, to
   Tipplers of Beere, and such like: amongst others, one mother
   Mampudding (as they termed her) for many yeares kept this
   house, or a great part thereof, for victualing' (*Survey*, I, 137).
   Nashe, in *Lenten Stuffe*, refers to 'The nurse or mother
   Mampudding' (III, 200), and in a note on the passage, F. P.
   Wilson (*Works*, V, 59) cites a reference to 'that mampodding
   madge' in R. B.'s *Appius and Virginia* (1575), B1.

266.0.2 *a sennate.* 'A set of notes played on a trumpet as a signal
   for the approach or departure of a procession' (*Shakespeare's
   England*, II, 45).

275 *Suckets, and Marmilads.* Cf. *The Return from Parnassus*, Part
   One, lines 406–408: 'and now the time is come I hope what
   ere I make will beare marmelett and sukket in the mouthe'.
   And Greene, *A Quippe for an Upstart Courtier*, XI, 249, of the
   'queasie maister veluet breeches': 'tush he cannot disgest his
   meate without conserues, nor end his meale without suckats'.
   'Suckets' were 'sweetmeats of candied fruit' (*O.E.D.*, *s.v.*
   Succade).

275 *Marchants*, 'a kind of plum' (*O.E.D.*, *s.v.* Merchant. *sb.* 5,
   citing the present passage as its only example).

299 *compleat steele. Hamlet*, I.iv.52. *L.D.*, IV.ii.88.

332 *mankinde*, i.e. possessed of a more than feminine – in other
   words masculine – strength.

335 *let me see, by what.* Cf. Marston, *Antonio and Mellida*, II.i.295–
   297:

> and thou and I will live –
> Let's think like what – and thou and I will live
> Like unmatch'd mirrors of calamity.

336 *long stocking. W.H.*, III.iv.77.

336–337 *skirtes, | Not made to sit vpon*, i.e. not to be injured, or
   annoyed. Cf. *S.D.S.*, E4: 'Dublets with little thick skirts (so
   short that none are able to sit vpon them)'. And Marston,
   Histriomastix, III.i (ed. Wood, III, 272):

> *Phil.* Your Lord-ships doublet-skirt is short and neate.
> *Mav.* Who sits there, finds the more uneasie seate.

The phrase 'to sit upon (somebody's) skirts' means to injure, or annoy, or take revenge upon him. See *W.H.*, IV.ii.211, n.

IV.i

2 *nuncions*, 'a light refreshment taken between meals; a lunch' (*O.E.D.*, *s.v.* Nuncheon). *M.G.*, p. 119: 'but how far must we march now like tottred Souldiers after a Fray, to their Nuncions?'

8 *makes hounds of vs.* The term 'brace' was used originally of dogs (*O.E.D.*, *sb.*² III.15.a, where the present passage is cited).

13 *hipocritnes.* Sir Vaughan's mispronunciation involves both the meaning 'hypocrisy' and 'hippocras', wine flavored with spices; he will drink a toast in it (and does so at lines 43 ff.).

32–33 *small timber'd.* Sir George Paule, *The Life of the Most Reverend and Religious Prelate John Whitgift, Lord Archbishop of Canterbury* (1612), p. 93: 'For his small timber, he was of good quicke strength, straight and well shaped in all his limbes.'

36–37 *bolts . . . soone shot.* Tilley, F515.

37 *let all slide.* Tilley, W879.

39 *Comfits . . . Carrawaies.* Cf. Deloney, *Gentle Craft*, Part Two, p. 142: 'whom her mistres had sent thither to buy Comfets and Carawayes, with diuers other sweet meates, for that they had a banket bespoken by diuers gallant Courtiers, which that night appointed to come thither'. 'Comfits' were sweetmeats 'made of some fruit, root, etc., preserved with sugar' (*O.E.D.*); 'Carrawaies' were sweetmeats or confections containing caraway-seeds (*O.E.D.*). Among the eccentric dishes described in 'The Bankrouts Banquet' at the end of *S.H.R.*, F4v, are '*Tarts* of seuerall Fruites, stucke with *Muske-comfits* of purpose, to sweeten the mouth, . . . *Annis-seed comfits*, . . . *March-panes*, which shewed like *Bucklers*, yᵉ long *Orange-comfits* standing vp like *Pikes*, & in the midst of euery *March-pane* a goodly sweet *Castle*, all the bottomes being thickly strewed with *Careawaies*'. *S.D.*, IV.i.271.

40 *it does him good to sweare*, i.e. because he swears by such comforting, carefree and conserving oaths. For the joke, cf. Heywood, *1 The Fair Maid of the West*, V.i.125–127: 'I will make bold to march in towards your banquet and there comfit myself, and cast all caraways down my throat, the best way I have to conserve myself in health.'

55 *stucke a nose*. Cf. *G.H.*, C4v, quoted in the note on lines 100–101, below.

56 *weare two faces vnder one hood*. Tilley, F20. *S.H.R.*, E3: 'Hee [Hypocrisy]...dwelt with a Vizard-maker, and there hee was the first who inuented the wearing of two faces vnder a hood.' *W.H.*, IV.ii.95.

58 *tallest*, boldest.

64–65 *For...royall*. Cf. *G.H.*, C3v: 'For the *Head* is a house built for *Reason* to dwell in.'

67 *high Court of Parliament*. *M.E.*, 1495.

69 *This little Ile of Man*. Day, *The Parliament of Bees* (1641), D1v:

> had my Barber
> Perfum'd my lowzy thatch (this nitty harbour)
> These pi'd-wingd Butterflies wud know me than,
> But they nere landed in the Ile of *Man*.

71–72 *crowne's the Haire:...stands awry*. Cf. *S.T.M.*, 3: 'I am deposde: my Crowne is taken from mee.'

78–81 *when we dye...graue*. From the *Calvitii Encomium* of Synesius, translated by Abraham Fleming in 1579 as *A Paradoxe, Prouing by reason and example, that Baldnesse is much better than bushie haire*, C6v: 'The haire is a dead and senselesse superfluitie, & in dead things they haue their nourishment. The *Aegyptians* shauing off the hair of their dead bodies, euen to the very stumpes: founde notwithstanding their haire growne againe, and their beardes shot out in length the yeare next following.'

87–88 *When her lasciuious armes the Water hurles, | About the shoares wast, her sleeke head she curles*. Cf. *D.T.*, B2v (Westminster speaks of the Thames): 'Sometimes does shee chaunge her selfe into a Girdle of Siluer, and then doe I weare it about my middle. Sometimes lookes shee like an Amazon, (a long curled hayre hanging loosely about her shoulders) and then dooes shee fight with the windes.' *O.F.*, IV.ii.9.

89 *rorid,* dewy.

91–94 *You see the Earth...blade.* Cf. *G.H.*, C4v:

> Grasse is the haire of the earth, which so long as it is suffred to grow, it becomes the wearer, and carries a most pleasing colour, but when the Sunne-burnt clowne makes his mowes at it, and (like a Barber) shaues it off to the stumps, then it withers and is good for nothing, but to be trust vp and thrown amongst Iades.

95–97 *Besides...rend this Head-tyre off.* Cf. *G.H.*, C4v: 'which beauty in men the Turkes enuying, they no sooner lay hold on a Christian, but the first marke they set vpon him, to make him know hees a slaue, is to shaue off all his haire close to the scull'.

100–101 *So, if faire haire...vile and base.* Cf. *G.H.*, C4v: 'How vgly is a bald pate? it lookes like a face wanting a nose: or like ground eaten bare with the arrowes of Archers, wheras a head al hid in haire, giues euen to a most wicked face a sweet proportion, & lookes like a meddow newly marryed to the *Spring.*'

103 *scalded,* affected with the 'scall', a scaly or scabby disease of the skin, especially of the scalp (*O.E.D.*). Hence, scurvy, paltry, contemptible. Cf. *Sat.*, IV.i.145; V.ii.320; *1 H.W.*, I.ii.98; *2 H.W.*, II.i.180; *W.B.*, V.ii.152; *P.G.*, III.ii.115.

107 *enameld,* enamoured (Miniver's malapropism).

111 *Harper.* Addressed to Sir Vaughan, with reference to the bardic tradition of the Welsh.

112 *cracknels,* 'small pieces of fat pork dried crisp' (*O.E.D.*). Spenser, *The Shepheardes Calender,* Januarye, 57–58: 'His clownish gifts and curtsies I disdaine, / His kiddes, his crack-nelles, and his early fruit.'

113–114 *shoote...Suger pellets.* Cf. *S.H.R.*, F4:

> After all this, a *Capias* with a *Latitat,* went from one to one, but none touched those dishes, yet they were heaped full to the brim with *Sugar-pellets,* and cakes of *Gynger-bread* piled round about them: But the *Pellets* when they were shot did scarce hit, and the *Gynger* so bit their tongues, and set their mouths in a heat, that none at the Table toucht them.

I.T.B.N., III.ii.23. And the anonymous *Dick of Devonshire* (M.S.R.), lines 454–455: 'And my Devonshire blade, honest Dicke Pike, / spard not his Sugar pellets among my Span-yards.'

115 *Cadwallader.* Drayton (in his annotations to *Englands Heroicall Epistles*, 'Owen Tudor to Queene Katherine', line 77) ident-ifies him thus: 'the last King of the *Britaines*, descended of the Noble and ancient Race of the *Trojans*; to whom an Angell appeared, commanding him to goe to *Rome* to Pope *Sergius*, where he ended his life' (*Works*, II, 213). *N.H.*, IV.i.41.

117 *Sering.* A quarto misprint for 'string'; addressed to Asinius, who at line 169 is called 'Lute-stringe' by Tucca. See T. M. Parrott's review of Scherer's edition of *Satiromastix* (*Modern Language Review*, 6 (1911), 401).

118 *scowring-sticke*, i.e. ramrod, specifically one fitted with a wad or sponge for cleaning out the bore of a gun. *I.T.B.N.*, V.iii.18.

121 *Fye'st.* The word involves a quibble on 'fist', an alternate form of 'foist' meaning (1) a rogue, and (2) a stench. For the latter, cf. *1 H.W.*, III.iii.70: 'spurne your hounds when they fyste'. It is common in vulgar usage, as in *Eastward Ho*, IV.ii.141: 'Mary, fyste o'your kindnesse.' For 'foist' as rogue, cf. *Every Man in his Humour*, IV.vii.131–132: 'you whoreson foist, you'. And *July and Julian* (M.S.R. (1955), prepared by G. Dawson), line 997: 'he ys a cogger, and fister'. 'Foist' in cant language means 'pickpocket'. Cf. *B.L.*, H2v: 'He that pickes the pocket is called a *Foist*.' And *J.M.M.*, E1v: 'others that haue been *foysts, [Marginal note: 'quasi. pickpockets.'] all or the most part of their time'. The implica-tion of stench is probably also present in the insult which Tucca hurls at Horace at IV.ii.47: 'I smelt the foule-fisted Morter-treader.'

121 *my name's Hamlet reuenge.* Shakespeare's play was entered in the Stationers' Register on 26 July 1602, as 'a booke called the Revenge of *Hamlett* Prince Denmarke [*sic*] as yt was latelie Acted by the Lord Chamberleyne his servantes' (Arber, III, 212). The present passage may refer either to this or to the

pre-Shakespearean *Hamlet* which had been holding the London stage at least since 1589 (when Nashe made his famous allusion to it in the Preface to Greene's *Menaphon* (*Works*, III, 315)). Henslowe records a performance at Newington Butts on 9 June 1594 (*Diary*, p. 21); and there is the well-known and here very pertinent passage in Lodge's *Wits Miserie* in 1596, H4v: 'he walks for the most part in black vnder colour of grauity, & looks as pale as the Visard of ye ghost which cried so miserally at ye Theator like an oister wife, *Hamlet, reuenge*'. For other references by Dekker to the play, cf. *D.T.*, G3:

Sometimes would he ouertake him, and lay hands vppon him (like a Catch-pole) as if he had arrested him, but furious *Hamlet* woulde presently eyther breake loose like a Beare from the stake, or else so set his pawes on this dog that thus bayted him, that with tugging and tearing one anothers frockes off, they both looked like mad *Tom* of Bedlam.

L.C., H2: 'But if any mad *Hamlet* hearing this, smell villanie, & rush in by violence to see what the tawny Diuels are dooing: then they excuse the fact.' *W.H.*, V.iv.50–51: 'but when light Wiues make heauy husbands, let these husbands play mad *Hamlet*, and crie reuenge'.

122 *Parris garden.* See III.i.228, n. *J.M.M.*, F3 (of the haunts of the pickpocket): 'his common wealth to liue in, or ground to encamp in, is the antient great grand father Powles, & all other little churches his children, besides Parish garden, or rather (places of more benefit) publick, & by your leaue priuate play houses'.

123 *I ha plaide Zulţiman.* Ward thought this was a reference to Kyd's *Soliman and Perseda* (A. W. Ward, *A History of English Dramatic Literature to the Death of Queen Anne*, new and rev. ed. (3 vols., London, 1899), I, 311, n. 3). Herford and Simpson label the suggestion 'improbable' (I, 13–14, n. 2); 'Zulziman' they call 'a part in a lost play on some Eastern theme' (I, 14).

127 *Fulkes.* The name of a bear?

127–128 *call'st Demetrius Iorneyman Poet.* I.ii.137–138.

129–130 *Player...couldst not set a good face vpon't.* Regarding Jonson as an actor, and his apparent lack of success in that profession, see Herford and Simpson, I, 13–14.

130 *leather pilch,* i.e. leather coat, regularly cited as the dress of a laborer. Nashe, *Pierce Penilesse,* I, 158: 'a Carre-man in a lether pilche'; and *Lenten Stuffe,* III, 179: 'the patchedest *Leather piltche laboratho*'.

131–132 *took'st mad Ieronimoes part.* I.ii.355–356, n.

132 *Stagerites.* With a pun on 'Stagirite' (Aristotle). *W.A.,* BIV: '*Tearme* times, when the *Two-peny Clients,* and *Peny Stinkards* swarme together to heere the *Stagerites*'.

133 *Ile of Dogs,* a marsh opposite Greenwich. The reference is to Nashe's satirical comedy, *The Isle of Dogs,* performed in the summer of 1597; it was judged by the Privy Council to contain 'very seditious and sclanderous matter', and in consequence the play itself was suppressed, some of the actors (including Jonson) arrested and imprisoned, and a warrant issued on 28 July closing all the London theatres until the following November. Jonson not only acted in the play but almost certainly had a hand in its authorship. Nashe, who fled London when the uproar broke, says in a marginal note to *Lenten Stuffe* that he wrote only the induction and the first act of the play, and that 'the other foure acts without my consent, or the least guesse of my drift or scope, by the players were supplied, which bred both their trouble and mine to' (*Works,* III, 153–154). The Privy Council on 15 August 1597 reported that among the players already 'apprehended and comytted to pryson' there is one who 'was not only an actor but a maker of parte of the said plaie' (*Acts of the Privy Council,* new series, XXVII (1597), p. 338; quoted in McKerrow, *Works of Nashe,* V, 31; reprinted in Herford and Simpson, I, 217–218). That Jonson was involved in the affair is known from the issue by the Privy Council on 8 October 1597 of warrants for the release of Gabriel Spencer, Robert Shaa, and Benjamin Jonson from the Marshalsea (*Acts of the Privy Council,* new series, XXVIII, 33, reprinted in Herford and Simpson, I, 218, and quoted in McKerrow, V, 30). That he is

to be identified with the 'maker of parte of the said plaie' was first urged by E. K. Chambers (*Modern Language Review*, 4 (April 1909), 410–411). According to Herford and Simpson, 'The principal if not the only hand employed [in the completion of *The Isle of Dogs*] was unquestionably Jonson's' (I, 15). The present passage supports the identification, the implication seeming to be that after his experience of *The Isle of Dogs* Horace (Jonson) turned satirist and has been snarling ever since.

133–135 *Ile of Dogs . . . Ban-dog . . . Parris-garden.* Cf. *W.A.*, BIV:

> What merry *Gale* shall wee then wish for? vnles it bee to *Ferry* ouer the *Hellespont*, and to crosse from *Sestus* to *Abidus*, that is to say, from *London* to the *Beare Garden*? The company of the *Beares* hold together still; they play their *Tragi-Comaedies* as liuely as euer they did:. . . Into this Ile of *Dogs* did I therefore transport my selfe.

Dekker makes repeated reference to the noise of the bear- and bull-baiting dogs of Paris Garden. Cf. *B.L.*, C3v: 'yes, yes, wee will, roared al the Kennell as though it had beene the Dogs of Paris Garden'. *R.G.*, V.i.III. For 'Ban-dog', see I.ii.326, n.

133–134. *villanous Guy.* Penniman (p. 428) suggested that 'the name as here used may have been that of a dog at the Beargarden,' but both he and Scherer (p. 109) see a reference to Guy of Warwick, and given Tucca's habit of loading his speech with the names of romance, ballad, and stage figures, such a reference is possible. Both as metrical romance and ballad, the story of Guy of Warwick was very popular. Cf. Puttenham, *The Arte of English Poesie* (ed. G. D. Willcock and A. Walker (Cambridge, 1936), pp. 83–84:

> blind harpers or such like tauerne minstrels that giue a fit of mirth for a groat, & their matters being for the most part stories of old time, as the tale of Sir *Topas*, the reportes of *Beuis* of *Southampton*, *Guy* of *Warwicke*, *Adam Bell*, and *Clymme* of the *Clough* & such other old Romances or historicall rimes, made purposely for recreation of the common people at Christmasse diners & brideales, and in tauernes & alehouses and such other places of base resort.

A ballad titled 'a pleasante songe of the valiant actes of Guy of Warwicke' was entered in the Stationers' Register on 5 January 1592 (Rollins, no. 2118; and see Chappell, I, 171–172; Simpson, 283–285). There may have been a play about him *c.* 1593 (see *Annals,* p. 58). On 14 October 1618, John Taylor the Water Poet saw 'a play of the life and death of *Guy of Warwicke,* played by the Right Honourable the Earle of *Darbie* his men' at the Maydenhead tavern in Islington (Bentley, v, 1347). This may have been the same as the 'Play Called the life and Death of Guy of Warwicke written by Iohn Day and Tho: Decker' that was entered for publication in the Stationers' Register on 15 January 1620. *The Tragical History, Admirable Atchievments and various events of Guy Earl of Warwick,* published in 1661 with a titlepage ascription to 'B.J.' is certainly not by Ben Jonson, and Bullen (ed.), *Works of John Day,* p. 645, thought it too badly written to be the one by Dekker and Day, which is generally accounted lost.

In the last decades of the sixteenth century, romances of the type of Guy of Warwick were coming under attack; this might account for Tucca's epithet 'villanous'. Edward Dering in the preface 'To the Christian Reader' of his *Briefe and necessary Instruction* (1572) had included *Guy of Warwicke* among books of 'childish follye', and in Francis Meres' *Palladis Tamia* (1598), *Guy of Warwicke* stands second in a list of twenty-four romances deemed 'hurtfull to youth'. See R. S. Crane, 'The Vogue of *Guy of Warwick*', *PMLA,* 30 (1915), 125–194.

136 *saue thy selfe and read,* as Jonson had done in October 1598 when standing trial at the Old Bailey for having killed his fellow-actor Gabriel Spencer in a duel on the previous 22 September. He confessed the indictment of felony, and escaped the gallows by claiming benefit of clergy. He was dismissed with confiscation of all his goods, and the mark of Tyburn branded on his thumb (Herford and Simpson, I, 18–19). The episode is alluded to elsewhere in the play at I.ii.117; IV.ii.61–62; IV.iii.105–106.

138 *Farding,* farthing (Scherer).

138 *Candle.* See I.ii.0.1, n.

139 *Damboys*. Presumably a reference to Bussy D'Ambois, the celebrated French courtier (murdered in 1579) who is the subject of Chapman's tragedy written in 1603–1604, shortly after the death of Elizabeth. The present allusion may refer either to the historical Bussy D'Ambois, or to a pre-Chapman play dealing with recent French history such as Dekker and Drayton's lost trilogy (with an introductory play by Dekker) titled *The Civil Wars of France*, for which Henslowe records payments between 29 September 1598 and 20 January 1599 (*Diary*, pp. 98–103). See T. M. Parrott, 'The Date of *Bussy D'Ambois*', *Modern Language Review*, 3 (1907–1908), 130.

142–143 *arise...Eccho*. A parody of *Cynthia's Revels*, I.ii.14: 'Arise, and speake thy sorrowes, *Eccho*, rise.'

142 *sprite ath Buttry*, literally, the spirit of wine. Stubbes, *Anatomie of Abuses*, p. 107:

> You shal haue them there sitting at the wine and goodale all the day long, yea, all the night, too, peraduenture a whole week together, so long as any money is left; swilling, gulling, & carowsing from one to another, til neuer a one can speak a redy woord. Then, when with the spirit of the buttery they are thus possessed, a world it is to consider their gestures & demenors, how they stut and stammer, stagger & reele too & fro like madmen.

P.G., V.ii.299; *N.H.*, V.i.380; *W.K.*, III.i.108. And cf. *Tarltons Newes out of Purgatorie* (1590), BIV: '*Hob Thrust, Robin Goodfellowe* and such like spirites (as they terme them of the buttry) famored in euerie olde wiues Chrinicle for their mad merry pranckes'. *L.C.*, D4: 'The *spirit* of the *Deuils Buttry* hearing this, made a legge to *Pride* for her counsell.'

142 *Herring-bone*, silk or velvet with a herring-bone pattern. Cf. Marston, *Scourge of Villanie*, VII, 18–22:

> Seest thou yon gallant in the sumptuous clothes,
> How brisk, how spruce, how gorgiously he shoews,
> Note his French-herring bones, but note no more,
> Vnlesse thou spy his fayre appendant whore
> That lackyes him.

As Davenport observes in his note on the passage (p. 328), *O.E.D.* does not record 'herring-bone' before 1659.

147 *Metheglin,* Welsh *meddyglyn.* It was the national drink of the time, of which, according to Harrison, 'the Welshmen make no lesse accompt and not without cause if it be well handled than the Greekes did of their Ambrosia or Nectar' (*Description of England,* ed. Furnivall, I, 161). Sir Thomas Elyot described it in *The Castle of Helthe* (1541), f. 36: 'Metheglyn, which is moste used in wales, by reason of hotte herbes boyled with hony, is hotter then meade, and more comforteth a colde stomake, if it be perfectly made, and not new or very stale.' *N.H.,* II.i.223; *W.E.,* II.ii.116.

147–148 *my old whore a Babilon.* There is no reason to suppose an allusion here to Dekker's *Whore of Babylon,* printed in 1607. The phrase, with its anti-Roman reference, was in constant use, by Dekker and his contemporaries. Cf. *N.F.H.,* B3; *D.P.,* B2v; *S.D.S.,* G3.

150 *Feede and be fat my faire Calipolis.* A conflation of two much-parodied lines from Peele's *Battle of Alcazar:* 'Feede then and faint not faire Calypolis' (line 548, repeated at line 561), and 'Feede and be fat that we may meete the foe' (line 568). Cf. Shakespeare, *2 Henry IV,* II.iv.179; Marston, *What You Will,* V.i.i. *S.H.,* V.ii.188.

151 *wriggle-tailes.* Cf. Spenser, *The Shepheardes Calender,* Februarie, 7–8: 'They wont in the wind wagge their wrigle tailes, / Perke as Peacock.'

152 *table-man,* a gaming piece; one of the figures used in playing at tables, or backgammon. Used of gamesters in *L.C.,* D4v: 'and knowing that your most selected Gallants are the onelye table-men that are plaid with al at *Ordinaires,* into an *Ordinary* did he most gentleman like, conuay himselfe in state'. Dekker uses the word figuratively in the sense of 'blockhead' in *G.H.,* B1v: 'You *ordinary Gulles,* that through a poore and silly ambition to be thought you inherit the reuenues of extra-ordinary wit, will spend your shallow censure vpon the most elaborate Poeme, so lauishly, that all the painted table-men about you, take you to be heires apparant to rich *Midasse*'.

152–153 *sincke point,* 'cinque point (Back gammon), the fifth point from the end on either side of the board' (Scherer, p. 110).

155–156 *Buffe Ierkin.* III.i.203, n.

163 *Cumrade,* 'obs. form of COMRADE' (*O.E.D.*).

167–168 *winter-plummes.* *R.A.*, B3v: 'no my countrie-men, neuer
beate the bush so long to finde out Winter, where he lies like
a beggar shiuering with colde, but take these from me as
certaine, and most infallible rules, know when Winter-plomes
are ripe & ready to be gathered'. *S.H.R.*, G2: 'the last winter-
plum the sad Comfit-maker threw at their heads'. Brome,
The Court Begger, II.i (ed. Shepherd, I, 201): 'sir *Raphael*
Winter-plum. / . . . That old witherd piece'.

169 *Sir Eglamour.* The metrical romance of *Sir Eglamour of Artois*
was printed by Wynkyn de Worde in 1500; subsequent
editions in English were printed in Edinburgh, 1508; in London
by W. Copland, *c.* 1548–1569; and London, *c.* 1570. A book
of *Sir Eglamour* was entered in the Stationers' Register on 15
January 1582 (Arber, II, 405). A burlesque account of his fight
with a dragon is given in Samuel Rowlands, *The Melancholie
Knight* (1615), E2–E3. The romance is found in *Bishop
Percy's Folio,* ed. J. W. Hales and F. J. Furnivall, II, 338–389.
See also *Roxburghe Ballads,* III, 607; Simpson, pp. 666–667.
Syr Eglamoour is among the romances in Captain Cox's
library, according to Laneham's *Letter* describing the Queen's
entertainment at Kenilworth in the summer of 1575 (Nichols,
Progresses of Queen Elizabeth, I, 452).

170 *Skinker,* tapster. *G.H.*, B2v: 'Awake thou noblest drunkerd
Bacchus, . . . you soueraigne Skinker.' *V.M.*, II.i.21.

171 *Codpeece point,* the lace fastening the codpiece to the hose.
Field, *Amends for Ladies,* IV.iv.90–91: 'I'le cut your codpeice
point Sir with this thrust, / And then downe goes your breeches.'
S.H., V.ii.167; *M.M.L.*, II.i.193; *V.M.*, II.iii.58–59; *W.E.*,
II.i.120.

173–174 *binde thee to the good forbearing.* Marston, *What You Will,*
IV.i.220–221: 'her eye promiseth she will be bound to the
good abearing'.

175 *Hobby-horse.* *W. of E.*, II.i.53, n.

181–182 *to Mum.* Short for 'mum-chance', a game of dice (suggested by T. M. Parrott in his review of Scherer's edition of

Satiromastix, Modern Language Review, 6 (1911), 405). See
W.H., II.ii.7, n. Cf. *Sat.*, IV.iii.263.

184 *playes mum-budget*, i.e., keeps silent. Deloney, *The Gentle Craft,*
Part Two, p. 158: 'looke you play mum-budget, and speake
not a word of this matter to any creature'. And *Look About
You* (M.S.R. (1913), prepared by W. W. Greg), line 833:
'Mum budgit not a word as thou louest thy life.' Tilley,
M1311.

186 *sing*, i.e. swinge, thrash.

189–190 *beget you the reuersion of the Master of the Kings Reuels.*
Jonson in fact was granted the reversion of this office in a
warrant of 5 October 1621 (reprinted in Herford and Simpson,
I, 237–239), but the grant availed him nothing because Sir
John Astley, who held the post, survived him. Malone
(*Variorum Shakespeare* (London, 1821), I, 418) assumed from
the evidence of the present passage that some attempt to obtain
this post for Jonson must have been made during the reign of
Elizabeth.

190 *Lord of Mis-rule*. Stow writes: 'In the feaste of Christmas,
there was in the kinges house, wheresoeuer hee was lodged, a
Lord of Misrule, or Maister of merry disports, and the like
had yee in the house of euery noble man, of honor, or good
worshippe, were he spirituall or temporall' (*Survey*, I, 97).
For an account of the tradition, see Hazlitt, *Popular Antiquities*,
I, 272–281.

195 *purging Comfits. S.H.R.*, F4: 'Next those dishes, were brought
in, a number of *Outlaries*, thwackt with *Purging-comfits*, for
they are able to make a man flye ouer nine hedges.'

204 *I hope he and I are not Paralels. Poetaster*, I.ii.26–28: 'is this
thy desseignes and thy discipline, to suffer knaues to bee
competitors with commanders and gent'men? are wee
paralells, rascall? are wee *paralells*?'

211 *I owe God a death. 1 Henry IV*, V.i.126: 'Why, thou owest
God a death.' Tilley, G237.

IV.ii

1 *Free₃e gowne watch man.* Cf. *R.A.*, B3v: 'When *Charity* blowes
   her nailes, & is ready to starue, yet not so much as a Watchman
   will lend her a flap of his freeze Gowne to keepe her warm'.
   For 'Freeze', see *W.H.*, II.ii.14, n.

14 *Pasquils-mad-cap.* The title of a verse satire by Nicholas Breton,
   published in 1600. *G.H.*, B4–B4v:

> Come, come, it would be but a bald world, but that it weares a periwig.
> The body of it is fowle (like a birding-peece) by being too much heated:
> the breath of it stinks like the mouthes of Chamber-maides by feeding
> on so many sweet meats. And though to purge it wil be a sorer labour
> then the clensing of *Augeaes* stable, or the scowring of Moore-ditch: yet
> *Ille ego, qui quondam*, I am the *Pasquilles mad-cap*, that will doot.

The name Pasquil, or Pasquin, is said to have been that of
a tailor (or a barber, or a shoemaker, or a schoolmaster) who
lived in Rome in the vicinity of the Piazza Navona where an
antique statue (said to represent a gladiator) had been dis-
interred and set up in 1501 by Cardinal Caraffa. The statue
came to be called Pasquin, and as the custom arose of decking
it out in verses of a satirical kind on St Mark's Day, the term
'Pasquinade' became a general name for squibs or lampoons,
and 'Pasquin' a name for the anonymous writer of such verses.
In the England of 1601, the name Pasquil had recently been
made particularly notorious from having been adopted by the
author of the anti-Martinist pamphlets (1589–1590).

14 *mother Bee.* A character in the Interlude titled *The Marriage
   between Wit and Wisdom.* The play is preserved in a manuscript dated 1579 in the British Library (Add. MS 26782);
   the name of Francis Merbury is appended to the epilogue.
   W. W. Greg (*Bibliography of the English Printed Drama to
   the Restoration* (4 vols., Oxford, 1939–1959), II, 963–964) has
   suggested that the manuscript is a transcript of a copy of a lost
   edition; evidence in support of this is discussed by Trevor
   N. S. Lennam in the introduction to his Malone Society
   edition of the play (1971, for 1966), pp. ix–x. 'The mariage
   of witt and wisedome' is in the repertoire of the company of

players who appear in *Sir Thomas More* (M.S.R.), line 922, though the version of it performed at lines 1029ff. bears little resemblance to the extant play.

16 *Basket hiltes*, swords furnished with a hand protection fashioned from narrow plates of steel curved into the shape of a basket. It was an old-fashioned weapon, and the term is used derisively. 'Basket Hilts' is the name of Squire Tub's guide and governor in Jonson's *A Tale of a Tub*; and Cokes, in *Bartholomew Fair*, calls his governor Waspe 'a fellow that knowes nothing but a basket-hilt, and an old Fox in't' (II.vi.59–60). In *2 Henry IV*, II.iv.131–132, Doll calls Pistol a 'basket-hilt stale juggler'.

21 *against the haire*. The phrase ordinarily means 'against the grain'. For its punning application here, cf. Chapman, *May Day*, IV.ii.186–190:

> For I have noted a most faithful league
> Betwixt him and his barber now of late;
> And all the world may see he does not leave
> One hair on his smooth chin, as who should say
> His hapless love was gone against the hair.

And *Blurt, Master-Constable*, II.ii.216–217: 'But now those beards are gone, our chins are bare; / Our courtiers now do all against the hair.' *W.H.*, I.i.163; *M.M.L.*, IV.v.3; *W. of E.*, III.iv.44. Tilley, H18.

23 *whir*. *2 H.W.*, I.i.49.

24 *Scanderbag*, a corruption of Iskanderbeg or Iscander Bey ('Lord Alexander'), the Turkish name of George Castriot (1405–1468), the patriot chief who was celebrated for his battles in the cause of Albanian freedom and of Christianity. An account of *the warres of the Turcke against George Scanderbeg, prince of Epiro, and of the great victories obteyned by the sayd George, aswell against the Emperour of Turkie, as other princes, and of his other rare force and vertues, worthye of memorye, translated oute of Italian into Englishe by John Shute* appeared in 1562; and in 1596, with a prefatory sonnet by Spenser, *The History of George Castriot Surnamed Scanderbeg, King of Albanie. Containing his famous actes, his noble deedes of Armes, and memorable victories against the Turkes, for the*

Faith of Christ...By Iaques de Lavardin...Newly translated out of French into English by Z. I., Gentleman. In 1601 he was the subject of a recent play (now lost); 'The true historye of George Scanderbarge as yt was lately playd by the right honorable the Earle of Oxenforde his servantes' was entered in the Stationers' Register on 3 July 1601 (Arber, III, 187). He is often mentioned. Nashe, in *Lenten Stuffe* (III, 191), speaks of 'a child that will be a souldiour and a commaunder before hee hath cast his first teeth, & an *Alexander*, a *Iulius Caesar*, a *Scanderbeg*, a *Barbarossa* he will proue ere he aspire to thirtie'. And cf. Jonson, *Every Man in his Humour*, I.iii.26–27; G. Markham and L. Machin, *The Dumb Knight*, Act I (ed. Hazlitt, *Old Plays*, X, 118); Dryden, *Sir Martin Mar-all*, IV.i.46; V.i.415; V.ii.71. *S.H.*, II.iii.92.

29 *my red flag is hung out.* Scherer compares Marlowe, *1 Tamburlaine*, IV.ii.116–118:

> But if he stay until the bloody flag
> Be once advanc'd on my vermilion Tent,
> He dies, and those that kept us out so long.

Cf. also *N.F.H.*, CI–CIV: 'Nay, since my flag of defiance is hung forth, I will yeelde to no truce, but with such *Tamburlaine-like* furie march against this great Turke, and his legions.' And *J.M.M.*, H3: 'It thundered and lightened all night, yet was it a faire day the very next morning for furious *Tamberlaine*, who as you heard was cutting out 3 sorts of banners for his 3 sworne enemies.'

32 *Turke-a-ten-pence.* A term of derision, expressive of the Christian's contempt for the infidel Turk. It gained currency from the use of figures, painted to represent Turks, as marks for archers to shoot at, as in Finsbury Fields. Marlowe, *The Jew of Malta*, IV.ii.38–39: 'what gentry can be in a poore Turke of ten pence?' Cf. *W.H.*, IV.ii.193; *S.H.*, II.iii.55–56, n.

36 *Cornelius.* The allusion (taken together with the 'fire' and 'burnt' of the preceding line) is to the tubs used in the sweating cure for venereal diseases, which were called 'Cornelius tubs'. Some of the many references (such as the present one) are oblique. Cf. the allusion to 'Frier *Cornelius*' in Hall,

Virgidemiarum, IV.iv.113; to '*Mother Cornelius Meridian*' in
Nashe, *Pierce Penilesse* (I, 182, marginal note); to 'mother
Cornelius' dry-fats' in *Blurt, Master-Constable*, I.ii.15–16;
and Webster's Character of 'An Improvident young Gallant'
(IV, 33): 'a Scholer he pretends himselfe, and saies hee hath
sweat for it: but the truth is, hee knowes *Cornelius*, farre
better then Tacitus', with the notes of the commentators.
Chapman, *Monsieur D'Olive*, III.ii.67–75:

D'Ol. Thy name first, I pray thee?
Cor. Cornelius, my lord.
D'Ol. What profession?
Cor. A surgeon, an't please your lordship.
D'Ol.. . .our ambassage is into France, there may be employment for
thee; hast thou a tub?

R.A., D2v: 'when Men ride (the second time) to Bathe, and
carry another *Cornelius* Tub with them'.

36 *Respice funem*, 'remember the rope' (i.e. the hangman), an
alteration of the well-known Latin tag *respice finem*. Nashe
employs it in *Strange Newes* (I, 268), where it is a fling at
Gabriel Harvey's father's trade of rope-maker: 'Somewhat
hee mutters of *defamation and iust commendation*, & what a hell
it is for him, that hath built his heauen in vaine-glory, to bee
puld by the sleeue and bidde *Respice funem*, looke backe to his
Fathers house.' And cf. *The Comedy of Errors*, IV.iv.41–43:
'Mistress, *respice finem*, respect your end, or rather, the proph-
ecy like the parrot, "beware the rope's end". '

37 *my little Cutlers Shoppe*, addressed to Tucca's sword-and-
buckler-laden boy.

42 *Huon.* The hero of the romance titled *Sir Huon of Bordeaux*,
translated from the French by John Bourchier, Lord Berners,
c. 1534. A third edition was published in 1601. *Huon of Burdeaux*
is listed among the romances in Captain Cox's library as
these are reported in Laneham's *Letter* describing the Queen's
entertainment at Kenilworth (Nichols, *Progresses of Queen
Elizabeth*, I, 451). Nashe, in *The Anatomie of Absurditie* (I, 11)
includes it in his denunciation of the romances of King
Arthur and similar literature ('the fantasticall dreames of those

exiled Abbie-lubbers, from whose idle pens proceeded
those worne out impressions of the feyned no where acts, of
Arthur of the rounde table, Arthur of litle Brittaine, sir
Tristram, Hewon of Burdeaux, the Squire of low degree, the
foure sons of Amon, with infinite others'). Henslowe records
three performances (on 28 December 1593 and 3 and 11 January 1594) by the Earl of Sussex' men of a play (now lost)
called 'hewen of burdoche' (*Diary*, p. 20).

43 *licke-trencher*, a parasite.

45 *cranke*, aggressively high-spirited, 'cocky' (*O.E.D.*). Haughton,
    Englishmen for my Money, lines 1468–1469: 'and if you be
    so crancke, Ile call the Constable'.

47 *Morter-treader*. Another allusion to Jonson's trade as a brick-
    layer. Cf. I.ii.139, and IV.iii.169–170. For 'foule-fisted', cf.
    IV.i.121, n.

50–51 *Horace is valliant, and a man of the sword. Poetaster*, IV.vii.
    16–18:

> *Pyrg.* I, but Master; take heed how you giue this out, *Horace* is a man
> of the sword.
> *Cris.* 'Tis true, in troth: they say, he's valiant.

53 *pennie-bench Theaters.* Cf. *G.H.*, E2v: 'your *Groundling*, and
    Gallery Commoner buyes his sport by the penny'.

53 *Squirrell*, prostitute.

53–54 *cracking nuttes.* For this well-known habit of Elizabethan
    audiences, cf. Beaumont and Fletcher, *The Scornful Lady*,
    IV.ii.64–67, where a gallant refers contemptuously to

> fellowes that at Ordinaries dare eat
> Their eighteene pence thrice out before they rise,
> And yet goe hungry to a play, and crack
> More nuts than would suffice a dozen Squirrels

And Jonson, *The Staple of Newes*, the prologue for the Court,
lines 4–8, where it is hoped the play

> may produce delight:
> The rather, being offered, as a Rite,
> To *Schollers*, that can iudge, and faire report

The sense they heare, aboue the vulgar sort
Of Nut-crackers, that onely come for sight.

54 *Mermaid*, another slang term for prostitute. *1 H.W.*, IV.i.133;
2 H.W., I.ii.154.

55 *Satyr'd, and Epigram'd*. Cf. Marston, *Histriomastix*, Act II (ed.
Wood, III, 257–258):

> How you translating-scholler? you can make
> A stabbing *Satir*, or an *Epigram*,
> And thinke you carry just Ramnusia's whippe
> To lash the patient.

And *G.H.*, E4:

> if the writer be a fellow that hath either epigramd you, or hath had a flirt
> at your mistris, or hath brought either your feather or your red beard, or
> your little legs &c. on the stage, you shall disgrace him worse then by
> tossing him in a blancket, or giuing him the bastinado in a Tauerne, if in
> the middle of his play, (bee it Pastorall or Comedy, Morall or Tragedie)
> you rise with a skreud and discontented face from your stoole to be
> gone.

Cf. *Hamlet*, II.ii.343–344, concerning the stage quarrel:
'many wearing rapiers are afraid of goose-quills, and dare
scarce come thither'.

55–57 *Satyr'd...on's humour*. Cf. Tucca in *Poetaster*, III.iv.188–
191: 'I would faine come with my cockatrice one day, and
see a play; if I knew when there were a good bawdie one:
but they say, you ha' nothing but *humours*, *reuells*, and
satyres, that girde, and fart at the time, you slaue.' Jonson's
Every Man in his Humour was acted at the Curtain in 1598,
and *Every Man out of his Humour* at the Globe in 1599;
both plays were performed by the Chamberlain's men.

58 *shoulder-clappers*, sergeants; the term comes from their practice
of clapping a man on the shoulder to signify his arrest. *L.C.*,
L1v: 'Now did they boldly step into some priuiledged Tauerne,
and there drinke healthes, dance with Harlots, & pay both
Drawers and Fidlers after mid-night with other mens money,
& then march home againe fearelesse of the blowes that any
showlder-clapper durst giue them.' *Comedy of Errors*, IV.ii.37.
I.T.B.N., V.ii.37; *W.H.*, V.iv.192. Cf. *V.M.*, III.iii.194–196.

61 *Horastratus.* A combination of the names of Horace and Hero-
   stratus, who made himself notorious by setting fire to the
   temple of Diana at Ephesus in order 'to purchase himselfe an
   euerlasting fame' (*The excellent and pleasant worke of Iulius
   Solinus Polyhistor*, trans. Arthur Golding (1587), sig. Aa4.
   For Dekker's knowledge of this work, see the note on lines
   62–63, below).

61–62 *killing a Player.* IV.i.136, n.

62–63 *wilde-man...Anthropophagite.* Cf. the reference to 'the
   Anthropophagiʒde Satyr' in *S.H.R.*, E4, with Dekker's
   marginal note: 'The Man-eating Monster. *Anthropophagi* were
   Scythians (now *Tartars*) so called for eating men, & drinking
   bloud in their sculs'; he cites as his authority Polyhistor, i.e.
   Gaius Julius Solinus, the author of *Collectanea rerum memora-
   bilium*, an epitome in Latin of Pliny's *Natural History*; it was
   published in an English translation by Arthur Golding in
   1587 (see note on line 61, above). *W.Y.*, p. 26: 'arme my
   trembling hand, that it may boldly rip vp and Anatomize the
   vlcerous body of this *Anthropophagiʒed* plague': a passage
   that is also provided with a marginal note ('Anthropophagi
   are Scithians that feede on mens flesh'). *V.D.*, KIv–K2:
   'This *Homo-Daemon* (Man-Diuell) when hee is once *Anthropophagiʒed*, and longs for humane flesh, no furie is so cruell.'

63 *Macænasses.* For the pun, cf. the dedication to *G.H.*, A3, where
   Dekker asks of 'all Guls in generall': 'Whom can I choose
   (my most worthie *Mecæn-asses*) to be Patrons to this labour
   of mine fitter then your selues?' And Jonson, *The Case is
   Altered*, I.ii.52–53: 'Why, you shal be one of my *Mæcen-
   asses*, I'le giue you one of the bookes.' Cf. *Sat.*, I.ii.332:
   'Pithyasse', and *N.H.*, II.i.122: 'Manasses'.

69 *Palinodicall rimester.* I.ii.100–101, n.

70 *Solœcismes.* An echo of Horace's aside in *Poetaster*, III.i.103–
   106, when unable to rid himself of the importunate Crispinus:

> This tyrannie
> Is strange, to take mine eares vp by *commission*,
> (Whether I will or no) and make them stalls
> To his lewd *solœcismes*, and worded trash.

76 *Quiddits*, captious niceties in argument; quibbles (*O.E.D.*). *S.D.S.*, B2 'by his wise instructions, if a Puny were there amongst them, he might learne more cases, and more quiddits in law within seuen dayes, then he does at his Inne in fourteene moneths'.

80 *Monsieur Machiauell.* Henslowe records performances of a play (now lost) titled 'matchavell' on 2 March, 3 April, and 29 May 1592 (*Diary*, pp. 16, 17, 18). That Machiavelli should be named here, after Tucca has accused Horace of hypocrisy and deceit, is characteristic of the Elizabethan view of the Florentine statesman. Deceit 'studies *Machiauell*' in *W.A.*, D4. Marston in *Certaine Satyres*, II, 87ff. depicts 'Humility', who seems 'The perfect image of faire Curtesie' but is in fact 'a damn'd Macheuelian': 'within a haughty malecontent, / Though he does vse such humble blandishment'. And Guilpin, *Skialetheia* (1598), C3v, describes 'great *Faelix*' who politely greets all whom he passes in the streets and seems the image of 'perfect curtesie', but is in fact puffed up with ambitious thoughts:

> *Signior Machiauell*
> Taught him this mumming trick, with curtesie
> T'entrench himselfe in popularitie.

81 *Troglodite. S.H.R.*, F3: 'the *Troglodites*, who eate Serpents'.

82–84 *hot oathes...Iestes.* Cf. Carlo Buffone of Macilente in *Every Man Out*, I.i.214–216: ''ware how you offend him, he carries oile and fire in his pen, will scald where it drops: his spirit's like powder, quick, violent: hee'le blow a man vp with a jest.'

84 *Salt-peter Iestes.* Cf. Guilpin, *Skialetheia*, C3-C3v:

> Thys leaden-heeled passion is to dull,
> To keepe pace with this Satyre-footed gull:
> This mad-cap world, this whirlygigging age:
> Thou must haue words compact of fire & rage:
> Tearms of quick Camphire & Salt-peeter phrases,
> As in a myne to blow vp the worlds graces,
> And blast her anticke apish complements.

85 *Maligo-tasters.* Cf. *W.A.*, E1v: 'the inexplicable ioy of Poets,

who did nothing but pen encomious Gratulatorie[s] to bid her welcome, drinking healths in rich malago to the honour of her, and their mistresses, (the nine Muses) '. 'Maligo' is a white wine which takes its name from Malaga, the port in the south of Spain.

86 *Cinocephalus,* one of a fabled race of men with the heads of dogs. Cf. *P.G.,* V.i.18–19, n.

87 *excellent infernall.* Cf. Dryden, *Love Triumphant,* Act II (ed. Summers, VI, 432): 'Prethee, sweet Devil, do not ogle me, nor squeeze my Palm so feelingly, thou dear Infernal, do not.'

90 *there's no faith to be helde with Heritickes and Infidels.* An allusion to Jonson's conversion to Roman Catholicism which, he told Drummond, came to pass through the offices of a priest who visited him during his imprisonment for the killing of Spencer in the fall of 1598; 'thereafter he was 12 yeares a Papist' (Herford and Simpson, I, 139). But for the sinister twist which this sort of relativism had recently been given on the stage, cf. Barabas in Marlowe's *The Jew of Malta,* II.iii.310–313:

> *It's no sinne to deceive a Christian;*
> *For they themselves hold it a principle*
> *Faith is not to be held with Heretickes;*
> *But all are Hereticks that are not Jewes.*

92 *Alexander and Lodwicke.* Henslowe records fifteen performances by the Admiral's men of a play of this title between 14 January and 15 July 1597 (*Diary,* pp. 51, 56, 57, 58, 59). It was evidently still holding the stage in the spring of 1599, when 'divers thinges' were bought for it on 31 March (*Diary,* p. 106). It is now lost. There is a ballad on the subject in the Pepys collection (reprinted, *Pepys Ballads,* ed. Hyder E. Rollins (8 vols., Cambridge, Mass., 1929), I, 136ff.): 'The Two Faithful Friends, the pleasant History of Alexander and Lodwicke, who were so like one another, that none could know them asunder; wherein is declared how Lodwicke married the Princess of Hungaria, in Alexander's name, and how each night he layd a naked sword betweene him and the Princess, because he would not wrong his friend.' For the

sources of the story, see F. L. Lucas' note on *The Duchess of Malfi*, I.i.572 (where 'the old tale' is mentioned) in *Works of Webster*, II, 142.

93–94 *Perithous... Theseus.* At Perithous' bidding, Theseus accompanied him in an expedition to Hades to abduct Persephone. The scheme failed, and they were both imprisoned by Pluto until eventually rescued by Hercules. The episode probably figured in the two-part play of *Hercules* that was being acted by the Admiral's men throughout 1595. Henslowe records eleven performances of Part One between 7 May 1595 and 6 January 1596, and eight performances of Part Two between 23 May and 25 November 1595 (*Diary*, pp. 28–34). The plays were still in the repertoire in December 1601 (*ibid.*, p. 185). Both are lost.

97–98 *shoote thy quilles... Porcupine.* Topsell, *The Historie of Four-footed Beastes* (1607), p. 588, of the Porcupine: 'When they are hunted the beast stretcheth her skin, and casteth [its quills] off, one or two at a time, according to necessity vpon the mouths of the Dogs, or Legs of the Hunters that follow her, with such violence that many times they stick into trees & woods.' *V.D.*, L2v: 'An offi[c]er of this Character [a gaoler], hath not a bosome like a Doues (all Downy) but rather the backe of a Porcupine, stucke full of Quils, ready to be shot euery minute, because euery minute he shall bee made angry.' *T.T.*, 313–314.

99 *Heliconistes. Poetaster*, V.iii.157 (Tucca to Horace): 'Giue mee thy wrist, *Helicon*.'

99–100 *Dialogues... Lucian.* One of Lucian's satirical dialogues, the *Lexiphanes*, provided Jonson with the model for the purging of Crispinus' vocabulary in *Poetaster*, V.iii.

102 *Parcell-Poets*, part poets. Tucca uses the term of Crispinus in *Poetaster*, III.iv.159–160: 'hee is a gent'man, parcell-*poet*'; and Crispinus uses it of himself (IV.vi.29): 'Your gentleman, parcell-*poet*, sir', to which Caesar replies: 'O, that prophaned name!'

104 *in Forma Pauperis*, i.e. exempted from the costs of a legal action. *N.F.H.*, B1: 'the Deuill would hardly (like a Lawyer

in a busy Terme) be spoken with, because his Clyent had not
a penny to pay fees, but sued *in Forma pauperis*'. *P.W.*, F3v:
'shall I goe a'th score, or drinke *in forma pauperis*, my Pockets
hauing such gay lynings in them'. *W.H.*, II.i.112–113.

107–108 *Sticke...like a sprig of Rosemary*. The reference is to the
use of the herb for seasoning. Cf. Beaumont, *Knight of the
Burning Pestle*, v.3–4: 'a good peece of beefe, stucke with
rose-mary'. *W.Y.*, p. 34: 'And those that could shift for a
time...went...miching and muffled vp & downe with Rue
and Wormewood stuft into their eares and nosthrils, looking
like so many Bores heads stuck with branches of Rosemary,
to be serued in for Brawne at Christmas.'

115 *Thomas Thomasius*. Scherer (p. 115) saw in the name an
allusion to the Cambridge printer and lexicographer (1553–
1588). T. M. Parrott, reviewing Scherer's edition of *Satiromastix* (*Modern Language Review*, 6 (1911), 406), doubted the
reference, and accounted thus for the name: 'Tucca, who is
addressing a Welshman, gives him a characteristically Welsh
name, one of the numerous Welsh duplications, Thomas
Thomas, John Jones, Griffith Griffiths, etc.' But Scherer is
right. As Penniman (p. 433) noted, 'The allusion is fixed by
the reference to "ten thousand words".' And 'Thomas
Thomasius' is the way the author signs himself at the end of
the prefatory epistle to his *Dictionarium Linguae Latinae et
Anglicanae*, first published in 1587. By the date of *Satiromastix*,
four subsequent editions of the dictionary had appeared (in
1592, 1594, 1596, 1600).

121 *fetches...fegaries*. 'Fetches' are dodges, tricks (*O.E.D.*, sb.[1] 2).
'Fegaries' is a corruption of 'vagaries', frolics or pranks of
a freakish nature (*O.E.D.*). Cf. Barry, *Ram-Alley*, III.i (ed.
Hazlitt, *Old Plays*, x, 313): 'We old men have our crotchets,
our conundrums, / Our figaries, quirks, and quibbles'; and
V.i (p. 366): 'What trick? what quiddit? what fegary is this?'
O.F., II.ii.115; *R.G.*, IV.ii.238.

124 *cry Mum*, keep silent, with a quibble on the meaning, 'to
gamble', as at IV.i.181–182. *B.L.*, I1v: 'if their last host
follow them with a Bailiffe or a Sergeant, they only hold vp a

finger, naming a Purseuant and cry *Mum*, no more mine Host, you wot what, which words are of more power to blow him away, than if you firde him thence with traines of gunpowder'. Cf. *Sat.*, IV.i.184, n.

125–126 *winke-a-pipes*, the eyes (*O.E.D.*, *s.v.* wink-a-peep).

128 *Sampson*. A play on the subject was acted at the Red Lion Inn in 1567 (Chambers, II, 380), and shortly after the composition of *Satiromastix* the Admiral's men were to have a new one. Henslowe on 29 July 1602 records payment 'for the Boocke of Samson' (*Diary*, p. 204). Chambers (II, 367) identifies this with the 'tragicomedy of Samson and the half tribe of Benjamin' which Duke Philip Julius of Stettin-Pomerania attended at the Fortune theatre in the afternoon of 14 September 1602.

139 *Trangdo*. Bang, quoted by Scherer (p. 116), identified the word with 'trangdido', to which he suggested that it bore the same relation as the word 'dildo' to 'dildido'. He cited Ford, *The Lover's Melancholy*, IV.ii (1629), IIv: 'I will firke his Trangdido'; and Ford's *The Fancies, Chaste and Noble*, IV.i (1638), G4: 'nay I will tickle their Trangdidoes'; also Haughton, *Englishmen for my Money*, line 1855: 'With Trandido, Dil-dido, and I know not what'. Bang thought 'trangdido' to mean 'buttocks', 'arse'. Penniman (pp. 433–434) too thought the word meant 'buttocks', though he noted that 'it is also a term for a phallus, and a contemptuous term for a man or boy' – which latter seems to be closer to the meaning here. Cf. Chapman, *Monsieur D'Olive*, V.i.33–34, where a Page says, 'My name is Dildo' and is told 'Sirrah, leave your roguery.' The word is common in ballad refrains. Cf. 'A new Ballad of ye dauncing on ye ropes to ye tune of a rich Merchant man, &c', attributed to 'Tho: Decker' in MS.V.a.160 in the Folger Shakespeare Library, Washington, D.C.:

> I sing of a wonder strange,
> But not soe strange as true,
> Of a woeman that daunces on ye ropes,
> And soe does her husband too.
> With a trang dildoe dee

With a trang dildoe dee
To see her comes K^{ts} & gay ladyes
And squires of low degree.

And so on for five stanzas more. The poem has been regarded as a Collier forgery, but see F. D. Hoeniger, 'Thomas Dekker, the Restoration of St Paul's, and J. P. Collier, the Forger', *Renaissance News*, 16 (1963), 181–200, where a text of the ballad is reprinted from the manuscript. Cf. Wil Cricket's song to his Pegge in *Wily Beguilde* (M.S.R.), lines 2451–2452: 'Thou art my Ciperlillie: / And I thy Trangdidowne dilly.'

142 *by the crosse a this sword and dagger*, here swearing by the sword and dagger crossed. Cf. *O.F.*, III.i.292.

147–148 *beard-brush. M.M.L.*, II.i.197.

148–149 *raw-head and bloudy-bones*. Both terms were common expressions for a bugbear. Cf. Peele, *The Battle of Alcazar*, lines 238–239: 'And shall we be afraide of Bassas and of bugs, / Rawe head and bloudie bone?' Nashe, *Have With You* (III, 98): 'Some lofty tragicall Poet helpe mee, that is dayly conuersant in the fierce encounters of Raw-head and bloody bones.' *O.P.*, M2: 'These [Abram men], walking vp and downe the Countrey, are more terribl[e] to women and Children, then the name of *Raw-head* and *Bloudy-bones*, *Robbin Good-fellow*, or any other *Hobgobling*.' Tilley, R35.

149–150 *another brat* (*of those nine common wenches*). Cf. I.ii.279, n.

153 *button-cap*, i.e. Flash, also referred to by his 'blew coate' (line 154) and his 'flawne' (literally, a kind of pancake, used figuratively of a flat cap, line 155). Cf. *1 Return from Parnassus*, 249–250, Ingenioso to a Servingman: 'Why man, I am able to make a pamphlet of thy blew coate and the button in thy capp.' There is a character named *Flawn* in Marston's *Jack Drum's Entertainment*.

IV.iii

24–25 *it sets / Our end before our eyes*. Cf. Synesius, *A Paradoxe*, C6: 'Baldnesse therefore is the end of nature, which end euery one hath not ye gift to attaine'.

35 *full-cheekt Moone*. Marston, *Antonio's Revenge*, III.i.187: 'Now barks the wolf against the full-cheek'd moon.'

37 *blazing Starres*. Cf. *A Paradoxe*, C2:

Now, if you saie that a blasing starre is a hairie starre, it resteth to be proued first that it is a starre in deede: but doubtlesse it is no starre, although it be termed so amisse: neither doeth it continue aboue foure daies, and then consumeth awaie by litle and litle. But suppose it were a starre, and consider what a mischeeuous and euill thing the haire thereof is, which bringeth decaie euen to the starre it selfe (if it be a starre:) besides innumerable miseries whereof it is a foretoken, all which I passe ouer in this place. Haue we euer read that anie good starre wasted to nothing? But this starre with crisped haire vanisheth, and the substance thereof dieth.

39–41 *mans fiue-folde sence...balde*. Cf. *A Paradoxe*, B5:

The fiue senses are precious things, and those partes whereby all liuing creatures haue life and feeling, are excellent things: among all which, the sight is the quickest, the liueliest, the most necessarie, and (you knowe) the eies haue their smoothnesse and baldnesse. That therefore which in man is of this kinde, deserueth most honour. So it followeth in conclusion, that the verie best things are bald.

41–43 *the haires...stormes*. Cf. *G.H.*, C3v: 'The two Eyes are the glasse windowes, at which light disperses it selfe into euery roome, hauing goodly penthouses of haire to ouershaddow them.'

49–50 *natures But...Arrow*. Cf. *F.B.N.A.*, p. 239: 'The grave is a But at which all the arrowes of our life are shot; and the last arrowe of all hits the marke.' *W.E.*, III.i.101.

50–52 *what man...vncouer'd*. Cf. *A Paradoxe*, C6: 'Name me anie one man, that hauing liued out his full age, hath not bene bald.'

54 *The Head is Wisedomes house*. Cf. *A Paradoxe*, B6–B6v:

For the head is the castell of knowledge, and wisedome. This comparison is not perceiueable to the vnskilful. Bushie haire is a beautie vnto youth, in whom wisedome is not yet growne to her floure: but when age is come vpon vs, which breedeth in vs vnderstanding and experience: what meane we (olde doting fooles) to be proud of our hairie lockes? If an old fellowe be curious & delicate in trimming of his haire: surelie he is brainesicke.

G.H., C3v: 'the *Head* is a house built for *Reason* to dwell in'.

54 *Haire...thatch.* Cf. *G.H.*, C4: 'Nature therefore has plaid the *Tyler*, and giuen it [the head] a most curious couering, or (to speake more properly) she has thatcht it all ouer, and that *Thatching* is haire.' *N.S.S.*, II.i.11.

56 *This Prouerbe...wit.* Cf. *A Paradoxe*, C8: 'If *Achilles* (as *Dion* reporteth) had long haire, it was in the heat and flower of his youth, when his minde was prone and inclinable to anger', and the marginal note: 'Of such speaketh the common prouerbe, More hair than wit.' *Sir Thomas More* (M.S.R. (1911), prepared by W. W. Greg), Addition IV, lines 202–204: 'thy head is for thy shoulders now more fitt / thou hast less haire vppon it but more witt'. Tilley, B736.

58 *Bush-naturall.* Cf. *G.H.*, C4: 'But let thine [hair] receiue his full growth that thou maiest safely and wisely brag tis thine owne *Bush-Naturall.*'

60 *most intanglingst beautie in a woman.* Cf. *G.H.*, C4v: 'long haire is the onely nette that women spread abroad to entrappe men in; and why should not men be as farre aboue women in that commodity, as they go beyond men in others?'

68.1 *this Paradox.* The *Calvitii Encomium* of Synesius, translated by Abraham Fleming in 1579 as *A Paradoxe, Prouing by reason and example, that Baldnesse is much better than bushie haire, etc. Written by that excellent Philosopher Synesius, Bishop of Thebes, or (as some say) Cyren.* Nashe, in 'The Epistle Dedicatorie' to *Have With You* (III, 7) mentions '*a Defence of short haire against Synesius and Pierius*: or rather, in more familiar English to expresse it, a Dash ouer the head against baldnes, verie necessary to be obserued of al the *looser* sort, or *loose* haird sort, of yong Gentlemen & Courtiers'. Nashe attributes the book to Richard Harvey. McKerrow (in his note on the passage, IV, 305) says that nothing is known about the book, which may or may not have been by R. Harvey, but that it did exist, 'for it was entered in the Stationers' Register to John Wolf on Feb. 3, 1592–93, as "A defence of shorte haire &c."' The Pierius named by Nashe was Valeriano Bolzano, who wrote a satirical work, *Pro Sacerdotum Barbis Defensio* (McKerrow, IV, 305).

In *Lenten Stuffe* (III, 176), Nashe speaks of philosophers who 'come sneaking in with their paradoxes of pouertie, imprisonment, death, sickenesse, banishment, and baldnesse'. See McKerrow's note on this passage (IV, 389) regarding the late Renaissance taste for composing '*encomia* on unworthy or ridiculous subjects'. Dekker has a particular penchant for the paradoxical set-piece. There is the 'praise of long haire' in Chapter 3 of *G.H.* (sigs C3v–C4), from which quotation has been made in the preceding notes; a 'Paradox in prayse of going to law', 'A Paradox in praise of a Pen', 'A paradox in praise of Vacations' (with reference to the law courts), and an 'Inuectiue against a Pen' in *D.T.* (sigs. C2, C3, E4v, F1); 'an *Encomiastick Paradoxicall* Oration in praise of a prison' in S.D.S. (sig. B1v); 'an Oration in praise of *Beggerie*' in B.L. (sig. C3); 'A Paradox in praise of Sergiants, and of a Prison' in *J.M.M.* (sig. H1v); and a celebration of war and the military throughout *W.W.W.*, that is acknowledged (sig. D3v) to be 'a *Paradox*' though it has not been initially labeled as one. Cf. *O.F.*, II.ii.57ff. for 'a Paradox in commendations of hunger'.

69 *Wit whether wilt thou.* Tilley, W570.

70 *Poeticall Furie*, Crispinus–Marston, whose style is parodied in the figure of Furor Poeticus in *The Return from Parnassus*, Part Two. Tucca addresses Demetrius by the term in *Poetaster*, IV.iii.108.

70 *hit it to a haire.* Tiley, H26.

73 *malepartly*, impudently. Lyly, *Gallathea*, V.iii.177–178: 'What are these that so malepartlie thrust themselues into our companies?'

73 *mych*, skulk. *W.Y.*, p. 34: 'And those that could shift for a time, ...yet went they (most bitterly) miching and muffled vp & downe.'

87 *Thalimum*, i.e. epithalamium. I.ii.37.

87–88 *crosse-stickes*, i.e. acrostics. I.ii.90.

88 *Polinoddyes*, i.e. palinodes. I.ii.100–101.

88 *Nappy-grams*, i.e. epigrams. Cf. IV.i.141.

93 *by my Fan.* A fashionably affected oath. Cf. *Cynthia's Revels*,

II.iv.72–73: 'By this fanne, I cannot abide any thing that sauours the poore ouer-worne cut.'

94 *Sinamon water*, water percolated through cotton moistened with oil of cinnamon; a restorative. Jonson, *The Magnetick Lady*, III.iii.20–22:

> Cure a poore wenches falling in a swoune:
> Which a poore Farthing chang'd in *Rosa solis*,
> Or *Cynnamon* water would.

W.H., II.ii.26; V.i.210.

96 *randes*, rants. *Poetaster*, III.iv.164, Tucca to the Histrio of Crispinus: 'hee will teach thee to teare, and rand, Rascall'. *W.Y.*, p. 24: 'The worst players boy stoode vpon his good parts, swearing tragicall and buskind oaths, that how villainously soeuer he randed,...he would...be halfe a sharer (at least).' *J.M.M.*, H4v: 'making fooles of the poore country people, in driuing them like flocks of Geese to sit cackling in an old barne: and to swallow downe those playes, for new, which here euery punck and her squire...can rand out by heart.' And Marston, *The Malcontent*, IV.iv.4: 'O, do not rand, do not turn player.' *N.H.*, IV.i.261.

96–97 *the poore fellow vnder Ludgate*, an inmate of the debtor's prison at Ludgate; the reference is to the cries of the prisoners for food as they begged through the grating to passers-by. *S.D.S.*, B1v: 'it was a bird pickt out of purpose (amongst the *Ludgathians*) that had the basest and lowdest voice, and was able in a Terme time, for a throat, to giue any prisoner great ods for yᵉ box at the grate.' *R.R.*, pp. 148–149:

> Where shall the wretched prisoners haue their Baskets filled euery night and morning with your broken meat? These must pine and perish. The distressed in *Ludgate*, the miserable soules in the Holes of the two *Counters*, the afflicted in the *Marshallseas*, the Cryers-out for Bread in the *Kings Bench*, and *White Lyon*, how shall these be sustayned?

105–106 *his white necke-verse*. I.ii.117; IV.i.136, n. 'White' is often used as a term of favor or endearment, as in the phrase 'white boy' or 'white son'. Cf. the reference to 'my white Poet' in *N.H.*, IV.i.214.

109 *Peter is my Salamander*. Cf. III.i.45.

111 *Clipst the Kinges English.* The phrase with its quibble on 'clip' (to mispronounce the language and to deface the coinage by fraudulently paring the edges of coins) is twice repeated in *W.Y.*: of a Dutchman (p. 40): 'away sneakes my clipper of the kings english'; and of a drunkard (p. 52): 'If he had clipt but a quarter so much of the kings siluer, as he did of the Kings English, his carkas had long ere this, bene carion for Crowes.' The latter passage implies the treasonable nature of the crime against the monarch's coinage which Sir Vaughan alludes to in line 112. Cf. *Henry V*, IV.i.227–229: 'but it is no English treason to cut French crowns, and tomorrow the king himself will be a clipper'.

118 *Adam Bell,* one of the three northern outlaws in the ballad of 'Adam Bell, Clym of the Clough, and William of Cloudeslee'. It is frequently mentioned. Captain Cox had a copy in his library (Laneham, *Letter*, in Nichols, *Progresses of Queen Elizabeth*, I, 454). And cf. Brome, *Covent Garden Weeded*, II.i (ed. Shepherd, II, 23):

Cross. Get *Bells* work, and you can, into the bargain.
Belt. Which *Bell*, Sir? *Adam Bell*, with *Clim o'th'Clough*, and *William* of *Cloudesley.*

For the ballad's numerous entries in the Stationers' Registers between 1557–1558 and 1655, see Rollins, nos. 10 and 11. It is included in *Bishop Percy's Folio* (ed. J. W. Hales and F. J. Furnivall), III, 76ff. See the quotation from Puttenham in the note on IV.i.133–134, above. *R.G.*, I.ii.120.

119–121 *bald-pate...vineger-bottle.* For the pun on 'vinegar' as a term for bitterness, satire, and as a part of the cure for venereal disease (of which baldness was one of the often-mentioned effects), cf. Nashe, *Pierce Penilesse* (I, 182):

Pish, pish, what talke you of old age or balde pates? men and women that haue gone vnder the South pole, must lay off their furde night-caps in spight of their teeth, and become yeomen of the Vinegar bottle: a close periwig hides all the sinnes of an olde whore-master; but *Cucullus non facit Monachum*: tis not their newe bonnets will keepe them from the old boan-ach.

And the Epistle 'To the Reader' in the 1594 edition of *Christs*

Teares (II, 185): 'To them I discend by degrees of Apologie, who condemne me all to vinegar for my bitternesse. It will bee some of their destinies to carrie the vinegar bottle ere they die, for being so desperate in preiudice.' With both passages, cf. *Return from Parnassus*, Part Two, lines 118–122, where Ingenioso is generally acknowledged to be a portrayal of Nashe:

Iudicio. What, *Ingenioso*, carrying a Vinegar bottle about thee, like a great schole-boy giuing the world a bloudy nose?
Ingenioso. Faith, *Iudicio*, if I carry a vinegar bottle, it's great reason I should confer it vpon the bald pated world.

Cf. Marston's Dedication to *Antonio and Mellida*, lines 9–10: 'O thou sweetest perfection, female beauty, shield me from the stopping of vinegar bottles.'

126 *Boniface.* Penniman (p. 435) suggests a quibble on 'bony face' and cites Tucca's later reference (V.ii.262) to Horace as a 'leane...hollow-cheekt Scrag'.

145 *groate*, worth 4d.

146 *teston*, sixpence.

149 *my light-vptailes all. S.H.*, I.ii.61, n.

151 *bag-pudding. 1 H.W.*, I.i.142, n.

152 *As blunt as the top of Poules.* Cf. Marston, *Jack Drum's Entertainment*, Act IV (ed. Wood, III, 221):

Bra. Ju. Brother how like you of our moderne witts?
How like you the new Poet *Mellidus*?
Bra. Sig. A slight bubling spirit, a Corke, a Huske.
Pla. How like you *Musus* fashion in his carriage?
Bra. Sig. O filthily, he is as blunt as *Pawles*.

The spire of St Paul's Cathedral was struck by lightning and burned on 4 June 1561, and it had not yet been replaced a century later when the entire church was destroyed in the fire of 1666. In the complaint voiced by Paul's steeple in *D.T.*, the cathedral's present headless condition and its continued ruinous state are stressed; after describing the fire of 1561, and the subsequent measures taken by the Queen and the London citizens to repair the losses (in which 'some good was done vnto mee, and much good left vndone'), the steeple continues: 'This last blow was to mee fatall and deadly, for now am I both headlesse, and honourlesse: my shoulders being daily troden vpon in scorne, branded with markes and Letters, and scoared vppon with the points of kniues and Bodkins' (D3v–D4). And cf. the allusion in 'The Picture of a Jesuit' in *D.P.*, A4v:

> When *Church* or *Church-men* he misvses,
> A *Rookes* or *Martins* nest hee chooses:
> Else hee's that prating bird that fowles,
> The (now *Vn-trimd*) bald head of *Powles*.

See *W.E.*, V.iii.88–90, n.

152 *Aloe*, 'A drug of nauseous odour, bitter taste, and purgative qualities, procured from the inspissated juice of plants of the genus *Aloe*' (*O.E.D.*). G.H., Biv: 'As for thee *Zoylus*, goe hang thy selfe: and for thee *Momus* chew nothing but hemlock, & spit nothing but the sirrup of *Aloes* vpon my papers, till thy very rotten lungs come forth for anger.'

152 *Cicatrine*, obsolete form of 'socotrine'; thus '*Socotrine aloes*, a drug prepared from the juice of the *Aloe socotrina* (or *perryi*) and originally obtained from the island of Socotra' (*O.E.D.*, citing the present passage).

154 *bulchin*, bull-calf. *M.G.*, p. 119: 'Sfoote, the mad Bulchin squeakes shriller then the Saunce Bell at *Westminster*.' *W.B.*, V.vi.45.

155 *rounciuall*, i.e. a giant, a great fat woman. Cf. Deloney, *Gentle Craft*, Part Two (p. 159): 'my Master cannot abide that great rounsefull should come in his company'. And Nashe, *Have With You* (III, 36): 'a fat *Bonarobe* and terrible *Rounceuall*'.

155 *Lanthorne and Candle-light*, the night watchman's cry, warning the householders to hang up at their street doors the lighted lantern which it was legally incumbent upon them to provide for the illumination of the streets. A ballad (now lost) with this title was entered in the Stationers' Register during the period 1569–1570 (Rollins, no. 1469). Dekker's pamphlet which takes its title from the cry, *Lanthorne and Candle-light, or The Bell-Mans second Nights-walke*, was first published in 1608, and all the subsequent expanded editions retain the cry

as part of their revised titles: *O per se O, or A new Cryer of Lanthorne and Candle-light* (1612); *Villanies Discouered by Lanthorne and Candle-light* (1616); *English Villanies...discovered by Lanthorne and Candle-light* (1632).

157 *Godboygh.* Cf. III.i.82.

157–158 *honest trade...Brickes.* IV.ii.47, n.

160 *railes, such as stand on Poules head.* Another allusion to the ruinous condition of the spire of St Paul's since the fire of 1561. Cf. *G.H.*, D3, where the gallant is advised, when first he visits the Cathedral, to pay his 'tribute to the top of *Powles-steeple* with a single penny: And when you are mounted there, take heede how you looke downe into the yard; for the railes are as rotten as your great Grand-father'.

162 *I am sir Salamanders.* Cf. line 108.

167–168 *blanket...tosse him.* An old form of punishment. Cf. e.g. the *Secunda Pastorum* in the Towneley Plays (ed. A. W. Pollard and G. England, Early English Text Society (London, 1897) where Mak is tossed in a sheet (line 628). *Dick of Devonshire* (M.S.R. (1955), prepared by J. G. and M. R. McManaway), lines 1769–1770: 'blanketts in wch fooles / & wrangling Coxcombes are tossd'. Cf. the passage from *G.H.*, E4–E4v, quoted in the note to IV.ii.55. *R.G.*, IV.ii.130. The punishment here was doubtless suggested by *Cynthia's Revels*, III.ii.6–8 (Anaides to Hedon of Crites): 'Hang him, poore grogran-rascall, pray thee thinke not of him: I'le send for him to my lodging, and haue him blanketted when thou wilt, man.'

167 *Venice glasses. M.M.L.*, I.iv.129, n.

168 *wag-tailes*, whores. *M.M.L.*, I.iv.128.

168 *bandy*, stroke (used of a tennis ball).

169 *why when?* I.ii.373.

169–170 *Tamberlaine.* For other references in Dekker to Marlowe's famous stage figure, cf. *W.Y.*, p. 31: 'Death (like a Spanish Legar, or rather like stalking *Tamberlaine*) hath pitcht his tents.' *S.D.S.*, F1: 'If therefore you, and *Fiue* companies greater then yours, should chuse a Colonel, to lead you against this mightie *Tamburlaine*, you are too weake to make him *Retire*.' *N.F.H.*, C1–C1v: 'Nay, since my flag of defiance is hung forth, I will yeelde to no truce, but with such *Tambur-laine-like* furie march against this great Turke, and his legions.' *J.M.M.*, H3: 'furious *Tamberlaine*...was cutting out 3 sorts of banners for his 3 sworne enemies'. *S.H.*, V.iv.53; *O.F.*, I.i.192.

170 *Morter vnder thy feete.* IV.ii.47, n.

172 *a bandy*, i.e. 'Let's have a game of tennis.' Cf. Marston, *Certaine Satyres*, I, 129–130: '*Tullus*...when ere he me espies / Straight with loud mouth (*a bandy Sir*) he cries.'

184–186 *entred Actions of assault and battery, against...Fathers of the law.* Cf. the 'Apologetical Dialogue' at the end of *Poetaster*, 81–82: 'Why, they say you tax'd / The Law, and Lawyers.'

188 *skip-Iacke*, 'A pert shallow-brained fellow; a puppy, a whipper-snapper' (*O.E.D.*). The horse courser's boys who participate in the cony-catching scheme described in Chapter 10 of *L.C.* 'are called *Skip-iacks*' (K1).

189–190 *Arrogance, and Impudence, and Ignoraunce, are the essen-tiall parts of a Courtier.* A response to *Cynthia's Revels*, II.ii.77–79 (Mercury of Anaides): 'he has two essential parts of the courtier, pride, and ignorance;...'Tis *impudence* it selfe, *Anaides*'; and III.iii.27 (Crites of Hedon and Anaides): 'Both impudent, and ignorant inough'.

191–192 *puncke, and pincke, and pumpe.* 'Puncke' = punch, 'with perhaps a play on "punk".' 'Pincke' = 'to pierce with a rapier or sword'. 'Pumpe' = 'to drain or exhaust, perhaps here referring to the motion in tossing in a blanket' (Penniman, p. 437).

194 *ptrooh.* For this vulgar interjection, cf. *Blurt, Master-Constable*, IV.iii.159: 'Hence, ptrooh!' And *Sat.*, V.ii.281.

195 *Flat-caps*, a term of derision for London citizens. *2 H.W.*, I.iii.21–22, n.

195–196 *banckrupts...punckes...cockatrices.* For the accusation, see *Poetaster*, IV.iii.61–64:

> *Cris.* Cousin, 'pray you call mistris Chloe; shee shall heare an essay of my *poetrie*.
> *Tvcc.* I'le call her. Come hither, cockatrice: here's one, will set thee vp, my sweet punke; set thee vp.

Tucca calls Albius, Chloe's husband, 'bankerupt' at IV.iii.87 and 158.

196 *cockatrices*, whores. *L.C.*, H4: 'What a wretched wombe hath a strumpet, which being (for the most part) barren of Children, is notwithstanding the onely *Bedde* that breedes vp these *serpents?* vpon that one stalke grow all these mischiefes. *Shee* is the Cockatrice that hatcheth all these egges of euills.' *1 H.W.*, III.iii.20: 'You, goody Punck, *subaudi* Cockatrice'. *W.H.*, III.iii.13; *N.H.*, IV.i.180; *V.M.*, II.i.11.

197 *arraigned*. Cf. 'To the World', 29, n.

199 *blacke Fryers*, where both *Cynthia's Revels* and *Poetaster* were acted. Cf. Epilogus, 7–8.

203 *one of these part-takers*, apparently meaning both one who takes a part (i.e. an actor) and one who is a sharer ('Partaker') in the company.

203–204 *Copper-lac'd.* I.ii.141.

208–226 *What could I doe…set in golde*. Quoted by Lamb, I, 203.

209–210 *they enuy me | Because I holde more worthy company*. A glance at the oath administered to the poetasters at the end of Jonson's play. They bind themselves never 'to maligne, traduce, or detract the *person*, or writings of *Qvintvs Horacivs Flaccvs*; or any other eminent man, transcending you in merit, whom your enuy shall find cause to worke vpon, either, for that, or for keeping himselfe in better acquaintance, or enioying better friends' (*Poetaster*, V.iii.595–600).

228–229 *that broken seame-rent lye of thine, that Demetrius is out at Elbowes*. I.ii.325, n.

230 *Crispinus is falne out with Sattin*. I.ii.324, n.

230–231 *bloate-herring*. The reference is to a process of curing herring 'which leaves them soft and only half-dried', as opposed to the shrivelled dryness of dried or red herring (*O.E.D., s.v.*, Bloat, v^1).

235 *Perpetuana*, 'a durable fabric of wool manufactured in England from the sixteenth century' (*O.E.D.*). Hedon has said of Crites in *Cynthia's Revels*, III.ii.28–31: 'By this heauen, I wonder at nothing more than our gentlemen-vshers, that will suffer a piece of serge, or *perpetuana*, to come into the presence.'

Marston, *What You Will*, II.i.7–8, Laverdure of Quadratus:
'I'll not see him now, on my soul: he's in his old perpetuana
suit.' Dekker speaks of 'the sober *Perpetuana* suited Puritans'
in *S.D.S.*, D3. There is a character so-named in *Histriomastix*.

236–237 *waxt ouer; th'art made out of Wax.* The allusion is to the
wax on the seals of the bonds that Horace has entered into
when he bought his clothes on credit, and which are still
owing. Cf. *O.F.*, I.ii.104–105, nn.

238 *hagler.* The Queen of Gold and Silver addresses all Engrossers
in *W.A.*, F2:

> I will prepare a certaine people that shall giue you your owne asking,
> and buy vp all you bring by the great, who shall afterwards sell it
> deerer then it was bought, by three parts... The people whom thus I
> promise to haue in a readines, are well knowne what they are, some call
> them *Huksters* or *Haglers*, but they are to me as honest *Purueyers* and
> *Takers*, and these politicke smooth faced *Harpyes*, shall out of a dearth
> raise a second deerenesse.

> *G.H.*, E2v: 'buyes his sport by the penny, and, like a *Hagler*,
> is glad to vtter it againe by retailing'.

238 *best-be-trust*, 'most to be trusted' (*O.E.D.*, *s.v.* Best, B.2.b).
Nashe, *Pierce Penilesse*, I, 163: 'he that hath no mony in his
purse, must go dine with sir Iohn Best-betrust, at the signe
of the chalk and the Post'. A ballad titled 'beste be truste' was
entered in the Stationers' Register during the period 1569–
1570 (Rollins, no. 186).

243–244 *whilst we haue Hiren heere.* The phrase is supposed to
come from Peele's lost play, *The Turkish Mahomet and Hiren
the Fair Greek*. It is much quoted, often with a quibble on
'Hiren'/'iron' (used for a sword): e.g., in *2 Henry IV*,
II.iv.159–160, by Pistol: 'down, faitors! have we not Hiren
here?' Cf. as well Jonson, Chapman, and Marston, *Eastward
Ho*, II.i.107–108; Middleton and Rowley, *The Old Law*,
IV.i.55–56; Day, *Law Tricks*, V.i (ed. Bullen, p. 203); Ford,
The Queen, III.i (1653), D1v.

247–248 *fooles Cap...couer'd your Poetasters*, alluding to the
sentence pronounced by Virgil near the close of *Poetaster*,
V.iii.576–581:

Demetrivs Fannivs, thou shalt here put on
That coate, and cap [of a fool]; and henceforth, thinke thyselfe
No other, then they make thee: vow to weare them
In euery faire, and generous assembly,
Till the best sort of minds shall take to knowledge
As well thy satisfaction, as thy wrongs.

Earlier (line 562) Virgil has instructed that Crispinus should be attired 'in that robe', which Herford and Simpson (IX, 580) assume to be 'the same as Demetrius' fool's coat and cap'.

262 *Grumboll*, 'a peevish, discontented person; a confirmed grumbler' (Wright, *English Dialect Dictionary*). Cf. *Misogonus*, IV.i.32 (ed. Bond), where the word is used as a term of reproach to a woman: 'ant had not bene for the[e] saddlebackt grombole Ide gott well by this shifte'. 'Grumboll' as a name for one of the devils occurs in *I.T.B.N.*, I.i.81, 114.

263 *Mum*. Penniman (p. 439) suggested as a possible meaning to 'be a mummer, in the maske', but cf. IV.i.182. The term is probably used simply in the sense of 'play with us', with the implication of 'gamble' – 'take your chances' – 'with us'.

263 *skneakes-bill*. A quarto misprint for 'sneakes-bill', as Scherer (p. 123) suggested. Halliwell quotes Cotgrave concerning 'sneak-bill': 'A chichiface, micher, sneake-bill, wretched fellow, one out of whose nose hunger drops'.

266 *occupied*. The word had bawdy implications, as Doll Common attests, *2 Henry IV*, II.iv.147–150: 'A captain! God's light, these villains will make the word as odious as the word "occupy", which was an excellent good word before it was ill sorted.' Marlowe, *The Massacre at Paris*, lines 806–810 (Folger manuscript reading): 'Now ser to you y^t dares make a dvke a cuckolde and vse a counterfeyt key to his privye chamber thoughe you take out none but yor owne treasure yett you putt in y^t displeases him and fill vp his rome y^t he shold occupie.' *S.H.*, I.i.143.

V.i

3 *Tenters. 2 H.W.*, IV.iii.20, n.

23–27 *Must... Shall... Will.* Cf. III.i.313.

24 *Must, is the King himselfe.* Cf. *P.G.*, IV.ii.142.

29–161 *Why didst thou sweare?... virgin dyes.* Quoted by Lamb,
I, 199–203 (with omissions at lines 60–63 and 158–160), who
comments as follows:

> The beauty and force of this scene are much diminished to the reader
> of the entire play, when he comes to find that this solemn preparation
> is but a sham contrivance of the father's, and the potion which
> Cælestina swallows nothing more than a sleeping draught; from the
> effects of which she is to awake in due time, to the surprise of her
> husband, and the great mirth and edification of the King and his
> courtiers. As Hamlet says, they do but 'poison in jest'. The sentiments
> are worthy of a real martyrdom, and an Appian sacrifice in earnest.

37 *if one be numbred.* An allusion to the proverb 'one no number
is'. Cf. *2 H.W.*, IV.i.294, n.

60 *a poast. L.D.*, II.iii.110, n.

135 *Thou rare Apothecary.* Cf. *Romeo and Juliet*, V.iii.119: 'O true
apothecary!'

141 *dyet-drinke.* II.i.210.

153 *standing house.* 'A domestic establishment' (Halliwell). Cf.
Donne, *An Anatomy of the World*, 7–8: 'When that Queene
ended here her progresse time, / And, as t'her standing house
to heaven did climbe.'

168 *sh's deathes Bride... maidenhead.* Cf. *Romeo and Juliet*,
IV.v.35–37:

> O son, the night before thy wedding day
> Hath Death lain with thy wife. There she lies,
> Flower as she was, deflowered by him.

V.ii

0.1 *an arm'd Sewer... seruice.* The 'sewer' (aphetic form of Old
French *asseoir*, 'to cause to sit, seat') was 'an attendant at a
meal who superintended the arrangement of the table, the

seating of the guests, and the tasting and serving of the dishes' (*O.E.D.*). The 'service' consisted of the provision for the table, as in Heywood, *A Woman Killed With Kindness* (1607), F1: '*Enter Butler, and Ienkin with a table cloath, bread, trenchers, and salt.*' Cf. *Macbeth*, I.vii.0.1–2: '*Enter a* Sewer, *and divers* Servants *with dishes and service over the stage.*' And Jonson, *The Case is Altered*, I.iii.0.1–2: '*Enter an armed Sewer: some halfe-do̜en in mourning coates following, and passe by with seruice.*' *W.K.*, III.i.148.1–2.

5–6 *Ioues page...Nectar. L.D.*, I.i.50–51.

37 *The Watch-word in a Maske is the bolde Drum.* Cf. Benvolio's 'Strike, drum' as the maskers set off to the Capulet ball in *Romeo and Juliet*, I.iv.114. And see the description of the Drum that heralds 'The Catch-Pols Masque' in *S.H.R.*, F1–F1v.

40 *Fees*, tributes or offerings to a superior (*O.E.D.*, citing this example).

42 *night peece*, a painting representing a night scene. Cf. Webster, *The White Devil*, V.vi.299.

89 *a constant wife.* V.i.157.

102–103 *trie...constancie.* Cf. *Blurt, Master-Constable*, V.iii.110–111: 'This was a plot of mine, only to try / Your love's strange temper.' And *L.D.*, V.i.290–291: ' 'twas but a trick to try, / That which few women have, true constancy'.

113–114 *to wed a Comicall euent, / To presupposed tragicke Argument.* Cf. the end of *Blurt, Master-Constable*, V.iii.185: 'tragic shapes meet comical event'. And of *L.D.*, V.iii.181: 'With Comick joy to end a Tragedie'.

118 *the whip of men.* Alluding presumably to Asper in the induction to *Every Man out of his Humour*, 16–20:

> But (with an armed, and resolued hand)
> Ile strip the ragged follies of the time,
> Naked, as at their birth:...
> ...and with a whip of steele,
> Print wounding lashes in their yron ribs.

And cf. *Sat.*, I.ii.225–237.

129–130 *Therefore be thou our selfe . . . Sceane of wit.* So Caesar
makes way for the arraignment in *Poetaster*, V.iii.161–163;

> You haue your will of Caesar: vse it *Romanes.*
> Virgil shall be your *Prætor*; and our selfe
> Will here sit by, spectator of your sports.

141–142 *all his Masesties most excellent dogs.* These, says Scherer
(p. 124), are the bellmen; Penniman (p. 440) agrees and cites
the preface, signed by 'The Bel-man of London' in Dekker's
pamphlet of that name: 'my *Bell* shall euer be ringing, and
that faithfull seruant of mine (the Dog that follows me) be
euer biting of these wilde beastes, till they be all driuen into
one heard, and so hunted into the toiles of the *Lawe*' (A2v).
The Bellman and his dog are represented in the woodcut on
the titlepage of the 1608 editions of the pamphlet. The allusion
to the night watch is carried on at line 156 ('He's reprehended
and taken').

153 *play at bo-peepes. P.G.,* I.ii.2–3.

154 *cryes all-hidde*, the cry at hide-and-seek. *Love's Labour's Lost*,
IV.iii.76: '"All hid, all hid" – an old infant play'.

157 *a New-found Land.* This does not necessarily refer to the
island at the mouth of the St Lawrence. There were many new-
found lands in the late sixteenth and early seventeenth centuries.

160 *place-mouth*, i.e. plaice-mouth, wry mouth. *2 H.W.,* II.i.6, n.

161 *Gurnets-head.* The gurnard or gurnet is 'a species of fish
characterized by a large spiny head with mailed cheeks'
(*O.E.D.*). Marston, *Scourge of Villanie*, VI, 41–42: 'His guts
are in his braines, huge Iobbernoule, / Right Gurnets-head,
the rest without all soule.' And *Blurt, Master-Constable*,
II.ii.179–181: 'I wonder what this gurnet's head makes here!
Yet bring him in; he will serve for picking meat.' Cf. *1 H.W.,*
II.i.201, n.

165 *Sultane Soliman. S.H.,* V.iv.52, n.

169 *hot Seruice.* Cf. Marston, *Certaine Satyres,* I, 107–114:

> What newes from *Rodio?*
> *Hote seruice, by the Lord, cryes* Tubrio.
> Why do'st thou halt? *Why six times throgh each thigh*
> *Pusht with the Pike of the hote enemie.*

Hot seruice, hote, the Spaniard is a man,
I say no more and as a Gentleman
I serued in his face. Farwell. Adew.
Welcome from Netherland, from steaming stew.

For the identification of Tucca with the Tubrio of Marston's satires, see I.ii.394, n.

172 *Tawsoone* (Welsh *Taw sôn*), 'hold your tongue'. *S.H.*, I.i.161, n.

174 *graines.* 'An old word for the fork of the body, the lower limbs; hence also bough or branch. Tucca means, probably, that he is one of the King's chief supporters' (Penniman, p. 441).

177 *Mandilian-Leaders.* Cf. III.i.54, n.

178 *Pantilius Tucca*, the name as given in *Poetaster*, I.i.29.

179 *fy—fy—fy—*. Tucca stutters, as below at line 185. See I.ii.133, n.

181 *whirligig. S.H.*, V.iv.51.

182 *Tamor Cham*, Timur Khaun. He was a perennially popular figure on the London stage. A two-part play bearing his name (usually given as 'tamber came'; cf. *P.G.*, V.i.18) was being acted by Strange's men throughout 1592; Henslowe records six performances of what he usually designates as Part Two between 28 April 1592 and 19 January 1593 (*Diary*, pp. 18, 19). The play was revived, probably in a revised form, by the Admiral's men in 1596; Henslowe records nine performances of Part One and four of Part Two between 6 May and 8 July (*Diary*, pp. 36, 37, 47, 48). The play is lost. The dramatic 'plot', or outline for prompter's use, of Part One which Steevens reprinted in the Variorum edition of Shakespeare (1803), III, 414 (the original is now lost), contains a list of actors' names which attests to a still later revival by the Admiral's, probably in the fall of 1602 (see *Diary*, pp. 332–333).

194 *to retyre me from the world*, as Jonson seems to have done in the wake of the storm produced by *Poetaster*. Cf. Herford and Simpson, 1, 30: 'For a few months he seems to have withdrawn himself literally into a sombre and sullen seclusion,

even from his home.' And they quote the famous entry by
Manningham in his Diary for February 1602/3: 'Ben Jonson
the poet now lives upon one Townesend, and scornes the
world.'

195 *Timonist.* B.*L.*, B3–B3v: 'hauing wandred long (like a
Timonist) hating men because they dishonoured their creation.'
G.H., B4v: 'to shew that you truly loath this polluted and
mangy-fisted world, turne [*T*]*imonists*, not caring either for
men or their maners'.

200 *Bug-beare. W.B.*, V.ii.27.

200 *a Campe royall,* i.e. a very large number. Nashe, *The Terrors of
the Night* (I, 349): 'What do we talke of one diuel? there is
not a roome in anie mans house, but is pestred and close
packed with a campe royall of diuels.' Middleton, *The Black
Book* (ed. Bullen, VIII, 29): 'passing through Birchin-lane,
amidst a camp-royal of hose and doublets'.

201 *you Nastie Tortois.* The allusion is to Jonson's slowly labored
compositional pace. Cf. I.ii.363, n.

202–203 *Christmas, but once a yeare.* In November 1602, a year
after *Satiromastix,* Dekker collaborated with Heywood,
Webster and Chettle in the authorship of a play (now lost)
titled *Christmas Comes but Once a Year* (Henslowe, *Diary,*
pp. 219–220). The phrase is proverbial (Tilley, C369).

204 *Tyber,* or Tybert, or Tybalt; the name of the cat in the *History
of Reynard the Fox.* Cf. Nashe, *Have With You* (III, 51):
'*Tibault...* Prince of Cattes'; and *Romeo and Juliet,* II.iv.18–
19.

225 *huckster,* pedlar, hawker. The word is again used of poets in
2 *Return from Parnassus,* lines 163–166: 'Considering the
furyes of the times, I could better endure to see those young
Can quaffing hucksters shoot of[f] their pellets so they would
keepe them from these English *flores-poetarum.*' Cf. the
quotation from *W.A.*, F2, cited in the note on 'hagler' at
IV.iii.238, above.

228 *coate pull'd ouer mine eares.* III.i.28–29, n.

235 *Callin-oes.* The reference is to the ballad tune titled 'Callino
Casturame', 'an English rendering of an Irish phrase, the

first element of which has come into modern usage as *colleen*' (Simpson, p. 79). A ballad titled 'Callin o custure me' was entered in the Stationers' Register on 10 March 1582 (Rollins, no. 259). 'A Sonet of a Louer in the praise of his lady. To Calen o Custure me: sung at euerie lines end' is included in *A Handefull of pleasant delites* (1584), ed. H. E. Rollins (Cambridge, Mass., 1924), pp. 38–39; and see Rollins' note, pp. 99–100. It is the tune to 'A pleasant Song made by a Souldier' (Stationers' Register, 24 April 1588; Arber, II, 488), and printed in *Roxburghe Ballads*, VI, 284–285. Here, as in the poem in *A Handefull of pleasant delites*, the Irish refrain is to be interpolated repeatedly within each stanza. Thus, as Simpson suggests (p. 79), John Davies of Hereford (*Works*, ed. A. B. Grosart (2 vols., Edinburgh, 1878), II, 16) alludes to the refrain in an epigram in his *Scourge of Folly*:

> No word proceeds from his most fluent tong,
> But it is like the burden of the song
>   Call'd Callino, come from a forraine Land,
>   Which English people do not vnderstand.

Pistol uses the Irish words in his gibberish reply to the French soldier in *Henry V*, IV.iv.4, where the 1623 folio reads: 'calmie custure me', and most editors adopt Malone's emendation of 'calmie' to 'Calen o'. For music to the tune, see Chappell, II, 793 and (a fuller account) Simpson, pp. 79–80.

238 *Biggin*, a night-cap, but also a skull-cap of lawn or silk worn by lawyers (as in *Volpone*, V.ix.5). The latter sense is present here for it prompts the pun on 'Lawrefyed' in the next line (where the meaning is both to be made a lawyer and to be made a poet laureate crowned with laurel). Horace in fact will be neither. He will be a poet, not a lawyer (the reference is to *Poetaster*, and the dilemma of Ovid, who would be a poet, but whose father would have him be a lawyer); but he will be crowned with nettles, not bays.

242 *roddes in Pisse*, i.e. rods in pickle; proverbial for 'punishment in store' (Tilley, R157). Guilpin, *Skialetheia* (1598), E1v: 'The double volum'd *Satyre* praised is, / And lik'd of diuers for his Rods in pisse.' Middleton, *The Family of Love*, V.i.39–

42: 'satires whet their tooths, and steep rods in pisse, epigrams lie in poetry's pickle, and we shall haue rhyme out of all reason against you'. Marston, *Scourge of Villanie*, I, 44; Chapman, *Monsieur D'Olive*, I.i.263.

243 *the Whipping a'th Satyre.* The title of a verse satire by W. I. which appeared in 1601, attacking the work of three authors: a satirist, an epigrammatist, and a humorist. For the identification of the three as Marston, Guilpin, and Jonson, see Arnold Davenport, *The Whipper Pamphlets*, Part One (University of Liverpool Press, 1951), pp. v–vii. W. I. has been identified as William Ingram, but Davenport (*ibid.*, pp. vii–xi) argues persuasively that he was John Weever. *The Whipping of the Satyre* elicited two responses: (1) *No Whippinge, nor trippinge: but a kinde friendly Snippinge* (1601) sought to resolve the quarrel of the satirists; the author of it is generally agreed to be Nicholas Breton; and (2) *The Whipper of the Satyre his Pennance* (1601), the anonymous author of which has been identified by Davenport as Guilpin, defending himself against W.I.'s attack (*The Whipper Pamphlets*, Part Two (Liverpool, 1951), pp. vi–vii). Herford and Simpson (IX, 581) find an allusion to *The Whipping of the Satyre* at the end of *Poetaster*, V.iii.604–605, where Crispinus and Demetrius are warned against 'ambitiously, affecting the title of the *vntrussers*, or *whippers* of the age', but that seems unlikely if *Poetaster* were produced (as Herford and Simpson maintain that it was) in the spring of 1601, for *The Whipping of the Satyre* was not presumably published until sometime after its entry in the Stationers' Register on 14 August. See Introduction, p. 181, n. 5; and see Commentary, above, 'Titlepage' (note on 'vntrussing').

244 *the Whipping of the blinde-Beare.* Cf. I.ii.319, n.

249 *King Cambises.* Thomas Preston's *Lamentable Tragedie, mixed full of pleasant mirth, containing the life of Cambises King of Percia* was acted *c.* 1561. It was entered in the Stationers' Register in 1569–1570 (Arber, I, 400), and subsequently published in two undated editions (the first *c.* 1570, the second *c.* 1585). The play, full of emotional and rhetorical extrava-

gance, was a great popular success. Falstaff has a well-known reference to speaking in passion and doing it 'in King Cambyses' vein' (*1 Henry IV*, II.iv.386–387). Dekker alludes to the play again in *G.H.*, E2v, when speaking of the gallants' practice of sitting on the stage at the theatre: 'on the very Rushes where the Commedy is to daunce, yea and vnder the state of *Cambises* himselfe must our fethered *Estridge*, like a peece of Ordnance be planted'.

251–252 *terrible mouth...Leuiathan.* *F.B.N.A.*, pp. 51–52: 'save our soules from the great *Leviathan*, whose jawes are ever open to devoure'. *D.D.*, D3:

> a shoare
> Made all of *Rocks*, where huge *Leuiathans* lay
> Gaping to swallow *Soules*, new cast away;

there are marginal references to 'Iob 27' and 'Esay. 57' (i.e., presumably, Job 41 and Isaiah 27: 1). *W.K.*, III.i.159.

251 *thy beard's afraide to peepe out.* Cf. I.ii.289, n.

252 *heere's the sweete visage of Horace.* Tucca here produces one of the two pictures which his boy has entered with (line 158.1). The other (of Horace–Jonson) is exhibited at line 263 ('heere's the Coppy of thy countenance').

253 *perboylde-face,* thoroughly boiled, hence red-faced. Cf. Nashe, *Terrors of the Night* (I, 353): 'Women they vnderhand instruct to pownce and boulster out theyr brawn-falne deformities, to new perboile with painting their rake-leane withered visages.' And Jonson, *The Staple of News*, II.iv.51–52: 'such a per-boil'd visage! /...His face lookes like a Diers apron, iust!' *S.D.S.*, E2: 'their [the Players'] houses smoakt euerye after noone with Stinkards, who were so glewed together in crowdes with the Steams of strong breath, that when they came foorth, their faces lookt as if they had been perboylde'.

258–259 *his face puncht full of Oylet-holes.* Porter, *The Two Angry Women of Abingdon*, lines 2971–2972: 'Twill be a good while, ere you wish your skin full of Ilet holes.' Cf. *W.E.*, III.i.103–104, n.

262 *so leane a hollow-cheekt Scrag.* Cf. Carlo Buffone's description of Macilente in *Every Man Out*, I.i.212–213: 'a leane mung-

rell, he lookes as if he were chap-falne, with barking at other mens good fortunes'. For 'scrag', cf. *L.D.*, IV.iv.52.

281 *Red-cap.* III.i.190, n.

281 *ware hornes. O.F.*, V.i.181.

295 *bumbast*, swell out, render grandiose with bombastic language (*O.E.D.*). Cf. the famous reference in *Greenes Groatsworth of Wit* (XII, 144) to the 'vpstart Crow' who 'supposes he is as well able to bumbast out a blanke verse as the best of you'. *R.G.*, 'To the Comicke Playreaders', 3: 'huge bombasted plaies'. *W.E.*, V.iii.106.

296 *Temples Reuels.* Revels, usually at Christmas time, were traditional at the Inns of Court, and the 'Prince D'Amour' revels at the Middle Temple during the holiday season of 1597–1598 had recently been notable for their satiric sophistication. See Finkelpearl, *John Marston*, chapter 4 (especially p. 61, where the present passage is cited).

297 *Tango.* Cf. IV.ii.139: 'my little Trangdo', also addressed to Sir Vaughan, and the note on that passage. In Haughton's *Englishmen for my Money*, lines 1387–1388, a daughter says of the foreign suitors whom her father wishes her and her sisters to marry: 'These horeson Canniballs, these *Philistines*, / These tango mongoes shall not rule Ore me.'

298–301 *sit in a Gallery...afraide to take your part.* Cf. *Cynthia's Revels*, induction, 160–166, where one of the child actors says of the author:

> wee are not so officiously befriended by him, as to haue his presence in the tiring-house, to prompt vs aloud, stampe at the booke-holder, sweare for our properties, curse the poore tire-man, raile the musicke out of tune, and sweat for euerie veniall trespasse we commit, as some Authour would, if he had such fine engles as we.

305 *the Lordes roomes.* They were boxes located in a gallery above and behind the public-theatre stage. See Richard Hosley, 'The Gallery over the Stage in the Public Playhouse of Shakespeare's Time', *Shakespeare Quarterly*, 8 (1957), 24, where the present passage is cited. Cf. *Every Man out of his Humour*, II.iii.189–193, Carlo Buffone of Fastidius Briske's professed familiarity with the nobility: 'There's ne're a one of these,

but might lie a weeke on the rack, ere they could bring forth his name; and yet he powres them out as familiarly, as if he had seene 'hem stand by the fire i' the presence, or ta'ne tabacco with them, ouer the stage, i' the lords roome.' *G.H.*, Biv: 'at a new play you take vp the twelue-penny roome next the stage, (because the Lords & you may seeme to be haile fellow wel met)'. Later in *G.H.* (sig. E2v), Dekker says that the most fashionable place to sit at a play is on the stage itself, and that the lords' room 'is now but the Stages Suburbs', but he was writing of the fashion that had come to prevail by 1609.

311 *vp-sitting*, sitting up after an illness, used especially of women after childbirth. *S.H.R.*, E4v: 'At the birth of euery one these Monsters, were particular Triumphes, but aboue all the rest, one had the glory to be graced with a Masque, and it was at an vpsitting, when the *Gossips* and many great *States* were there present'; and Beaumont and Fletcher, *The Woman Hater*, II.i.367–368: 'I was entreated to invite your Lordship to a Ladies upsitting.' *W.H.*, V.i.173.

312 *Whitson-Ale*. Stubbes describes them thus:

> In certaine Townes where drunken *Bachus* beares all the sway, against a *Christmas*, an *Easter*, *Whitsonday*, or some other time, the Church-wardens...of euery parish...prouide half a score or twenty quarters of mault,...which mault, beeing made into very strong ale or beere, it is set to sale, either in the Church, or some other place assigned to that purpose. Then, when the *Nippitatum*, this Huf-cap (as they call it) and this *nectar* of lyfe, is set abroche, wel is he that can get the soonest to it, and spend the most at it; for he that sitteth the closest to it, and spends the moste at it, he is counted the godliest man of all the rest (*Anatomy of Abuses*, ed. Furnivall, p. 150).

N.F.H., D4v: 'drink more in two dayes, then all Maningtree do's at a Whitsun ale'.

316 *Holofernes*. His story in the apocryphal book of Judith was familiar. He was the subject of a ballad, 'The ouerthrow of proud *Holofernes*, and the triumph of vertuous Queene *Iudith*', printed in the second part of Deloney's *Garland of Good Will* (*Works*, pp. 355–361). This had presumably been in broadside circulation for some years before Deloney's

collection was first published in 1593. A ballad of 'the historye of Judith and Holyfernes' was entered in the Stationers' Register in the period 1566–1567 and again on 23 March 1588 (Rollins, nos. 1120, 1805). There are characters named Holofernes in *Love's Labour's Lost* and Marston's *What You Will*.

320 *tooth and nayle. P.G.*, I.ii.1–2.

320–321 *scalde...Iestes.* IV.i.103, n. Guilpin, *Skialetheia* (1598), A3v:

> Whose hap shall be to reade these pedler rimes,
> Let them expect no elaborat foolery,
> Such as Hermaphroditize these poore times,
> With wicked scald iests, extreame gullerie

320–321 *wry-mouth.* Cf. above, line 160, n.

321 *Iestes vpon his Knight-hood.* 'Wherever Jonson used the word "Knight" in the quarto of *Poetaster* he substituted another word in the folio, evidently as a result of criticism or a command from someone in authority' (Penniman, pp. 444–445).

323 *Doctor Doddipol*, a proverbial name for a blockhead (Tilley, D429). Middleton, *The Family of Love*, V.i.90–91: 'well, if I pepper ye not, call me doctor Doddipoll'. The term often carries the implication of a learned fool, a pseudo-scholar. Cf. Nashe, *Have With You*, III, 14: 'there haue been Doctors of thy Facultie, as Doctor *Dodipowle* for example'. *L.C.*, F2v: 'Upon two leane hackneies were these two *Doctor doddipols* horst, Ciuilly suited, that they might carry about them some badge of a Scholler.' A comedy, *The Wisdom of Doctor Dodypoll*, acted by the Children of Paul's *c.* 1599, was entered in the Stationers' Register on 7 October 1600 and printed in the same year. *O.F.*, IV.ii.105.

325 *crye Mew.* I.ii.94. And cf. *Every Man Out*, induction, 158–176.

328–333 *when you Sup in Tauernes...Carlo Buffon.* Herford and Simpson (IX, 428) find the point of this in Macilente's attack on Carlo Buffone in *Every Man out of his Humour*, I.i.191–193: 'Though yours bee the worst vse a man can put his wit

to, of thousands, to prostitute it at euery tauerne and ordinarie'.
The character of Buffone is described by Jonson as

A Publike, scurrilous and prophane Iester; that (more swift then
Circe) with absurd *simile's* will transforme any person into deformity...
A slaue, that hath an extraordinary gift in pleasing his palat, and will
swill vp more sacke at a sitting, then would make all the Guard a
posset. His religion his rayling, and his discourse ribaldry. They stand
highest in his respect, whom he studies most to reproch (Herford and
Simpson, III, 423–424).

330–332 *Epigrams...the Shot.* The 'Shot' was the tavern bill.
Cf. *G.H.*, D4v:

If you be a Poet and come into the Ordinary...order yourself thus:...
take occasion (pulling out your gloues) to haue some *Epigram*, or
Satyre, or *Sonnet*, fastned in one of them, that may...offer it selfe to
the Gentlemen:...and rather then you should sit like a dumb Coxcomb,
to repeat by heart either some verses of your owne, or of any other
mans..., it may chaunce saue you the price of your Ordinary.

And F2: 'But in such a deluge of drinke, take heede that no
man counterfeit him selfe drunck, to free his purse from the
danger of the shot.' *1 H.W.*, III.iii.32.

339 *Poet-Apes.* II.ii.43.

347 *Hearbe-a-grace*, rue, perhaps, as Penniman suggests (p. 445)
with a play 'on the name Ru-fus, as [Tucca] plays on the
name William'.

348–349 *Lady Furniuall.* Scherer (pp. 130–131) noted the presence
in Chapman's *Sir Giles Goosecap* (III.i.174–175) of a character
named Lady *Furnifall* who 'is never in any sociable veine
till she be typsie'. Though thus alluded to, no such character
appears in the printed text of the play (Quarto 1606). For the
suggestion that the 'drinking humor' of Lady Furnifall
contained a personal reference to which objection was made,
resulting in the suppression of her scenes, see T. M. Parrott,
'The Authorship of *Sir Giles Goosecap*', *Modern Philology*, 4
(1906–1907), 29, 34. The allusion in the present passage need
not refer to Chapman's play, Lady Furnifall (or Furnivall)
being 'apparently a familiar, not to say notorious character in
the London of Chapman and Dekker' (Parrot in his review of

Scherer's edition of *Satiromastix*, *Modern Language Review*, 6 (1911), 404).

351 *hit the Mistris.* The phrase is from the game of bowls, the 'mistress' being the small ball.

351–352 *fore-game...rubbers.* Cf. *Blurt, Master-Constable*, III.iii. 170–173: 'If we can keep but this bias, wenches, our goodmen may perchance once in a month get a fore-game of us; but, if they win a rubbers, let them throw their caps at it.' For 'rubbers', cf. *R.G.*, III.ii.166.

Epilogus

4 *Tantara*, the Latin onomatope for the sound of a trumpet. Cf. Puttenham, of *Onomatopeia*:

> Then also is the sence figuratiue when we deuise a new name to any thing consonant, as neere as we can to the nature thereof, as to say: *flashing of lightning, clashing of blades, clinking of fetters, chinking of money*: & as the poet *Virgil* said of the sounding a trumpet, *ta-ra-tant, taratantara* (*Arte of English Poesie*, ed. Willcock and Walker, p. 182).

Thus Stanyhurst's translation of *Aeneid*, II.324: 'Thee townsmen roared, thee trump taratantara ratled' (ed. 1583, p. 29). The sound is much employed by the dramatists. Cf. *The Tragicall Raigne of Selimus* (ed. Grosart, *Works of Greene*, XIV, 204), lines 247–248; 2 *Tamburlaine*, IV.i.66–67; Chapman, *May Day*, IV.iii.65–67. *N.H.*, II.i.256; *I.T.B.N.*, I.ii.244.

7–8 *when once (in an assembly of Friers) I railde*, referring to the Tucca of *Poetaster*, acted at the Blackfriars by the Chapel Children (and thus the allusion to 'when stiffe *Tucca* was a boy' in lines 9–10). Cf. *Sat.*, IV.iii.199.

10–11 *The Deuill and his Angels.* Scherer compares *K.C.*, G2: 'hee can put himselfe vpon none but the diuel and his Angels: and they (to make quick worke) giue him his Pasport'.

11 *Kings-truce. 1 H.W.*, II.i.202.

13–14 *dance Friskin.* Cf. *W.H.*, II.iii.13–14: 'Why *Tenterhooke* pray thee lets dance friskin, and be mery.' *L.D.*, II.iii.28. And cf. *Sat.*, III.i.116.

15 *your two pence a peice*, the price of admission to the Gallery

(cf. line 6). *S.D.S.*, E2: 'sit in the two-pennie galleries amongst the Gentlemen'. *L.C.*, D3v: 'pay thy two-pence to a *Player*, in his gallerie maist thou sitte by a Harlot'. *R.G.*, V.i.257–258.

28 *this colde weather*. Herford and Simpson compare *Poetaster*, III.iv.328–329, where Histrio says: 'this winter ha's made vs [the players] all poorer, then so many staru'd snakes'. But *Satiromastix* was almost certainly acted in the fall of 1601, not in the spring as *Poetaster* presumably was.

APPENDIX

Quotations from *Satiromastix* in Edward Pudsey's Commonplace Book

Bodleian Library MS. Eng. poet. d.3 fol. 42v

Pl[ay]: vntruss: of yᵉ Poet Dekker

weddings	fflowers srewd in yᵉ Bryds way becaus it is a most sweet thing to ly wᵗʰ a mā [I.i.1, 13, 14, 17–18]
tonge	A tong lyke a womā Bitten wᵗʰ fleas, nevʳ lyes still [I.i.44–45]
gay cloths	Lyke sumpter horses yᵗ carry good cloaths [I.ii.126] Evʳ since one hit mee in yᵉ teeth wᵗʰ yᵉ greatˢᵗ cks [I.ii.188–189]
musick	His musicke catcht mee by the eares. [II.i.73–74] I will com to yoʷ incontment &c [III.i.53]
womē	Woemen are earthly moones yᵗ nevʳ shyne till night yᵉᵗ chang their orbs &c [II.i.206–208]
countʳfeit	Yoʷ have his words as right as if hee had spit them in to yoʳ mouth [II.ii.19–20]
witt	Yoʳ great bellied witt longs for evʳy thing [II.ii.27]
a gloue	A glove in a hatt, a lether brooch: [III.i.121–122] worth thus much in bare velvett [III.i.204] hee fights wᵗʰ skill, but does most vyly Lye [III.i.252] I smell thy meaning tho I stop my nose [III.i.264–265]
curtesy	ffor a true furnish courtier hath such force, though his tonge faint, his very leggs discorse [III.i.304–305] And hee is no full-made courtier nor well strung that hath not evʳy ioint stuck wᵗʰ a tonge. [III.i.307–308]
Baldnes	Yf then stuck a nose & 2 eys on a Bald pate hee might weare two faces vnder one hood. [IV.i.55–56]

Yo^w blaze yor ignorance [IV.i.61]

chardg thy spirits to wait more close & neer thee [IV.i. 207–208]

thrust ther fing^{rs} in to ye fur of yor muff [*Blurt, Master-Constable*, III.iii.112–113]

Speech   Hee that speaks not well keeps not a good tong in his head [IV.iii.114–115]

Off all parts ye head (beeing ye seat of discours witt iudgm^t & all vnd^rstanding faculties) is ye cheefest, And ye hair is ye crowne of that the want whereof must needs bee a great blemishe [IV.i.64–72]

Against   At o^r birth wee possesse it, at o^r death it leavs vs not growes

Baldnes   in o^r graves & looks fresh when all o^r other beauties are gone [IV.i.76–82]

The 4 elem^{ts} (to prove ye excellencie of it [)] take pryde in ye fashion of it. When ye Fyre burnes most bright ye flames are lyke golden locks. When ye wat^{rs} hurles her lascivious armes about ye shores wast, her head shee curles: And rorid clouds beeing suckt into ye Ayre, when ye melt down lyke siluer hayre hangs. The Earth (whos head so oft is shorne) frighted wth ye rude tearing of her locks, her hair stands an end, & thorough fear ev^ry hair is turned to a green naked blade: Besides in o^r greatest greefs wee rend y^t off wch doth most beautifye beeing ye head tyre. [IV.i.83–97]

A Bald reason it is termd wch hath no hairs vpon it a scurvy scald reason [IV.i.102–103]

the oth^r pts Legitimate. Blu: [*Blurt, Master-Constable*, II.ii.139]

In prays   A bald head (lyke a dead mans skull) puts vs in mynd of death [IV.iii.23–25]. Heauen

of it   ye head or crown of earth, is bald & all creatures in it as ye sun moon & starrs, except som illboding blasing starres [IV.iii.29–37]

The Ey cheefest sense is bald [IV.iii.39–41]

nev^r was mā truly wise except bald [IV.iii.52–53]

The head is wisdoms hous hair but ye thatch. & prv^{rbs} prve ye vilenes of it – he has more hair then witt [IV.iii.54–56] bush naturall [IV.iii.58]

SIR THOMAS WYATT

INTRODUCTION

Sir Thomas Wyatt represents – in the abridged and verbally gar-
bled shape of a memorially reconstructed text – all that remains of
the 'playe called Ladey Jane' for which Henslowe paid Chettle,
Dekker, Heywood, Wentworth Smith, and Webster in October
1602. Two payments are recorded, on 15 and 21 October, the latter
'in fulle'.[1] On 27 October, Henslowe paid 5s. to Dekker 'in earnest
of the 2 p[ar]te of Lady Jane',[2] but nothing more is heard of this,
at least under that title. 'The playe of the overthrowe of Rebelles'
for which Henslowe on 6 November 1602 paid £5 (for 'a sewt of
satten'[3]) has often been identified conjecturally with the play of
Lady Jane; it may possibly represent the second part. That a
second part of *Lady Jane* could have been contemplated must
mean that the heroine had not met her end in Part One, but it
may have been that little of her story remained to be told except
for her trial and execution. Wyatt's rebellion, occurring historic-
ally between the plot to put Lady Jane Grey on the English throne
in the summer of 1553 (the subject presumably of Part One), and
the execution of her and her husband, Guilford Dudley, in February
1554, might be expected to have a place in any dramatization of
the events of these months. Accounts of it exist side by side in the
chronicles of Grafton, Stow and Holinshed with accounts of the
plot to make Lady Jane queen.

It seems reasonable to assume, then, that a sequel (under what-

[1] *Henslowe's Diary*, p. 218. The identification of *Wyatt* with *Lady Jane* (Parts
One and Two) was first made by Dyce in his edition of Webster (1830), II, 251, and
has never been seriously questioned.

[2] *Diary*, p. 219. The small amount, and the lack of further mention in the *Diary*
of a second part, have caused some doubt as to whether the sequel was ever written.
Harold Jenkins has suggested that the 10s. paid to Smith and the 3s. to Chettle on
12 November (*Diary*, p. 220) 'may also have been to the account of the continuation'
(*The Life and Work of Henry Chettle* (London, 1934), p. 241).

[3] *Diary*, p. 219.

311

ever title) to the play of *Lady Jane* was in fact written, and that the extant text of *Sir Thomas Wyatt* represents an abridgement of the two parts. The division into parts may be reflected in the break in subject matter which has been noted at the beginning of Act III of the extant text.[1] Acts I and II of *Sir Thomas Wyatt* dramatize the conspiracy to make Jane queen, the failure of this, and the accession of Mary; these scenes presumably represent Part One of *Lady Jane*. Acts III–V of *Sir Thomas Wyatt* dramatize the threat posed to Mary's throne by Wyatt's rebellion, the overthrow of this, his execution, and the execution as well of Jane and her husband; these scenes presumably represent *Lady Jane*, Part Two, which may otherwise have been known as *The Overthrow of Rebels*. The original play (whether in one or two parts) presumably ended with Mary's marriage to Philip of Spain. The titlepage of the 1607 quarto of *Sir Thomas Wyatt* makes reference to this (as it does also to Mary's coronation), but Philip does not appear in the extant text (see below, p. 316). If an original two-part play is in question, however, it would be wrong to assume that Wyatt appeared only in Part Two. The appropriation to him of the historical role played by Judge James Hales as the only Justice who supported Mary when Jane was proclaimed queen suggests that the drama must in some sense have been built around him from the outset (see below, p. 315).

The sad story of Lady Jane Grey and her young husband, Lord Guilford Dudley, had a prominent place in the historical accounts of the tense years just before the accession of Queen Elizabeth I. Foxe memorialized their fates among the Protestant martyrdoms of the *Actes and Monuments* (1563), Grafton recounted their story in his *Chronicle* of 1569, and in later decades it was kept before the public in successive editions of the *Chronicles* of Holinshed (1577, 1587) and the *Annales* of Stow (1580, 1592, 1600, 1601). In the meantime, their story had become known in more popular forms. Within a decade of her death, Lady Jane had become a subject for ballad and song. At least two ballads dealing with her were

---

[1] See W. W. Greg's edition of *Henslowe's Diary* (London, 1904–1908), II, 233. See also Jenkins, *Henry Chettle*, p. 242, and P. Shaw, '*Sir Thomas Wyat* and the Scenario of Lady Jane', *Modern Language Quarterly*, 13 (1952), 234.

entered in the Stationers' Register in the early 1560s.[1] There are two poems on 'Queen Jane' in Ulpian Fulwell's *Flower of Fame* (1575). In the decade just before Henslowe's quintet of dramatists adapted her story to the stage, Warner had recounted it in *Albions England* (1592) Book 8, chapter 40; and two of the most popular verse letters in Drayton's *Englands Heroicall Epistles* (1597) were those exchanged between Lady Jane and Dudley.[2]

Henslowe's dramatists turned to Foxe, Grafton, Stow and Holinshed for Lady Jane's story, and as the Commentary that follows will show, the works of all four are drawn on heavily in the course of the play. In Grafton, Holinshed and, especially, Stow the dramatists could also find detailed accounts of Wyatt's rebellion which followed a few months after the plot to make Jane queen.[3] The importance of Stow's *Annales* among the dramatists' sources has been pointed out by M. F. Martin.[4] The sequence of events as set forth in the *Annales* is in effect the sequence of actions which the play's plot attempts to encompass. A copy of Stow's volume (in either its 1600 or 1601 edition) was demonstrably open before the dramatists more than once while the play was

[1] See Rollins, nos. 1391 (where reference is made to a song with music about Lady Jane in Egerton MS 2009, f. 11v, beginning 'She that was named Queene & neuer crowned') 1450, 1455, 1457 ('The lamentacion that Ladie Jane made / Saiyng for my fathers proclamacion now must I lese my heade').

[2] For the popularity of these epistles, see the note by K. Tillotson and B. H. Newdigate in the Hebel edition of Drayton's *Works*, v, 134.

[3] The earliest published account is *The historie of Wyates rebellion* by John Proctor (1554). This is the basis of the account in Holinshed's *Chronicle*. Stow had access to the diary containing the eyewitness account of the Tower Chronicler, later published as *The Chronicle of Queen Jane, and of Two Years of Queen Mary, and especially of the Rebellion of Sir Thomas Wyat. Written by a resident in the Tower of London.* Edited by John Gough Nichols, Camden Society, no. 48 (1850).

[4] First in her 'Critical Edition of the Famous History of Sir Thomas Wyat' (University of London manuscript thesis, 1930), chapter 4, pp. 57ff., and subsequently in 'Stow's "Annals" and "The Famous Historie of Sir Thomas Wyat"', *Modern Language Review*, 53 (1958), 75–77. Earlier scholars (e.g. E. E. Stoll, *John Webster* (Boston, 1905), p. 45; F. E. Pierce, *The Collaboration of Webster and Dekker*, Yale Studies in English, no. 37 (New York, 1909), p. 151; Hunt, p. 76; Lucas (*Works of Webster*, IV, 239) held Holinshed's *Chronicles* to be the sole source for *Wyatt*, misled presumably by the fact that much of Holinshed's account of the historical events dramatized in the play is drawn from Stow.

being written, but it should be stressed that no one source will account for all the historical details which the play exhibits.[1] Foxe, Grafton, Stow and Holinshed were all drawn on, if not in equal degrees, then in notable ways. The quotations from these sources in the Commentary will indicate the use to which the dramatists put their chronicle materials. Since the action of the play is not always comprehensible as the result of the derangements that have been visited on its plot and language from its abridgement and the memorial reconstruction of its text, the quotations from the sources may also serve as a series of glosses on the dramatic events and their historical significance in individual scenes.

Sir Thomas Wyatt deals with events in English history extending from the death of King Edward VI in early July 1553 to the execution of Wyatt in early April 1554. In between come Northumberland's plot to divert the succession from the Princess Mary in favor of his daughter-in-law, Lady Jane Grey; the failure of his effort when the country rallies to the support of Mary; the troubles into which her reign as Queen promptly enters as she defaults on her promise to her supporters to maintain the Protestant religion and as she makes clear her determination to join herself in marriage with Philip of Spain; the revolt led by Wyatt in protest against this; the suppression of his rebellion and Wyatt's end on the gallows. So far as historical chronology is concerned, Wyatt's execution (11 April 1554) represents the latest event in the period covered by the play, but the dramatists have violated chronology by devoting the final scene to the execution first of Jane and then of Dudley (which had in fact taken place two months earlier, on 12 February). It is hard not to see the hand of Webster in the structural design if nothing else of this final scene. With its depiction of the death first of one and then of the other of a pair of lovers, it seems like a first tentative sketch of the dramatic ground plan that would

---

[1] The most conspicuous occasion when a copy of Stow's *Annales* was open before the dramatists was when some one of them adopted its misspelled name for the Spanish ambassador ('Edmond' for 'Egmond'; see Commentary on III.i.59–61). For the importance of Foxe, Grafton and Holinshed as supplements to Stow in accounting for the play's sources, see Shaw, '*Sir Thomas Wyat*', pp. 227–238; and Jones-Davies, I, 123, n. 138.

fashion the elaborately suspended catastrophes of his later tragedies: the beheading first of Jane and then of Dudley is to *Sir Thomas Wyatt* what the murder first of Brachiano and then of Vittoria is to *The White Devil*, and the murder first of the Duchess and then of Antonio is to *The Duchess of Malfi*.

This is not the only place in the play where the shaping power of one or the other of the dramatists involved is to be seen. The achievement of dramatic coherence is always a first concern of the playwright working with chronicle materials, and whoever was responsible for the opening scene of *Wyatt* (it may have been Webster) can be seen altering his source material in a way that is crucial for the accomplishment not only of dramatic unity but also for providing the character of Wyatt with an occasion of decisive choice which casts its long, ironic shadow over all that subsequently happens to him. In the chronicle sources, Wyatt appears out of nowhere in January 1554, leading a revolt in his native Kent in protest against the Queen's determination on a Spanish marriage. In Foxe's account of the manner in which Northumberland, having prevailed upon the dying King Edward to divert the succession from Mary to Jane, then set about obtaining the consent of the council to the King's revised will, the author of I.i of *Wyatt* read of Judge James Hales, the only Justice who refused to agree to the change in the order of succession. The dramatist attributes this stand to Wyatt (see I.i.31ff.), thereby laying the foundation for potentially tragic and ironic resonances which – however imperfectly they may sound in the verbally decimated extant text – must have been evident in the original version. By making Wyatt a principal agent to Queen Mary's accession, the dramatist assures that his later disenchantment with her policies and his eventual revolt against them will be shadowed with the irony and the pathos that attend on the frustration and despair of one who has himself brought about in some measure the events which drive him to his ruin.[1]

[1] Judge Hales' own fate was no less ironic and pathetic. Upon Queen Mary's accession he continued, with strict legality, to enforce King Edward's laws against the old religion. Foxe relates how,

'notwithstanding he had ventured his life in queene Maries cause, in that he woulde not subscribe to the disheriting of her by the kinges will, yet for that he did at a

Wyatt thus becomes the play's central figure, dominating it from beginning to end in a way he could never have done if confined to his historical role of leading the Kentish rebellion. His fate endows the play with a pattern of reversal that seems to have been a principal quality of the dramatic rhythm as originally conceived. Wyatt, the overthrower of rebels (specifically of Northumberland and his followers), becomes himself finally a rebel overthrown, and his fate has its parallel in the fates of the play's two feminine antagonists: Jane who begins by being proclaimed Queen and ends on the block, Mary who initially appears under threat of being deprived of her royal rights and ends installed on her throne.

This raises the question of the play's original ending. The title-page of the 1607 quarto promises 'the Coronation of Queen Mary, and the coming in of King Philip'. Of this there is nothing in the extant text, but it is tempting to wonder if in the original version the play might not have ended in some such burst of spectacle by way of confirming the extent of Mary's triumph, her rebellious subjects now reduced to order. There is much to recommend the speculation that, in the course of its theatrical evolution in one or two parts – sometime, presumably, between 27 October and 6 November 1602 – the play that was first known as *Lady Jane* in fact became *The Overthrow of Rebels*. That at any rate is what, in its extant text, it is about. Produced on the stage in the last weeks of 1602, virtually on the eve of Queen Elizabeth I's death and the succession crisis it was feared that that might bring, the play by whatever name it was known, with its parade of pretenders to the throne and would-be powers behind it and high-principled but

quarter Sessions giue charge vpon the statutes made in the time of king Henrie the eight, and Edward the sixt, for the supremacie and religion, hee was imprisoned in the Marshalsey, Counter, and Fleete, and so cruellie handled and put in feare by talke, that the Warden of the Fleete vsed to haue in his hearing, of such tormentes as were in preparing for heretickes (or for what other cause God knoweth) that hee sought to ridde himselfe out of this life, by wounding himselfe with a knife: and afterward was contented to say as they willed him: whereupon hee was discharged, but after that hee neuer rested till he had drowned himselfe in a riuer, half a mile from his house in Kent' (*Actes and Monuments* (1596), p. 1282).

The fact that Hales, like Wyatt, was a knight of Kent may have confirmed the identification of the two for the dramatist.

deluded defiers of the royal prerogative who pass across the stage to the scaffold, must have told a timely and a cautionary tale.[1]

That the titlepage of the 1607 quarto of *Sir Thomas Wyatt* attributes the play to Dekker and Webster is not to be taken to mean that their work alone is represented in the extant text. By 1607 Dekker had emerged as the most prominent of the five dramatists who had originally written the play; and his name coupled with Webster's may have had some advertising value on a titlepage in that year, which also saw the publication of *Westward Ho* and *Northward Ho*, both advertised as theirs. In any case, the 1607 quarto attribution of *Sir Thomas Wyatt* to them is not exactly false; it is simply not the whole truth. The quarto text is quite certainly an abridgement of the entire text of the original *Lady Jane* play (or plays), not simply of Dekker and Webster's shares in it (or them).[2] It is not wise to attempt to go very far in attributing authorial shares of a memorially reconstructed text of an abridged

[1] Five prominent characters are thus shown proceeding to their doom: Northumberland, Suffolk, Wyatt, Jane and Dudley. However much the age might have been inclined to sympathize with the religious and patriotic motives of Wyatt, orthodox political opinion had to proclaim him a rebel. See the account of his arraignment in Grafton, for example, where he is reported to have spoken with exemplary self-recrimination:

'Lo here & se in me the same end which all other commonly had, which haue attempted like enterprice from the begynning. For peruse the Chronicles through, and you shall see that neuer rebellion attempted by subiectes against their prince and countrye from the begynning did euer prosper or had better successe, except the case of king Henry the fourth, who although he became a Prynce: yet in his act was but a Rebell, for so must I call him. And though he preuayled for a time, yet was it not long, but that his heires were depriued and those that had right againe restored to the kingdome and crowne, and the vsurpation so sharpely reuenged afterward in his blood, as it well appered that the long delaye of Gods vengeaunce was supplyed with more grieuous plague in the third and fourth generation' (*A Chronicle at large and meere History of the affayres of Englande* (1569), pp. 1339–1340).
It should be noted, however, that the Wyatt of the play exhibits no such repentant mood as he faces his end. Concerning the play's 'strong political implications', see Irving Ribner, *The English History Play in the Age of Shakespeare* (Princeton, 1957), p. 217.

[2] The possibility of this was acknowledged by Pierce (*Collaboration of Webster and Dekker*, p. 159), and more forcibly stated by such later scholars as Jenkins (*Henry Chettle*, p. 243), Lucas (*Works of Webster*, IV, 240), Shaw ('*Sir Thomas Wyat*', p. 238), and Jones-Davies (II, 362).

version of a presumptive two-part play written originally by five dramatists of whom one was such a relatively unknown quantity as Henry Chettle and another such a totally unknown quantity as Wentworth Smith. Nonetheless a few points can be made. Two scenes (I.iii and III.i) have been plausibly identified by M. F. Martin as containing the work of Heywood (see the Commentary). Dekker's share in the play can be most clearly traced in IV.ii–iii; there are fainter traces of his presence in II.iii and IV.i. There are signs of Webster in I.i–ii and V.i and (as already suggested) in the design of V.ii. If, in the Commentary that follows, the connectives that have been suggested between these scenes and the acknowledged work of Dekker or Webster or Heywood seem inadequate as evidence for determining authorial shares, as they are, they nonetheless provide a contrast with certain other scenes of the play where there are no connectives at all with the acknowledged work of these three dramatists. The section of the text that extends from I.iv through II.ii, for example, exhibits nothing that suggests the presence of Dekker, Webster or Heywood, and one can only conclude that it represents portions of the original play that were composed either by Chettle or Smith or by both. Two later scenes (III.ii and IV.iv) are equally devoid of familiar signs. It should be understood that the passages cited from acknowledged works are intended merely to indicate some of the points at which this dramatically disjointed and verbally mangled text approaches (or seems to approach) the recognizable manner of Dekker or Webster or Heywood. There is no question of attributing entire scenes to any one of them, for the scene as an authorial unit is bound to be suspect in a text of this kind. What constitutes a scene in the 1607 quarto may very well represent two or more scenes (originally perhaps the work of two or more authors) that have been compressed into a single one, either intentionally as the result of abridgement, or accidentally through failure of memory in the process of the text's memorial reconstruction.

The play that was first called *Lady Jane* and then may have been called *The Overthrow of Rebels* and came eventually to be known as *Sir Thomas Wyatt* was written for the Earl of Worcester's Company.¹ Within a month of its completion, Dekker, Chettle, Heywood and Webster were working together on another play seasonably titled *Christmas Comes but Once a Year* (payments recorded by Henslowe on 2, 23 and 26 November 1602, the final one 'in fulle'²). Smith was at work with Day, Hathway and another on *The Black Dog of Newgate*, Part One. *Sir Thomas Wyatt* apparently continued in the repertoire of Worcester's Men until after the accession of King James, when the Company came under the patronage of Queen Anne;³ the titlepage of the 1607 quarto proclaims the play to have been 'plaied by the Queens Maiesties Seruants'.

When and under what circumstances the reported text printed in the quarto was prepared, we have no way of knowing.⁴ It is interesting to note that a play with which *Wyatt* has much in common (including a shared author), Heywood's *If You Know Not Me, You Know Nobody*, Part One, had been printed in a reported text two years before *Wyatt*, in 1605. Years later, Heywood complained that his play had been drawn into print by means of 'Stenography' with 'scarce one word trew'.⁵ Both plays were acted by the Queen's Company, and both cover some of the same historical ground.⁶ What they principally have in common is their depiction of Queen Mary and the suffering of English men and

¹ Playing either at the Boar's Head or at the Rose, which they were occupying by May 1603 and possibly earlier. See Chambers, II, 225–226.

² *Diary*, pp. 219–220.

³ The change in patronage 'was probably effected by Christmas [1603], and certainly by 19 February 1604' (Chambers, II, 229).

⁴ For the view that the quarto text represents a shortened form of the play, prepared by the actors themselves for performance in the provinces, and thus is not a pirated text, see W. L. Halstead, 'A Note on the Text of the *Famous History of Sir Thomas Wyatt*', *Modern Language Notes*, 54 (1939), 585–589. Such a view fails, however, to take into account the fact that, as Jenkins has observed (*Henry Chettle*, p. 243, n. 3), 'the text has evidently been produced by someone who had small regard for the exigencies of the verse, and perhaps very little understanding of them'. Jenkins suggests the possibility 'that the two parts of *Lady Jane* had at some time been reduced to one, perhaps for a revival, and that the extant text is a pirated quarto of the resultant version' (*ibid.*, p. 244, note).

⁵ 'A Prologue to the Play of Queene Elizabeth as it was last revived at the Cock-pit, in which the Author taxeth the most corrupted copy now imprinted, which was published without his consent', printed in Heywood's *Pleasant Dialogues and Dramas* (1637), pp. 248–249.

⁶ Mary Forster Martin in '*If You Know Not Me, You Know Nobodie*, and *The*

women under her Romish rule. Heywood's play provides at least part of what the titlepage of the 1607 quarto of *Wyatt* promised and failed to deliver: 'the coming in of King Philip'; it does not present Queen Mary's coronation, though she enters in much state near the beginning. The popularity of *If You Know Not Me*, even in its unsatisfactory verbal and dramatic condition, is attested to by its numerous editions in the years that followed (1606, 1608, 1610, 1613, and later). *Sir Thomas Wyatt*, rather surprisingly, had a second edition in 1612. There was clearly an audience among both readers and theatre-goers for the kind of nationalistic, anti-papal play represented by these two pieces. Dekker would address himself to it explicitly in *The Whore of Babylon*.

Reference is made in the Commentary to the work of the following editors of *Sir Thomas Wyatt*: A. Dyce in vol. 1 of his *Works of John Webster*, 1st ed. (London, 1830; rev. ed. 1857); and W. Hazlitt (in vol. 1 of his *Dramatic Works of John Webster* (London, 1857).

COMMENTARY

I.i

What time king Edward by long sicknesse began to appeare more feeble and weake, in the meane while during the time of this his sicknesse, a certain mariage was prouided, concluded & shortlie also upon the same solemnized in the moneth of May, betweene the lord Gilford, sonne to the duke of Northumberland, & the ladie Iane the Duke of Suffolkes daughter, whose mother being then aliue, was daughter to Mary king Henries second sister, who first was maried to the French king, and afterward to Charles duke of Suffolke. But to make no long tariance hereupon, the mariage beeing ended, and the king waxing

Famous Historie of Sir Thomas Wyat', *The Library*, 4th series, 13 (1933), 280–281, plausibly accounts for this as follows:

at some date subsequent to the production of *Sir Thomas Wyat*, probably afer tthe death of Queen Elizabeth, while she was still very much in the hearts and minds of her people, Heywood was suddenly called upon to write a play about her. With his reading in Fox and Holinshed fresh in his mind, and the play *Lady Jane* recently in the repertory, Heywood set to work and wrote *If You Know Not Me, You Know Nobodie*, using many incidents and ideas that he had used in the former play.'

euerie daie more sicke then other, whereas indeede there seemed in
him no hope of recouerie, it was brought to passe by the consent not
onlie of the Nobilitie, but also of all the chiefe Lawyers of the Realme,
that the king by his Testament did appoint the foresaid ladie Iane,
daughter to the duke of Suffolke, to be inheritrice unto the crowne of
England, passing ouer his two sisters Mary and Elizabeth.

To this order subscribed all the kings counsell, and chiefe of yᵉ
Nobilitie, the Maior and citie of London, and almost all the Iudges and
chiefe Lawyers of this Realme, sauing onlie Iustice Hales of Kent, a man
both fauouring true religion, and also an upright iudge as any hath
beene noted in this realme, who giuing his consent unto Ladie Marie
woulde in no case subscribe to ladie Iane... The causes laid against
Ladie Marie were as well for that it was feared shee woulde mary with
a stranger, and thereby intangle the crowne: as also that she would
cleane alter religion, used both in king Henrie hir father, and also in
king Edward hir brothers daies, and so bring in the Pope, to the utter
destruction of the realme, which indeed afterward came to passe.
(Foxe, *Actes and Monuments* (edn. 1596), p. 1278).

1–2 *cheerely...as a dying man.* Cf. the proverb 'A Lightening
(lightning) before death' (Tilley, L277). Professor Bowers
(I, 455) has commented on the corruption of lines 2–3. Presumably the implicit allusion to 'lightening/lightning' in the
proverbial reference that informs lines 1–2 suggested the next
simile, 'Like to quicke lighting' in line 3, another proverbial
allusion (Tilley, L279). Webster makes use of both in *The
White Devil*: at I.ii.259 ('Woe to light hearts! – they still
forerun our fall!') and I.ii.4–5 ('I am prompt / As lightning
to your service').

33 *surprise,* take possession of.

60 *though death his body doe disseuer.* 'King *Edward* being about the
age of 16. yeeres ended his life at Greenewich, on the sixt of
Iuly, when he had raigned sixe yeeres, fiue moneths, and odde
daies, and was buried at Westminster' (Stow, *Annales* (edn.
1601), p. 1029).

I.ii

The 8. of Iuly, the lord maior of London was sent for to the court then
at Greenewich, to bring with him sixe aldermen, as many merchants
of the staple, and as many merchant aduenturers, unto whom by the
councell was secretly declared the death of king *Edward,* and also how

he had ordained for the succession of the crowne by his letters pattents, to the which they were sworn, and charged to keepe it secret.

The 10. of Iuly in the afternoone about 3. of the clocke, lady Iane... was conuaied by water to the tower of London, and there receiued as Queene. After fiue of the clocke the same afternoone, was proclamation made of the death of king *Edward* the sixt, and how he had ordained by his letters pattents, bearing date the 21. of Iune last past, that the ladie *Iane*... should be heire to the crowne of England, and the heire males of hir body, etc. (Stow, *Annales*, pp. 1029–1030).

13 *I haue no thoughts so ranke.* Cf. Northumberland's address to his followers regarding 'the sacred and holie oth of alleageance made freelie by you to this vertuous lady the queenes high-nesse, who by your and our enticement, is rather of force placed therein, than by her owne seeking and request' (Stow, *Annales*, p. 1031).

21 *flattering belles.* Cf. Webster, *The White Devil*, III.ii.96–97: 'those flattering bels have all one tune / At weddings, and at funerals', and V.vi.275: 'Let no harsh flattering Bels resound my knell.'

27 *Night-cap... Crowne.* Cf. *M.M.L.*, I.iv.63–65.

35 *aue*, acclamation (Latin *ave*, hail!). Webster (and Heywood?), *Appius and Virginia*, V.ii.7: 'Whose station's built on Avees and Applause'. *W.B.*, I.i.12.

63 *O propheticke soule.* Hamlet, I.v.40.

64–66 *Lo we ascend into our chaires of State, | Like funerall Coffins, in some funerall pompe | Descending to their graues. But we must on.* Fractured though this be, it is not perhaps merely fanciful to feel a Websterian movement in the verse, like unto that in such a speech as Flamineo's beginning 'Wee are ingag'd to mischiefe and must on' in *The White Devil*, I.ii.341ff.

64 *chaires of State.* Webster, 'A Monumental Columne', 115.

I.iii

The Ladie Mary a little before liyng at Honesdon in Hartfordshire, hauing intelligence of the state of the king her brother, and of the secret practise against her, by the aduice of her friendes with all speede tooke her iourney towarde her house of Keninghall in Norffolke, entend-ing there to remaine vntill she coulde make her selfe more strong of her friendes and allies: neuerthelesse vnderstanding by them that she could not lie there in surety, being a place open and easy to be approched, remoued from thence vnto her Castell of Fremingham standing in a wood Countrie, and not so easie to be inuaded by her enimies (Grafton, *A Chronicle*, p. 1324).

For the relation of this scene to Heywood's *If You Know Not Me, You Know Nobody*, Part One, see Martin, '*If You Know Not Me*, and *Wyat*', pp. 272–281.

7–14 *all their pride . . . this land.* With Queen Mary's soliloquy on the virtues of the Roman Catholic Prayer-Book, Martin compares Queen Elizabeth's speech in praise of the English Bible at the end of Heywood's *If You Know Not Me* (ed. Shepherd, I, 246):

> Thou art the way to honor; thou to blisse.
> An English Bible! Thankes, my good Lord Mayor,
> You of our body and our soule haue care,
> This is the iewel that we still loue best;
> This was our solace when we were distrest.
> This book, that hath so long conceald itself,
> So long shut vp, so long hid, now, lords, see,
> We here vnclaspe: for euer it is free.
> Who lookes for ioy, let him this booke adore;
> This is true food for rich men and for poore.
> Who drinkes of this is certain ne'er to perish:
> This will the soule with heauenly vertue cherish.

14.1 *Sir Henry Beningfield.* The name is given as Sir Henry Bedingfield in Stow (*Annales*, p. 1030), where it occurs among a list of knights attendant on Mary at Kenninghall. The form of the name in the present passage seems to derive from Foxe (*Actes and Monuments*, p. 1337), where it occurs as 'Benefield' and 'Benifielde'. Foxe relates how Elizabeth, upon her release from the Tower in May 1554, was put into the keeping of Benifielde at Woodstock, and how he 'both forgetting her estate, and his own duty. . . shewed himselfe more hard and streight vnto her, then either cause was giuen of her part, or reason of his owne part would haue led him'. He is a prominent figure in Heywood's *If You Know Not Me*, where he is represented 'as a petty tyrant, currying favour with Mary by his unkindness to her sister, and in turn seeking Elizabeth's favour on her accession' (Martin, '*If You Know Not Me* and *Wyat*', p. 280, who compares his entrance with the news of Mary's accession in the present scene with his arrival bearing news of Elizabeth's accession near the end of Part One of Heywood's play (ed. Shepherd, 1, 245)). Martin parallels his arrival in *Sir Thomas Wyatt* 'with the wrong news – for Wyat follows him immediately with the report of the Lords' recognition of Jane as the rightful Queen' – with his tardiness (for which he is ridiculed) in reaching Elizabeth in *If You Know Not Me*, where three others arrive before he does with the word that she is Queen. Heywood, in his account of Elizabeth's keeper in *England's Elizabeth* (1631), gives the name as 'Sir Henry Benningfield' (p. 147).

36–38 *the tenants... | Denide their ayde.* Cf. Stow, *Annales*, p. 1032: 'word of a greater mischiefe was brought to the Tower, that is to saie, that the Noblemens tenantes refused to serue their lords against queene *Marie*'.

43 *from Framingham.* Read 'to Framingham'. All the chronicles are agreed that Mary went from Kenninghall in Norfolk (where the present scene must be assumed to take place) to Framlingham in Suffolk. Cf. the passage from Grafton, quoted at the head of the present scene. And Stow, *Annales*, p. 1032: 'By this time word was brought to the tower, that the Lady *Mary* was fled to Flamingham castle in Suffolke; where the people of the countrey almost wholy resorted to hir.' Foxe reports how Mary, having 'tossed with much trauell up and downe, to worke the surest waie for her best aduantage', withdrew 'into the quarters of Northfolke and Suffolke,...and there gathering to her such aide of the commons in euery side as shee might, keepeth her selfe close for a space within Fremingham Castle' (*Actes and Monuments*, p. 1279). That her stay at Framlingham was subsequent to the period of the action represented by the present scene is clear from III.i.22–23.

47–48 *I lou'd the Father...death will run.* Cf. Wyatt's declaration at his trial: 'I serued hir highnesse against the duke of Northumberland, as my lord of Arundell can witnesse...My

father also serued king Henrie the eight to his good contenta-
tion, and I also serued him, and king Edward his son. And in
witnesse of my bloud spent in his seruice, I carrie a name'
(Holinshed, *Chronicles* (edn. 1587), III, 1103). Martin ('*If
You Know Not Me* and *Wyat*', p. 280), compares the present
passage with two passages from Heywood's *If You Know
Not Me*, Part One: 'As you did loue her Father, or her
Brother' and 'You seru'd her father, and he lou'd you well:/
You seru'd her brother, and he held you deare' (ed. Shepherd,
I, 199, 217).

I.iv

By speedie counsell it was there concluded, that the Duke of Suffolke
with certaine other noblemen, should go towards the ladie *Mary*, to
fetch hir vp to the tower: this was first determined: but by night of the
same daie [12 July], the said voiage of the Duke of Suffolke was cleane
dissolued by the speciall meanes of the lady *Iane* his daughter, who
taking the matter heauilie, with weeping teares made request to the
whole councell, that hir father might tarry at home in her company:
whereupon the counsell perswaded with the duke of Northumberland,
to take that voiage vpon him...Well (quoth the duke then) since ye
think it good, I and mine wil go, not doubting of your fidelity to the
queens maiesty which I leaue in your custody (Stow, *Annales*, pp. 1030–
1031).

1 *Captaine Bret*. Later, one of the captains in Wyatt's forces (see
below, headnote to IV.i–IV.iii.8). His introduction here, in
the company of Northumberland and Suffolk, is unhistorical.

5 *arain'd*, i.e. arranged, set in order (Hazlitt).

24 *seisure*, possession.

31–41 *My Lord, most lou'd...with teares*. Cf. Stow, *Annales*,
p. 1032:

Then as the Duke came through the counsell chamber, hee tooke his
leaue of the Earle of Arundell, who praied God bee with his grace,
saying, he was sorie it was not his chance to go with him, and beare
him companie, in whose presence he could find in his heart to spend his
bloude, euen at his feete.

Drayton notes the incident in his 'Annotations' to *Englands
Heroicall Epistles*, 'Guilford Dudley to Lady Jane Gray'
(ed. Hebel, II, 307).

37 *traile a pike*, serve as a common soldier. The reference is to the marching posture, with the pike carried in the right hand in an oblique position with the head forward and the butt nearly touching the ground. The phrase is common. Cf. Fletcher and Massinger, *The Spanish Curate*, I.i (1647), p. 26):

> how proud,
> In the service of my Country, should I be,
> To traile a pike under your brave command.

A.G., D1; *W.B.*, V.vi.50.

45 *Commend vs to the Queene.* Some confusion here; Arundel's words at lines 33–37 declare that he is staying with the Queen (i.e. Jane), and his presence at the Tower in the next scene makes it clear that he does.

I.v

The duke thought long for his succors, and wrote somewhat sharpelie to the counsell at the tower in that behalfe, as well for lacke of men as of munition, but a slender answere had he againe: And from that time forward certaine of the counsell, to wit, the earle of Pembroke, and sir *Th. Cheyney* lord Warden, and other, sought to get out of the Tower to consult in London, but coulde not yet (Stow, *Annales*, pp. 1032–1033).

The same 16. of Iuly, the lorde Treasurer was gone out of the tower to his house in London at night, and forthwith about 7. of the clocke the gates of the tower vpon a sodain were shut vp, and the keies born vp to the lady Iane, which was for feare of some packing in the L. treasurer, but he was fetched again to the tower, about 12. of the clocke in the night (*ibid.*, p. 1033).

0.1 *Treasurer*, William Paulet, first Marquis of Winchester (?1485–1572). He was Lord Treasurer from 1550 until his death. Cf. the opening stage direction to the following scene. He is not to be confused with the Bishop of Winchester who appears later in the play.

31 *the Duke is but newly arrested.* The reference is to Suffolk, who was sent to the Tower on 28 July 1553. He was released 'and had the queenes pardon' on 31 July (Stow, *Annales*, p. 1035).

I.vi

20 *nice*, 'delicate', 'needing tactful handling' (*O.E.D.*).

55 *ceased her*, i.e., 'given her seizure of', 'put her in possession of'. Cf. I.iv.24.

57–59 *we haue armed the Dukes with power,* | *Giuen them commission vnder our owne handes* | *To passe against the Lady.* An important point, of which the council is reminded later by Guilford (V.i.83–85).

59 *the Lady*, i.e., Mary.

59 *You*, i.e., the council. The sense of the passage that follows seems to be that the council has entered upon a course of action that is bound to bring it into hostilities with the adherents of Mary, and that the irascible spirit of Northumberland, which they of the council have themselves countenanced 'vnder our owne handes' (line 58), will not be curbed (called to check) by letters repealing his commission.

88 *refeld*, refuted.

100–108 *Why then giue order... hold our audience.*

> The 19. of Iulie, the Counsell, partlie mooued with the right of the ladie *Maries* cause, partlie considering, that the most of the realme was wholy bent on her side, chaunged their mindes, and assembled them-selues at Bainardes castle, where they communed with the Earle of Pembrooke: And the earle of Shrewsburie, with Sir *Iohn Mason* Cleark of the Councell, spoke to the lorde Maior secretlie, that he with the Sheriffes and such other of the Aldermen with the Recorder, as he thought best, to meete him and the Councell at Bainardes Castle, within lesse than an houre: which they did, where the councell declared to the lorde Maior and his brethren, that hee and they must ride with them into Cheape to proclaime a newe Queene, which was the ladie *Maries* grace, daughter to King *Henry* the eight; and they riding from thence to Paules Church-yarde, and into Cheape, the people were so assembled, that the Lordes coulde not ride by them to the Crosse, where Maister *Gartar* king at armes in his rich Coate of Armes, with a Trumpet beeing readie, the Trumpet was sounded, and then they proclaimed the ladie *Mary*, Daughter to King Henry the eight and Queene *Katherine*, Queene of Englande, Fraunce, and Irelande, defender of the faith, etc. Which Proclaimation ended, the Lorde Maior, and all the Coun-cell rode to Paules Church, where the Canticle of *Te Deum* was soung. And the same night the Earle of Arundell, and the Lorde Paget, rode in Poste to Queene *Mary* with thirtie horse with them (Stow, *Annales*, p. 1033).

327

II.i

1 *Lance persado*, i.e. 'lanceprisado':

> a military name taken over from the Italian *lancia spezzata* and the
> French *lancepessade* meaning broken or spent lance. The term is said
> to have originated during the wars of Francis I and Henry II of France
> against the Emperor Charles V and his brother-in-law, the Duke of
> Savoy. It was applied to a trooper that had broken his lance and lost
> his horse in battle, but that received his full pay as a trooper until he
> could rehabilitate himself. As time passed, however, such an unfortunate
> was, instead, made companion of the corporal whom he assisted, and
> finally became an officer under him – the lowest non-commissioned
> officer in the army, receiving only a private foot-soldier's pay. From
> his title came the distinctive 'lance' prefixed to the titles sergeant and
> corporal (E. A. W. Bryne, on Massinger's *The Maid of Honour*,
> III.i.47, in her edition of that play (London, 1927), p. 116).

> *L.C.*, H3: '*Lucifers Lansprizado* that stood aloof to behold
> the mustrings of these Hell-hounds took delight to see them
> Double their Fyles so nimbly.' *V.M.*, II.i.17.

7 *take tooles of the pies and the aple-women.* Cf. the induction to
Jonson's *Bartholomew Fair*, where the Stage-keeper complains
that the play contains no 'little *Dauy*' – i.e., no swaggering
bully – 'to take toll o' the Bawds' at the fair (lines 14–15).
'Pies' (magpies) are whores, and 'aple-women' (like their
male counterparts 'apple-squires') are bawds.

12 *this is a famous Vniuersitie.* The scene is Cambridge; see the
head-note to the following scene.

30 *descant.* A musical term: 'A melodious accompaniment to the
plainsong, sung or played above it: the earliest form of
counterpoint' (*O.E.D.*). Here, the term implies 'to comment
on censoriously'.

II.ii

The 20. of Iulie, *John* Duke of Northumberlande, beeing then in
Cambridge, and hauing sure knowledge, that the ladie *Mary* was by
the Nobilitie and others of the Counsell remaining at London proclaimed Queene; about fiue of the clocke the same night, he with such
other of the nobilitie as were in his companie, came to the market
crosse of the towne, and calling for an Herault, himselfe proclaimed
queene *Mary*, and among other he threw vppe his owne cappe, and

within an houre after he had letters from the counsell, by the handes of
Richard Rose herault: Dated at Westminster the 20. of Iune [read
'July'] in forme following.

In the name of our Soueraigne Lady *Mary* the Queene to bee declared to the duke of Northumberland, and all other of his band of what
degree soeuer they be.

Yee shall command and charge in the Queenes highnesse name, the
saide Duke to disarme himselfe, and to cease all his men of war: and
to suffer no part of his army to doe any villanie, or any thing contrary
to the peace: and himselfe to forbeare his coming to this citie vntill
the Queenes pleasure be expressedly declared vnto him. And if he will
shewe himselfe like a good quiet subiect, we will then continue as wee
haue begunne, as humble suters to our soueraigne lady the Queenes
highnesse for him and his, as for ourselues. And if he do not, we will
not faile to spend our liues in subduing him and his.

Item, yee shall in all places where yee come, notifie it, If the Duke
of Northumberland do not submit himselfe to the Queenes highnesse,
Queene *Marie*, he shall be accepted as a traytour. And all we of the
nobilitie that were counsellers to the late king, will to the vttermost
portion, persecute him and his to their vtter confusion. *Thom. Cant.*
archbishop, *Thomas Elie* Chancelor, *Will Winchester* Marquesse,
I. Bedforde Earle, *H. Suffolke* duke, *F. Shrewsburie* Earle, *W. Pembrough*
Earle, *Thomas Darcy* Lorde Chamberlaine, *R. Cotton, W. Peter*
secretarie, *W. Cecill* second secretarie, *I. C. I. Baker* Chancelor of the
tenths, *I. Mason* master of requests, *R. Bowes* master of the Rols.

The rumour of these letters was no sooner abroad, but euery man
departed. And shortly after, the Duke was arrested in the Kings
Colledge by one master *Slegge*, Sergeant at armes. At the last letters were
brought from the counsell at London, that all men should go each his
way: Whereupon the Duke said to them that kept him, Yee doe me
wrong to withdraw my libertie, see yee not the Counsels letters without
exception, that all men should go whither they woulde? At which
wordes, they that kept him and the other Noble men, set them at
libertie, and so continued they for that night, insomuch, that the Earle
of Warwicke was readie in the morning to haue rode awaie, but then
came the Earle of Arundale from the queene to the Duke into his
Chamber, who sent out to meete him, and as soone as hee sawe the
Earle of Arundale, hee fell on his knees, and desired him to be good to
him, for the loue of God, consider (saieth hee) I haue done nothing but
by the consents of you and all the whole Counsell: My Lord (quoth
the Earle of Arundell) I am sent hither by the Queenes maiestie, and in
her name I doe arrest you: and I obey it my Lord (quoth he) I beseech
you my Lorde of Arundell (quoth the Duke) use mercie towardes mee,
knowing the case as it is: my Lorde (quoth the Earle) yee should haue
sought for mercie sooner, I must doe according to my commandement,

and therewith he committed the charge of him, and of other to the guard and gentlemen that stood by (Stow, *Annales*, pp. 1033–1034).

1–2 *My Lord tis true, you sent vnto the Counsell | For fresh supplies, what succour.* Cf. Stow, *Annales*, pp. 1032–1033, quoted in the head-note to I.v.

32–34 *In Baynards Castle...proclaime Queene Mary.* Cf. Stow, *Annales*, p. 1033, quoted in the note on I.vi.100–108.

50 *Lord Huntington.*

And so the duke of Northumberland, beeing by counsell and aduise sent forth against her, was left destitute and forsaken alone at Cambridge, with some of his sonnes, and a fewe other, among whom the earle of Huntington was one: who there were arrested and brought to the tower of London, as traitors to the crown, notwithstanding that he had there proclaimed her queene before (Foxe, *Actes and Monuments*, p. 1280).

57.1 *Maister Roose.* See Stow, *Annales*, pp. 1033–1034, quoted in the head-note to the present scene.

77 *Commission.* Northumberland is commenting bitterly on the commission he had received from the council to proceed against Mary. Cf. I.vi.57–58, and II.ii.89.

106 *your three Sons*, the Earl of Warwick, Lord Ambrose Dudley, and Lord Henry Dudley.

107 *Vnto the Tower.* 'The 25. of Iuly, the Duke with other were brought vp to the Tower of London, vnder the conduct of *Henry* Earle of Arundale, with a great number of light horse-men, bowes and speares' (Stow, *Annales*, p. 1035).

111 *O my Children.* At his arraignment (18 August 1553), Northumberland expressed the hope 'that her Maiestie will be gratious to my children, which maie heereafter do good seruice, considering, that they went by my commandement, who am their father, and not of their own free willes' (Stow, *Annales*, p. 1037).

II.iii

The .xxv. day of Ianuary next folowyng newes were brought to the Court of this sturre begon by the sayde Sir Thomas Wyat. And foorthwith after this it was knowne that Henry Duke of Suffolke father to the Ladie Iane (which Ladie Iane was yet aliue) was sodainely departed from the Court with his two brethren into Warwikeshire, and Leycestershire, there to rayse and gather a power of those Countries to ioyne with Sir Thomas Wyat. The Queene hearing of these tumults did first by her proclamation declare the saide Duke of Suffolke, and syr Thomas Wyat with other Traitors...

In this meane time as before you haue hearde, the Duke of Suffolke beyng come from London into Leycestershire, and Warwikeshire with a very small company (as the saiyng was) tooke vpon him there to publishe a Proclamation in his daughters name, purposing thereby to haue perswaded the subiectes, that Queene Marie entended to tourne the succession, of the Crowne of Englande unto straungers, namely unto Spanyardes, which Proclamation notwithstanding, the people kept themselues quiet. Queene Mary vnderstanding of this, sent Fraunces Erle of Huntyngdon to rayse power in those partes to withstande the sayde Duke, the which Erle sped his time so well that he preuented the seyde Duke from entring the Citie of Couentrie, where he had great hope of ayde among the common sort: By reason whereof, hee being nowe disappointed of his enterprise, with his two brethren, the Lorde Thomas and the Lorde John Graye fledde from thence to a Manor of his called Astley sixe miles from Couentry, and committed himselfe to a man of his being keeper of his parke, called Nicholas Laurence, the which keeper bestowed the Duke his maister in a hollow Oke within the saide parke, where he remained two or three dayes vndiscouered, vntill the sayde keeper (as it is saide) disclosed his case to the sayde Erle, who immediately apprehended the saide Duke, and brought him prisoner to the Tower of London (Grafton, *A Chronicle*, p. 1331).

4   *Cabin.* N.H., III.i.95.

8.1   *Homes.* The servant is named Nicholas Laurence in Grafton (quoted in the head-note to the present scene). Foxe (*Actes and Monuments*, p. 1289) says that the Duke 'committed himselfe to the keeping of a seruant of his named Underwood in Astley Parke, who like a false traitor bewraied him'. Stow makes no mention of the servant or of the Duke's betrayal. Holinshed (*Chronicles*, iii, 1095) states that 'through the vntrustiness of them, to whose trust they [Suffolk 'and the lord Iohn Greie his brother'] did committ themselues (as hath beene crediblie reported) they were bewraied to the earle of Huntington'.

16   *the hollow tree.* This detail is mentioned only in Grafton (quoted in the head-note, above). But cf. Heywood's account in *England's Eliȝabeth* of Suffolk's betrayal by

Vnderwood, a man raysed by him onely to a competent estate, vnto whose trust and gard hee committed his Person, was by him conueyed into a hollow tree, morning and euening relieued with sustenance by him, euery time of his appearance renewed his confidence vnto him, and engaged himselfe with millions of oathes for the performance of his truth and fidelity, yet easily corrupted with some small quantity of gold, and many large promises, *Iudas*-like betrayed his Master (1631, p. 90).

66 *shrimpe. N.S.S.*, III.ii.79.

67 *mouching*, i.e., munching. Cf. *P.G.*, II.i.2–3: 'my teeth water till I be mounching'; and V.i.4: 'mounch vp our victuals'.

67 *Colen*, the greater portion of the large intestine. The word is frequent in expressions of hunger. *R.A.*, B4v: 'such as walke snuffing vp and downe in winter euenings through Pye-corner, yet haue no siluer to stop Colon'. *V.M.*, III.iii.57.

89 *lusticke*, merry, jolly (Dutch *lustig*). Often used with reference to drinking; cf. *The Weakest Goeth to the Wall* (M.S.R. (1912), prepared by W. W. Greg), lines 869–870: 'heigh loustick'. And *All's Well that Ends Well*, II.iii.41: '*Lustick*, as the Dutchman says.'

III.i

Queene *Mary* came from Wansteed in Essex, to London on the 3. of August, being brought in with her nobles very honorably, and strongly, the number of veluet coats that did ride before her, as well strangers as others were 740. and the number of ladies and gentlewomen that followed was 180. The earle of Arundale riding next before her, bare a sworde in his hand, and Sir *Anthony Brown* did beare vp her traine. The lady *Elizabeth* her sister followed her next...A great peale of ordinance was shotte off at the Tower of London, when the Queene entered the Citie through Aldgate, vp to Leaden hall, then downe Grace streete, Fanchurch streete, Marke lane, Tower streete, and so into the Tower, where *Thomas* duke of Norffolke, doctor *Gardener* late Bishoppe of Winchester, *Edward Courtney* sonne and heire to *Henry* marquesse of Excester, the Dutchesse of Somerset, prisoners in the Tower, kneeling on the hill within the same tower, saluted her grace, and she came to them and kissed them, & said, these be my prisoners (Stow, *Annales*, pp. 1035–1036).

0.1 *Winchester*. This, as is evident from his speech at lines 72–77 (see note, below), is Stephen Gardiner, Bishop of Winchester,

not the Marquis of Winchester (the Lord Treasurer) who
appeared in I.v and I.vi.

1 *By Gods asistance, and the power of heauen.* The same line is
spoken by Queen Mary on her first appearance in Part One
of Heywood's *If You Know Not Me, You Know Nobody*
(ed. Shepherd, 1, 195), where the Queen expresses herself in
a vein similar to that of the present passage:

> By Gods assistance, and the power of heaven,
> We are instated in our Brothers throne,
> And all those powers that warred against our right,
> By help of heauen and your friendly aide,
> Dispersed and fled, here we may sit secure.
> Our heart is joyfull, lords, our peace is pure.

For an account of the subject materials common to the scene
in Heywood's play and the present one (e.g. Mary's refusal
to honor her promise to the Suffolk men concerning con-
tinuance of the Protestant religion in return for their support
at the time of Jane's accession; plans for Mary's marriage with
Philip and her joy at his expected arrival in England), see
Martin, '*If You Know Not Me* and *Wyat*', pp. 275–277.

13 *briefly,* in a short time, alluding to the promptitude with which
Mary intends to restore the Church to its former honours.
But see Professor Bowers' textual note (1, 457).

19–20 *giue release vnto such ancient Bishops | That haue lost their
honours.*

> Upon the receauing of this newe Queene, all the Byshops which had
> bene depriued in the time of king Edwarde the sixt her brother for the
> cause of religion, were nowe againe restored to their Bishoprickes. And
> such other as were placed in king Edwards time remoued from their
> Seas, and other of contrarie religion placed. Amongst whom Edmond
> Bonner Doctor of the lawes, late afore depriued from the Sea of
> London and committed prisoner to the Marshalsea by order of king
> Edwardes counsayle, was with all fauour restored to his libertie and
> Bishoprick, and Nicholas Ridley Doctor in Diuinitie late before ad-
> uaunced to the saide Sea by the sayd king was hastily displaced and com-
> mitted prisoner to the Tower of London (Grafton, *A Chronicle*, p. 1327).

Prior to this, upon her entry into the Tower when she arrived
in the city, Grafton reports that Mary had singled out Stephen

Gardiner, Bishop of Winchester, with especial favor, 'whome shee not onely released of imprisonment, but also immediately aduaunced and preferred to be Lorde Chaunselor of Englande, restoring him also to his former estate and Byshoprick, and remoued from the same one Doctor Poynet, who a little before was placed therein by the gift of king Edwarde the sixt' (*ibid.*, pp. 1326–1327). Stow reports the release on 5 August of Boner from the Marshalsea, and of '*Cutbert Tonstall* the olde bishop of Durham prisoner in the King's bench'; both 'had their pardons, and were restored to their Seas' (*Annales*, p. 1036).

21 *the Duke of Norfolke.* He was one of the prisoners presented to Mary upon her entry into the Tower (see the passage from Stow, quoted in the head-note to the present scene). He had been attainted of treason in the last year of Henry VIII. 'But in the Parliament holden in this first yere of Queene Marye, the saide supposed attayndor was by the aucthorities and act of parliament for good and apparunt causes alleaged in the sayde acte, declared to be vtterly frustrate and voyde' (Grafton, *A Chronicle*, pp. 1326–1327).

24 *the late Oath you tooke at Framingham.* At Framlingham, the Suffolk men had promised to aid Mary on condition 'that she would not attempt the alteration of the religion, which her Brother king Edward had before established by lawes and orders publicklie enacted'. Foxe comments: 'unto this condition she eftsoones agreed, with such promise made vnto them, that no innouation should be made of religion, as that no man would or could then haue misdoubted her'. He continues:

Thus Mary being guarded with the power of the gospellers, did vanquish the duke [of Northumberland], and al those that came against her. In consideration whereof, it was (me thinkes) an heauy word that she answered to the Suffolke men afterwardes, which did make supplication vnto her grace to performe her promise. For so much (saith she) as you being but members, desire to rule your head you shall one daie well perceiue that members must obey their head, and not looke to beare rule ouer the same (Foxe, *Actes and Monuments*, p. 1279).

The issue is dramatized in one of the early scenes of Heywood's *If You Know Not Me*, when one Dodds presents to Queen

Mary a petition from the Suffolk men reminding her of her promise to them. Urged on by Winchester, she scornfully rejects it, and Dodds is sentenced to stand three days in the pillory (ed. Shepherd, I, 195–196).

26 *shall a Subiect force his Prince.* In *If You Know Not Me*, Queen Mary says of the Suffolk men and their petition:

> They shall know,
> To whom their faithfull duties they doe owe:
> Since they, the limbs, the head would seeke to sway,
> Before they gouerne, they shall learne t' obey.
>   (ed. Shepherd, I, 196)

28–30 *release . . . Brothers daies.* 'Also the same day [4 September 1553] by proclamation, was pardoned the subsidie of foure s. the pound lands, and two s. eight d. the pound of mooueable goods, granted in the last parliament of king *Edward* the sixt' (Stow, *Annales*, p. 1041).

40–41 *The Duke of Suffolke | Is not yet apprehended.* Suffolk was arrested twice: first, on 28 July 1553, in connection with the plot to put Lady Jane on the throne (he was pardoned on 31 July; see above, I.v.31, n.), and again on 2 February 1554 as the result of his involvement with Wyatt's conspiracy. The present reference is in anticipation of his second arrest, which has already been shown in the preceding scene.

47 *the Daughter.* Actually, the grand-daughter: 'the Lady Iane eldest daughter of Henry Duke of Suffolk and the Ladie Fraunces his wife, who was the daughter of Mary second sister to king Henrie the eight, first maried to Lewys yᵉ French king, & after to Charles Brandon, Duke of Suffolke' (Grafton, *A Chronicle*, p. 1323). See p. 320.

57 *ostend*, show, exhibit.

59–61 *Count Egmond . . . Sonnes behalfe.* 'In the beginning of the month of Ianuary, the Emperor [Charles V] sent a noble man called *Edmond*, and certaine other Ambassadors into England to conclude a marriage betweene K. *Philip* his son, and Queene *Mary* of England' (Stow, *Annales*, p. 1043). The name of the ambassador as given in the foregoing quotation makes it clear that the Q1 reading *Edmond* – which Professor Bowers rejected

335

in favor of Q2 *Egmond* – is in fact what the authors wrote here and at lines 152 and 152.1, below. The Q1 form of the name is based on a misprint that appears in both the 1600 and 1601 editions of Stow's *Annales*. The name which Grafton gives (*A Chronicle*, p. 1330) as 'Countye Ayguemont' (reproduced in Holinshed, *Chronicles*, edn. 1577, p. 1724: 'Conte de Ayguemont'; and edn. 1587, p. 1093: 'Conte de Aiguemont') appears first in Stow (*Annales*, edn. 1580, p. 1077) as 'Ecmondane'. In the edition of 1592 (p. 1045) this becomes 'Ecmond', but in the edition of 1600 (p. 1043) the name has been altered to 'Edmond', and the error is repeated in the edition of 1601 (p. 1043). It is unlikely that the actors would themselves independently duplicate an error that stood in their authors' principal source. This point has also been made by Mary Forster Martin in her 'Stow's "Annals"', p. 76. Bearing in mind that the play is textually bad 'and that the error may have been made by the reporter or the compositor', she notes: 'If so, however, it would be a curious coincidence that in the first edition should be found the same mis-spelling as is found in the two most recent editions of an important sourcebook.'

72–77 *we haue cause to thanke our God | . . . will vouchsafe – | . . . | To grace our mightie Soueraigne with his . . . Title.*

The 14. of Ianuary, doctor *Stephen Gardener* bishop of Winchester, Lord Chancelor of England, in the chamber of presence at Westminster, made to the Lords, Nobility, and Gentlemen, an Oration very eloquent, wherein he declared that the Queenes Maiestie, partly for amity, and other waighty considerations had, after much suite on the Emperors and Prince of Spaines behalfe made, determined by the consent of the Counsell and Nobilitie, to match her selfe with the saide Prince in most godly and lawfull matrimonie: and declared further, that she should haue for her iointer 30000 duckets by the yeere, with all the low-countrey of Flanders, and that the issue (if there happened any) betweene the two lawfully begotten, should be heire as wel to the Kingdome of Spaine, as also to the said low-countrey. He said therfore that they were all bound to thanke God that so noble, worthy, and famous a Prince would vouchsafe so to humble himselfe, as in this marriage to take vpon him rather as a subiect, than otherwise, for the Queene and her councell should rule all things as she did before, and that there should be of the councel no Stranger, neither to haue the custody of any forts, or Castles, etc. nor beare any rule or office in the queenes house, or else-where in all England, with diuers other articles there by him rehearsed, wherefore he said the queens pleasure and request was, that like good subiects for her sake, they would most louingly receiue him with reuerence, ioy and honor (Stow, *Annales*, pp. 1043–1044).

87 *the mightie Cham*. O.F., I.ii.198, n.

120–121 *his head once in,* | *The slender body easily will follow*. I.T.B.N., I.iii.202. Webster, *The White Devil*, IV.i.136. Tilley, F655.

124 *seauenteene famous Prouinces*. M.E., 438–439, n.

157–166 *And ere hee land... defend*.

But this mariage was not well thought of by the Commons, nor much better liked of many of the Nobilitie, who for this, and for the cause of religion, conspired to rayse war rather then to see such chaunge of the state. Of the which conspiracie though there were many confederats, yet the first that shewed force therein, was one sir Thomas Wyat a knight in Kent, who by open Proclamations published there that the Queene and her Counsaile woulde by this forreyne maryage bring this realme into most miserable seruitude and bondage of straungers (Grafton, *A Chronicle*, pp. 1330–1331).

III.ii

The twentie two of August, *Sir Iohn Gage* Lieuetenant of the Tower, deliuered to the Sheriffes of London, by Indenture these prisoners following: first Sir *Iohn Gates* was brought foorth, and set at the Garden Gate, then the Duke of Northumberlande, was likewise brought foorth, and Sir *Thomas Palmer* after him (Stow, *Annales*, p. 1038).

21 *dreames...contrarie prooue*. Tilley, D588.

23–28 *people stand in heapes...swarmes*. Cf. *L.D.*, III.iv.25–26: 'This heap of fools, who crowding in huge swarms, | Stood at our Court gates like a heap of dung'.

38–39 *great Northumberland,...lost his head*. Northumberland was arraigned at Westminster Hall on 18 August 1553, and executed on Tower Hill on 27 August.

41–42 *His sinnes...Epitaph*. Dyce compares *1 Henry IV*, V.iv.100–101: 'Thy ignominy sleep with thee in the grave, | But not rememb'red in thy epitaph.'

44–1 *Suffolke garded foorth.* 'The tenth of Februarie, the Earle of Huntington, and other Gentlemen, and to the number of 300. horseman, brought into the Tower as Prisoner the D. of Suffolk, and the L. *Iohn Grey* his brother from Couentry' (Stow, *Annales*, pp. 1051–1052).

53 *Deathes lesson...adue.* Suffolk was beheaded on 23 February 1554 (*ibid.*, p. 1053; 21 February according to Foxe, *Actes and Monuments*, p. 1293, and Grafton, *A Chronicle*, p. 1338).

57 *Till your Arrainement.* Jane and Dudley were arraigned at the Guildhall on 13 November 1553 (Stow, *Annales*, p. 1043).

IV.i—IV.iii.8

The 29. of Ianuary, the D. of Norffolke lieutenant of the army, and with him the earle of Arundell, M. *Henry Iernigham* captaine of the guarde, with a great number of the guard, and other souldiers, and the captaine and souldiers that were sent from London, minded to assault Rochester Castle, where *Wyat* and his people laie, so that vppon Mundaie they were set in arraie towardes Rochester bridge, which was kept by *Wyats* companie, and furnished with 3. or 4. double cannons: but before the setting forwarde of these men, the D. sent master *Nory* an Herault vnto Rochester, with the Q. proclaimation of pardon to all such as would desist from their purpose, who comming to the bridge, would haue gone through into the citie, but they that kept the bridge would not suffer him till that the captaine came, who at the last graunted the same to be read in the citie, but holding a dag against him, cried, speake softlie, or els they would shoot him through, so that they would not suffer the people to heare the Proclamation: which beeing ended, each man cried they had doon nothing wherefore they should need any pardon, and in that quarrel which they had taken in hand, they would liue and die: neuertheles, at the last Sir *George Harpar* receiued the pardon outwardly, and being receiued vnder the D. of Norffolks protection, came on forward against the Kentishmen, and euen as the companie were set in a readines, and marched forward toward the bridge, *Bret* beeing captaine of the 500. Londoners, of which, the more parte were in the foreward, turned himselfe about, and drawing out his sword, saide these or like words: Masters wee go about to fight against our natiue Countrymen of England and our friends, in a quarrel vnrightful, & partly wicked, for they, considering the great miseries which are like to fall vpon vs, if wee shall be vnder the rule of the proude Spaniards or strangers, are here assembled to make resistance of their comming, for the auoiding of so great inconueniences likely to light, not onely vpon themselues, but on euerie of vs & the whole realme,

wherefore I thinke no English hart ought to say against them, much
lesse by fighting to with stande them: wherefore I and others (meaning
such as were in that ranke with him) will spend our blood in the quarrel
of this worthie captaine M. *Wyat*, and other gentlemen here assembled:
which words once pronounced, each man turned their ordinance against
their followers ['fellowe' in the diary of the Tower Chronicler –
Stow's source for this passage – printed in *The Chronicle of Queen Jane,
and of Two Years of Queen Mary*, ed. J. G. Nichols, Camden Society,
48 (1850), p. 39], and therupon cried, a *Wyat*, a *Wyat*, of which
sodaine noise, the Duke, the captaine of the guard and other, beeing
abashed, fled forthwith: immediatlie came in master *Wyat* and his
companie on horsebacke, rushing in amongst as well the guard as the
Londoners, and said, so manie as will come and tary with vs shall bee
welcome, and so manie as will depart, good leaue haue they, and so
all the Londoners, part of the gard, and more than three parts of the
retinue, went to the campe of the Kentishmen, where they still remained.
At this discomfiture, the Duke lost eight Peeces of Brasse, with all other
munition and ordinance, and himselfe with fewe other hardly escaped
(Stow, *Annales*, pp. 1045–1046).

IV.i

6 *cannot put vp crosses. W.H.*, III.ii.60, n.

9 *Shall now get Crownes, marry they must be crackt.* For the quibble,
see *P.G.*, II.i.219–220, n.

10 *white money*, silver. *L.C.*, K2v: 'But because he is verie
shortly...*to trauaile to Venice*, to *Ierusalem* or so, and would
not willingly be disfurnished of *Golde*, he dooth therefore
request the Cittizen to lend...so much in white money.'
2 H.W., III.i.45–46; *V.M.*, II.iii.232.

15 *light crownes.* Cf. *W.H.*, I.ii.9: 'light gold', and note.

26 *A Wyat, a Wyat, a Wyat.* For this rallying cry, cf. *1 Henry VI*,
II.i.77.1–2: '*Enter an English Soldier, crying* "A Talbot! a
Talbot!"' And *2 Henry VI*, IV.viii.53–54: '*All.* A Clifford!
a Clifford! we'll follow the King and Clifford.' The 'A' is
usually regarded as the indefinite article, but it may represent
French *à*. Cf. *L.D.*, IV.ii.26–27.

45 *passe and repasse*, a conjurer's term; thus the reference to
'iuggle'. See *O.F.*, V.ii.10, n.

47 *Set foorth thy brasen throate.* Cf. *Troilus and Cressida*, I.iii.6–25

257: 'Trumpet, blow loud, / Send thy brass voice through all these lazy tents.'

50 *Lime-twigs*. *O.F.*, I.ii.76, n.

62 *Herrald...armes*. Cf. *N.H.*, IV.iii.166–167.

77 *silken faces*. Cf. *O.F.*, III.i.115: 'a Spruce silken face Courtier'.

78 *wrinckles*, betokening an angry countenance.

92–93 *false sir George | Is fled*. Holinshed (*Chronicles*, p. 1094) records that following the skirmish at Wrotham 'sir George Harper departing from sir Thomas Wiat, and coming to the duke of Norffolke, submitted himselfe vnto his grace, & the duke receiued him'.

97–98 *Harpers...nine pence*. The allusion is to the Irish coin which bore the figure of a harp and was known as a harp shilling, but was worth only 9d. in English money. Cf. *The Fair Maid of the Exchange* (M.S.R., (1963, for 1962), prepared by P. H. Davison and A. Brown), lines 681–683: 'they cost thee an English shilling at a word, mary it followes in the text, that your shilling proou'd but a harper'. And *W.A.*, GIV: 'send (at least) some of thy Harpers to sound their nine-penie musicke in our eares'.

IV.ii

[The duke of Norfolk] being sent with fiue hundred Londoners, and certaine of the gard for his better defense, to go against the Kentishmen thus assembled with sir Thomas Wiat, was come downe to Grauesend, [and] set foorth from thence on mondaie the nine and twentieth daie of Ianuarie, about ten of the clocke in the forenoone, marching towards Stroud on this side of Rochester, & about foure of the clocke in the after noone of the same daie, he arriued at Stroud neare vnto Rochester, hauing with him sir Henrie Ierningham capteine of the gard, sir Edward Braie, sir Iohn Fog, knights, Iohn Couert, Roger Appleton, esquiers, Maurice Griffith the bishop of Rochester, Thomas Swan gentleman, with certeine of the gard, and others, to the number of two hundred or thereabout, besides Bret and other fiue capteins, who with their bands taried behind at spittle hill neere vnto Stroud, whilest the duke went to Stroud to see the placing of the ordinance, which being readie charged & bent vnto the towne of Rochester, and perceiuing by sir Thomas Wiat and his men by hanging out their ensignes, little to regard him, the duke commanded one of the peeces to be fired and shot off into Rochester, and as the gunner was firing the peece,

sir Edward Braies eldest son came in all hast to the duke, and told him
how the Londoners would betraie him (Holinshed, *Chronicles*, p. 1094).

For Stow's account of Brett's defection, and his address to the
soldiers, see the head-note to IV.i–IV.iii.8.

23 *hot shots. I.T.B.N.*, II.i.104.

24 *shrink for a wetting*. A proverbial expression; cf. Fletcher,
Massinger, Field, *The Knight of Malta*, II.i (1647), p. 76:
'My tough knave welcom: thou wilt not shrink ith' washing.'
And see *W.H.*, II.i.41–42, n. *I.T.B.N.*, II.i.51.

24–25 *beare off any thing with head and shoulders*. Cf. Tilley, H274.

34 *Kentishmen...taile*. A quibble on the proverbial expression
'Kentish longtails' (Tilley, K17). Cf. *N.H.*, I.iii.176, n.

34–35 *hang'd – like a Iuell in the Kingdomes eare*. Cf. Blurt, *Master-
Constable*, IV.i.19–20: 'if now my friend thou stand, / I'll hang
a jewel at thine ear, sweet night'. *Romeo and Juliet*, I.v.45–46.
W.B., prologue, 2–3.

39–40 *Spittle-houses and Hospitalles*. The distinction is preserved
as well in *B.L.*, D2v: 'a pattent to beg for some Hospitall or
Spittle house'. 'Spittle-houses' were hospitals, especially for
foul diseases.

44–45 *keepe King Phillip out,...giue the Land such a Phillip*. The
pun on 'fillip' is repeated in *L.D.*, V.iii.16–17.

48 *Hot-cockles. Sat.*, III.i.199, n.

51 *Camocho*, from Italian *camoscio*, defined by Florio as 'a kinde of
stuffe worne in Italie'. As a term of contempt, cf. Jonson,
Every Man out of his Humour, V.iii.73–74: 'out of my sight,
goe, hence, speake not: I will not heare thee: away *camouccio*'.
And *Blurt, Master-Constable*, I.ii.82–83: 'Whosoever says
you have a black eye, is a camooch.'

51 *Callimanco*, i.e. 'calamanco', a glossy woollen stuff made in
Flanders, twilled and chequered in the warp, so that the checks
are seen on one side only (*O.E.D.*). Cf. Nashe, *Strange Newes*,
I, 330: 'What a *Calimunco* am I to plead for him, as though I
were as neere him as his owne skinne.'

52 *Dondego*, i.e. 'Don Diego' ('James'), a name for a Spaniard.
Thus Subtle of the disguised Surly in Jonson's *Alchemist*,
IV.iii.36–39:

Yes, the *Casa*,
My precious *Diego*, will proue faire inough,
To cossen you in. Doe you marke? you shall
Be cossened, *Diego*

and IV.v.106: 'Will you goe fetch *Don Diego* off, the while?'
And *Dick of Devonshire* (M.S.R. (1955), prepared by J. G.
and M. R. McManaway), line 770: 'now Don Diego, & Don
Thunderbolt, or Don Divell I defye thee'. *O.F*, II.ii.267, n.

53 *Stockfish. W.H.*, V.iv.104–105, n.

53 *poore Iohn*, dried and salted hake, often mentioned as a type of
inferior food. For its association with the Spanish diet, cf.
Blurt, Master-Constable, I.ii.209–210: 'What meat eats the
Spaniard? /...Dried pilchers and poor-john.' *P.G.*, I.ii.127.

54 *Viliago*, 'villain', from the Italian *vigliacco*. The word's association with Spanish may derive from the phrase 'Fuora villiacco',
their watchword at the sack of Antwerp in 1574. Cf. *A Larum
for London* (M.S.R. (1913), prepared by W. W. Greg), line
1129: 'Fuora villiaco'. The Spaniard Don John uses the word
in *Dick of Devonshire* (M.S.R.), line 771: 'oh Viliaco, Diablo,
Anglese.' Cf. *Sat.*, I.i.72, n.

56–57 *There came but one Dundego...and hee made all Paules
stincke.* The earliest of the numerous references to this notorious
incident seems to be in Nashe's letter to one William Cotton,
written in the early fall of 1596 (*Works*, v, 195). Cf. *Blurt,
Master-Constable*, IV.iii.135–137:

Laz. I am kin to Don Dego, the Spanish adelantado.
Blurt. If you be kin to Don Dego that was smelt out in Paul's, you pack.

There are allusions as well in Heywood, *1 Fair Maid of the
West*, IV.iv.110–111; Webster, *The White Devil*, II.i.299–
300; Fletcher and Rowley, *The Maid in the Mill*, II.i (1647),
p. 6.

64–66 *yard...giue an inch hee'le take an ell. W.H.*, II.i.20–21.

70 *flat Caps*. The characteristic head-dress of the London citizens.
See 2 *H.W.*, I.iii.21–22, n.

71 *Neates-leather*. Lyly, *Mother Bombie*, I.iii.44–46: 'they saie he
is as goodly a youth as one shall see in a Summers daie, and

as neate a stripling as euer went on neats leather'. *S.H.*, IV.iii.36.

71–72 *Spanish Leather. 1 H.W.*, I.ii.33, n.

72 *a figge. O.F.*, I.ii.173.

78 *licke-pennies*, those who 'lick up the pennies' (i.e., make the money go).

> And to prooue this Eastcheape to bee a place replenished with Cookes, it may appeare by a song called *London lickepennie*, made by *Lidgate* a Monke of Berrie, in the raigne of *Henrie* the fift, in the person of a Countrie man comming to London, and trauelling through the same. In West Cheape (saith the song) hee was called on to buy fine lawne,... in Cornhill to buy old apparell, and houshold stuffe,...in Candlewright streete Drapers profered him cheape cloath, in East cheape the Cookes cried hot ribbes of beefe rosted, pies well baked, and other victuals:...but he wanted money to abide by it, and therefore gat him into Grauesend barge, & home into Kent (Stow, *Survey*, I, 217).

Tilley, L228.

IV.iii

1 *eight brasse peeces.* See Stow, quoted in the head-note to IV.i– IV.iii.8.

9 *The Lawyers plead in Armour steede of Gownes.* 'On the friday, which was Candlemas day [2 February 1554], the most part of the housholders of London, with the maior and aldermen were in harnesse, yea this daie and other daies the iustices, sergeants at the law, and other lawyers in Westminster hall, pleaded in harnesse' (Stow, *Annales*, p. 1046). And John Proctor, *The historie of Wyates rebellion* (1554), p. 73: 'This daye [Ash Wednesday, 7 February] the Iudges in the Commen Place at Westminster satte in armoure.'

12–19 *this is Ludgate...Auaunt thou Traitor.* 'Thus some of *Wyats* men, some say it was *Wyat* himselfe, came euen to Ludgate and knocked, calling to come in, saying there was *Wyat*, whome the queene had granted to haue their requests, but the lord *William Howard* stoode at the gate, and saide, auaunt traitor, thou shalt not come in heere' (Stow, *Annales*, p. 1050).

12.2 *Pembroke.* Stow (*ibid.*, p. 1046) writes: 'vnderstanding that many in London did fauour *Wyats* part, she [Mary] appointed lord *William Howard* lieutenant of the Citie, and the earle of Pembroke generall of the field, which both prepared all things necessary for their purpose'. But cf. lines 31–32.

22 *cost the liues of twentie thousand.* Holinshed reports that on 31 January Sir Edward Hastings, Master of the Queen's Horse, and Sir Thomas Cornwallis came to Wyatt at Dartford 'to vnderstand the cause of his commotion' (*Chronicles*, p. 1095). 'There was long & stout conference betweene them, in so much that the maister of the horse said: Wiat, before thou shalt haue thy traitorous demand granted, thou shalt die, and twentie thousand with thee' (*ibid.*, p. 1096).

33 *Are you Lord Maior?* Grafton (*A Chronicle*, p. 1333) reports that 'the Lorde Wylliam Howard was associate with the Lord Maior of London, whose name was Sir Thomas White, for the protection and defence of the Citie'.

44–45 *O London...broke, thy promise to thy friend?* Cf. Dekker's allusion to the City's failure to support Wyatt in *S.D.S.*, F iv:

mark in what triumphant and proud manner, he is marshalled through *Newgate*: At which *Bulwarke* (& none other) did he (in policy) desire to shew himself. First, because he knew if the Citie should play with him as they did wᵗ *Wiat*, *Newgate* held a number, that though they were false to all the world, would be true to him.

49 *buy.* 'Probably for *abye*, or suffer the consequences of' (Hazlitt). Cf. Sackville and Norton, *Ferrex and Porrex, or Gorboduc*, IV.i.29–30 (ed. E. Creeth, *Tudor Plays* (New York, 1966)): 'Thou, *Porrex*, thou this damned dede hast wrought, / Thou, *Porrex*, thou shalt dearely bye the same'.

50–51.1 *Wold I could steale away...they all steale away.* Brett's desertion had occurred before the arrival at Ludgate, during the march on London.

And so about 11. of the clocke, *Wyat* with his band, without resistance marched towardes London, meaning to haue beene at the court gate before day of the next morning. They came almost to Brainford or euer they were descried by yᵉ queens scouts, who there by chance meeting *Bret* & his company, *Bret* said to the scout, backe villaine, if thou go further to discouer any thing here, thou shalt die out of hand, so the scout returned in great haste: but as God would haue it, before he came within sixe miles of the citie, staying vpon a piece of his great ordinance, which was dismounted by breach of the wheeles, his comming was discouered, & it was 9. of the clocke of the day following, before he came to Hide parke... Whilest *Wyat* and his counsell were deuising how to raise his ordinance dismounted, many of his society slipped from him, among the which, M. *Harper* was one, who went to the court, and opened al the premises aforesaid, to the Q. and Councel, where *Wyat* was, what had chanced, and what was his intention. The breaking of the said gun was such an hinderance to his enterprise, that all about him were amazed, and at their wits end, because by that means, the houre was broken of appointment, wherefore, *Vaughan*, *Bret*, and other approoued souldiers and counsellers, such as had wise heads in other affaires, as doctor *Poinet* and other, did counsell the said *Wyat* to march forwards and keepe his appointment, and to let the gun lie, which in no wise he could be perswaded to do. Doctor *Poinet* therefore, considering how many of his confederacie was stolne away from him, he began to perswade with captaine *Bret*, and other his friends to shift for themselues, as he would do, and at that very place where the gun did breake, he tooke his leaue of his secret friends, and said he would pray vnto God for their good successe, and so did depart, and went into Germany, where he died (Stow, *Annales*, p. 1048).

IV.iv

1–9 *Pembroke reuolts...raisde this slander.*

At Charing crosse there stoode sir *Iohn Gage* lorde chamberlaine with the garde, and a number of other, being almost a thousand, the which vpon *Wyats* comming, shot at his company, but at the last fled to the court gates, which certaine pursued, and forced with shot to shut the Court Gates against them. In this repulse the said lord chamberlain and others were so amazed, that manie cried treason in the court, and had thought that the Earle of Pembrooke, who was assaulting the taile of his enemies, hadde gone to *Wyat*, taking his part against the Queene (Stow, *Annales*, pp. 1049–1050).

13–26 *Wiat is marcht downe Fleete-streete...Lords I yeeld.*

Wyat a while staied [at Ludgate], and rested him vppon a Stall ouer-against the Bell Sauadge gate, and at the last seeing hee could not get into the citie, and beeing deceiued of the aide hee hoped for, returned backe againe in arraie towardes Charing Crosse, and was neuer stopped till hee came at Temple barre, where certaine horsemen which came from the Fielde, mette them in the face, and then beganne the fight againe, till *Clarentius* an Herault came and sayde to Maister *Wyat*: Sir, you were best by my counsell to yeelde, you see this daie is gone against you, and in resisting, you canne get no good, but bee the death of all

these your souldiers, to your great perill of soule: perchance you maie
finde the Queene mercifull, and the rather, if yee stint so great bloude-
shead as is like heere to be. *Wyatt* herewith being somewhat astonied
(although he saw his men bent to fight) said, Well, if I shall needes
yeelde, I will yeeld me to a gentleman, to whom sir *Mawrice Barkeley*
came straight, and bad him leape vp behinde him, and an other tooke
Thomas Cobham and *William Kneuet*, and so carried them behinde
them vpon their horses to the court, then was taking of men on all
sides (*ibid.*, p. 1050).

34 *Though you say Traitor, I am a Gentleman.* When Wyatt and
   the principal rebels were brought to the Tower,

sir *Philip Denny* receiued them at the bulwarke, and as *Wyat* passed by
he saide, go traitor, there was neuer such a traitor in England: to
whom sir *Thomas Wyat* turned and said, I am no traitor, I woulde thou
shouldest well knowe, thou art more traitor than I, it is not the pointe
of an honest man to call mee so, and so went foorth (*ibid.*, p. 1051).

V.i

34–43 *Our answere...vnto our deathes.* Mary Forster Martin
('Stow's "Annals"', p. 76) has suggested that 'The trial of
Lady Jane and her husband, Guilford Dudley, nowhere
described by the historians, in the play bears some resemblance
to that of Sir Nicholas Throgmorton, one of the rebels, as
related in Holinshed alone', and cites the present passage in
comparison with the following from Holinshed (III, 1105):

Throckmorton. Maie it please you my lords and maisters...to giue me
   leaue to speake a few words...before I answer to the indictement...?
Bromleie. No, the order is not so, you must first plead whether you be
   giltie or no.
Throckmorton. If that be your order and law, iudge accordinglie to it.
Hare. You must first answer to the matter wherewith you are charged,
   and then you maie talke at your pleasure.
Throckmorton. But things spoken out of place were as good not
   spoken...So I satisfie my selfe, sith I shall not speake, thinking
   you all know what you haue to doo, or ought to know.

Martin suggests plausibly that the word omitted from Q1 in
line 35 and which Professor Bowers supplies as 'if' might,
when the passage is 'read in conjunction with the presumed
source', more likely be 'ere' (thus, Holinshed: 'before I

answer to the indictement'; Dekker, Webster, *et al*: 'ere wee confesse the inditement').

52 *Timelesse*, untimely. *Richard III*, I.ii.117–118: 'the causer of the timelesse deaths / Of these Plantagenets'. *L.D.*, III.ii.175: 'her timelesse grave'.

72–76 *And will you count...Royaltie*. Cf. *The White Devil*, III.ii.211–214:

> Condemne you me for that the Duke did love mee?
> So may you blame some faire and christall river
> For that some melancholike distracted man,
> Hath drown'd himselfe in't.

82 *Wast not by your consents?*

> Thus the xii. day of February...was beheaded the Lady Iane, & with her also the Lord Gilford her husband, one of the duke of Northumberlandes sonnes, two innocentes in comparison of them that sate vpon them. For they did but ignorantly accept that which the others hadde willingly deuised, and by open proclamation consented to take from others and giue to them (Foxe, *Actes and Monuments*, p. 1293).

And cf. Drayton, *Englands Heroicall Epistles*, 'Guilford Dudley to Lady Jane Gray', lines 77–82:

> When *Dudley* [i.e., Northumberland] led his Armies to the East,
> Of our whole Forces gen'rally possest,
> What then was thought his Enterprise could let,
> Whom a grave Councell freely did abet,
> That had the Judgement of the pow'rfull Lawes,
> In ev'ry Point to justifie the Cause?

83–85 *I haue your hands to show...wage armes*. Cf. I.vi.57–59.

99–100 *Great men like great Flies, through lawes Cobwebs breake, / But the thin'st frame, the prison of the weake*. Cf. *The Defence of Conny-Catching* (Greene's *Works*, XI, 51): 'But you play like the Spider that makes her webbe to intrap and snare litle Flyes, but weaues it so slenderly, that the great ones breake through without any damage.' And *Dick of Devonshire* (M.S.R.), lines 1767–1768: 'Law? yes; ye Spiders Cobweb, out of wch great flyes breake, / & in wch ye litle are hangd'. The image is proverbial (Tilley, L116), and a favorite of Dekker's. Cf. *N.G.*, p. 97:

Tis now the Beggers plague, for none
Are in this Battaile ouerthrowne
But Babes and poore: The lesser Fly
Now in this Spiders web doth lie.
But if that great, and goodly swarme
(That has broke through, and felt no harme,)
In his inuenom'd snares should fall,
O pittie!

I.T.B.N., II.i.10–11; *M.M.L.*, IV.i.58–60.

146 *Great griefes...least are dumbe.* Dyce suggested that the
dramatist wrote: 'Least griefs speak louder, when the great
are dumb', after Seneca, *Hippolytus*, 607: 'Curae leves loquun-
tur, ingentes stupent.' Cf. Drayton, *Englands Heroicall
Epistles*, 'Lady Jane Gray to Guilford Dudley', lines 23–24
in their original version: 'From strongest woe, we hardly
language wrest, / The depth of griefe, with words is sounded
least.' The lines were altered in editions after 1608. See the
Hebel edition of Drayton's *Works*, v, 134.

V.ii

5 *them that wrong'd their country, and their friend.* Thus Wyatt in
Grafton (*A Chronicle*, p. 1341):

for I had thought that other had bene as farre forward as my selfe,
which I found farre otherwise: So that being bent to kepe promise with
al my confederates, none kept promise with me: For I lyke a Moyle
went through thick and thinne with this determination, that if I should
come to any treaty, I should seeme to bewray all my friendes.

28 *We come to bring you to your execution.* 'The 11. of Aprill, sir
Th. Wyat was beheaded on the tower hill, and after quartered,
his quarters were set vp in diuers places, and his head on the
gallowes at Hay hill neere Hyde parke, from whence it was
shortly after stolne and conueied awaie' (Stow, *Annales*,
p. 1054).

81–82 *you reioyc'd to see / The fall of Cromwel.* Foxe, after stating that
Cromwell's 'chiefe and principall enimie...was Steuen
Gardiner Bishop of Winchester', reports that, when Cromwell
was committed to the Tower in July 1541,

as many good men which knew nothing but truth by him did lament,
and prayed hartily for him, so moe there were on the contrary side that
reioyced, especially of the religious sort, and of the Clergy, such as had
beene in some dignitie before in the Church, and now by his meanes
were put from it. For in deed, such was his nature, that in all his doings
he could not abide any kinde of Poperie, nor of false religion creeping
vnder hypocrisie, and lesse could he abide the ambitious pride of Popish
Prelacie, which professing all humilitie, was so elated in pride, that
Kings could not rule in their owne Realmes for them. These snuffing
Prelates as he could neuer abide, so they againe hated him as much,
which was the cause of shortning his dayes, and to bring him to his ende
(Foxe, *Actes and Monuments*, pp. 1084–1085).

106–107 *the Lady Iane must first suffer death*. The dramatists have
reversed the order of the deaths as reported in the Chronicles.

The 12. of February being Monday, about tenne of the clocke, there
went out of the tower to the scaffold on the tower hill, the L. *Guilford
Dudley*, son to the D. of Northumberland, husband to the lady Iane
Grey, daughter to the D. of Suffolke, who at his going out, tooke by
the hands sir *Anthony Browne*, M. *Iohn Throckmorton* and many other
gentlemen, praieng them to pray for him: and without the bulwarke
gate M. *Thomas Offley* one of the sherifs of London receiued him and
brought him to the scaffold, where after a small declaration, he kneeled
down and said his praiers, then holding vp his eies and hands to heauen,
with teares, at the last he desired the people to pray for him, and after
was beheaded: his body beeing laide in a car, and his head in a cloth,
was brought into the chappell within the tower, where the lady *Iane*,
whose lodging was in master *Partridges* house, did see his deade
carcasse taken out of the car, aswell as shee did see him before aliue
going to his death, a sight to hir woorse than death.

By this time was there a scaffold made vpon the greene, ouer-against
the white tower, for the ladie *Iane* to die vpon, who with hir husbande
was appointed to haue been put to death on the Friday before, but was
staied till then: this lady being nothing at all abashed, neither with
feare of her owne death, which then approched, neither with the sight
of the dead carcasse of her husband when he was brought into the
chappell, came forth, the lieutenant leading her, with countenance
nothing abashed, neither her eyes anie thing moistened with teares
(although hir gentlewomen *Elizabeth Tilney* and mistresse *Helen*
woonderfully wept) with a booke in her hand, wherin she praied
vntil she came to the said scaffold, wheron when she was mounted, she
was beheaded: whose deathes were the more hastened for feare of
further troubles and stir for hir title, like as hir father had attempted
(Stow, *Annales*, p. 1052).

112–149 *Forgiue me Lady . . . to the blocke to die.*

First when she mounted vpon the scaffold, she said to the people standing thereabout: Good people, I am come hither to die, and by a lawe I am condemned to the same. The fact against the Queenes highnesse was vnlawfull, and the consenting thereunto by me: but touching the procurement and desire thereof by me or on my behalfe, I doe wash my hands therof in innocencie before God, and the face of you, good Christian people, this daie: and therewith she wroong hir hands, wherein she had hir booke. Then saide she, I pray you all, good christian people, to beare me witnes that I die a true christian woman, and that I doe looke to be saued by no other meane, but only by the mercie of God in the bloud of his onlie sonne Iesus Christ: and I confesse that when I did know the worde of God, I neglected the same, loued my selfe and the worlde, and therefore this plague and punishment is happlie and worthily happened vnto mee for my sinnes: and yet I thanke God of his goodnesse that he hath thus giuen mee a time and respite to repent: and now, good people, while I am aliue I pray you assist mee with your praiers. And then kneeling down she turned hir to Frecknam saying: shall I saie this psalme? and he saide, yea. Then said she the Psalme of *Miserere Mei Deus* in English, in most deuout maner throughout to the end, and then she stood vp and gaue her maiden maistresse Ellen hir gloues and handkercher, and her booke to maister Bruges, & then she vntied hir gowne, and the hangman pressed vppon hir to helpe hir off with it, but she desiring him to let hir alone, turned towards her two gentlewomen, who helped hir off therwith, and also with hir frowes paast [i.e. 'frow's paste', a head-dress] and necker chiefe, giuing to hir a faire handkerchiefe to knit about hir eies.

Then the hangman kneeled downe and asked hir forgiuenesse, whom she forgaue most willinglie. Then hee willed her to stand vpon the straw: which dooing she saw the blocke. Then she said, I pray you dispatche me quickly. Then shee kneeled downe, saying: will you take it off before I lay me downe? and the hangman said, no Madame. Then tied shee the kercheife about her eies, and feeling for the blocke shee said: what shall I doe, where is it? where is it? One of the standers by guiding her thereunto, she laid her head downe vpon the blocke, and then stretched forth her bodie, and said: Lord into thy hands I commend my spirite, and so finished her life in the yeare of our Lord God. 1553. the 12. daie of February (Foxe, *Actes and Monuments*, p. 1293).